COSMOPOLITAN FILM CULTURES IN LATIN AMERICA, 1896–1960

New Directions in National Cinemas
ROBERT RUSHING, *editor*

COSMOPOLITAN FILM CULTURES IN LATIN AMERICA,
1896–1960

Edited by

RIELLE NAVITSKI
and NICOLAS POPPE

INDIANA UNIVERSITY PRESS

This book is a publication of

Indiana University Press
Office of Scholarly Publishing
Herman B Wells Library 350
1320 East 10th Street
Bloomington, Indiana 47405 USA

iupress.indiana.edu

© 2017 by Indiana University Press

All rights reserved

No part of this book may be reproduced or utilized in any form or by any means, electronic or mechanical, including photocopying and recording, or by any information storage and retrieval system, without permission in writing from the publisher. The Association of American University Presses' Resolution on Permissions constitutes the only exception to this prohibition.

♾ The paper used in this publication meets the minimum requirements of the American National Standard for Information Sciences—Permanence of Paper for Printed Library Materials, ANSI Z39.48–1992.

Manufactured in the United States of America

Library of Congress Cataloging-in-Publication Data

Names: Navitski, Rielle editor. | Poppe, Nicolas editor.
Title: Cosmopolitan film cultures in Latin America, 1896–1960 / edited by Rielle Navitski and Nicolas Poppe.
Description: Bloomington : Indiana University Press, 2017. | Series: New directions in national cinemas | Includes bibliographical references and index.
Identifiers: LCCN 2016041001 (print) | LCCN 2016054378 (ebook) | ISBN 9780253025722 (cl : alk. paper) | ISBN 9780253026460 (pb : alk. paper) | ISBN 9780253026552 (eb)
Subjects: LCSH: Motion pictures—Latin America—History—20th century. | Motion pictures—Social aspects—Latin America.
Classification: LCC PN1993.5.L3 C68 2017 (print) | LCC PN1993.5.L3 (ebook) | DDC 791.43098/0904—dc23
LC record available at https://lccn.loc.gov/2016041001

1 2 3 4 5 22 21 20 19 18 17

To the archivists, librarians, collectors,
and cinephiles who make the recuperation
of lost histories of film culture possible

CONTENTS

Acknowledgments   IX

Introduction / *Rielle Navitski and Nicolas Poppe*   1

Part I. The Silent Era: *Between Global Capitalism and National Modernization*

Primary text: "The Lumière Cinematograph," *El Monitor Republicano* (Mexico City), August 16, 1896   15

1 Gabriel Veyre and Fernand Bon Bernard, Representatives of the Lumière Brothers in Mexico / *Aurelio de los Reyes*   18

Primary text: Tic-Tac (Carlos Villafañe), "The Show on June 15th," *Películas* (Bogotá), June 1919   34

2 Films on Paper: Early Colombian Cinema Periodicals, 1916–1920 / *Juan Sebastián Ospina León*   39

Primary text: Enrique Méndez Calzada, "The Lover of Rudolph Valentino," from *And Christ Returned to Buenos Aires* (1926)   66

3 Manipulation and Authenticity: The Unassimilable Valentino in 1920s Argentina / *Giorgio Bertellini*   73

Part II. The Interwar Period: *Between Hollywood and the Avant-Garde*

Primary text: Felipe de Leiva, "Memoirs of an Extra," *Cinelandia* (Hollywood), November–December 1927   101

4 Mediating the "Conquering and Cosmopolitan Cinema": US Spanish-Language Film Magazines and Latin American Audiences, 1916–1948 / *Rielle Navitski* — 112

    Primary text: Octávio de Faria, "Russian Cinema and Brazilian Cinema," *O Fan* (Rio de Janeiro), October 1928 — 147

5 Parallel Modernities?: The First Reception of Soviet Cinema in Latin America / *Sarah Ann Wells* — 151

    Primary text: Guillermo de Torre, "The 'Cineclub' of Buenos Aires," *La Gaceta Literaria* (Madrid), April 1, 1930 — 176

6 A Gaze Turned Toward Europe: Modernity and Tradition in the Work of Horacio Coppola / *Andrea Cuarterolo* — 180

Part III. The Golden Age of Latin American Film Industries: *Negotiating the Popular and the Cosmopolitan*

    Primary text: John Alton, "Motion Picture Production in South America," *International Photographer* (Hollywood), May 1934 — 213

7 John Alton in Argentina, 1932–1939 / *Nicolas Poppe* — 217

8 The Golden Age Otherwise: Mexican Cinema and the Mediations of Capitalist Modernity in the 1940s and 1950s / *Ignacio M. Sánchez Prado* — 241

    Primary text: Gabriel García Márquez, "The Mambo," *El Heraldo* (Barranquilla), January 12, 1951 — 267

9 Bad Neighbors: Pérez Prado, Cinema, and the Politics of Mambo / *Jason Borge* — 269

Part IV. The Afterlives of Moving Images: *Cinephilia and Cult Spectatorship*

    Primary text: Thomas E. Sibert, "Fox Film de Cuba, S.A.'s Continuing Competition for Scholarships to Summer School at the Universidad de La Habana" (unpublished circular, June 1956) — 295

10 Film Culture and Education in Republican Cuba: The Legacy of José Manuel Valdés-Rodríguez / *Irene Rozsa* — 298

11 The Secret History of Aztlán: Speculative Histories, Transnational Exploitation Film, and Unexpected Cultural Flows / *Colin Gunckel* — 324

INDEX — 349

ACKNOWLEDGMENTS

THANKS ARE IN ORDER, first and foremost, to our contributors for their labor and dedication, their suggestions of primary texts for inclusion in this volume, and their efforts in securing rights and permissions for copyrighted material.

The publication of this volume was made possible in part by the generous support of Middlebury College's Scholarly Publication Fund.

At Indiana University Press, we thank editor Raina Polivka for championing the project from its very first stages, editor Janice Frisch and director Gary Dunham for guiding it to completion, and Kate Schramm for her assistance during the production process. We would also like to express our gratitude to Zuzana Pick for her insightful comments on an earlier version of the manuscript.

Preliminary versions of Rielle Navitski's essay "Mediating the 'Conquering and Cosmopolitan Cinema': US Spanish-Language Film Magazines and Latin American Audiences, 1916–1948," Sarah Ann Wells's essay "Parallel Modernities?: The First Reception of Soviet Cinema in Latin America," and Ignacio M. Sánchez Prado's essay "The Golden Age Otherwise: Mexican Cinema and the Mediations of Capitalist Modernity in the 1940s and 1950s," were presented at the 2014 Society for Cinema and Media Studies conference at a panel organized by the editors. We thank the audience members in attendance for their feedback on the presentations.

The editors and publisher gratefully acknowledge the permissions granted to reproduce copyrighted material and items from archival collections in this book. We thank the Biblioteca Miguel Lerdo de Tejada, Secretaría de la Hacienda y Crédito Público (Mexico City); Biblioteca Nacional de Colombia; Biblioteca Nacional de España; Fundación Cinemateca Argentina;

Guillermo Gómez-Peña; Hemeroteca Digital Brasileira; Philippe Jacquier and the Jacquier-Veyre Archive; Museo del Cine Pablo Ducrós Hicken (Buenos Aires); Billy Rose Theater Division, the New York Public Library for the Performing Arts, Astor, Lenox and Tilden Foundations; Pedro Noa Romero; and Video Data Bank for permission to reproduce images.

The editors thank the author and the Instituto de Investigaciones Estéticas–Universidad Nacional Autónoma de México for permission to publish a slightly modified English translation of Aurelio de los Reyes's essay "Gabriel Veyre y Fernand Bon Bernard, representantes de los hermanos Lumière en México," *Anales del Instituto de Investigaciones Estéticas* 67 (1995), 119–137.

The editors also thank the author and the Centro de Fotografía in Montevideo, Uruguay, for permission to publish a slightly modified English translation of Andrea Cuarterolo's essay "Con la mirada en Europa: Modernidad y tradición en la obra de Horacio Coppola" from her book *De la foto al fotograma. Relaciones entre cine y fotografía en Argentina (1940–1933)* (Montevideo: Centro de Fotografía, 2013), 223–250.

Brief portions of Sarah Ann Wells's essay "Parallel Modernities?: The First Reception of Soviet Cinema in Latin America" appeared in a slightly different form in her article "Mass Culture and the Laboratory of Late Modernism in Patrícia Galvão's *Parque industrial*." *Luso-Brazilian Review* 53, no. 1 (2016): 55–76. © 2016 by the Board of Regents of the University of Wisconsin System. Reproduced courtesy of University of Wisconsin Press.

Octávio de Faria, "Cinema russo e cinema brasileiro," *O Fan* (Rio de Janeiro), October 1928, 1, 3, appears in translation by permission of André do Carmo Seffrin.

Guillermo de Torre, "El 'cineclub' de Buenos Aires," *La Gaceta Literaria* (Madrid), April 1, 1930, 5, © Herederos de Guillermo de Torre, appears in translation by permission of Miguel de Torre Borges.

Gabriel García Márquez, "El mambo," in *Obra Periodística* Vol. 1, *Textos Costeños, 1948–1952*, © Gabriel García Márquez y Herederos de Gabriel García Márquez, appears in translation by permission.

Thomas E. Sibert's "Fox Film de Cuba, S.A.'s Continuing Competition for Scholarships to Summer School at the Universidad de La Habana" and the images reproduced in chapter 10 have been preserved thanks to the admirable work of the researcher Pedro Noa Romero in his digitization of materials belonging to the archives of the Extension School of the Universidad de la Habana and are reproduced with permission.

Every effort has been made to trace copyright holders and to obtain their permission for the use of copyrighted material. The publisher apologizes for any errors or omissions in the above list and would be grateful if notified of any corrections that should be incorporated in future reprints or editions of this book.

Nicolas would like to express his gratitude to colleagues at Middlebury College and beyond. From scholars whose research has formed and challenged his work to colleagues whose support has been inestimable, this project has only emerged through people like Joshua Finnell, Enrique García, Lisa Kuriscak, Chris Luke, David Miranda Hardy, Lucía Rodríguez Riva, Ryan Schmitz, and Paola Vega. He is also appreciative of institutional assistance, particularly the Interlibrary Loan Departments at Ball State University and Middlebury College, the Office of the Dean for Faculty Development and Research at Middlebury College and Dean Jim Ralph, and the Museo del Cine Pablo Ducrós Hicken in Buenos Aires. He is especially indebted to Erin Jones-Poppe and Sebastian Poppe for their encouragement and love.

Rielle thanks her colleagues Antje Ascheid, Marla Carlson, Richard Neupert, David Saltz, Emily Sahakian, and Chris Sieving for their encouragement, with special thanks to Richard for his kind assistance with images. She would also like to express her appreciation to those who provided advice and aid regarding rights and permissions: Mara Fortes, Fernando Macotela, Daniela Michel, Raúl Miranda, and especially David García and Klaus Vervuert. She is grateful for the work of the staffs of the Billy Rose Theater Division of the New York Public Library and the Interlibrary Loan Department at the University of Georgia Library; to Paulo Henrique Caetano and Alexander Spektor for offering their expertise regarding thorny points that emerged in the final stages of editing; to Regina Edmonds for her insightful suggestions and perspective; and to Al Navitski, Alanna Navitski, and José Guadalupe Vázquez Zavala for their support.

This volume is dedicated to those who make our work possible through the often difficult labor of preserving and making accessible the artifacts of Latin American and Latino/a film cultures.

COSMOPOLITAN FILM CULTURES IN LATIN AMERICA, 1896–1960

Introduction

Rielle Navitski and Nicolas Poppe

THE PAST TWO DECADES have witnessed an explosion of scholarly interest in Latin American cinema as the globalization of production, distribution, and reception has fueled the resurgence—and, in some cases, the emergence—of commercially viable film production in several Latin American nations. Thanks to new programs of government subsidies, growing opportunities for international coproductions, and increased visibility on the international festival circuit, a diverse group of films from the region has enjoyed impressive distribution and critical attention outside their countries of origin. Yet if, as Elizabeth Ezra and Terry Rowden have suggested, cinema's social functioning "is being drastically reshaped by the possibilities for global and transcultural knowledge that underpin the film festival as a site for the fashioning of cosmopolitan citizenship," the very mechanics of film funding acknowledge the historical inequalities that necessarily shape the parameters of this citizenship.[1] The existence of funding bodies that target film production in the so-called Global South—such as the Hubert Bals Fund of the Rotterdam Film Festival and the Berlinale's World Cinema Fund—signals that the disparities between world regions, shaped by the intertwined histories of colonialism and capitalism, continue to inform global media culture in profound and sometimes unexpected ways.

Grappling with an audiovisual culture that is increasingly produced and consumed on a planetary scale and across a range of devices and platforms, scholars have sought to define "global," "world," or "transnational" cinemas in terms that are both specific and flexible enough to account for contemporary trends and historical developments. In the process, they have framed new objects of inquiry, focusing attention not only on the cross-border exchanges that shape contemporary digital media culture but also those that have defined its celluloid past. Given the parallels between late nineteenth- and early twentieth-century imperialism and present-day global capitalism, both of which have been closely intertwined with the circulation of moving images, for many contemporary film scholars "borders are seen to have been always permeable, societies always hybrid, and international film history to have been key to the processes of globalization."[2] Despite this consciousness of the long history of transnational currents in film culture, historical studies (especially in the Latin American context) have largely been limited to moments when Hollywood's hegemony was actively contested, such as the transition to sound or the politicized New Latin American Cinema movements of the 1960s.

Rethinking well-worn accounts that oppose Hollywood cultural imperialism to audiovisual expressions of a national identity often presented as stable and homogeneous, *Cosmopolitan Film Cultures in Latin America, 1896–1960* investigates the international horizons of film production and consumption in Latin America during a period that scholars have examined almost exclusively through the lens of national cinema.[3] Most scholars of transnational tendencies in Latin American cinema have focused on the present moment, with some critical interest also devoted to the continental—and tricontinental—scope of the political modernist cinema of the 1960s and 1970s.[4] Following Argentine militant filmmakers Fernando Solanas and Octavio Getino, these movements are often theorized as variants of Third Cinema, a formulation that resonated with anticolonial filmmaking in Africa and Asia.[5] In addition to a small number of recent studies of the transnational exchanges that shaped the transition to sound, scholars of Latin American cinema have devoted some attention to collaborative initiatives between US and Latin American nations under the auspices of the Good Neighbor policy, when World War II increased the strategic and economic importance of Latin American nations for the United States.[6]

Whether focusing on short-lived collaborations between Hollywood and national industries or overt economic or stylistic/ideological challenges to North American cinema, these accounts tell only part of the story, not only because they tend to sharply divide the world between Hollywood and its other(s) but also because they almost invariably privilege specific aspects of production and film style over distribution, exhibition, reception, and the associated practices of film criticism and fan culture. In the first half of the twentieth century, the market dominance of imported cinema in Latin American nations helped facilitate a thriving exhibition and fan culture, as well as social practices that provided novel means of participating in the public sphere for emergent social actors in growing cities—particularly immigrants, internal migrants to urban centers, the working classes, and women. At the same time, film culture made possible new modes of affiliation that spanned class lines and national borders.

The term "cosmopolitan" implies the unhampered movement of individuals and capital across borders, forms of prestige tied to a specifically international brand of cultural capital, and experiences of global citizenship exceeding alliances to the nation-state. Building on these associations, and in some cases critiquing them, this volume seeks to outline how film culture—understood as the confluence of moving images, the economic and social institutions linked to their production and circulation, and the public discourses and social practices surrounding them—intersected with cosmopolitan projects in Latin America in the first half of the twentieth century.

In previous scholarship, cosmopolitan affiliations tend to appear as a function of the mobility and cultural competency of a few individual creators, such as Sergei Eisenstein, Orson Welles, and Luis Buñuel.[7] There are a handful of exceptions to both tendencies: Maricruz Castro Ricalde and Robert McKee Irwin's work on Mexican Golden Age cinema explores the global reception of its films and coproductions with other Spanish-speaking nations, while Laura Isabel Serna's study of Hollywood cinema's presence in Mexico in the teens and twenties demonstrates how the consumption of US cinema proved surprisingly central to the modernizing projects of postrevolutionary nationalism.[8] Expanding the initial insights of these recent works to geographic contexts outside Mexico, this volume examines configurations of production, distribution, exhibition, print culture, and fan cultures in Argentina, Brazil, Colombia, Cuba, Mexico, and the United States, tracing a network of unexpected interconnections within patterns of cultural circulation shaped by the legacies of colonialism and the expansion of industrial capitalism.

Following Nataša Ďurovičová, we understand the term *transnational* "in contradistinction to 'global,' a planetary category bound up with the philosophical conception of totality, and in contrast to 'international,' predicated on political systems in a latent relationship of parity, as signaled by the prefix 'inter-,'" while also observing the historical significance of the state in Latin America's audiovisual culture. For Ďurovičová, "the prefix 'trans' implies relations of unevenness and mobility," inviting scholars to reckon with the unequal flows of people, capital, and cultural goods alongside the openness and interconnectedness purported to accompany globalization.[9] In this vein, Will Higbee and Song Hwee Lim have called for the field of film studies to cultivate a "critical transnationalism" that addresses the "political imbalances as well as the unstable and shifting identifications between host/home, individual/community, global/local, and indeed, national/transnational," remaining "attendant to the dynamics of the specific historical, cultural, and ideological contexts involved in the production and reception of each particular film."[10] The studies contained in this volume demonstrate the productivity of examining cultural exchanges "above the level of the national but below the level of the global," sketching a transnational imaginary that highlights alternative genealogies for the industrial-capitalist modernity so closely linked to the emergence and spread of cinema in the first half of the twentieth century.[11]

As postcolonial theorist Walter Mignolo has argued following Enrique Dussel, the colonial histories of the territories now known as Latin America must be viewed as constitutive rather than external to this industrial-capitalist modernity. Interrogating the intersection between colonialism, capitalism, and "emancipatory" projects with a global scale, Mignolo opposes top-down processes of globalization, which he defines as "a set of designs to manage the world," to cosmopolitanism, which he characterizes as "a set of projects toward planetary conviviality" that can be used to either support or critique "global designs" ranging from nineteenth-century imperialism to present-day neoliberalism.[12] In doing so, he revises canonical models of cosmopolitanism traced from Kant, which implicitly or explicitly reassert a Western philosophical universalism tied to the values of the northern European Enlightenment. To borrow Scott Malcomson's term, Mignolo is interested in an "actually existing cosmopolitanism" that is situated in subaltern experience and ethical practice, rather than a falsely universalizing theory.[13] In insisting on the links between cosmopolitanism, colonialism, and capitalist modernity, Mignolo provides a productive point of departure for rereading Latin American film culture and examining how the dynamics of globalization "from above" made possible new forms of social experience that held emancipatory potential, even as they intersected with global hierarchies of power and hegemonic processes of state formation. (As María Fernández has argued in the case of Mexican visual culture, "nationalism need not preclude cosmopolitanism; rather, it frequently presupposes it.")[14]

In his taxonomy of the "flows and phases of world cinema," Dudley Andrew suggests that in cinema's first two decades, before North American producers effectively gained a hold on international markets during World War I, global film culture was marked by an "expansive cosmopolitanism," as cultured spectators in major cities experienced the presence of cinema as a marker of "internationalism" that offered a sense of simultaneity with metropolises across the globe.[15] The essays collected in this volume interrogate how, during the first six decades of the twentieth century, this network of cinematic texts and associated practices facilitated physical or imagined mobility for consumers, generated forms of cultural capital specific to particular local and national contexts, and made possible forms of cultural consumption and belonging articulated on a scale that exceeds the national.

The notion of a cosmopolitan transnationalism—that is, an approach to transnationalism that insists on the political, ethical, and even utopian dimensions of cultural exchange—in moving-image culture allows for fresh approaches to debates regarding the meanings of cultural modernity, which have been hotly debated both within film studies and Latin American cultural studies. Miriam Hansen's influential formulation of "vernacular modernism," which posits that the classical Hollywood cinema constituted "the first global vernacular" due to its ability to address the transformations of sensory experience under industrial capitalism, has been criticized for reinscribing "a dyadic pattern involving Hollywood with each of innumerable peripheral cinemas," rather than attending to the dynamics of intraregional or South-South exchange.[16]

Models of Latin American cultural hybridity also face challenges when attempting to decenter narratives that frame North Atlantic industrial/imperialist powers as agents of modernization. Néstor García Canclini's influential conception of the "multitemporal heterogeneity" of Latin American societies "where traditions have not yet disappeared and modernity has not yet completely arrived" runs the risk of reinscribing teleological temporalities of modernization that frame Latin American modernity as deficient and delayed.[17] *Cosmopolitan Film Cultures in Latin America, 1896–1960* seeks to nuance these models by attending closely to case studies of film culture, indicating complex points of intersection between local cultural hegemonies and forms of cultural affiliation exceeding the bounds of the national.

Combining critical essays with primary texts, which have not previously been translated into English, *Cosmopolitan Film Cultures in Latin America, 1896–1960* argues for the significance of Latin American and Latino/a film culture's engagement with the global circulation of moving images before the anti-imperialist and internationalist moment of New Latin American Cinema. Given the precariousness or complete absence of self-sustaining film industries, Latin American film cultures consistently looked beyond national horizons, forging discourses and social practices that worked both to constitute and to contest public spheres and nationalist projects. The book's four sections focus on the emergence of Latin American film cultures in the silent era, the negotiations between Hollywood cinema and international modernism during the interwar period, the transnational flows that shaped national film industries in the 1930s through the 1950s, and the afterlives of moving images in both cinephilic and cult spectatorship in the region. Understanding the cosmopolitan as an optic that foregrounds the inherently political nature of global cultural markets, we use it to illuminate how the production and consumption of cinema has participated in negotiations between the local and the global and the popular and the elite.

Exploring distinct facets of the circulation of motion pictures during the silent era—arguably the first age of global media—the first section, "The Silent Era: Between Global Capitalism and National Modernization," addresses initial film exhibition, early distribution networks, the development of film criticism, and local (dis)engagements with Hollywood's star system. Paired with a report on the first press screening of the Lumière Cinématograph in Mexico City in August 1896, Aurelio de los Reyes's essay "Gabriel Veyre and Fernand Bon Bernard, Representatives of the Lumière Brothers in Mexico" not only details how two Lumière agents introduced residents of Mexico City to the spectacle of the moving image but also how their actuality films shaped the emergence of film production in Mexico. Juan Sebastián Ospina León addresses how the circulation of imported films shaped a film culture that was simultaneously cosmopolitan and nationalistic in his essay on the Colombian reception of Italian and US films from 1916 to 1920. Focusing on the magazine *Películas*, associated with the distribution and exhibition empire controlled by Italian immigrants Francesco and Vincenzo Di Domenico, Ospina León traces how Italian cinema was enlisted in a project of conservative modernization that would advance national progress while preserving social and racial hierarchies. Ospina León's essay is accompanied by "The Show on June 15," a humorous account of an audience in need of reform in the Di Domenico's flagship movie theater by Tic-Tac (a pen name of writer Carlos Villafañe), a keen observer of daily life in early twentieth-century Bogotá. Similarly focusing on the forms of cultural capital attached to Italian identity by silent-era film audiences in Latin America, Giorgio Bertellini's essay "Manipulation and Authenticity: The Unassimilable Valentino in 1920s Argentina" examines the Argentine reception of the Hollywood star. Through an examination of previously neglected Italian-language publications and other sources, Bertellini shows that rather than enthusiastically embracing Valentino as a Hollywood star, Argentine spectators never hailed him as an icon. Stereotyped images of Argentina in Hollywood films such as *The Four Horsemen of the Apocalypse* proved much less appealing to audiences than the hybridized representations of Italians in popular theater and Argentine films such as *Nobleza gaucha* (*Gaucho Nobility*, 1915). Yet as Bertellini suggests, Valentino's sexual allure did inspire a degree of moral panic in Argentina that recalls his reception in the United States. In the accompanying short story "The Lover of Rudolph Valentino" by writer Enrique Méndez Calzada, the fanaticism inspired by the actor threatens to derail a courtship and, by extension, the upward mobility of the female protagonist.

The volume's second section, "The Interwar Period: Between Global Hollywood and the Avant-Garde," traces frequently opposing cultural formations that were heavily mediated by print culture: Hollywood cinema and international modernism. In her essay—complemented by "Memoirs of an Extra," an account by Felipe de Leiva of the labor of Latino/a immigrants in a racially stratified Hollywood—Rielle Navitski examines the lengthy runs of *Cine-Mundial* (1916–1948) and *Cinelandia* (1926–1948). These Spanish-language film magazines published in the United States acted as intermediaries between Hollywood studios and local distributors, exhibitors, and fans. Furthermore, as Navitski suggests, *Cine-Mundial* and *Cinelandia* gave prominence to multiple sites of film production and consumption, including growing Spanish-speaking communities in Los Angeles and New York. Sarah Ann Wells similarly focuses on the role of print culture as a site for mediating Hollywood and its alternatives in her essay on the initial reception of Soviet cinema in Latin America from the mid-1920s to the mid-1940s, which was registered in critical texts like the one included in the volume, Octávio de Faria's "Russian Cinema and Brazilian Cinema." Emphasizing how Soviet cinema offered both aesthetic possibilities and strategies for industrial film production for Latin American intellectuals, Wells argues that the reception of Soviet cinema allowed writers to imagine forms of cinematic modernity that circumvented Hollywood's hegemony. Linking the cultural contexts discussed in Wells's essay and a piece by Andrea Cuarterolo on Buenos Aires photographer and filmmaker Horacio Coppola, the primary text "The 'Cineclub' of Buenos Aires" by avant-garde writer and critic Guillermo de Torre describes how Coppola and other local intellectuals cultivated cinephilic forms of spectatorship in one of the Americas' foremost movie-going capitals. For her part, Cuarterolo argues that Coppola's movement between experimental film and photography was exemplary of the currents of transatlantic modernism that marked his career. More specifically, Cuarterolo analyzes the ways in which Coppola, who would become the emblematic photographer of modern Buenos Aires, adapted and reformulated the visual aesthetics of European and North American modernism to address local forms of urban experience.

The volume's third section, "The Golden Age of Latin American Film Industries: Negotiating the Popular and the Cosmopolitan" focuses on the transnational dimensions of Latin American film industries from the 1930s through the 1950s. The primary text "Motion Picture Production in South America," written by cinematographer John Alton, foregrounds the international roots of these early sound films. In a 1934 letter to the editor of *International Photographer*, Alton surveys film production in Latin America, primarily in Argentina, arguing that local industry will only materialize through the organization of foreigners, especially technicians. Evaluating the influence of Euro-American film labor on emerging Latin American film industries through the contributions of one celebrated cinematographer, Nicolas Poppe's essay examines Alton's work in Argentina between 1932 and 1939. Through detailed formal analysis, Poppe examines two distinct periods in Alton's career in Argentina: an experimental phase in which he collaborated on projects with several incipient studios and a more mainstream one in which he adapted and applied the lighting conventions of classical Hollywood genres for Argentina Sono Film, the first major local studio. In both periods, Alton's work foreshadowed the visual stylization and contrasting tones of film noir for which he would become renowned in the 1940s and 1950s. Stressing the global character of Mexico's film culture during this midcentury period, in his essay, Ignacio M. Sánchez Prado reconsiders the nation's cinematic "Golden Age" in his analysis of the range of imported and domestically produced films exhibited in Mexico City during a representative week in 1950. Rather than participating in a form of spectatorship circumscribed by the nationalistic bent of Mexican cinema, mid-century filmgoers in Mexico negotiated the transformations of subjectivity that accompanied the capitalist growth of the so-called Mexican Miracle through their consumption of both domestic and foreign productions. Similarly charting how the circulation of cultural goods can generate powerful affective and sensuous responses across national borders, Jason Borge's study of the cinematic uses of mambo, which hybridized Cuban rhythms with American big-band style, observes how both US and Mexican musicals featuring bandleader Dámaso Pérez Prado playfully inverted the North American hegemony initially reinforced by Hollywood films of the Good Neighbor era. "The Mambo," a primary text by celebrated novelist Gabriel García Márquez, who was also a prolific film critic in the 1950s, describes how the infectious music of artists like Pérez Prado circulated internationally and locally in Barranquilla, Colombia.

The book's final section, "The Afterlives of Moving Images: Cinephilia and Cult Spectatorship," focuses on the cultural meanings attached to films viewed at a historical and geographic remove from the site of their production. Irene Rozsa traces how José Manuel Valdés-Rodríguez articulated a pedagogy of film spectatorship in his pioneering course "Cinema: Industry and Art of Our Times," offered at the Universidad de La Habana from 1942 to 1956. In addition to shaping a sophisticated film audience through his course and published film criticism, Valdés-Rodríguez guided young cinephiles of the late Republican era who would later become important figures in Cuban cinema of the 1960s. The primary text, "Fox Film de Cuba, S.A.'s Continuing Competition for Scholarships to Summer School at the Universidad de La Habana," demonstrates one way in which Hollywood studios attempted to engage local cinephiles. Signed by Thomas E. Sibert, the company's president, it is also an example of how studios promoted new technologies like Cinemascope abroad. From the construction of Cuban cinephilia in dialogue with European and US cinema, the next essay moves to the US-Mexico border to examine a cultural dialogue that took place in a considerably less rarified register. Colin Gunckel teases out an alternative genealogy that sidesteps the aesthetic, economic, and political paradigms of New Latin American Cinema and subsequent film movements. In demonstrating affinities between the science fiction and horror films that circulated between the United States and Mexico in the 1940s and 1950s and Chicana/o art of the 1960s and 1970s,

Gunckel argues that the tropes of exploitation film later proved uniquely fruitful for imagining alternate histories and cultural geographies.

Cosmopolitan Film Cultures in Latin America, 1896–1960 situates the individual trajectories of camera operators, entrepreneurs, filmmakers, and stars in the first half of the twentieth century within the collective cinematic imaginaries forged through the engagement of fans, cinephiles, and critics with moving images and discourses on cinema that connected their daily experiences with distant spaces. It charts how film culture staged intersections, both pleasurable and fraught, between media forms and between multiple spatial scales—the movie theater or classroom, the city, the nation, the Spanish-speaking world, the Americas, and the globe. Ultimately, it demonstrates how currents of modernism and experiences of capitalist consumption held the potential both to reinforce and to contest hierarchies of race, class, and nation. Moving images facilitated novel forms of affective and intellectual experience, giving rise to a cosmopolitanism that was inseparable from early forms of globalization, yet nevertheless allowed for a creative negotiation with unequal cultural flows.

> RIELLE NAVITSKI is Assistant Professor of Theater and Film Studies at the University of Georgia. She is the author of *Public Spectacles of Violence: Sensational Cinema and Journalism in Early Twentieth-Century Mexico and Brazil* (Duke University Press, 2017).

> NICOLAS POPPE is Assistant Professor of Spanish at Middlebury College. His work on Latin American cinema and cultural studies has appeared in several edited volumes, as well as journals such as *Arizona Journal of Hispanic Cultural Studies*, *Cinema Journal*, and *Journal of Latin American Cultural Studies*.

NOTES

1. Elizabeth Ezra and Terry Rowden, "What Is Transnational Cinema?" in *Transnational Cinema: The Film Reader* (New York: Routledge, 2006), 3–4.

2. Kathleen Newman, "Notes on Transnational Film Theory: Decentered Subjectivity, Decentered Capitalism," in *World Cinemas, Transnational Perspectives*, eds. Nataša Ďurovičová and Kathleen Newman (New York: Routledge, 2010), 4.

3. For an important corrective to this model in other geographic contexts, see Melvin Stokes and Richard Maltby, eds., *Hollywood Abroad: Audiences and Cultural Exchange* (London: British Film Institute, 2004).

4. The regional scope of these filmmaking movements is implied in the title of Zuzana M. Pick's study, *The New Latin American Cinema: A Continental Project* (Austin: University of Texas Press, 1993). See Stephanie Dennison, ed., *Contemporary Hispanic Cinema: Interrogating the Transnational in Spanish and Latin American Cinema* (London: Tamesis, 2013); Carolina Rocha and Cacilda Rêgo, eds., *New Trends in Argentine and Brazilian Cinema* (London: Intellect, 2010); *Contemporary Latin American Cinema: Breaking into the Global Market*, ed. Deborah Shaw (Rowan & Littlefield, 2007).

5. See Anthony R. Guneratne and Wimal Dissanayake, *Rethinking Third Cinema* (New York: Routledge, 2003).

6. On the transition to sound, see Lisa Jarvinen, *The Rise of Spanish-Language Filmmaking: Out from Hollywood's Shadow, 1929–1939* (Rutgers, NJ: Rutgers University Press, 2012); Colin Gunckel, *Mexico on Main Street: Transnational Film Culture in Los Angeles before World War II* (Rutgers, NJ: Rutgers University Press, 2015). On the Good Neighbor policy, see Allen L. Woll, "The Good Neighbor Policy: The Latin Image in American Film," *Journal of Popular Film* 3, no. 4 (1974): 278–293; Ana M. López, "Are All Latins from Manhattan? Hollywood, Ethnography and Cultural Colonialism," in *Mediating Two Worlds: Cinematic Encounters in the Americas*, eds. John King, Ana M. López and Manuel Alvarado (London: British Film Institute, 1994), 67–80; Julianne Burton-Carvajal, "'Surprise Package: Looking Southward with Disney," in *Disney Discourse: Producing the Magic Kingdom*, ed. Eric Smoodin (New York: Routledge, 1994), 131–147.

7. See especially Ernesto R. Acevedo-Muñoz, *Buñuel and Mexico: The Crisis of National Cinema* (Berkeley: University of California Press, 2003); Masha Salazkina, *In Excess: Sergei Eisenstein's Mexico* (Chicago: University of Chicago Press, 2009); Laura Podalsky, "Patterns of the Primitive: Eisenstein's *"¡Que Viva México!"* in *Mediating Two Worlds: Cinematic Encounters in the Americas*, eds. John King, Ana M. López, and Manuel Alvarado (London: British Film Institute, 1993); Catherine Benamou, *It's All True: Orson Welles' Pan-American Odyssey* (Berkeley: University of California Press, 2007).

8. See Maricruz Castro Ricalde and Robert McKee Irwin, *El cine mexicano "se impone": Mercados internacionales y penetración cultural en la época dorada* (Mexico City: Universidad Nacional Autónoma de México, 2011) and Robert McKee Irwin and Maricruz Castro Ricalde, eds., *Global Mexican Cinema: Its Golden Age* (New York: Palgrave Macmillan / British Film Institute, 2013); Laura Isabel Serna, *Making Cinelandia: American Films and Mexican Film Culture before the Golden Age* (Durham, NC: Duke University Press, 2014).

9. Ďurovičová, "Preface," in *World Cinemas, Transnational Perspectives*, eds. Nataša Ďurovičová and Kathleen Newman (New York: Routledge, 2010), x.

10. Will Higbee and Song Hwee Lim, "Concepts of Transnational Cinema: Towards a Critical Transnationalism in Film Studies," *Transnational Cinemas* 1, no. 1 (2010): 12–13.

11. Ďurovičová, "Preface," ix.

12. Walter D. Mignolo, "The Many Faces of Cosmo-polis: Border Thinking and Critical Cosmopolitanism," *Public Culture* 12, no. 3 (2000): 721.

13. Scott L. Malcomson, "The Varieties of Cosmpolitan Experience," in *Cosmopolitics: Thinking and Feeling Beyond the Nation*, ed. Pheng Cheah and Bruce Robbins (Minneapolis: University of Minnesota Press, 1998), 238.

14. María Fernández, *Cosmopolitanism in Mexican Visual Culture* (Austin: University of Texas Press, 2014), 3.

15. Dudley Andrew, "Time Zones and Jet Lag: The Flows and Phases of World Cinema," in *World Cinemas, Transnational Perspectives*, ed. Nataša Ďurovičová and Kathleen Newman (New York: Routledge, 2010), 64.

16. Miriam Hansen, "The Mass Production of the Senses: Classical Cinema as Vernacular Modernism," *Modernism/Modernity* 6, no. 2 (1999): 59–77; Dudley Andrew, "An Atlas of World Cinema," in *Remapping World Cinema: Identity, Culture, and Politics in Film*, eds. Stephanie Dennison and Song Hwee Lim (London: Wallflower Press, 2006), 24.

17. Néstor García Canclini, *Hybrid Cultures: Strategies for Entering and Leaving Modernity*, trans. Christopher L. Chiappari and Silvia L. López (Minneapolis: University of Minnesota Press, 1995), 3, 1.

PART I

The Silent Era:
*Between Global Capitalism and
National Modernization*

"The Lumière Cinematograph," *El Monitor Republicano* (Mexico City), August 16, 1896

> *This unsigned account of one of the earliest exhibitions of moving images in Mexico City emphasizes not only the curiosity produced by the apparatus and its naturalistic reproduction of motion but also its proximity to other popular amusements, including the magic lantern and the circus, in a modernizing capital city.*

THE NIGHT BEFORE LAST, on the top floor of the Plateros Drugstore (the second block of Plateros Street, number 9), an exhibition of the apparatus called the "Lumière Cinématograph" dedicated to the press of this capital took place.

The cinematograph is a type of magic lantern that projects a luminous cone onto a white screen placed in front of the spectators.

In the luminous field of the screen, scenes full of life and movement unfold, caught unawares by inventor's photographic apparatus.

The night before last we viewed the following scenes: *The Arrival of a Train, Rollercoasters, A Cavalry Charge, Card Party, The Baby's Meal, Workers Leaving the Factory, The Sprinkler Sprinkled, Demolition of a Wall,* and *Swimming in the Sea.*[1]

Each scene is more marvelous than the last.

In the arrival of the train, one sees the locomotive advance with all its natural movements, followed by the cars carrying the passengers, who disembark hurriedly and move away.

The scene is so natural that one almost seems to hear the noise of the train and the bustling of the passengers.

In the rollercoasters, a scene is shown similar to the one we saw in the pantomime *A Baptism during Carnival* at the Orrín Circus: a small boat that slides down a ramp and breaks the surface of the water, scattering it into a fine spray that envelops the vessel for a moment.

In the cavalry charge, one clearly sees the immense cloud of dust kicked up by the hooves of the horses, which envelops the field of operations in a dense haze.

In the card players, one can see the sometimes pensive, sometimes fevered attitude of the players, while the waiter approaches with a tray and bottles of beer and peeks behind the head of one of the players to see the cards in his hand, while a third player pours the beer from the bottles into the glasses.

The baby's meal is a scene in the home of M. Auguste Lumière, inventor of the apparatus. One can see, seated at the table, M. Lumière on one side; his son, a young child, in the middle; and on the other side, Lumière's wife M. Lumière gives sweets to the boy, while his wife serves coffee.

The exit from the Lumière factory shows the moment in which a large number of female workers leave the factory.

The gardener and the boy is a comic scene. The gardener waters the garden with a rubber hose; the boy steps on the hose and prevents the water from flowing. When the gardener inspects the mouth of the hose, the boy lifts his foot and the water shoots out, soaking the gardener's face.

In the demolition of a wall, M. Lumière again appears, directing the operation: the wall falls and a cloud of dust envelops the workers.

In the bathers, they are seen on a beach diving into the sea; one observes the movement of the waves and the splashing of the water as the bathers tumble.

In all of these scenes, the movements are perfectly photographed: there is natural life and animation in them, and all of this produces the most marvelous effect.

Translated by Diana Norton and Rielle Navitski

RIELLE NAVITSKI is Assistant Professor of Theater and Film Studies at the University of Georgia. She is the author of *Public Spectacles of Violence: Sensational Cinema and Journalism in Early Twentieth-Century Mexico and Brazil* (Duke University Press, 2017).

DIANA NORTON is a PhD candidate at the University of Texas in Austin, currently writing her dissertation on *Hispanidad* and the star discourses of Hollywood and Latin American actresses in Spain.

NOTES

1. *Editors' Note:* For clarity, we have used common English-language versions of the film titles. The titles used by the journalist differ slightly; we have preserved them in the wording of following paragraphs, in which the author briefly describes each of the films without referring to them by title.

Chapter 1

Gabriel Veyre and Fernand Bon Bernard, Representatives of the Lumière Brothers in Mexico

Aurelio de los Reyes

STUDYING THE HISTORY OF cinema in Mexico allows one to better comprehend its society, especially if one takes the beginnings of the medium as a point of departure, as it allows us to delve into the habits and mores, in the politics of church and state, given that as a mass phenomenon, both would regulate, police, and condition it. Fortunately, in the case of Mexico we have detailed knowledge about the arrival of the cinematograph thanks to the press, the historical archive of the capital, and the letters written by Gabriel Veyre, Lumière agent, to his mother. Since the publication of the first book of the author of these lines, *Los orígenes del cine en México 1896–1900* (*The Origins of Cinema in Mexico, 1896–1900*), in 1972, research on the first years of cinema in Mexico has continued.

In early July 1896, Gabriel Veyre, a technician for the Lumière Cinématograph, and Claude Fernand Bon Bernard, a representative authorized to commercialize the apparatus in Mexico, Venezuela, the Guianas, and the Antilles, embarked from Le Havre for New York. Mexico City was their final destination and, after traveling five days by train from New York, they arrived on the twenty-fourth: "Overall, a very good trip. The five days we spent on the train were a little tiring and we slept soundly last night. I'll do the same tonight. I hear from my window an *orgue de barbarie* [a barrel organ]; it reminds me of a peculiarity of the trip: near Laredo, nearing Mexico, there is also another tall tree called 'organo,' which means *orgue*. ... *de barbarie*. Just like, without a doubt, like figs!"[1]

It is probable that Veyre and Bernard met each other and joined forces in Lyon. The cinematograph offered them the possibility of seeing the world, of crossing borders, of choosing adventure over stability.

Veyre came from a family of good social standing in Lyon, the city where the Lumière brothers invented the cinematograph. His father, a notary in Saint-Alban du Rhône (located in the department of Isère about thirty kilometers from Lyon) where he lived with his family, died in 1893. His employment gave him social status; Gabriel studied pharmacology because he had assumed the responsibility of providing for his mother, three brothers, and two sisters, but the cinematograph intervened in his life's journey. Bernard, a mysterious character, appears to have descended from German residents of Santa Fe, New México. The reasons for his presence in France and the conditions of his association with Veyre are unknown.

They stayed at the Hotel de la Gran Sociedad on the Calle del Espíritu Santo, now known as Isabel la Católica, in the heart of Mexico City. On July 25, Veyre related his impressions of the trip and the beginning of his Mexican adventure to his mother.[2] He told her that someone—he does not say who—referred them to Fernando Ferrari Pérez, who in turn introduced them to the "Commander-in-Chief of the Mexican army," most assuredly Felipe Berriozábal, the secretary of war, who rented the mezzanine of the Plateros drugstore, located at Plateros 9, headquarters of the Mexican Stock Exchange, on their behalf. Before the first exhibition, they resolved various technical difficulties, including the low wattage of the electrical power. After six anxiety-filled days, Veyre combined two projector bulbs in order to achieve enough brightness to project the films with clarity. He notes that others who tried to commercialize a similar apparatus faced the same problem. It is probable that Veyre is referring to Edison's Vitascope, which began its exhibitions in the Circo Orrín one month after Veyre and Bernard began their sessions. He writes, "Have faith, dear mother; trust and patience. This could be the beginning of the end of all our worries."

On August 1, *L'Echo de Mexique*, the local French-language newspaper, acknowledged receipt of an invitation from the two gentlemen to attend an exhibition of the apparatus, previously displayed in the principal European capital cities, where it had provoked admiration and excitement.[3] General Berriozábal promised to carry out some military exercises so that they could be recorded by the cinematograph, and to arrange for the invention to be exhibited for General Porfirio Díaz, president of the republic, who was offered the first film exhibition in Mexico on Thursday, August 6, at his residence, the Castillo de Chapultepec. The president, his wife, and some forty guests attended, "leaving incredibly pleased." The hosts invited Lumière's emissaries to dinner and, afterward, they continued viewing moving pictures "until one in the morning."[4]

Veyre and Bernard, fearful that there would be no audience at a screening for the press and "scientific groups" scheduled for Friday, August 14, invited more than fifteen hundred people.[5] So many people arrived that they did not know where to put them. "We predict a great success from their applause and shouts of 'Bravo!' and all the cries of 'how lovely!' 'how lovely!' The girls above all, as Joseph would say, and the boys applauded to the end. In short, a splendid debut evening."[6]

It is not known what films were exhibited at the first showing because several sessions had to be held at thirty-minute intervals in order to keep up with demand. Each program consisted of eight different short films, which they tried to avoid repeating in the following session. A journalist from *Gil Blas* counted eleven: *The Gardener and the Boy* (*L'Arroseur arrosé*), *The Card Players* (*Partie de cartes*), *The Arrival of a Train* (*L'Arrivée d'un train en gare de La Ciotat*), *Babies' Quarrel* (*Querelle enfantine*), *Grass Burners* (*Les Brûleurs d'herbe*), *Child's Play* (perhaps *Scène d'enfants*), *Imperial Procession in Budapest* (likely *Cortège de la couronne* or *Cortège du sceptre royal*), *A Plaza in Lyon* (perhaps *Place Bellecour*), *Bathing in the Sea* (*Baignade en mer*), *Baby's Meal* (*Repas de bébé*), and *Rollercoasters* (*Montagnes russes sur l'eau*).[7] A reporter from *El Monitor Republicano* counted nine: *The Arrival of a Train at La Ciotat Station*, *Rollercoasters*, *Cavalry Charge* (perhaps *Lanciers de la reine, défilé*), *The Card Players*, *Baby's Breakfast*, *Workers Leaving the Lumière Factory* (*Sortie d'usine*), *The Gardener and the Boy*, *Demolition of a Wall* (*Démolition d'un mur*), and *Bathing in the Sea*.[8] It is likely that the enthusiasm of the spectators obliged the Lumière emissaries to show more films than planned.

The first paid exhibition took place on the fifteenth, a rainy Saturday. In spite of the bad weather, enough people attended to turn a profit. Veyre writes, "I believe there will be a crowd because this morning many people came to watch, but we could only make the apparatus work after five p.m., the hour when the electricity powers up. . . . I end my letter hastily. I stretch myself in all directions trying to write it between shows, but so many people are coming that I have no time. In five sessions, we have had more than 100 people."[9]

Fig. 1.1a Veyre dressed in a Mexican suit. Jacquier-Veyre Archive, courtesy of Philippe Jacquier.

In general terms, the spectacle impressed the public and journalists. Exhibitions took place daily from five to ten at night. The price of the ticket—elevated—was around fifty cents, the same that one would pay to sit in the shade at a bullfight or on the patio of the Arbeu Theater for an opera performance. In the program, handed out at the entryway, the Lumière emissaries demonstrated their pride in the invention, describing it as the "only apparatus

Fig. 1.1b The Pane swimming pool, the subject of one of Veyre's actualities. Jacquier-Veyre Archive, courtesy of Philippe Jacquier.

that has been able to win and retain the admiration of the most enlightened peoples of the Old World for more than a year. The president of the Mexican Republic, General Porfirio Díaz, the president of the French Republic, Felix Fauré, the German emperor, the Russian Tsar, the queen regent of Spain—in short, all the world's notable people—have assured and applauded its success."[10]

The spectacle pleased the public; the Lumière emissaries were obliged to offer exhibitions every day. It seems that the heterogeneity of the audience bothered a certain segment of society because they asked for exclusive showings every Thursday after August 27, at twice the price, one peso, for a tableaux of twelve short films instead of eight.

The press did not record the moment when Gabriel Veyre began shooting films in Mexico City. On August 16, Veyre told his mother that a few days previously he had recorded a panorama of the president walking through the park and that on the fourteenth, the day of the press screening, he had filmed in the Colegio Militar and with some swimmers who were doing dangerous dives in the Pane swimming pool.[11] On the eighteenth, *El Correo Español* announced the upcoming exhibition of "a portrait of General Porfirio Díaz,

Fig. 1.2 A program dedicated to General Porfirio Díaz, president of the Republic, on August 27. Jacquier-Veyre Archive, courtesy of Philippe Jacquier.

the students of the Military School practicing various maneuvers and other scenes that will already be familiar to us when exhibited."[12]

On the twenty-third, "General Díaz and some members of his family in movement, a scene in the Pane swimming pool, another in the Colegio Militar and . . . one in the Viga Canal" were shown in the Castillo de Chapultepec. *Gil Blas* added that "a group of the most well-known writers in Mexico" would be organized "so as to be recorded by the Cinématograph," but this film was never exhibited, if it was in fact shot.[13]

Four days later, Veyre and Bernard returned to Chapultepec in order to show *The President of the Republic Riding a Horse in the Forest at Chapultepec Castle*, along with another twenty-six shorts of varying themes and places: *Fight amongst Women* (*Bataille de femmes*), *Babies' Quarrel, Pork Butcher in Chicago* (not identified), *The Tuileries Palace of Paris* (*Bassin des Tuileries*), and so on, divided into two sessions of thirteen films each.[14]

On Sunday the thirtieth, *Gil Blas* published an invitation for the well-to-do families who wished to see their carriages recorded by the cinematograph as they promenaded on the Paseo de la Reforma between three and four o'clock in the afternoon, "if the sky is clear, at this hour we will be shooting views of the esplanade, being unable to do so at a later time due to the lack of light."[15] It was announced that General Díaz and his wife might be in attendance.

People did not come as expected; Doña Carmen Romero Rubio de Díaz, the president's wife, a group of her relatives, and "perhaps some cyclists and pedestrians wandering by were the only ones captured in the instant photographs."[16] Eight days later, the invitation was repeated; no other information is available about what was in the film, as it was never shown in later screenings.

On September 13, 1896, *El Tiempo* commented on the new films "of Mr. President waving goodbye to his ministers and taking a carriage" and another that shows "a group of Indians at the foot of the *Árbol de la Noche Triste*."[17] The report adds that scenes of historical sites around Mexico City would be shot; nevertheless, the films were never shown.

On September 15, Veyre captured the transfer of the Independence Bell, on its way down Juárez Avenue, precisely at the stretch then known as the San Francisco Bridge, between San Juan de Letrán and Calle López.[18]

It is said that seven scenes of *fiestas patrias* were shot, but I have only been able to identify five: *Parade of Peasants in the Fiestas Patrias, Arrival of the Historic Bell on September 16, The President of the Republic Crossing the Plaza de*

Fig. 1.3 The charge of the *rurales* on the aqueduct of the Villa de Guadalupe. Jacquier-Veyre Archive, courtesy of Philippe Jacquier.

la Constitución on September 16, *Parade of Rurales at a Gallop* on September 16, and *The President and his Retinue* on September 16.[19]

The military exercise arranged by General Berriozábal resulted in the films *Students of Chapultepec with Bayonets*, *Students of Chapultepec on Parade*, and *Charge of the Rurales in the Village of Guadalupe*.

On October 13, Veyre captured scenes of the execution of Antonio Navarro, "from the time that the defense lawyer Gonzálo Suárez handed the blindfold over to Father Clemente Miró, until the execution was over." In spite of having been promised, they were never exhibited.[20]

On October 19, the Lumière emissaries began exhibitions in the Boys' Academy of Guadalajara. The spectacle was not a novelty because the Edison Vitascope had been successfully exhibited since September 26. Veyre traveled to the Atequiza hacienda:

> An hour's train ride to shoot landscapes. I filmed a lassoing by some Indian horsemen, but the bull they were chasing moved out of the camera's field of view, so you only see it for a short period of time. But as the horsemen were numerous and quite odd, I think that the view will hold a certain interest.

> The second view is an Indian riding bareback astride a bull. The bull jumps and tosses its horns right and left to throw the rider. At the end of the view, the bull leaps high and falls along with its rider. This view will be quite lovely and strange for European viewers.[21]

In the same letter to his mother, he adds:

> On Sunday and Monday we had grand celebrations for All Saints' Day and The Day of the Dead, which in this country is a national festival. All the streets are invaded by itinerant vendors seated on mats on the floor; everywhere there are sugar death's heads which are sold to children: the skull, the skeleton, everything made of sugar! Many sell sugarcane that looks like the fishing rods that we used in Saint-Alban; you chew this stick which is full of sugared juice. I would like to send you a piece, but it does not keep and would arrive sour and fermented.[22]

In Guadalajara, they shot *Lassoing, Cockfight, A Horse Breaker, Selection of Yokes for a Drove of Oxen, Horses Bathing, Mexican Dance,* and *Lassoing of a Wild Ox*, which premiered on November 12.[23]

The season ended on November 15, when Veyre returned to Mexico City. While the films that Veyre shot of the president were on their way from Lyon along with a second apparatus that they had requested, Bernard traveled to Monterrey in order to investigate the possibility of exhibiting the cinematograph in the city where General Berriozábal lived when he was the military commander of Nuevo León and Coahuila.

After November 27, the Lumière emissaries offered simultaneous exhibitions in Guadalajara and Mexico City: Bernard in the old Colegio Leon XIII and Veyre at 4 Espíritu Santo Street, in the lower levels of the Hotel de la Gran Sociedad.[24] Veyre mentioned to his mother that he had already talked with his colleague about dissolving their partnership.[25]

On November 25, General Díaz apologized to Veyre for not attending the cinematograph screenings; Veyre may have invited him for the opening of the new season.[26] Instead, Carmen Romero Rubio attended on the first of December, accompanied by a notable group of female friends and relatives. The military commander of Mexico City sent the cavalry band to make the session more pleasant.[27] The exhibitions continued throughout the month of December and into the first week of January 1897.

Among the films shot in Mexico by Veyre that were exhibited at this time, we find *Parade of Rurales at a Gallop on September 16, The President of the Republic Returning to Chapultepec in a Carriage, The President of the Republic and his Ministers at Chapultepec Castle on September 16*, in addition to *Arrival of the Historic Bell on September 16* and *The President of the Republic Crossing the Plaza de la Constitución on September 16*.[28] *The Palace Governor and Honor Guard on Horses; Gymnastics Class at the Colegio de la Paz, Formerly Vizcaínas; Dance of the Spanish Procession at the Tívoli del Eliseo*; and a film titled *Señorita Andrea*, which may have been a portrait of one of General Berriozábal's nieces with whom Veyre fell in love during a ball.[29] Although according to a letter her name was Virginia, he may have changed it for commercial reasons: "I spoke to you about three young girls who were playing the mandolin. One of them is quite remarkable. She seemed to be one of the prettiest girls in Mexico. She is 16 years old, and is the niece of the general. I am sending you her portrait, which can only give a pale idea of her loveliness, because she is not only beautiful, but also charming and good. Certainly, if I were intending to marry, it's very possible I would make her my wife."[30]

El Universal announced "that photographs of the entrance and exit on foot and by carriage of the president to the Chapultepec Palace have now been taken."[31] The last film that Veyre seems to have shot in Mexico City, which caused quite a commotion, was a reconstruction of a pistol duel that had taken place some years before between two congressman. One of them died, causing a stir in local society.[32] On January 9, General Porfirio Diaz appeared at the cinema accompanied by relatives in order to bid good-bye to Veyre. So that the president would be comfortable, the audience that had been waiting at the door for the exhibition to start was barred entrance.[33]

Bernard stayed in Mexico with the other apparatus in order to continue its commercialization. Veyre decided to dissolve the partnership because of Bernard's character and because Bernard seemed nostalgic for Santa Fe; Veyre doubted that Bernard would be successful because, beyond his personality, he did not have the ability to resolve technical problems, as evidenced by the lighting difficulties that had occurred upon their arrival in Mexico.

He was right, because, after a short period of time, Bernard sold his apparatus to Ignacio Aguirre, who continued profiting from it in the establishment at number 4, Espíritu Santo Street, according to the permit granted to him by the local Mexico City government.[34] With the money, Bernard was able to return to his beloved Santa Fe in New Mexico.

On January 11, Veyre, as an authorized dealer and technician, left for Veracruz on the train at seven in the morning. He writes, "Absolutely marvelous trip. This train line is the most picturesque in the world. Suspended in the peaks, one descends from the height of the mountains over the course of about three hours. From afar, one can perceive a microscopic city, a thousand meters below. Truly marvelous."[35]

The steamboat Lafayette transported him to Havana.[36] Before leaving, it seems that he shot the film *Hurricane, or Tempest in Veracruz*, his last film in Mexican territory.[37]

Translated by Diana Norton

AURELIO DE LOS REYES is a researcher at the Instituto de Investigaciones Estéticas at the Universidad Nacional Autónoma de México, and a distinguished historian of Mexican cinema, particularly its silent era. He is the author of *Cine y sociedad en México, 1896–1930* (Universidad Nacional Autónoma de México, 1983, 1993, 2013), comprising three volumes to date, and a three-volume *Filmografía del cine mudo mexicano* (Universidad Nacional Autónoma de México, 1986, 1994, 2000), as well as *Orígenes del cine en México, 1896–1900* (Fondo de Cultura Económica, 1983); *Con Villa en México: Testimonios de los camarógrafos norteamericanos en la Revolución* (Universidad Nacional Autónoma de México, 1985); *Medio siglo de cine mexicano* (Editorial Trillas, 1987); *Dolores del Río* (Grupo Condumex, 1996); *Tercera llamada! Tercera! Programas de Espectáculos Ilustrados por José Guadalupe Posada* (Instituto Cultural de Aguascalientes, 2005), among others.

DIANA NORTON is a PhD candidate at the University of Texas in Austin, currently writing her dissertation on *Hispanidad* and the star discourses of Hollywood and Latin American actresses in Spain.

APPENDIX
Films That Gabriel Veyre Shot in Mexico, According to the Press, Playbills, and the Lumière Catalogue

1. *Alumnos de Chapultepec con la esgrima del fusil* (*Students of Chapultepec with Bayonets*); extant in the Archives du Film (Paris) as *Exercice à la baïonnette*, Lumière catalogue no. 349
2. *Alumnos de Chapultepec desfilando* (*Students of Chapultepec on Parade*)

3. *Un amansador* (*A Horse Breaker*), filmed in Guadalajara; extant in the Archives du Film (Paris) as *Cavalier sur un cheval rétif*, Lumière catalogue no. 356
4. *Baile de la romería española en el Tívoli del Eliseo* (*Dance of the Spanish Procession at the Tívoli del Eliseo*); extant in the Archives du Film (Paris) as *Bal espagnol dans la rue*, Lumière catalogue no. 358
5. *Baño de caballos* (*Horses Bathing*), filmed in Guadalajara; extant in the Library of Congress; extant in the Archives du Film (Paris) as *Baignade de chevaux*, Lumière catalogue no. 357
6. *El canal de la Viga* (*The Viga Canal*); extant in the Archives du Film (Paris) as *Marché indien sur le canal de la Viga*, Lumière catalogue no. 355
7. *Carga de rurales en la Villa de Guadalupe* (*Charge of the Rurales in the Village of Guadalupe*); extant in the Archives du Film (Paris) as *Ruraux au galop*, Lumière catalogue no. 347
8. *Carmen Romero Rubio de Díaz y familiares en carruaje en el Paseo de la Reforma* (*Carmen Romero Rubio de Díaz and Relatives in a Carriage on the Paseo de la Reforma*)
9. *Clase de gimnasia en el Colegio de la Paz, antiguas Vizcaínas* (*Gymnastics Class at the Colegio de la Paz, Formerly Vizcaínas*); extant in the Archives du Film (Paris) as *Défilé de jeunes filles au Lycée*, Lumière catalogue no. 36
10. *Comitiva presidencial del 16 de septiembre* (*The President and his Retinue on September 16*)
11. *Danza mexicana, o jarabe tapatío* (*Mexican Dance, or Jarabe tapatío*), filmed in Guadalajara; extant in the Archives du Film (Paris) as *Danse mexicaine*, Lumière catalogue no. 353
12. *Desayuno de indios* (*Indians at Breakfast*); extant in the Library of Congress; extant in the Archives du Film (Paris) as *Repas d'indiens*, Lumière catalogue no. 351
13. *Desfile de rurales al galope el 16 de septiembre* (*Parade of Rurales at a Gallop on September 16*); extant in the Library of Congress
14. *Un duelo a pistola en el bosque de Chapultepec* (*Pistol Duel in Chapultepec Forest*); extant in the Archives du Film (Paris) as *Duel a pistolet*, Lumière catalogue no. 35
15. *Elección de yuntas en una bueyada* (*Selection of Yokes for a Drove of Oxen*); extant in the Archives du Film (Paris) as *Lassage des bœufs pour la labour*, Lumière catalogue no. 354
16. *Escena en los baños Pané* (*Scene at the Pane Baths*)
17. *Grupo de indios al pie del árbol de la Noche Triste* (*Group of Indians at the Foot of the Tree of the Night of Sorrows*)
18. *Grupo de los literatos más conocidos de México* (*Group of the Most Well-Known Men of Letters in Mexico*)

19. *Grupo en movimiento del general Díaz y de su familia* (*General Diaz and His Family on the Move*)
20. *Lazamiento de un buey salvaje* (*Lassoing of a Wild Ox*); extant in the Archives du Film (Paris) as *Lassage d'un bœuf sauvage*, Lumière catalogue no. 352
21. *Lazamiento de un caballo salvaje* (*Lassoing of a Wild Horse*); extant in the Library of Congress; extant in the Archives du Film (Paris) as *Lassage d'un cheval sauvage*, Lumière catalogue no. 350
22. *Llegada de la campana histórica el 16 de septiembre* (*Arrival of the Historic Bell on September 16*); extant in the Archives du Film (Paris) as *Transport de la cloche de l'Independence*, Lumière catalogue no. 346
23. *Manganeo* (*Lassoing*), filmed in Guadalajara
24. *Huracán, o temporal en Veracruz* (*Hurricane, or Tempest in Veracruz*)
25. *Pelea de gallos* (*Cockfight*), filmed in Guadalajara; extant in the Library of Congress; extant in the Archives du Film (Paris) as *Combat de coqs*, Lumière catalogue no. 26
26. *El presidente de la república despiéndose de sus ministros para tomar un carruaje* (*The President of the Republic Waving Goodbye to his Ministers in Order to Climb Aboard a Carriage*); extant in Archives du Film (Paris) as *Le Président prenant congé de ses ministres*, Lumière catalogue no. 345
27. *El presidente de la república, en carruaje, regresando al castillo de Chapultepec* (*The President of the Republic Returning to Chapultepec Castle in a Carriage*)
28. *El presidente de la república entrando a pie al castillo de Chapultepec* (*The President of the Republic Entering Chapultepec Castle on Foot*)
29. *El presidente de la república entrando en coche al castillo de Chapultepec* (*The President of the Republic Entering Chapultepec Castle by Coach*)
30. *El presidente de la república paseando a caballo en el Bosque de Chapultepec* (*The President of the Republic Riding a Horse in the Forest at Chapultepec Castle*); extant in Library of Congress; extant in Archives du Film (Paris) as *Le Président en promenade*, Lumière catalogue no. 348
31. *El presidente de la república recorriendo la plaza de la Constitución el 16 de septiembre* (*The President of the Republic Crossing the Plaza de la Constitución on September 16*)
32. *El presidente de la república saliendo a pie al castillo de Chapultepec* (*The President of the Republic Leaving Chapultepec Castle on Foot*)
33. *El presidente de la república con sus ministros el 16 de septiembre en el castillo de Chapultepec* (*The President of the Republic with his Ministers at Chapultepec Castle on September 16*)

34. *El proceso del soldado Antonio Navarro* (*Prosecution of Soldier Antonio Navarro*)
35. *Señorita Andrea*

* In 1972, the Universidad Nacional Autónoma de México published my book, *The Origins of Cinema in Mexico, 1896–1900*. Since then, little has been added to the information that I presented regarding the Lumière emissaries in Mexico. The present account, based on newspaper information that I compiled a long time ago, was enriched by the letters that Gabriel Veyre sent to his mother; correspondence that Veyre's great-grandson, Philippe Jacquier, kindly gave to me and authorized me to publish. Along with the letters, Jacquier found some photographs that Veyre took and a Mexican suit that he bought in the attic of the family home, in addition to many photographs and objects from Veyre's trip to Japan. When I wrote the book there was no way to travel to Lyon or Paris in order to verify if the films taken by Veyre in Mexico still existed. There were no books in Mexico regarding the Lumière brothers, nor was there any way of coming into contact with the Cinémathèque Française or with any Lumière descendants. Subsequently: (1) The short book *Louis Lumière*, written by Georges Sadoul arrived in Mexico. This book includes an appendix with a catalogue of Lumière films: not all of the titles that I found in the press are included among those from Mexico; however, the catalogue does include titles of which the press does not have a record. (2) I encountered film programs that allowed me to add titles not registered by the press or by Sadoul. (3) I became acquainted with the Lumière films made in Mexico that, based on exchanges between cinémathèques, arrived at the film section of the Library of Congress in Washington, DC. These are listed in the appendix with the three films included in the film *Lumière*, which was exhibited in the film club of the Institut Français de l'Amérique Latine. (4) The celebration of the 100th anniversary of film in Lyon allowed me to add the titles of the films preserved in the Lumière archives, all of which offers a more complete panorama regarding the exhibition and shooting of films by Lumière emissaries. Pending are the personal anecdotes of Veyre included in his letters, whose translation I will make known at another time. I do not dare to say that this will be the definitive article regarding the Lumière emissaries in Mexico because it lacks the materials that can be found in the Lumière archives, which are closed to researchers, and in other archives yet to be explored, but I do expect it to have lasting effect.

Notes

1. Letter from Gabriel Veyre to his mother, July 25, 1896. Archive Jacquier-Veyre (abbreviated hereinafter as AJV), uncatalogued.
2. Ibid.
3. "Faits divers," *L'Echo du Mexique*, August 1, 1896, 2. [*Editor's note*: All periodicals cited are published in Mexico City unless otherwise noted.]
4. "En Chapultepec: Sesión cinematográfica," *El Universal*, August 29, 1896, 2.
5. "El cinematógrafo de Edison en México," *El Correo Español*, August 6, 1896, 2.
6. Letter from Gabriel Veyre to his mother, August 16, 1896, AJV, uncatalogued.
7. "El cinematógrafo Lumière, la maravilla del siglo," *Gil Blas*, August 16, 1896, 3.
8. "El cinematógrafo Lumière," *El Monitor Republicano*, August 16, 1896, 3.
9. Letter from Veyre to his mother, August 16, 1896, AJV, uncatalogued.
10. Undated handbill, uncatalogued.
11. Letter from Veyre to his mother, August 16, 1896, AJV, uncatalogued.
12. "Noticias generales," *El Correo Español*, August 18, 1896, 2.
13. "El cinematógrafo Lumière," *Gil Blas*, August 23, 1896, 3.
14. Invitation, August 27, 1896, AJV, uncatalogued.
15. "El cinematógrafo en la Reforma," *Gil Blas*, August 30, 1896, 2.
16. "Noticias del día," *El Tiempo*, September 1, 1896, 2.
17. "Notas de la semana," *El Tiempo*, September 13, 1896, 1–2. [*Editor's Note:* The *Árbol de la Noche Triste* (Tree of the Night of Sorrows) stood on the site where conquistador Hernán Cortés supposedly wept after the defeat and expulsion of his forces from Tenochtitlan in 1520.]
18. "La campana de la Independencia," *El Municipio Libre*, September 16, 1896, 1.
19. "Gacetilla," *El Tiempo*, September 23, 1896, 3. [*Editor's Note: Fiestas patrias* are independence day celebrations. See appendix for original Spanish-language titles.]
20. "Le cinematograph Lumière," *L'Echo du Mexique*, October 14, 1896, 4; "Gacetilla," *El Globo*, October 16, 1896, 3.
21. Letter from Veyre, November 6, 1896, AJV, uncatalogued.
22. Letter from Veyre, Guadalajara, November 6, 1896, AJV, uncatalogued.
23. "El cinematógrafo Lumière," *El Universal*, December 6, 1896, 6.
24. "El cinematógrafo Lumière," *El Nacional*, November 17, 1896, 2.
25. Letter from Veyre, November 6, 1896, AJV, uncatalogued.
26. Letter from General Díaz to Veyre, November 25, 1896, AJV, uncatalogued.
27. "Gacetilla," *El Tiempo*, December 2, 1896, 3.
28. "El cinematógrafo Lumière," *El Nacional*, November 27, 1896, 2.
29. "Información," *El Correo Español*, November 28, 1896, 2; "Gacetilla," *El Tiempo*, December 30, 1896, 3.
30. Fragment of an undated letter, AJV, uncatalogued.
31. "El cinematógrafo Lumière," *El Universal*, December 6, 1896, 6.
32. "Simulacro de duelo," *El Nacional*, December 14, 1896, 2.
33. "Visita del señor general Díaz," *Gil Blas*, January 10, 1897, 3.
34. Archivo Histórico del Ex Ayuntamiento de la Ciudad de México, Diversas Publicaciones en General, 1891–1898, box 9, year 1897, file 861, 1.

35. Letter from Veyre, January 15, 1897, AJV, uncatalogued.
36. Ibid.
37. Veyre tells his mother that he enjoyed his trip from Veracruz to Havana; however, it is possible that the day before he boarded the ship there was a wind from the north that violently agitated the waters. Generally disappearing after three days, it left the sea tranquil once again and in conditions for safe navigation. A traveling salesman, whose projector—no doubt—was a Lumière, exhibited the film in Mérida during the first two weeks of February 1897 under the name *Hurricane in Veracruz*. He also exhibited it under the name *Tempest in Veracruz*, while others also exhibited a film entitled *North Wind in Veracruz*, which could be the same.

We might attribute this film to Veyre because we cannot confirm the presence of other men traveling all over Mexico shooting films. Veyre was in Veracruz on January 10, while the Lumière Cinematographic Committee exhibited the film in Mérida on February 1. In addition, they announced the films *Military Exercises by the Cadets at the Mexican Academy* and *Pool at the Moment in which Large Numbers of Swimmers Enter*, which correspond to *Students of Chapultepec with Bayonets* and *Scene at the Pane Baths*, both of which were shot by Veyre. The doubt that Veyre might have shot this film arises from the short amount of time that passed between when the film was shot and its exhibition: twenty nine days. According to his letters, mail from Lyon took around sixteen to eighteen days to arrive in Mexico because the boats had a layover in New York and Le Havre, to which we must add the layovers that the exhibitor from the Cinematograph Committee would have had on his voyage to Mexico. Perhaps the routes between Havana and the port of Progreso did not stop in New York, and it is probable that Veyre sent the film to Lyon from Havana.

Tic-Tac (Carlos Villafañe), "The Show on June 15th," *Películas* (Bogotá), June 1919

Colombian writer Carlos Villafañe (1881–1959), also known by his pseudonym Tic-Tac, was a poet, avid bullfighting fan, and prominent journalist who published widely in Bogotá newspapers. This vivid chronicle of an evening at the flagship movie theater of the Di Domenico entertainment empire was originally published in El Diario Nacional *and reprinted in the magazine* Películas, *a publication sympathetic to the Di Domenicos. The impresarios were likely pleased to have their venue written about by Villafañe, even if it placed their exhibition practices—including changes to the program to appease rowdy spectators—in a less than flattering light.*

THE CELEBRATED JOURNALIST TIC-TAC wrote the following charming chronicle on the theme of the June 15 show at the Salón Olympia, during which the films "Winning Grandma," with Marie Osborne, and "Emir, the Police Horse" were exhibited.[1]

PROLOGUE IN THE STYLE OF UNAMUNO[2]

Before I get into the agenda for the night, note the following: my movie theater is the Olympia. I prefer it because it is large, cool, and comfortable. And above all, for the orchestra. I go to the movies to pass the hours, not to see what passes by on the screen. To kill time, not to inform myself on cinematic events. The conventionalism of the cinema irritates me. The artificial destiny of the cinema is tiresome. The psychology of the cinema is like a cheap trinket. The conventionalism of the cinema is quite common. Merchandise from Piñalosa.

But at the movies, I kill half an evening. I listen to music. I observe people. I congregate with my fellow citizens. And at the appointed time, I sleep like a congressman. I have my spot "marked" as if from a watchtower. The right side, next to the orchestra, so close I can see the whites of their eyes. From my spot on the bench I observe. And . . .

I note with sympathy that the musicians, who give the show its flavor, cannot watch the film because they are scrupulously "taking note." All of them have to attend to their "papers," to the "holy scripture."[3] Eminent experts perform in the orchestra. Carillo's meritorious clarinet. Cuervo's enchanted flute. Soto's terrific trumpet. Figueroa's venerable violin. Peralta the virtuoso, etc. And next to the trombone, the one-man band, the gentleman with seven instruments, Professor Romero. The double bass player has to play standing up. A bad business, playing double bass. Excessive dimensions. Excessive volume. On past nights there was a full house. There wasn't a single spot. The double bass player's seat was empty. It tempted me to take it and sit down on it (the stool). But then I thought: when he's finished, he'll sit down and end up on the floor. His instrument will fall and could kill him. No easy task to get free of that heap of wood. And if a fret pokes him, he might burst.

Last Night's "Soirée"

Last night, the impresario Domenico offered us a film with the child actress Marie Osborne. I must confess that this girl's films are more suited to a matinée full of little ones than a show for "grown" people. I prefer a spasmodic contortion by Bertini or the erotic languor of Don Casto to Osborne's mischief.[4]

During the first act, the audience was discontented with the film; they began to shift about and shortly after, the whistling started. The impresario thought the audience was stomping in displeasure at the musicians and went into the orchestra pit to ask them to change the waltz they were scraping and wheezing out. One of the musicians, his pride as an artist wounded, told Domenico: "The heat's in the sheet." That is, what the audience was booing was the picture. But later the audience quieted down and they applauded the film.

Two Lovebirds Canoodling

There are lovers who go to the movies not to watch films, but to perform them: not to attend the show but to "give it." And they take certain liberties. . . . They think they can do in public what they do in private and that when the lights are off, no one is looking at them. They're wrong. The spectators are like cats: they see in the dark.

And so it is, ladies and gentlemen, that last night a boy and a girl, mere striplings, decided to start canoodling—and how! With the lights off, he started to "play" and she to "let him." And the kid—to be fair—"plays" very well. And he "leans in," as one says at the bullfights.[5] The way he leans! He should be in the orchestra playing both parts of a duet. At times they look like certain films: the shadows of their profiles merge. On a bench on in the back there was a Censor Board: a gentleman, two matrons, and two young ladies. What must the young ladies think? What the hell! Those lovebirds think they're in the treetops! The Censor Board observes. And they had to see what I saw: that those lovers traveled from "Pernambuco" to "Manaus" to "Bessarabia."[6]

I'm not one to frown and cross myself when I see these films. Nothing strikes me as new in this cinema called life. Everything can be explained satisfactorily within my system, and I know that love at twenty is the most audacious and the most enterprising. But there are things one shouldn't do in front of people, even if the lights are off. Love should be, above all, well mannered. In fact: in public it should seem not to be love. Any movement in the shadows is suspicious.

And so . . . you beginners: moderate your course a little in the future and don't disrespect your neighbors, since I am a respectable man. Just as it sounds: a man of res, peto and arepas.[7] If you are naughty again, your name and the origin of your debt will be published.[8]

At Half Past Ten

The film with the moppet Osborne has ended by this time. The screen announces a Pathé Journal newsreel, something light and pleasant, to act as a digestif. And the audience starts to make a fuss, demanding something else. So the Impresario—perhaps in revenge—decides, at this time of night, to unload the "Police Horse" film on us. At a quarter to eleven, the "rank and file" begins its melodrama. And little by little the show gets dull and people start peeling off. The poor musicians have to keep "enlivening the show with their select repertoire." What a deal! I manage to fall asleep while the horse performs its antics. When the show ends, the hall looks like it does on Tuesday nights: almost empty. The audience has snuck out. And rightly so. It's not right to rush through two shows in one just to please four louts who start stomping when they see "Pathé."

It was twenty past twelve when the screen announced "Good Night," and at this hour the horse was no longer swishing its tail, nor was the audience.[9] The horse wanted to go to its pasture and the audience to its lodgings. What a show!

I take a trolley, so as not to take two, and go back downtown. At the door of the Café Imperial I run into "Alé," the new bullfighter who is in town and whom we will see very soon in the San Diego Arena.

"Hello, Alé, how are you?"

"Good, n'you?"

"Let's get a private room."

"Let's."

And we start telling tall tales. Chatting about bulls and bullfighters (Pedro: bring me a beer, a ham sandwich, a hot chocolate, and a very hot *café con leche*).

Alé puts a record on and it starts to spin. He speaks delightfully. His conversation is an interesting "film." He knows lots about bulls and bullfighters. And he talks fluently. He could be a professor of bullfighting here. And we'll see him at the moment he "leans in." We'll see him with feinting with his red cape or stabbing from the inside out, or without his sword, soothing or chasing the bull.

At three in the morning, after running into "Juancé" in his coat and tails, I arrive at my lodgings and throw upon the pillow my head full of thoughts just plucked, purple and yellow.

If they'd shown another film at the Olympia, I would have arrived at my hovel at seven in the morning. That is, I would have arrived "the next day."

Translated by Rielle Navitski

RIELLE NAVITSKI is Assistant Professor of Theater and Film Studies at the University of Georgia. She is the author of *Public Spectacles of Violence: Sensational Cinema and Journalism in Early Twentieth-Century Mexico and Brazil* (Duke University Press, 2017).

Notes

1. (Unless otherwise indicated, all notes are from the editors.) *Winning Grandma* (1918) was directed by William Bertram. The second film is likely the Italian *Emir, the Circus Horse* (*Emir, cavallo de circo*, dir. Ivo Illuminati, 1917). Other foreign release titles for the film refer to a "police horse."

2. A reference to the Spanish writer Miguel de Unamuno.

3. I.e., their sheet music.

4. A reference to the Italian diva Francesca Bertini and the French actor Marcel Lévesque, known as Don Casto in some Spanish-speaking film markets.

5. In bullfighting, *arrimarse*, the verb used here, means to engage the bull at close quarters; in general, it means to "come close."

6. Referring to two locations in Brazil and a region on the Black Sea, the writer suggests how "far" the couple goes, while also punning on body parts and gestures: *boca* (mouth), *manos* (hands) and *beso* (kiss).

7. After asserting that he belongs to a "respectable" class, the writer puns on ingredients in a typical working-class meal: *res* (beef), *peto* (a corn-based beverage), and *arepas* (corn cakes).

8. This threat is a reference to periodicals' practice of printing the names of subscribers who owed money, along with the amounts owed.

9. This is likely a reference to the practice of projecting slides to communicate a message to the audience.

Chapter 2

Films on Paper: Early Colombian
Cine Periodicals, 1916–1920

Juan Sebastián Ospina León

IN MARCH AND AUGUST 1919, an argument took place between two specialized film periodicals: New York's *Cine-Mundial* and Bogotá's *Películas*. In *Cine-Mundial*, the Spanish-language edition of *Moving Picture World* designed to promote American cinema in Latin America, Mexican critic Rafael Bermúdez Zatarain published an article that criticized the artistic virtues of Francesca Bertini, Lyda Borelli, and Pina Menichelli—the great divas of early Italian cinema. In response, *Películas* condemned that criticism as an "expression" of American "patriotism."[1] It was a particularly delicate matter for the editors of *Películas*, as they proudly proclaimed, "By race we are Italophiles [*italianófilos*]." As unexpected as it may seem to find Spanish-language journalists passionately defending imported cinema, this reaction suggests the cultural significance attributed to foreign films in transnational contexts.

In its argument, *Películas* collapsed national and racial categories to insist on the impossibility of comparing artistic value across national borders: "Since artistic orientations vary by race ... you cannot compare Ruth Roland or Pearl White with Borelli or Bertini," the journalists claimed. *Cine-Mundial* responded to that assertion by looking to expose *Películas'* underlying agenda, namely, the fact that *Películas* depended on the largest distribution and exhibition circuit in Central America, the Lesser Antilles, and northern South America, administered by the Italian-born Di Domenico family. "[*Películas*] is a Di Domenico organ," *Cine-Mundial* decried. It then questioned the magazine's aesthetic principles: "What thrills [them] is not artistic effects ... but simply box-office effects."[2] This riposte, in fact, was only somewhat accurate;

while Di Domenico theaters exhibited and advertised American films and sold portraits of American serial queens, *Películas* systematically condemned American serials.[3] This discrepancy between discourse and practice sheds light on the rhetorical uses of foreign film by local exhibitors and distributors. *Películas* consistently incorporated discourses favoring Italian cinema and culture turned to the nationalist ends of forging a cultured Colombian film spectator. These pronouncements, which were likely aimed at protecting the Di Domenicos's commercial interests, resonated with and strategically catered to the racialized and even protofascist rhetoric that characterized Colombia's conservative yet modernizing society. *Películas*, as well as other local magazines, expressed anxieties about racial threats both outside and inside Colombia by supporting limits on immigration and drawing racialized distinctions between upper and lower classes. These claims drew on local associations between European cinema and upper-class tastes to discursively construct a social divide between those who they saw as the racially distinct, lower-class film spectators and the Colombian elite, who imposed their discursive authority on exhibition practices and local film culture.

Protofascist rhetoric found ripe terrain for growth in Colombia, a country in which the elite jealously guarded its cultural legitimacy. According to historian Juan Carlos Ruíz Vásquez, local fascism emerged in response to the "ideological instability" brought on by industrialization, growing urbanization, and the "erosion of old structures inherited from the colon[ial period] that questioned the power of diverse elite groups."[4] For Ruíz Vásquez, discourses of nationalism, racism, and corporatism dominated the local political and cultural landscape from the late 1910s to the 1930s. This rhetoric resonated with anxieties regarding emerging social actors. Even though fascism never evolved into a cohesive political faction in Colombia, the elites expressed protofascist positions through a range of social and political activities. Multiple groups spread fascist-inflected nationalist propaganda through associations, publications, and the cinema. These groups included Conservative Party officials, the Leopardos poetry circle, and even the Catholic Church, which held more influence over Colombian national politics and culture than any other Latin American nation at that time.[5]

Anxieties around urban expansion and the emergence of new social actors in early twentieth-century Colombia shaped local exhibition and distribution practices relating to imported films. These can be mapped out in local early film periodicals. As Ben Singer points out, "trade journal articles and editorials usually are valuable as historical evidence less for their ostensible content than for the wishful thinking and underlying discursive agendas they betray."[6] At a moment of unprecedented material and sociocultural transformations in Colombia, two racialized, class-driven discourses underpinned local cinema publications. First, press discourses developed a pedagogy of film viewing, striving to cultivate emergent spectatorship through print. Second, film periodicals deployed identitarian discourses that, in turn, rhetorically divided film spectators by class. In the remarkable example of *Películas*, the journal built a Colombian-Italian nationalist discourse that, rather than calling for national film production, aimed to defend European cinema as an art form that was essential to Colombian modernization.[7] Situated between these two agendas, *Películas* favored European cinema over American productions, in the face of Hollywood films' growing presence on local screens and increasing demand for them among popular audiences in the teens.

A pedagogy of proper film spectatorship and preferential exhibition of European films in service of national progress exemplified the ways in which Colombian film periodicals presented cinema as an inclusive modern venue, while they discursively divided society between popular sectors and the patrician elite. These periodicals defended the economic interests of local impresarios. At the same time, they drew on European productions to spearhead an exclusionary aesthetic, moral, and ideological enterprise premised on condemning the American fare on which these impresarios also capitalized. In these publications, European films rhetorically served as metonymies of Old World values akin to the values of local elites, while American serials represented the opposite. It was an appropriation of European films in stark contrast with other Latin American film cultures. In Mexico, for instance, Italian diva films were seen as incredibly destabilizing in terms of gender and sexuality at a time of fast-paced modernization.[8] Conversely, in Colombian film periodicals the promotion of European cinema, most notably Italian strongman and historical films, reproduced traditional social hierarchies against a backdrop of conservative modernization. By foregrounding how local film periodicals buttressed these existing forms of sociability, this article questions the simple opposition between the modern and the traditional in narratives around the advent of the cinematograph in so-called peripheral markets.[9] In the Di Domenico circuit, the visual medium of cinema sparked a renegotiation of elite discourses and practices, both in print media and in public life. Film periodicals in Colombia suggest that the arrival

Fig. 2.1 Promoting the Italian strongman film: Luciano Albertini in the lead role of *Samson against the Philistines* (*Sansone contro i filistei*, dir. Domenico Gaido, 1918). *Películas*, January 1919. Courtesy of the Biblioteca Nacional de Colombia.

of new mechanical reproduction technologies reshaped hierarchies in representation, which intellectually sophisticated elites quickly appropriated to repurpose existing models of conservative modernization across media.

Recent scholarship on the production, consumption, and reception of early Latin American film mainly draws on Argentine, Mexican, and Brazilian periodicals.[10] This predominance overshadows alternative ways in which other Latin American film cultures engaged with the global circulation of moving images. A case in point is the circuit built by Francesco and Vincenzo

Di Domenico, two Italian immigrants who established a distribution and exhibition empire, which has been largely underresearched. At its peak, this empire spanned Central America, the Lesser Antilles, Venezuela, Guyana and French Guiana, Panama, Ecuador, Peru, and Colombia, with its center in Bogotá. Within this circuit, some periodicals in the early twentieth century embraced the offerings of the Di Domenicos, while others rose up against their hold on the market through inflammatory articles. In an attempt to introduce to a larger public neglected silent-era Latin American cinema periodicals and their surprising uses of foreign cinema in the service of highly nationalistic discourses, I focus here on Colombian film periodicals—an uncharted territory for the majority of Latin American film scholars. Paying particular attention to the Di Domenico–friendly *Películas* (1916–1920) and in a lesser to degree to *El Cine Gráfico* (1914–1917) and *El Kine Universal* (1914–1916), I analyze the ways in which global film distribution intersected with local exhibition practices and film culture.

Voyage from Italy

Francesco and Vincenzo Di Domenico built their exhibition and distribution circuit on preestablished transatlantic trade routes between Italy, the Caribbean, and Colombia. They started as traveling exhibitors in 1909. Composed mostly of Pathé and Itala stock, their Cinema Olympia program circulated throughout the Caribbean and Central and South American countries, including Martinique, the Lesser Antilles, Panama, Colombia, and Venezuela. In 1910, Francesco brought his itinerant program to Bogotá. One year later, with the new name Di Domenico Brothers and Company, he established his center of operations in the Colombian capital. Through extended family networks, this traveling cinema business quickly developed into a distribution and exhibition powerhouse. By the end of the 1920s, Di Domenico Brothers, along with its parallel company, SICLA (Sociedad Industrial Cinematográfica Latinoamericana, or the Latin American Cinematographic Industrial Society), distributed and exhibited American and European pictures, produced newsreels and feature-length films, and managed about two hundred cinemas in several countries.[11]

Bogotá might seem like an unlikely center for film trade, given its early isolation from the coffee and transportation technology booms that had taken place in other Colombian regions. Nevertheless, nestled in the western mountain ranges, Bogotá partook in the unprecedented urban transformations experienced by Latin American capitals at the turn of the century. However, unlike urban reforms inspired by George-Eugène Haussmann's remodeling of Paris (as in Buenos Aires, Montevideo, and Rio de Janeiro), spontaneous demographic growth—the product of rural migrations to the urban center—physically and culturally expanded the original colonial city.[12] The checkerboard city layout grew outward, but kept traditional and new institutions of power (Catholic temples, the police department, city hall, and Congress) around the colonial central square. Thus, in a time of unprecedented material and sociocultural transformations, Bogotá reproduced colonial regulatory principles of "unity, planning, and rigorous order reflecting a social hierarchy."[13] The city was essentially colonial in its commitment to order and hierarchy, yet partaking in modern change. Particularly, Bogotá reproduced colonial sociability and mores through an obsessive relation to the written word and a mastery of language. According to historian Malcolm Deas, this obsession "was an important component" providing the intellectual elite with "a connection to the [colonial] past," during the "Conservative Hegemony," a period of unprecedented economic growth between 1885 and 1930, throughout which the Conservative Party kept political power while investing in reaffirming colonial values and suppressing any critiques of its government, including the loss of Panama to US interests.[14] Periodicals reproduced this cultural, political, and economic spirit, which was the essence of conservative modernization.

The Di Domenicos quickly adapted to the Bogotá milieu, catering to both emergent lower-class and elite spectatorship. In 1912 they opened the massive Salón Olympia. For John King, this celebrated three-thousand-seat film theater was "a symbol of the modernity of new picture palaces" in Latin America.[15] However, King overlooks how the unique physical layout of the Salón Olympia perpetuated social stratification. The picture palace had its screen located in the middle of the building, with the inexpensive seats situated behind it, thus forcing those spectators to read the intertitles backward.[16] Shared yet segregated spaces reveal the significant yet partial expansion of Bogotá's public sphere, paradoxically premised on social immobility. Tellingly, the theater's slogan in the press read, "The *rendez-vous* of Bogotá aristocracy."[17]

The immigrant brothers pulled spectacular publicity stunts during the teens, capitalizing on technological innovations and cultural traditions.

Appealing to local traditionalism, Francesco Di Domenico sent a petition to the Bogotá municipality demanding a piece of land in front of the Salón Olympia to be donated to the company. Supposedly, Di Domenico Brothers planned to erect a monument of Policarpa Salavarrieta, a heroine of the Colombian independence movement. Published in *Películas*, the petition drew on nationalist sensibilities, describing Salavarrieta as "the highest exemplar of virtue and Colombian female patriotism."[18] Using this national figure to allow the brothers to intervene commercially into the city's public space, which was most likely a pretext to expand the Salón Olympia lot, the periodical-promoted project functioned as a symbolic gesture to join Italian philanthropy with Colombian nation building. The Di Domenico patriarch, who was Hispanicized in the text as "Francisco Di Doménico," justified his demand by stating that he "considered [Colombia] his second Fatherland." Claims to a second fatherland, published through the sympathetic magazine *Películas*, were aimed to gain favor within the city's highest social circles by linking foundational history to the European novelty their films offered.

Despite the immigrant brothers' publicity stunts that evoked both progress and tradition, aimed at the higher echelon of Bogotá society, the Salón Olympia and other theaters partially opened up the public sphere, offering spaces for the social classes to come together. Consequently, the illustrated press mirrored the anxieties and titillation produced by juxtaposing polarized segments of the audience—the patrician elite and its popular counterpart. In confronting newfound, shared spaces in theaters, periodicals readily focused on viewing practices. The *Boletín de la Sociedad de Embellecimiento de Bogotá* (Bulletin of the Bogota Beautification Society), an elitist publication that linked urban life and beautification to social issues and civic pride, discussed physical threats to "ladies and respectable people" at the theaters.[19] Purportedly, lower-class patrons reacted aggressively to certain musical accompaniments, shouting or banging in protest, although the column does not describe the music or the reason for the patron's violent reactions. As a response, in an open letter to the governor, the Beautification Society demanded a new bill regarding public events: exhibitors were to publish the musical repertoire in film programs and posters in order to forestall lower-class outbursts of rage. When passed, this regulation legally permitted the police to arrest indignant patrons in the name of public order, on the grounds that they had been informed of the musical repertoire before going into the theater.

Other publications condemned new forms of gendered sociability in cinema theaters albeit voyeuristically. For example, renowned journalist Carlos Villafañe (writing under the pseudonym Tic-Tac) depicted the Salón Olympia as "a space apart and a space in between," to borrow Miriam Hansen's terms.[20] For Villafañe, its physical space permitted unprecedented displays of sexual expression. He complained, "There are lovers who go to the movies not to watch films, but to perform them. . . . They think they can do in public what they do in private and that when the lights are off, no one is looking at them. They're wrong. The spectators are like cats: they see in the dark."[21] Villafañe's provocative chronicle reveals anxieties about the increasingly diverse film spectator. From the safe distance of a participant observer, Villafañe reveled in recording transgressions of the public/private divide. As part of the elite, however, Villafañe's chronicle obliquely policed sexual liaisons through public shaming. Reproducing a common practice in local magazines—listing the names of subscribers who owed money and the relevant amounts—Villafañe warned, "If you are naughty again, your name and the origin [i.e., the reason] of your debt will be published."

The particular transformations of this social environment had significant consequences for the public dimension of film viewing. Unlike cities such as New York or Buenos Aires, where massive immigration and renegotiated social relations generated spaces for new forms of association, including at the cinema, conservative modernization in Bogotá did not condition the emergence of "alternative public spheres" in film theaters.[22] Premised on civic autonomy and a break with an earlier social order, the notion of alternative public spaces demands revision in the Colombian context. Foremost, the idea of public space did not emerge to delegitimize the sociocultural power of former colonial social structures. Rather, colonial values and mores endured, reproducing the values of the patrician elite: hereditary privilege, social immobility, and hierarchical divisions of space. Both periodicals and built environments revitalized traditional principles and practices in the modern setting. In this context, it is no surprise that film journals reproduced regulatory principles regarding film viewing and film taste, intending to impose prescribed norms of viewing conduct on their readership. Thus *Películas*, as well as its competitors, *El Kine* and *El Cine Gráfico*, aimed both to cultivate an ideal spectator and to legitimize local distribution and exhibition practices that favored European cinema.

Cinematic Decorum: Joining the Instructive with the Agreeable

In general, traditionalism affected the ways in which local audiences and distributors engaged with the global circulation of moving images, both on paper and in film. Periodicals were suffused with concerns about the need to regulate film and its effects on society. These anxieties were entangled with broader concerns about emergent social actors. Many periodicals saw film as a danger to its audiences—especially women, children, and the lower classes. The phenomenon was not unique to Colombia; in the 1910s and 1920s, moral panic went hand in hand with the policing of cinema across the globe. In the United States, female viewers aroused anxiety—particularly, of course, among men—about women's growing social and economic independence.[23] In Mexico, Brazil, and elsewhere, there was a fear that imported films would engender local emulators of international crime as seen on the silver screen.[24] In this climate of international anxiety over film's social repercussions, Colombian film exhibitors performed unique acts of discursive appropriation through film periodicals. As a response to the attacks on cinema in the press, exhibitors capitalized on the authority of the written word to defend their businesses, as well as their cultural and ideological positions. Through rhetoric that elevated their own cultural legitimacy and simultaneously depicted cinema as a potential boon to both spectators and the nation, local exhibitors safeguarded an exhibition niche, while cultivating racial and class divisions among spectators. In local film journals, cinema was the herald of both culture and material progress under the banner of conservative modernization.

Three exhibitors-distributors produced hybrid periodicals, positioned between the fan magazines that addressed a general (largely female) readership and film-trade journals, directed at (male) distributors, theater owners, and projectionists.[25] Di Domenico Brothers in Bogotá, Domingo Guzmán in Cúcuta, and Variety Theater in Cartagena respectively printed *Películas: Revista de Arte y Variedades* (1916–1920), *El Cine Gráfico* (1914–1917), and *El Kine Universal* (1914–1916).[26] The last's subtitle—"to instruct, to moralize, to delight"—best sums up these periodicals' primary aim.[27] Appropriating the Horatian advice to join the instructive with the agreeable, a common reference in Colombia periodicals at the time, *El Kine* announced cinema's utility in terms of morality and leisure.[28] These competing publications and their publishers found common ground fighting against censorship committees, taxation, and the self-proclaimed "Catholic press," which condemned the purported proclivity of filmgoers to imitate the crimes and brazen eroticism shown on screen. In the meantime, through their periodicals, the three impresarios lobbed accusations at each other: charges of smuggling film stock, of engaging in unfair competition, and even of damaging filmgoers' "optic nerves" by projecting scratched films.[29] Despite underlying agendas, two discourses dominated the Colombian film periodicals: the production of an "ideal spectator," and the ideological promotion of European films over American serials.

Local magazines gave priority to constructing the ideal spectator out of their expanding readership. In the context of conservative modernization, "the problem of the public" for film magazines began with establishing filmgoing in terms of social and economic exchanges. Exhibition practices, such as class-divided theaters, revealed partially inclusive yet ultimately segregationist film-viewing practices imposed from the top down. At the same time, practices from the bottom up resisted the capitalist exchanges exhibitors offered to patrons. For example, in a condescending editorial, *El Cine Gráfico* rebuked a practice that accompanied ordinary economic transactions—the ñapa, which referred to an "extra gift" shoppers would ask merchants for during bargaining to make the most out of a deal. According to the column, after viewing European "spiritually demanding dramas," filmgoers used to solicit, as ñapa, the "spicy gestures of Max Linder" and "other princes of laughter."[30] In response, exhibitors haughtily demanded decorum during film screenings: drama, "through which art placidly runs," should not conclude anticlimactically with slapstick films thrown in for good measure. Keeping with the "good taste" that *El Cine Gráfico* thought to impart to its readers, the column condemned ñapa practices: the "backward habit" should be left to "fruit sellers and milkmen." The column concluded with an appeal to the cultivated elite, extolling its "intellectual ... audience and [exhibitors] to safeguard the prestige of Art, in a joint effort." *El Cine Grafico*'s rebuke thus portrayed the customary practice of ñapa as an exclusively lower-class habit, antithetical to progress.

Colombian exhibitors responded to these gift economy exchanges with pedagogical and moralistic articles that aimed to discipline lower-class spectators and, at the same time, to elevate cinema's cultural status to the level of art. Ñapa, "a custom rooted in the soul of the people [*pueblo*]," was to be censored and controlled in the face of the popularization of leisure practices. Like the segregated spaces of the Salón Olympia, the attempted control of ñapa revealed considerable resistance to the presence of emergent social actors on the part of the elites. On the one hand, the column acknowledged the aesthetic progress of filmgoers: "With a precision that delights and excites [the columnist], today any son of the people can understand the most complicated plot [and experience] a quiver in the soul." However, the very terms used to refer to these patrons, the "people"—the *pueblo*—reveal the operation of exclusionary rhetoric in the cultivation of spectators. At the turn of the twentieth century in Latin America, emerging social actors gained unprecedented visibility in the press through vague terms such as "the people" or "the masses," which ambiguously made visible conflicting collectivities in the process of political and cultural modernization. As cultural critic Graciela Montaldo argues, rather than incorporating new subjects into the social body, periodicals depicted a heterogeneous national collective that resisted incorporation into dominant discourses "by escaping definition."[31] In a similar way, Colombian film periodicals aimed to nurture the pueblo into a modern spectator, but by virtue of representing new social actors in these terms, they ultimately doubted the success of such an endeavor. To cultivate the pueblo was "a utopic attempt," the aforementioned article concluded.[32] Through the written word, exhibitors positioned themselves as arbiters of propriety and film aesthetics, which sat in sharp contrast to lower-class patrons.

On the other hand, the practice of including a ñapa in film screenings also points to a tension between the variety program and emerging feature-film exhibition. *El Cine Gráfico* discursively differentiated exhibition forms in levels of cultural prestige, mustering forces against the desire for one-reel slapstick extras in favor of standardized feature-length screenings. The traditional ñapa further problematized the "conception of the *everyday* in terms of capitalist modernity," to borrow again from Hansen. In "Western modernity," Hansen argues, the modern everyday became the site in which the demands of capitalist production and consumption "were set off against, yet made to coexist, 'uneasily and unhappily,' with received social and cultural forms and relationships."[33] Extra-economic practices such as ñapa reveal how the standardization of film exhibition in Colombia collided with preexisting forms of exchange, much like the Japanese and Chinese cases Hansen studies. In the Colombian case, the clash between these forms opened up a space to reproduce received social structures through film periodicals and their renderings of everyday practices at the cinema.

The attempts of local film periodicals to cultivate an ideal spectator did not merely challenge traditional transactional practices. Film periodicals created a narrative of the global circulation of moving images in ways that favored distribution and exhibition of European over American productions. Ironically, periodicals praised action-driven Italian films and criticized American serials, not because the former had any high-art pretensions, but because of their nationality. *El Cine Gráfico, El Kine,* and most notably, *Películas*, printed Manichaean columns that opposed "true art" cinema, meaning European films, to American films, despite the increasing presence of American productions.[34] Columns praised European "cinematographic tendencies ... characterized by a real conception of Art and of life"—a "realism" that "educates and refines," in opposition to American productions that "exploit[ed] *feuilleton*-esque motifs woven from unrealities."[35] In addition to filmgoing propriety, journal editorials, film reviews, and opinion columns touted Italian and French films' superiority in terms of moral and aesthetic refinement. In their view, preference for European films was an indicator of good taste.

Películas aimed to associated European film production with the dignity and prestige of Old World values. The magazine glorified European historical films such as *Quo Vadis?* (dir. Enrico Guazzoni, 1913) and *Cabiria* (dir. Giovanni Pastrone, 1914), as well as films based on French and Italian literary works, most notably the Pasquali production company's adaptations of novels by Carolina Invernizio. Other periodicals, however, reveal that by 1919 the Colombian public primarily viewed American serials.[36] In response, *Películas* hyperbolically praised European productions even more. The magazine especially celebrated a particular feature-length Italian genre, which Monica Dall'Asta calls the "highly serialized epic-athletic genre of strong men," born from the international circulation and cross-influence of French feuilleton narratives and American serial-queen melodramas.[37] *Películas* published abundant reviews of many of the twenty-six *Cabiria* sequels starring muscleman Bartolomeo Pagano.[38] Ambrosio's shorter series of *Galaor* films (dir. Mariano Restivo, 1918) also received special attention. *Películas* promoted Italian musclemen films within what was then considered the "globalized [*mundializado*]" circulation of these types of films, evoking the fact that they were shown all over the world as a sign of their quality.[39] Despite Maciste's rather simple character development, a strongman who sides with the weak, *Películas* attributed his persona with complex moral qualities that made his character and these films superior to the international—i.e., American— competition. According to the magazine, Maciste's "bonhomie," "poise," and "valor" revealed not only moral but also filmic and acting superiority, or as one film critic put it, "masculine beauty in all its splendor." Maciste's "moral and physical" cultivation surpassed that of American athletes, such as Douglas Fairbanks and Eddie Polo, who were depicted as "educated" but less refined, and ultimately, deemed "rough" and "coarse" by Colombian critics.[40] Certain French serials more akin to American serials also got privileged column space in *Películas*, where Gaumont's *Judex* (dir. Louis Feuillade, 1916) and Phocea Film's *Mascamor* (dir. Pierre Marodon, 1919) received particular attention.

Colombian film culture presented tensions between the improvised variety program and feature-film exhibition, seen as forms with differing levels of cultural prestige, just as the critique of cinematic ñapa suggests. In the context of shifting exhibition formats, the tussle between European features and American serials took center stage in the periodicals. The dispute seems to have been quite intense, for it reached the pages of *Cine-Mundial*, published in New York City: "The [Colombian] audience is divided. The great audience ardently yearns for American [serials] while the feminine and elegant audience does not get tired of adoring the passionate gestures of Pina Menichelli, the violent dramatism of Francesca Bertini, or the contortions of Lyda Borelli."[41] Elite-oriented press discourses on serials were the clearest case of ideologically charged oppositions between American and Italian cinema. It is no surprise that serial formats were at the basis of the struggle, since "seriality" stimulated the "consistency and regulation" of film markets across the globe.[42] Episodic formats made possible the shift from the variety format of early cinema exhibition to more standardized sessions. In the early and mid-1910s, the serials' multireel format "offered a compromise" when feature-length films began to offer an "alternative model of standardizing motion-picture entertainment."[43] Local periodicals grounded their purportedly aesthetic agendas on opposing these two serial formats in their drive for aesthetic uplift and regularizing film exhibition in local circuits.

Serial cinema was "the most powerful vehicle in the emergence of a globalized, transnational culture," to quote Dall'Asta.[44] In this global context, she argues that national film cultures often reacted to the dangers of acculturation that were particularly associated with serial productions. Recent scholarship on the reception of foreign serials in Latin America

Fig. 2.2 Francesca Bertini in an advertisement for *Frou-Frou* (dir. Alfredo de Antoni, 1918). *Películas*, November 1919. Courtesy of the Biblioteca Nacional de Colombia.

stresses the ambivalent reactions that serials provoked in local circuits. For example, according to Laura Isabel Serna, in Mexico in the 1910s, American serials offered popular audiences "thrills and emotions that resonated with their experience of modern life."[45] Serials capitalized on stunts, suspense, and active female heroines. At the same time, however, Mexico's elite saw serials as importing "behaviors and attitudes . . . to reform and educate out of existence."[46] In a similar vein, Rielle Navitski foregrounds how the cross-pollination among feuilletons, imported crime serials, and sensationalist police reporting conferred new meanings to criminal activity: rather than a sign of backwardness, crime became proof of urban growth and modernity.[47]

Discourses on the ambivalent pedagogical properties of serials—schooling the masses in new forms of consumption, but also in new methods of crime—also permeated the Colombian press.[48] However, I am more interested in foregrounding the racialized and aestheticized elite discourses present in Colombian film periodicals and their relationship to film-exhibition practices. In this light, the privileging of Italian strongman films over American films comes into focus. As mentioned, *Películas* granted considerable space to Maciste films in columns and fiction tie-ins that accompanied film releases. Recent scholarship on Maciste stresses that, from the time of the character's birth as a black-bodied African slave in *Cabiria*, to the first spin-off, the eponymous *Maciste* (dir. Luigi Romano Borgnetto and Vincenzo Denizot, 1915), he changed radically into a white (northern) Italian. This transformation occurred during a transitional phase when Italian films "became more ideologically marked in support of nationalist policies." Simply put, "as a national symbol, [Maciste] had to be white" in order to evoke Roman victories pertinent to nationalist and colonialist enterprises that were then familiar to Italian spectators.[49] With this context in mind, it is important to consider the uses of these films in local circuits. *Películas* granted special visibility to Maciste spin-offs. When read in the light of broader discourses on race in *Películas*, both in articles written locally and Italian texts in translation, this emphasis on Maciste takes on greater significance, which I will examine in greater detail in the following section. *Películas* reveals how, at the level of circulation and reception, film magazines in Latin American consumer nations played a crucial role in determining national film cultures. In this case, film magazines leaned toward certain productions while rejecting others, based not only on profit but also on sociocultural agendas favoring Italian cinema and culture.

"For the Glory and Greatness of Italy": Nationalist Rhetoric in Crisis

In June 1920, *Películas* published a Spanish translation of "The American Danger," an angst-ridden article on the Italian exhibition market. Initially written for an Italian readership by the renowned journalist Diego Angeli, the article observed disapprovingly how "American films conquered all publics" and consequently led to Italian film production's decline.[50] He lamented that there were "no more historical dramas, no sentimental comedies, nor passionate tragedies ... [only] adventures and more adventures and always adventures." For Angeli, the greatest danger that American films brought about was acculturation, or in his terms, the "Americanization of national cinematography." Consequently, he proposed "to prepare for the invasion" through a filmic return to the national and the patriotic; namely, to go back to the *anni d'oro* of historical film.[51] In the years between 1908 and Italy's entry into the Great War in 1914, the anni d'oro films flaunted "spectacular *mises-en-scène* aimed at reaching both the verisimilar and the fantastic [while] they exploited the Italian public's desire to have its cultural patrimony affirmed."[52] Angeli tied spectacular historical film to an inherent sense of Italianness. Translated from Italian to Spanish in *Películas*, the Italian nationalist discourse of "The American Danger" served the purposes of the elite in the Colombian context.

Angeli's concern with transnational film markets was a response to the Italian experience. Nevertheless, it also resonated with then-current cultural anxieties in Colombia and in Latin America in general, evident in discourses of identity affirmation and cultural specificity that operated through "a dialectics of crisis," to use Carlos J. Alonso's terms.[53] One of the determining factors in the emergence of this dialectics was Pan-Americanism, a historic and political narrative through which the United States meant to facilitate its hegemony over the Americas at the turn of the century.[54] Local responses to the threat of Pan-Americanism varied from nation to nation. These discourses, which equated cultural autochthony with cultural production, necessarily came into conflict with Latin America's insertion into the early twentieth-century economic world order—overall, these discourses "narrate[d] the story of an essential cultural schism."[55] "The American Danger," translated into Spanish and published in *Películas*, hinted at a similar local crisis in Colombia, both addressing the construction of Colombian nationalism through a reaction to the other and insinuating an eminent threat to local film culture, which *Películas* portrayed as Italianist film culture.

In particular, the notion of cultural schism sheds light on the uses of foreign film in local film periodicals. "The American Danger," recontextualized in *Películas*, served as a cautionary tale for exhibitors and elites regarding

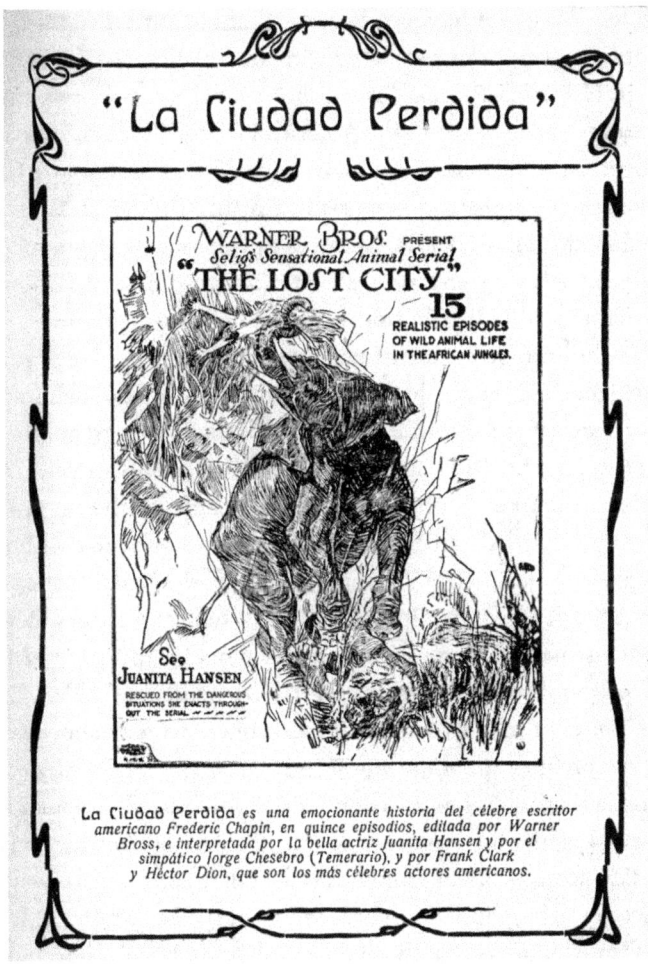

Fig. 2.3 Advertisement for *The Lost City of the African Jungle* (dir. E. A. Martin, 1920), published alongside "The American Danger" in *Películas*, July 1920. Courtesy of the Biblioteca Nacional de Colombia.

emergent threats to conservative modernization. It was one example of multiple articles, either original or translated, published in early film periodicals in Colombia that were repurposed to help shore up elite agendas.[56] Film periodicals polemically framed the global circulation of moving images, deploying articles that favored nationalist ideologies. Thus, "The American Danger" exhorted spectators to watch artfully crafted Italian historical films rather than formulaic American adventure serials. In the absence of local fiction films—which would not be produced in Colombia until the mid-1920s—the favoring of European films resonated with an elitist sense of refinement and social order. However, *Películas'* layout betrayed a schism between ideology and marketing—each page of "The American Danger" was accompanied by a compelling illustrated ad for *The Lost City* (dir. E. A. Martin, 1920), a Warner Brothers serial. The translation and reprinting of "The American Danger" in the local context suggested how elite anxieties about cultural influence, troublingly aligned with lower-class tastes, unfolded in new arenas of cultural conflict—namely, film distribution, exhibition, and reception.

Películas built a Colombian-Italian nationalist discourse that aimed to defend European cinema as an art form germane to Colombian modernization and patriotism. In addition to praising Italian strongman films via the pages of *Películas*, the Di Domenicos pushed Italian historical films in the local exhibition market, both in print and through exhibition practices. In a manner similar to the Italian strongman films, the historical films of Italy received special attention from Colombian film periodicals. In the exhibition market, in fact, they were manipulated to be close to mandatory viewing. The Di Domenicos made *Cabiria* (released in Colombia in 1916) the first local case of block booking.[57] Spearheading Di Domenicos' Golden Cycle program, *Cabiria* was a mandatory rental if exhibitors were to show other films, including Ambrosio's *Gli ultimi giorni di Pompeii* (*The Last Days of Pompeii*, dir. Mario Caserini, 1913) and "lesser" serials such as Gaumont's *Fantômas* (dir. Louis Feuillade, 1913), *Judex*, and Pathé Exchange productions, among other titles. If "Roman history films served [Italian] journalists well as points of reference for arguments that proposed the artistic and moral legitimacy of Italian film production," film criticism in Colombia, reinforcing the programming imposed by the Di Domenicos, attested to the desire to translate a rhetoric of artistic and moral superiority of European—predominately Italian—film productions, regardless of market fluctuations, to a Colombian setting.[58]

Throughout its run, *Películas* published a section titled "For the Glory and Greatness of Italy." This section contained translated fiction and poetry, as well as articles on Italian history, military might, international commercial relations, and cultural productions. In the first installment, the magazine declared that "only fervent love for our *second Fatherland* pushes us" to publish the section (emphasis added).[59] With an explicit claim to double nationalism, "For the Glory" transplanted Italian discourses and anxieties about a

Fig. 2.4 A transcription of a speech read at a Di Domenico fund-raiser for the Italian Red Cross in Panama, accompanied by a portrait of Italian Army General Luigi Cadorna. *Películas*, August 1917. Courtesy of the Biblioteca Nacional de Colombia.

shifting world order into a context where they resonated with local antagonisms. Many articles deployed protofascist rhetoric that spread throughout other sections of the magazine, such as translations of Gabriele D'Annunzio's work—then Italy's most famous writer, and an architect of Italian fascist practices—as well as articles about both the Great War and the Libyan

War.⁶⁰ For Lucia Re, the concept of race was essential to the formation of an "imaginary yet essential identity," comprising the racism, colonialism, and imperialism found in Italy in the 1910s (for which D'Annunzio was the primary spokesman). Discursive productions focused on colonial ambitions and the Libyan War "sought to unify Italians by displacing racism from inside to outside the body of the nation and its people."⁶¹ Appropriated in *Películas*, this rhetoric also procured racialized displacements. However, by contrast with Italian identity construction, this imported rhetoric was mobilized with regard to racial distinctions *inside* the Colombian body politic.

The racial dimension of protofascist rhetoric found a particular niche in local periodicals and culture. New social science discourses, such as the Italian school of criminology (Lombroso, Ferri, and Garofalo), rapidly spread across the social spectrum after elites were exposed to this writing through magazines and university penal law classes.⁶² In addition, popular magazines also disseminated these new ideas of criminology to a broader readership. Racial superiority, however, was not a novel, imported discourse—racialized hierarchies were already deeply embedded in the local culture. Exalting whitewashed physical traits "as a sign of power and supremacy," Ruíz Vásquez argues, racist discourse "was [widely] spread since colonial times."⁶³ Thus, meetings of the local intelligentsia, as well as university lectures, popular magazines, and other media, revitalized colonial racial hierarchies under the guise of social Darwinism. Regarding film journals, many film reviews seamlessly connected film appraisal and racialized reproach. For instance, a column on Maciste (most likely *Cabiria*'s Maciste, for the column lingers over his African racial traits) praised the strongman and at the same time questioned Afro-Colombians' contribution to material progress: "Maciste makes logical uses of his muscles. Our big blacks [*negros*], better yet: our big Macistes, neither tame bulls nor do they uproot the jungle."⁶⁴ Through these short yet amply scattered amounts of racialized commentary, film periodicals played a part in revitalizing racialized discourses during the first decades of the twentieth century.

Películas incorporated essentialist discourses of race on various levels. First, arguments of racial superiority sustained elitist critiques on local film taste. One film review, more nuanced than the example just quoted, critiqued American serials' appeal to lower-class audiences and stated with a note of sarcasm: "American cinematography has the seal of audacity and impudence that characterizes every intellectual and material manifestation of that original and massive people. Our race, half Latin and half indigenous, likes to feel strong emotions."⁶⁵ Attributing the popularity of sensational melodramas from the United States to the racial hybridity of the nation's population, the assertion also constructed a rhetorical distance separating the imagined reader of *Películas* from racially distinct—in this case indigenous—lower-class spectators while aligning him or her with a local (white) elite with European ("Latin") predilections. In the review, claims to bipartite identitary origins supported a social and cultural schism that ambiguously defined the Colombian nation as both miscegenized and segregated in racial and class terms. Based on "universal grounds," according to which "artistic inclinations vary by race," *Películas* claimed racial proximity to—and thus artistic proclivity for—Italian productions, as the article on film aesthetics and Italophilia that opened this essay suggests.[66] Most importantly, the use of pronouns, based on racialized premises in *Películas*, naturalized an exclusivist "we" that, classed and raced, favored European "refinement" while reproving lower-class filmic tastes. Second, going beyond questions of film reception and critique, *Películas* strongly supported immigration, with the explicit exception of "anything that entails danger against race and customs."[67] In Colombia, which had not yet been widely affected by major transnational migratory movements, this purportedly liberal stance betrayed a sense of conservative modernization. *Películas* warded off threats of miscegenation and moral decline through a racialized sense of modern "progress."

Throughout its sections, *Películas* articulated a sustained message: the idealized elite spectator should demand European films by contrast with lower-class patrons, who reveled in American serials. This rhetoric safeguarded a niche for European film distribution and exhibition, favoring the Di Domenicos's established business practices, despite the growing presence and advertising of American productions, including in their own magazines. Between profit and ideological agendas, *Películas* built a Colombian-Italian nationalist discourse that presented Italian cinema as an art form essential to Colombian modernization. This particular idea of "progress," inflected with racial overtones, conferred visibility on new social actors and their film-viewing practices, but it did so through a revitalized exclusionary discourse that was premised on social immobility, social Darwinism, and rhetoric bordering on protofascist.

Conclusion

The particular Colombian cultural dynamics in play in the 1910s inflected local exhibition practices and discourses in these publications. Local film periodicals deployed exclusionary notions of ideal spectatorship in tune with Colombia's distinct mode of conservative modernization, which exerted direct influence on the local circulation, consumption, and reception of international films. As is most evident in *Películas*, local film periodicals evoked hierarchies of taste and deployed a pedagogy of film viewing purposed to "cultivate" emergent spectatorship, discursively constructed as a lower-class, racialized other.

A struggle over audience preferences characterized the discursive agendas of Colombian film periodicals. This phenomenon emerged from "a dialectics of crisis" that accompanied discourses that affirmed the specificity of Colombian identity, ironically through reference to imported film. In the absence of local film production, *Películas*, *El Kine*, and *El Cine Gráfico* favored European—primarily Italian—films over those made in the United States. However, the appeal of American serials demonstrates a schism between press discourses and popular film-viewing practices, and the Di Domenicos's marketing and distribution practices as well. Exhibitors touted filmic Old World values through film reviews, articles, and editorials, concurrently recognizing American serials' appeal, yet choosing to inform the spectatorial palate against popular taste. Favoring European films did not only respond to profit margins, but rather adhered to cultural imperatives of elitism and hierarchy: the pillars of the patrician elite. In fact, American serials may have been seen by the Di Domenicos and other local impresarios as a necessary evil that, as in other global film cultures, stimulated consistency and regulated the film market in the shift from the variety program to feature-film exhibition. Local exhibitors might have turned toward American serials to consolidate a dependable audience, but they did not give up on their elitist agendas. Film periodicals revitalized exclusionary discourses proper to the Colombian Conservative Hegemony period in order to police filmic taste and viewing practices. Between societal reconfiguration and technologic innovation, film periodicals reproduced traditional discourses and their underlying social hierarchies to capitalize on the novelties of conservative modernization.

> JUAN SEBASTIÁN OSPINA LEÓN is Assistant Professor of Hispanic Studies at The Catholic University of America. His research focuses on the relations between melodrama, modernity, and shifting visual regimes in Latin American silent film and silent film culture.

Notes

1. "Leyendo la prensa cinematográfica," *Películas*, June 1919. Unless otherwise noted, all translations from the French, Spanish, and Italian into English are my own.

2. "Crónica de Bogotá," *Cine-Mundial*, August 1919, 639–640. I thank Rielle Navitski for bringing this article to my attention.

3. "Crónica de Colombia," *Cine-Mundial*, May 1921, 354.

4. Juan Carlos Ruíz Vásquez, *Leopardos y tempestades: Historia del fascismo en Colombia* (Bogotá: Javegraf, 2004), 238.

5. By the prerogatives conferred to the clergy in the 1886 Constitution and the 1887 Concordat, the church monopolized education for decades, consequently influencing Colombians' everyday lives. Furthermore, the church was represented on local censorship committees during the period of study. More research is needed regarding the church's use of moving images for pedagogical purposes before 1930. It is very likely that it resorted to film for its own purposes, based on the many Di Domenico "Charity" shows advertised in *Películas*. Another telling fact is that by the 1930s, the church owned 150 movie theaters throughout the country. See Jorge Nieto and Diego Rojas, *Tiempos del Olympia* (Bogotá: Fundación Patrimonio Fílmico Colombiano, 1992), 102–103, and Ruíz Vásquez, *Leopardos y Tempestades*, 102.

6. Ben Singer, "New York, Just Like I Pictured It," *Cinema Journal* 35, no. 3 (1996): 115.

7. The discourse elevating film to the stature of high art was a global phenomenon during the 1910s. See Kristin Thompson's brief introduction to a special edition on 1910s films, "International Cinema of the 1910s," *Film History* 9, no. 4 (1997): 339–340.

8. See Hipólito Seijas [pseud. Rafael Pérez Taylor], "El Menichelismo," *El Universal*, October 14, 1917, in Manuel González Casanova, *Por la pantalla: Génesis de la crítica cinematográfica en México 1917–1919* (Mexico City: Universidad Nacional Autnónoma de México, 200), 406–409. I thank Rielle Navitski for bringing this article to my attention.

9. A seminal piece on the relations between modern attractions, modernity, and the traditional is Ana M. López's "Early Cinema and Modernity in Latin America," *Cinema Journal* 40, no. 1 (2000): 48–78. Lopez defines Latin American modernity in terms of a "decentered, fragmented and uneven" process (49). Her argument, thus, presupposes center/periphery relations revealed by the import of foreign technology and its uses.

10. See, for instance, María Luisa Amador and Jorge Ayala Blanco, *Cartelera Cinematográfica 1912–1919* (Mexico City: Universidad Nacional Autónoma de México, 2009); Leonardo Maldonado, *Surgimiento y configuración de la crítica cinematográfica en la prensa argentina, 1896–1920* (Buenos Aires: iRojo, 2006); Jason Borge, *Avances de Hollywood: Crítica cinematográfica en América Latina* (Buenos Aires: Beatriz Viterbo Editora, 2005); González Casanova, *Por la pantalla*. Ana M. López had already recognized Argentine, Brazilian, and Mexican predominance in Latin American media history in her seminal essay "Early Cinema." Most recently, the Media History Digital Library has digitized thirty years of *Cine-Mundial* (1916–1946), which was published in New York. Thanks to digital access and scholarly interest, *Cine-Mundial* promises to become another vital source for analyzing film journals targeting a Latin American readership.

11. Nieto and Rojas, *Tiempos*, 13–42.

12. For historian José Luis Romero, these cities resorted to "demolition of the old to make room for the new . . . to epitomize the supreme triumph of progress." See his *Latin America: Its Cities and Ideas*, trans. Inés Azar (Washington, DC: Organization of American States, 1999), 222.

13. Ángel Rama, *The Lettered City*, trans. John Charles Chasteen (Durham: Duke University Press, 1996), 5, 7.

14. Malcolm Deas, *Del poder y la gramática* (Bogota: Tercer Mundo Editores, 1993) 28, 47.

15. John King, *Magical Reels: A History of Cinema in Latin America* (London: Verso, 2000), 25.

16. Nieto and Rojas, *Tiempos*, 9.

17. Ibid., 63.

18. "Homenaje a Policarpa Salabarrieta [sic]—La iniciativa de la SICLA," *Películas*, September 8, 1917.

19. "Oficial," *Boletín de la Sociedad de Embellecimiento de Bogotá*, June 10, 1918.

20. Miriam Hansen, *Babel & Babylon: Spectatorship in American Silent Film* (Cambridge, MA: Harvard University Press, 1991), 118.

21. "La función del 15 de julio," *Películas*, June 1919. The chronicle indicates that it was initially published in the conservative newspaper *El Diario Nacional*.

22. Hansen, *Babel*, 90.

23. Shelley Stamp, *Movie-struck Girls: Women and Motion Picture Culture after the Nickelodeon* (Princeton, NJ: Princeton University Press, 2000).

24. Rielle Navitski, "Spectacles of Violence and Politics: *El automóvil gris* (1919) and Revolutionary Mexico's Sensational Visual Culture," *Journal of Latin American Cultural Studies* 23 (2014): 133–152. In Japan, to mention a case outside the Americas, criminality also caused great concern. As a response to the French detective film *Zigomar, roi des voleurs* (*Zigomar, King of Thieves*; Victorin Jasset, 1911), intellectual authorities defined cinema as an alternative realm of experience in need of reform and control. See Aaron Gerow, "The Motion Picture as a Problem," in *Visions of Japanese Modernity: Articulations of Cinema, Nation, and Spectatorship, 1895–1925* (Berkeley: University of California Press, 2010), 40–65.

25. *Películas'* gendered pronouncements are most clear in its feuilleton section "Novelas de Películas." Beginning with Emilia Pardo Bazán's *La aventura de Isidro*, the section predicted that "[its] polite and good *lectoras* [female readers]" would "devour" the novel "with sincere pleasure" (*Películas*, February 17, 1917; my emphasis). In other Latin American nations, trade journals and film magazines demonstrated greater autonomy in terms of content and target readership. See Clara Kriger's *Páginas de cine* (Buenos Aires: Archivo General de la Nación, República Argentina, 2003).

26. Given the difficulty of determining actual print runs, dates in parentheses indicate archival holdings in the Biblioteca Luis Ángel Arango, Biblioteca Nacional, and the Fundación Patrimonio Fílmico Colombiano, all located in Bogotá.

27. *El Kine*, February 15, 1914. Other publications, such as *Olympia* (1913), the predecessor of *Películas*, also flaunted variations on the Horatian motto.

28. See Horace's *Ars Poetica* (ca. 19 BCE), particularly verses 333–334. *Olympia: Revista cinematográfica ilustrada* (1913) also adopts the motto.
29. "El peligro de las películas rayadas," *Películas*, February 17, 1917.
30. "La manía de la ñapa," *El cine gráfico*, June 15, 1917.
31. Graciela Montaldo, "La desigualdad de las partes," *A Contra Corriente* 7, no. 1 (2009): 14–44, 29.
32. "La manía."
33. Miriam Hansen, "Vernacular Modernisms: Tracking Cinema on a Global Scale," in *World Cinemas, Transnational Perspectives*, eds. Natasa Ďurovičová and Kathleen Newman (New York: Routledge, 2010), 287–314, 300. Emphasis in original.
34. Leaving underlying (pro-Hollywood) agendas aside, *Cine-Mundial*'s "Crónica de Colombia," as well as other chronicles on Bogotá and other major Colombian cities, hint at consistent growth in American serial imports between 1917 and 1923. In 1917, local correspondents mentioned a combination of Italian features and few American serials exhibited in local theaters. By 1923, however, American Pathé serials dominated and Italian films were seldom mentioned. For comparison, see "Crónica de Colombia," *Cine-Mundial*, January 1918, 40, and "Crónica de Barranquilla, Colombia," *Cine-Mundial*, January 1922, 34. Major newspapers, unaffiliated with film exhibitors, also reveal this tendency in film programs.
35. "Las tendencias cinematográficas," *Películas*, January 27, 1917. In other Latin American film cultures, lack of realism was not a reason for scorn. A Mexican critic described American serials as narratives in which "not even implausibility proved to be an obstacle," quoted in Laura Serna, *Making Cinelandia: American Films and Mexican Film Culture before the Golden Age* (Durham: Duke University Press, 2014), 26.
36. See note 34.
37. Monica Dall'Asta, "Italian Serial Films and 'International Popular Culture,'" *Film History* 12 (2000): 302.
38. Itala Film's *Maciste alpino* (*Alpine Maciste*, 1916), *Maciste atleta* (*Maciste the Athlete*; dir. Vincenzo Denizot and Giovanni Pastrone, 1918), *Maciste poliziotto* (*Maciste the Policeman*, dir. Roberto Roberti, 1918), *Maciste medium* (*Maciste the Medium*, dir. Vincenzo Denizot, 1918).
39. "Charlas cotidianas: Los atletas del cine," *Películas*, June 1920.
40. Ibid. It should be noted that Maciste's *mundialización* (globalization) went beyond circulation and exhibition in Latin America. In Mexico, *Maciste turista* (*Maciste the Tourist*, dir. Santiago Sierra) was released in 1917, attesting to the transnational success of the muscle-man genre. See Hipólito Seijas [pseud. Rafael Pérez Taylor], "Maciste turista," *El Universal*, May 28, 1917, repr. in González Casanova, *Por la pantalla*, 233–235.
41. "Crónica de Colombia," *Cine-Mundial*, May 1921, 354–355. Penned for a very different readership by a local correspondent, the chronicle still hints at irresolvable local class differences in cinema between the "great" and "feminine and elegant" audiences.
42. Rudmer Canjels, *Distributing Silent Film Serials: Local Practices, Changing Forms, Cultural Transformation* (New York: Routledge, 2011), 7.

43. Kaveh Askari, "An Afterlife for Junk Prints: Serials and Other 'Classics' in Late-1920s Tehran" in *Silent Cinema and the Politics of Space,* eds. Jennifer M. Bean, Anupama Kapse, and Laura Horak, (Bloomington: Indiana University Press, 2014), 108.

44. Dall'Asta, "Italian Serial Films," 302.

45. Serna, *Making Cinelandia,* 26.

46. Ibid., 76.

47. Navitski, "Spectacles," 135, 142.

48. A fascinating example is *Los misterios del crimen,* published in Bogotá between 1924 and 1926. Composed of a weekly novel based on real crimes and serialized essays on the causes of local criminality, the publication aspired to viscerally thrill its reader, as well as to advise them against foreign imports such as film serials and, somewhat ironically, serialized novels.

49. Jacqueline Reich, "The Metamorphosis of Maciste in Italian Silent Cinema," *Film History* 25, no. 3 (2013): 33.

50. Diego Angeli, "El peligro americano," *Películas,* July 20, 1920.

51. For a thorough historical study of Italian production's "golden years," see Paolo Cherchi Usai, ed., *Giovanni Pastrone. Gli anni d'oro di cinema a Torino* (Turin, Italy: Utet, 1986).

52. John David Rhodes, "'Our Beautiful and Glorious Art Lives': The Rhetoric of Nationalism in Early Italian Film Periodicals," *Film History* 12, no. 3, (2000): 309.

53. See Alonso's *The Spanish American Regional Novel* (New York: Cambridge University Press, 1990). Despite a somewhat misleading title, Alonso's study examines what Latin American scholarship terms the *novela de la tierra* (earth novel) or *criollista* literature. Rather than regionalist texts, these 1920s novels capitalized on a broader concern: Latin America's problematic relationship with modernity.

54. Carlos Alonso, "The Criollista Novel," in *The Cambridge History of Latin American Literature,* eds. Roberto González Echevarría and Enrique Pupo-Walker (New York: Cambridge University Press, 1996), 198.

55. Alonso, *The Spanish American,* 36.

56. *Películas* does not reveal the Italian source of "El peligro americano." Thus far, I have not found the original for comparison. Translation and appropriation of foreign film criticism describes to a great extent the overall tone of *Películas.* As ancillary material, translated foreign criticism suggests an editorial hand that favored anti-US sentiment on cinematic matters, among other topics. Another example taken from *El mundo cinematográfico,* published in Barcelona, reported with alarm on the US takeover of the Italian film market ("El mundo cinematográfico," June 1919). Other sections of *Películas,* such as the monthly "Por esos mundos," mostly focused on cinematic characteristics of then-current productions. The section systematically foregrounded faults in US films when compared to Italian and French films. Occasionally, the section mentioned Argentine and Mexican productions, describing them as great successes in those markets. There is no reference to imports of Latin American productions into the Di Domenico circuit.

57. Nieto and Rojas, *Tiempos*, 111.
58. Rhodes, "'Our Beautiful,'" 315.
59. "La propaganda de Italia," *Películas*, March 1919.
60. See Michael A. Ledeen, *D'Annunzio the First Duce* (New Brunswick, NJ: Transaction, 2009), xiii.
61. Re, "Italians and the Invention of Race: The Poetics and Politics of Difference in the Struggle over Libya, 1890–1913," *California Italian Studies Journal* 1, no. 1 (2010): 8–9.
62. Ricardo Arias Trujillo, *Los Leopardos: una historia intelectual de los años 1920* (Bogota: Universidad de los Andes, 2013), 66. The fact that criminology and the social sciences filtered into political discussions and elite thought through judicial theory further corroborates the lettered undergirding of the Colombian social order.
63. Ruíz Vásquez, *Leopardos y tempestades*, 198.
64. "Crónica: 'Maciste,'" *Películas*, October 7, 1917.
65. "Los estrenos en Bogotá," *Películas*, June 1919.
66. "Leyendo la prensa cinematográfica," *Películas*, March 1919.
67. "Notas editoriales," *Películas*, September 1919.

Enrique Méndez Calzada, "The Lover of Rudolph Valentino,"[1] from *And Christ Returned to Buenos Aires* (1926)

A critic and fiction writer, Enrique Méndez Calzada (1898–1940) was raised in Spain and later returned to his native Argentina, where worked as a journalist. In "The Lover of Rudolph Valentino," Méndez Calzada sketches a portrait of the middle and upper classes of Buenos Aires with keen observation and humor, suggesting how traditional rituals of heterosexual courtship can be disrupted by novel forms of mass consumption, including the pleasures of film fandom.

I WILL RECOUNT TO you the unhappy end of the love affair between my friend Roberto H. and an agreeable young lady.

First of all, as I believe is the common custom of scrupulous storywriters, I have the pleasure of introducing you to the characters:

She: Seventeen springs. Blonde, slender, and as already mentioned, very agreeable. She belongs to a family that, although they do not summer in Mar del Plata, or attend the "reveillons" of El Tigre, is very honorable.[2] Someone has told her that she looks like Pearl White, which gives her an excuse to wear fantastical velvet berets, which in reality are not very, or at all, flattering. Her given name is Leonor, but everyone (everyone that knows her) knows her as "Lita." (I note this fact for the undoubted historical importance it holds.)

He: is twenty-four; has some excellent qualities; expects to inherit. He is tall, elegant, affable and of a distinguished appearance. He has an automobile. He studies medicine, and in spite of being in his fifth year, still writes verses. (No, miss, don't be malicious: I haven't copied this "profile" from the section "Who Is Your Ideal Suitor?")

They met at a dance in Belgrano. (I admit that it could as well have been in Caballito, but I insist: it was in Belgrano.)[3]

Meeting each other, looking at each other, speaking with each other, and loving each other ... at first sight, and grammatically speaking, these are four reflexive verbs: but when it comes to lovers, there's no place to speak of reflection. These four reflexive verbs were on that occasion a single act. Upon leaving the aforementioned dance, Leonor and Roberto were engaged.

* * *

Two years had passed since the happy night on which our two young people had met, and the fervent love both professed had not cooled. To the contrary, their passion was growing. And when what I am about to narrate took place, the treasury departments of their respective families had lately been deliberating the inclusion of an exceptional item in their domestic budgets to defray wedding costs.

Leonor and Roberto were entirely happy. They saw laid out before their ecstatic eyes an endless and luminous path of uncounted joys. Their love was the divine communion of two young souls, possessed by the same longings; such was the harmony of these two harps that, vibrating in unison, intoned a single marvelous melody ...

In other words, everything suggested that the courtship begun at a dance in Belgrano would end in El Salvador or La Merced; and that fifty years later, the newspapers would publish photos of Roberto and Leonor, very elderly, and surrounded by children and grandchildren underneath letters half an inch high reading: "Golden Wedding Anniversary."[4]

* * *

> The leaves were falling. The agony
> of the sun was beginning, devastating
> and on the wind a whining old woman
> moaned her grave litany ...

... according to the lovely phrase of the lyric. It was in Palermo, and the lovers were sitting, very close together, at one of the borders of the Rose Garden.[5] It was a sweet, gentle, melancholy autumn afternoon. The leaves were falling, as they were wont to do at this time of year. And the cool breeze of dusk, full of pleasant aromas, gathered them together and swept them along. The hour held a deep romantic enchantment. One heard the sound of elegant automobiles gliding down the avenue that surrounded the Rose Garden and the lakes; one heard, measured and rhythmic, the trotting of thoroughbred horses, who were pulling sumptuous *landaus*; one heard, as well, the turning wheels of the modest carriages for hire, whose horses were not thoroughbreds, but who also trotted in their fashion. Along the paths of the Rose Garden, some couples were ruminating; and on a gloomy bench, a no less gloomy poet tried to ruminate as well, but his efforts along these lines were fruitless.

Leonor's chaperone—an ancient relic who could have held her own beside the Egyptian mummies in the Louvre—was reading a novel on a nearby bench. Considering this circumstance, one could introduce some variations into Carriego's stanza, which would thereby gain descriptive force; it could, for example, be altered thusly:[6]

* * *

> The leaves were falling. The agony
> of the sun was beginning, devastating
> and on the wind an old grumbler
> devoured Martínez Zuviría...[7]

The lovers talked, talked... What were they taking about? What were they saying? They were saying a thousand things, all of great importance; but let us not profane them trying to repeat them. The importance of those words did not extend beyond the ears of the two lovers. They were banal, puerile, insignificant, trivial in themselves; but full of significance for them.... Perhaps, if others heard them, "other people" would find them laughable: but what did they care about "other people's" opinion? Their sentences—the slightest of sentences—any old word—the most vulgar of words—had then an immense value, a vast significance.

I would like to transcribe onto paper some of these sentences of such overwhelming eloquence; but I am certain that any of my readers would ask upon reading them: "What! Is that all? And they go to Palermo to tell each other this 'hokum'?"

I'm convinced that publishing a volume composed of shorthand versions of conversations between lovers would be a complete commercial failure.

"Do you love me, Lita?" said Roberto.

"Yes, Roberto," Lita answered.

"You're not lying? You really love me?"

"I'm telling you yes!" she insisted. And remembering the notions of algebra that the Ursulines, through patient effort, had managed to drum into her, she added, with an enchanting grimace:[8]

> "I've already told you n times."
> Roberto, obstinate, would not be satisfied:
> "Lita, tell me $n + 1$ times."
> "How stubborn! I love you, Roberto. I love you very much."
> "But you say it with a voice that is unsure, timid, shaking, hesitant..."
> "I have a cold."

The dialogue continued, wittily ... (Here you can insert any witty lover's dialogue, taking it, for example, from some novel by Madam Braemé or the aforementioned Mr. Zuviría. The works of both writers abound in amorous dialogues appropriate to the case. I haven't time to spend on such trifles.)

The mental effort expended by Lita to come up with each of the scintillating phrases with which the conversation was embellished, caused her to get distracted and let her purse fall on the flagstones of the flowerbed: her lovely bag of black silk netting, with Chinese embroidery and an embossed silver closure.

Lita gave a small cry of shock.

Roberto picked up the purse; he stripped it—using his jacket sleeve as a brush—of the inevitable dusty-earthy particles that had attached themselves to the lovely object; and he was going to restore it to the owner—the owner of his heart and of the silk purse—when it occurred to him to say, "Lita, I'll let you go through my wallet if you let me go through your bag. This way, we will prove we have no secrets from each other."

Upon hearing the proposition, Lita probably went pale; but since she wore make-up, this went unnoticed. She tacitly accepted.

Roberto gave her the wallet. When she began to go through its contents, the first thing she found was the photograph she had inscribed to her suitor. Then rubbish of no importance: the bill of sale for a house, a deposit-only check, the waybill for a load of wheat... Aside from the photograph, nothing interesting. Lita returned his wallet, saying, "Roberto, I can see you have no secrets from me."

Then it was he who went through her wallet. There began to appear things of great importance: a little round mirror with an advertisement; a compact; a little square mirror, without advertisement; a powderpuff; a little hexagonal mirror, beveled; a bar of "crayon pour le soin des paupières et des sourcils,"[9] rouge, quite used . . . along with other no less important things.

"And my photograph?" Roberto asked anxiously.

"I have it in my 'secrétaire,'[10] kept safe," she answered.

Roberto continued with his requisition. At the bottom of the bag, softly wrapped in the lace of a lovely perfumed handkerchief, there was a photograph . . . His? No! A photograph of Rudolph Valentino!

Distraught, trembling, Roberto got up, and said curtly,

"Good afternoon, miss."
After this bit of laconic eloquence, he walked away.
Lita called to him:
"Roberto! Roberto! Let me explain."

Nothing. This new Othello, jealous of Rudolph Valentino . . . in effigy, continued his march.

From a distance, he looked disdainfully at "the unfaithful one," making a lofty gesture of farewell, but without doffing his hat, which, in any case, would have been impossible, since he didn't have it on. In his perturbation, he had forgotten it on the bench; and this detail reveals what an intense passion dominated Roberto. (Indeed, the hat cost forty pesos.)

Lita, in despair, burst into tears. She adored Roberto; she loved him with all her soul; she saw through her lover's eyes; she thought of no one but him. It was true that the elegance and the effeminate beauty of Rudolph Valentino "pleased" her, but as far as love went, she loved no one but Roberto. Of course, if his moral qualities were combined with the physical qualities of her favorite actor, her passion for him would be greater . . . Of course if he looked like Rudolph Valentino she would love him much more . . .

In sum: the one she was in love with—without knowing it, or rather without wanting to admit it—was Rudolph Valentino and not Roberto H.

The chaperone, seeing the girl cry, came over to offer comfort; but she didn't manage to pronounce anything more than a few foolish and meaningless phrases. There are certain readings that predispose one to incoherence.

The next day, Lita and Roberto returned each other's letters.

* * *

Leonor, the innocent young lady whom we know to be in love with Rudolph Valentino, lost, in the manner just related, an excellent opportunity to change her status under advantageous conditions, joining herself to a young, honorable man with a bright future, and has just married an old importer of Japanese fans who has already buried two or three wives, who wears a toupée, and, to clean his teeth, puts them in a glass of peroxide.

As far as Roberto goes, I'm unaware of his fate; but an advertisement that occasionally appears in the Classifieds section of the newspapers has given me much to ponder:

YOUNG exporter of agricultural products, good appearance, seeks to marry a woman who has never gone to the movies nor collects photographs of screen artists. Age, nationality, economic situation, weight and height are irrelevant. Write to R.H., box 115.

Girls, look at yourselves in Lita's mirror.

(In the mirror of her misfortune, not in her square mirror, nor in her round mirror, nor in her beveled mirror, nor in her unbeveled mirror.)

Translated by Rielle Navitski

RIELLE NAVITSKI is Assistant Professor of Theater and Film Studies at the University of Georgia. She is the author of *Public Spectacles of Violence: Sensational Cinema and Journalism in Early Twentieth-Century Mexico and Brazil* (Duke University Press, 2017).

NOTES

1. (Unless otherwise indicated, all notes are from the editors.) *Author's Note*: Dear reader of 1950 (if there is one): Rudolph Valentino was a film actor, who reached his peak of fame in the first quarter of this century. He died in mid-1926, in the flower of youth. The elect of the gods, he experienced the gifts of fame, fortune, and the idolatry of women, and he even had the luck not to experience rheumatism or baldness. Several nations dispute the honor of being his birthplace.

2. Respectively, a resort town in the province of Buenos Aires and a fashionable suburb just outside the city.

3. Two centrally located, middle- to upper-class Buenos Aires neighborhoods.

4. Two Buenos Aires churches.

5. The scene takes place in the Bosques de Palermo, a large park modeled on the Bois de Boulogne in Paris.

6. A reference to the poet Evaristo Carriego, subject of an eponymous book by Jorge Luis Borges.

7. *Author's Note:* Here I should advise the hypothetical reader of 1950 that in 1926, Mr. Martínez Zuviría was a popular novelist.—E. M. C. [*Editor's Note*: Author of the popular novel *Flor de durazno* (Peach Flower, 1911), Martínez Zuviría was better known by the pseudonym Hugo Wast.]

8. An order of nuns devoted to St. Ursula.

9. In French in original: "pencil for the care of eyelids and eyebrows."

10. "Desk," in French.

Chapter 3

Manipulation and Authenticity: The Unassimilable Valentino in 1920s Argentina

Giorgio Bertellini

THE POST–WORLD WAR I commercial success of American films around the world, caused among other factors by the weakening of European companies' competitiveness at home and abroad, brought an unprecedented degree of fame to Hollywood companies, directors, and stars.[1] In a process that domestically contributed to the commercial and cultural consolidation of Hollywood as the preeminent American entertainment and that abroad prompted the first charges of cultural hegemony and imperialism, the star system represented one of the key vectors of Hollywood's widespread appeal. Silent film scholars have thus been tempted to predict that the rise to fame of a Hollywood star indexed models of gender, racial, and national identification that not only applied to America as a whole but also to other nations.[2] Accordingly, the critical toolbox adopted to read Hollywood stars' mainstream American fame has been sanctioned as valid for fans of different cultural constituencies around the country and around the world. A more fruitful methodological approach should instead assume the opposite: a star's ability to embody modern imageries and new ideas of social difference and interaction is likely to exert different outcomes in different contexts, whether ethnic, regional, or international. Comparative discussions of different reception contexts may not legitimately rely on the critical framework used for just one of them.[3] Case studies about a star's circulation among America's ethnic groups or abroad may not only offer most cogent counterexamples to conventional and predictable receptions but also help in reformulating and fine-tuning given notions of broad-based appeal.

Rudolph Valentino has been quite central to the study of silent film stardom in the United States. In the last two decades, film scholars have read the American popularity of the Italian-born Hollywood actor as an index of his ability to embody appealing new ideas about masculinity and gender relationships, ethnic exoticism, and attendant heterosexual and queer imageries.[4] In my research on how Italian immigrants living in New York City embraced *and* rejected Valentino on the basis of internal cultural dynamics, I sought to complement earlier approaches, centered on ethnicity, gender, and sexuality, with perspectives of national and cultural difference.[5] My different approach meant the utilization of neglected sources of evidence—Italian newspapers of all political leanings—whose historiographical cogency, I would argue, extends beyond the research field of Italian American culture. For the scholar of American film culture of the 1920s, at a time when large sections of film audiences were still either immigrants or immigrants' descendants, the evidence of the ethnic press adds significant layers to the otherwise all too Anglo-American formulations of gender identity, sexual imagery, and consumer culture.[6]

The case study of Valentino's fame in Argentina may be fraught with comparable methodological assumptions and projections. In theory, several elements appear likely to have enhanced his national assimilation within the country's different constituencies. In his breakout film *The Four Horsemen of the Apocalypse* (dir. Rex Ingram, 1921), he played the role of an attractive and fiery Latin lover from Argentina, who excels at tango dancing and who becomes a patriotic-martyr in World War I Europe out of a romantic but hopeless love for a French woman. The temptation to posit the actor's popularity, especially but not exclusively among Argentine women (and homosexual men), on the basis of his physical attractiveness, passionate masculinity, and fondness for the national Argentine dance, is doubled when one considers his personal story as a successful Italian immigrant. For the largest Italian immigrant populations in Latin America, Valentino's personal biography—it may be easy to assume—meant a proud and unproblematic acceptance. The reality was very different: Valentino did not develop into a *national* icon either for Italian immigrants or for Argentines.

In this essay I discuss the reasons for such a missed alignment by examining different contexts of cultural encounter. I shall first consider how foreign film cultures, specifically from Europe and the United States, made the Latin American country into a charmingly wild and exotic other. Not only did Valentino's breakout film belong to such continuum of antagonist and clichéd representations, it also came from Hollywood, the capital of America's cultural empire. Against these hegemonic representations, since the early 1910s Argentine cinema sought to articulate its own national myths and figures by showcasing the ways in which the country's different social constituencies—inhabitants of the pampas versus urban dwellers, native whites versus Italian immigrants—could be integrated into unified national narratives. The unmatched result of these efforts was *Nobleza gaucha* (*Gaucho Nobility*, dirs. Humberto Cairo, Eduardo Martínez de la Pera, and Ernesto Gunche, 1915), which deserves extensive discussion. The film revealed how gauchos and Italian immigrants, through the mediation of a comedic tradition known as *cocoliche* that mimicked and mocked their cultural and linguistic shortcomings, could assimilate within the same universe of *argentinidad* by virtue of the dialogic quality of their characterizations.

Against these performances, Valentino's characterization, which did not at all appear in conversation with Argentine cultural constituencies, could not compete. The scarcity of references to him and his works in the key Italian newspaper, *La Patria degli Italiani*—a never-examined source of evidence for scholars of silent Argentine cinema—is thus unsurprising. *La Patria* favored a traditionalist model of actors and performers, mostly from the opera and traditional stage, over Hollywood's manufactured and make-believe celebrities and their artful stories. Spanish-speaking Argentine film culture largely failed to cover his films and performances as well, as I learned by examining the key film periodical *La Película*. Similarly, Argentine critics and intellectuals rejected him by describing his tango dancing style as inauthentic and thus extraneous to the true Argentine tradition, or by caricaturizing the reactions of Argentine men as unable to tolerate his disturbing appeal among women.

In the end, Valentino's unassimilability was the result of cultural debates—amounting to a tension of authenticating investments and othering distantiations—projected on such familiar figures as the gaucho, the immigrant, and the tango dancer. His unassimilability also reflected the uneasiness that mainstream Argentine culture felt for novel, destabilizing phenomena such as popular moviegoing, film stardom and related novel ideals of gender identity and relationships. Times have changed. It should not surprise us then that, decades later, the rejection of the "great lover" in 1920s Argentina has been all but forgotten.

Romance on the Frontier

From *The Four Horsemen* to his sudden death in late August 1926, Valentino was a global Hollywood icon praised for his unique combination of exotic glamor and uninhibited passion. That Argentina was one of the settings of his first film as leading man, after which he played the role of Arab sheik, Spanish toreador, and Russian military officer, was not a fortuitous circumstance. Adapted from the Spanish writer Vicente Blasco Ibáñez's best-selling 1916 novel *Los cuatro jinetes del Apocalipsis*, *The Four Horsemen* belonged to a series of cinematic representations that for years had romantically designated the vast Latin American nation as new Western frontier.[7] As a pristine land, site of timeless confrontations and exchanges between wilderness and humanity, Argentina appeared to recapture, nostalgically, the heroic spirit of North America's Wild West and its widely mythologized and commercialized figures.[8]

Cinema had contributed to this multimedia process since the beginning of the century. A number of British, French, Italian, and Brazilian films identified in Argentina the nostalgic reincarnation of the old western frontier, a charmingly untamed natural setting inhabited by primitive and colorful cowboys, the gauchos.[9] After World War I had dramatically weakened the distribution network of European film industries, Hollywood began flooding Argentina with his own heroes and heroines. The melodramatic *The Four Horsemen* was part of this process, soon followed by other titles and regularly featuring passionate characters played by such stars as Gloria Swanson, Antonio Moreno, Greta Garbo, and Nita Naldi.[10] By the time Douglas Fairbanks was filming *The Gaucho* (dir. F. Richard Jones, 1927), Argentina had fully emerged as a charming and exotic setting best suited for melodramas of romantic love and fierce independence. A year later, Hollywood and the Argentine film industry even collaborated on the historical film *The Charge of the Gauchos*, also known as *The Beautiful Spy* and *Una nueva y gloriosa nación*. Directed by Albert H. Kelley, the film featured one of Hollywood's greatest silent film stars, Francis X. Bushman, in the role of the leader of the 1810 May Revolution, Manuel Belgrano.[11] Hollywood dared to intrude into Argentina's pantheon of *libertadores*.

In reaction, the Latin American country viewed Hollywood as a modernizing force in the international broadcasting of national narratives and symbols, at once deserving of admiration but also anti-imperialistic denunciations for identical reasons: the scale of its production values, the hegemonic reach of its distribution networks, and the popular interclass appeal of its glamorous stars.[12] Not indifferent to stereotypical or even romanticizing projections, Argentine cinema sought to develop its own idiomatic film mythology by foregrounding its own romantic approach to national settings, narratives, and star figures.

Toward an Imperfect, but Authentic Assimilation

From the very beginning, Argentina sought to articulate consistent and recognizable national narratives—in both nonfiction and fiction cinema—notwithstanding the markedly multinational origins of its producers, filmmakers, and audiences. The *actualités* about Buenos Aires that the Frenchman Eugenio Py shot since 1897 and, even more consistently, the hundreds of episodes of newsreel series produced by Max Glücksmann and Federico Valle—*Actualidades Argentinas* and *Film Revista Valle*, respectively—addressed the profound social and geographic divisions of the nation. Week after week they granted comparable documentary and ideological significance to both center and periphery, capital city and interior regions, as well as to their iconic subjective correlatives—gauchos and *porteños* (as the inhabitants of Buenos Aires are known).

In terms of fictional cinema, the national film industry drew inspiration from founding historical events to produce patriotic or historical reenactments—from Mario Gallo's *La revolución de Mayo* (*The May Revolution*, 1909) and *La creación del himno* (*The Creation of the Hymn*, 1910) to *El último malón* (*The Last Indian Uprising*, dir. Alcides Greca, 1916)—and biopics of criollo heroism from *Güemes y sus gauchos* (*Güemes and His Gauchos*, 1910) to *Juan Moreira* (1910), both shot by Gallo.[13] Standing above all them was *Nobleza gaucha*, the country's longest film to date, a stepping-stone of national film culture and a paradigm builder of what could become inclusively (and populistically) popular.

Nobleza gaucha emerged out of a distinct historical context marked by the centennial celebrations of 1910 and by ensuing political debates on universal suffrage and literary ones on the nation-building value of the poems *Martín Fierro* (1872 and 1879) and *Santos Vega* (1877), written respectively by José Hernández and Rafael Obligado. Released the same year as D. W. Griffith's *The Birth of a Nation*, *Nobleza gaucha* was a romantic story of love and rescue loosely based on those poems. The film covered almost the whole gamut of Argentine society. It approached the landed elite of Buenos Aires as violent and decadent, embraced the icons of the horse-riding and poncho-wearing gaucho and the innocent *criollita* [creole girl] as unspoiled champions of moral integrity, authenticity, and heroism, and celebrated a version of Italian immigrants as amusingly whimsical and sympathetic characters. Through both ethnographic and fictional strategies, the film solicited a most appreciative identification with such somewhat exoticized yet fully nationalized characters and the nation's iconic settings, from the wide-open spaces of the interior regions to the capital's new imposing squares and avenues.[14] Ultimately, the film served as a proud display of *argentinidad*[15] and as such it belonged to an array of discourses and practices of national inclusion and regeneration that included the gauchesco poetry of Hernández's and Bartolomé Hidalgo, the pedagogical programs of Ricardo Rojas, as well as popular stage melodramas and linguistic farces, including the *sainete*, the *circo criollo*, and the *cocoliche*.[16]

The film's inclusion of the Italian Don Genaro, with his plebeian hat, long pipe and moustache, and broad gestures, represents a concession to one of these popular performative genres, the cocoliche. Linguistically, cocoliche identified an argot associated with Italian immigrants living in the countryside and made of Italian dialects, Spanish, gaucho speech, and *lunfardo*.[17] Performatively, the cocoliche identified a form of grotesque vaudeville comedy, quite popular among Argentina's nationally diverse lower classes, which allowed for amusing forms of cultural dialogism.[18] Cocoliche poked fun at Italian immigrants' linguistic mistakes and customs, but it also enabled them to ridicule the gaucho and his way of speaking through the Italian immigrants' initial ignorance of traditional Argentine customs. Through this transcultural and transnational genre, the Italian immigrant was not cast as an outsider, but as a key comedic interlocutor to more native figures like the gaucho. Ultimately, not despite but because of his many flaws—his ineptitude as a speaker, a husband, a farmer, and even his vulgar materialism—Don Genaro is made to play a *constitutive* role in the promotion of the gaucho to national icon. As Ana Cara-Walker put it, the cocoliche allowed for the "creolization of Italians and natives" in the sense of a "cultural redefinition negotiated by two or more diverse groups coming into contact." As such the cocoliche enabled "the sociocultural redefinition of Argentina's 'national character' . . . yield[ed] a new ethic and aesthetic order wherein the presence of each group becomes integral to the national whole."[19] Ultimately, by relying on this vernacular popular tradition, *Nobleza gaucha* performed a populist interethnic conciliation while maintaining an admiration for both the pampas' boundless wilderness and the capital city's towering magnificence.

The film's diegesis addressed the same pressing political questions of cultural hierarchy by relying on the *spatial mobility* of its characters. All of them, gaucho, *criollita*, *estanciero* (i.e., the owner of an *estancia*, a large estate), and immigrant, find themselves moving between city and countryside and experience forms of reterritorialization through different degrees of ease. Although not exactly a catalyst for socioeconomic uplift, their geographical mobility enhances a multiplicity of identificatory positions. The film in fact allows urban and nonurban Argentines alike to align themselves with, and thus adopt, a variety of characters' points of view. It is not surprising that by relying on and feeding a multidimensional mode of address, *Nobleza gaucha* was still doing commercially well in Argentina and in Latin America in general in 1917 and 1918, and beyond.[20]

Valentino's on- and off-screen embellished interpretations, beginning with *The Four Horsemen*, could not be compared to the rough authenticity that *Nobleza gaucha* granted its own characters. In the 1921 Metro film, the Italian actor played the role of Julio, the spoiled grandson of an abusive and patriarchal estanciero. Julio is an exceptionally charming and stylish individual who, despite his character's conversion from son of privilege to war martyr, ultimately represents only himself—a Hollywood star. He could not have been more distant from the virile yet virtuous Juan and his *gauchesca* genuineness. On the Italian side, the film actor's biographical reputation as a young and impeccably dressed dandy connoted a narcissistic attention to attire and couture that was unassimilable to the rough and humbly dressed Don Genaro.

Ultimately, it was not just a matter of different styles of characterizations or of different shooting locations—the Hollywood studio and the California desert versus the actual Argentine countryside. As stories, the two films' leading characters engaged very differently with Argentina's social and natural landscape. In *Nobleza gaucha*, the gaucho seeks and obtains justice in his homeland, where he most naturally belongs. In *The Four Horsemen*, the cosmopolitan Julio-Valentino, who is only half-Argentine (his mother married a Frenchman), completes his transformation from spoiled young man, committed to a life of drinking and smoking in *tangherias*, to virtuous and

Fig. 3.1a and Fig. 3.1b Strange urban bedfellows: The Gaucho and Don Genaro in *Nobleza gaucha* (*Gaucho Nobility*, dir. Eduardo Martínez de la Pera, Humberto Cairo and Ernesto Gunche, 1915).

self-sacrificing patriot by moving abroad, to the distant French war front. Argentina does not appear to house any conversion or salvation for him. All that is left is a mannered tango-dancing performance, limited to the film's first part and frozen in a culturally stereotypical and thus inauthentic timelessness.

Valentino and Italian Argentines

If the character of Julio had French and Spanish blood, the actor playing him had been an anonymous Italian immigrant before becoming a Hollywood royal. By contrast with the opera star Enrico Caruso, who used to leave his Fifth Avenue apartment to dine in Italian restaurants in the Lower East Side and even acted in a film, *My Cousin* (dir. Edward José, 1918) as both famous opera singer and poor Italian sculptor from Little Italy, Valentino did not show much sympathy or closeness to the lives of fellow migrants to America. Further, his film roles did not foreground any of the adaptational struggles experienced by actual immigrants, whether to the United States or Argentina, or engage in the sort of cultural dialogism that the cocoliche tradition eloquently enacted. Still, one could have legitimately expected that the Italian immigrants to Argentina embraced the Italian actor, given how his personal story of fame and success matched the classic rags-to-riches immigrant narrative. Further, since the beginning of the century, a proud patriotism had accompanied the visits of Italian celebrities, from Eleonora Duse to Caruso, the staging of Italian theatrical and opera shows, as well as the exhibition of Italian films.[21] By contrast, the Italian press, whose record is glaringly absent from histories of silent cinema in Argentina, remained virtually silent about Valentino.

My main primary resource has been the daily newspaper, *La Patria degli Italiani* (1876–1931), one of the oldest and most respected Italian dailies printed in Buenos Aires. *La Patria* covered the major news stories from Italy as well as the events and happenings related to the Italian communities in Argentina. Its pages celebrated both Italian and Argentine national figures and selectively reported on Italian films, particularly the newsreels about the war in Libya in 1911 and World War I in 1915–1918.[22] Not all Italian fiction films distributed in Argentina in the 1910s, even when celebrated in Italy for their patriotic and aesthetic qualities, found coverage in *La Patria*.[23] By the time the Fascist regime came to power in 1922, one year after Valentino's breakout film, the newspaper's patriotic editorial style did not translate into a blind toeing of the Fascist Party line. Instead, it combined a continuous support of the local Italian community with the praise for traditional artistic accomplishments associated to the distant homeland.[24] Valentino did not easily fit into such a news-making agenda. The only reference to him that I located is from April 5, 1925, in a snippet about his new contract with United Artists. The paper referred to the Italian actor as "the famous gallant figure of the film world" (*il famoso galante della cinematografia*).[25] When the late 1925 and early 1926 controversy between the regime and the actor found ample publicity in Italian and American papers, following Valentino's intention to acquire US citizenship for tax purposes (and relinquish his Italian nationality), *La Patria* ignored it. It was not an oversight given that the paper, "despite pressure from the embassy, relied on a United States news service" for much of its news coverage, including for Italian subjects.[26] And it was not a suppression motivated by political reasons. As mentioned earlier, *La Patria* wished to remain politically independent from any Fascist pressure. Of course, it extensively covered the newsworthy Mussolini, both as a political leader and a film character—for instance, as leading man in the regime's biopic *Camisas negras* (*A noi!*, dir. Umberto Paradisi, 1923).[27] What prompted the paper's silence about Valentino was its approach to culture. *La Patria* practiced a form of cultural patriotism that tended to equate Italian culture with an idealized notion of art, mainly represented by theater and literature—at the expense of what it viewed as commercially based film production, particularly if manufactured by Hollywood.[28]

Thus the newspaper gave extensive and regular space to the stage and literary works of established writers Gabriele D'Annunzio and Giovanni Verga, to the arrival in Buenos Aires of star performers and intellectuals, and through the column, Arte e Artisti (Art and Artists), to the staging of classical dramas and operas at the Teatro Coliseo or at the Teatro Colón in Buenos Aires.[29] Initially, the column also reported on nonfiction film productions with an Italian subject, but after February 21, 1923, it began publishing a dedicated subcolumn or section—entitled Tra Cinematografi e "Films" (Between Movie Theaters and "Films"). The decoupling of this section from Arte e Artisti is a significant event because it signaled the visible divorce of moving pictures—mostly nonfiction—from the domain of artistic productions.[30] In addition, the new column's attention to cinema was quite selective: it was mostly devoted to picturesque travelogues about Italy's natural and urban attractions (i.e., the series *Bellezza italiche* [*Beauties of Italy*, prod. unknown, 191?])

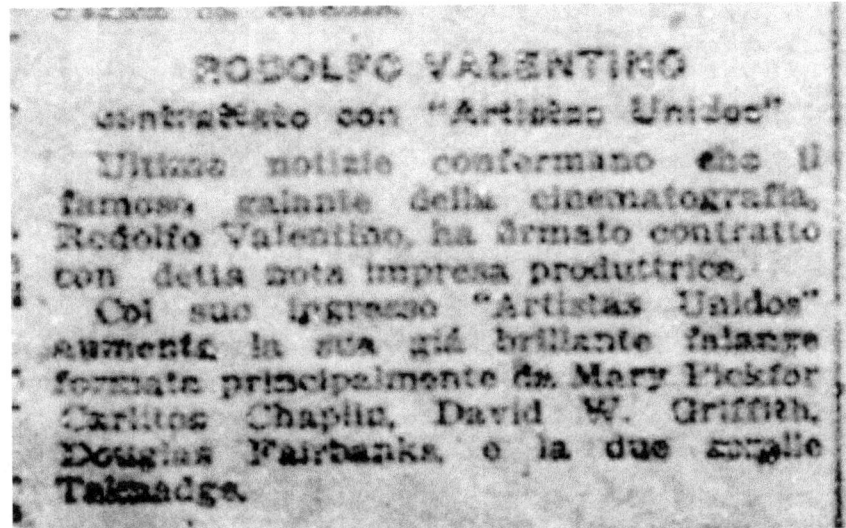

Fig. 3.2a "Rodolfo Valentino contrattato con United Artists," *La Patria degli Italiani*, April 5, 1925.

and to 1920s retakes on once-popular historical epics, including Enrico Guazzoni's 1924 film *Messalina* and *Quo Vadis?* (dir. Gabriellino d'Annunzio and Georg Jacoby).

Within such conservative cultural policy, the Italian actor appeared to be part of a cultural phenomenon—the American star system—that the paper likely viewed as a corruption of true artistic expression. It was a policy that promoted other forms of news suppression or that found explicit rhetorical formulations on those occasions when it covered Hollywood. For instance, the publication of an article devoted to "actresses and love" referred only to stage performers and failed to mention any of the famous *dive* of Italian cinema, from Francesca Bertini and Pina Menichelli to Lyda Borelli, as if they were not considered performers at all.[31] When the paper mentioned Hollywood comedian Harold Lloyd, it described him in dismissive terms as one of the "manufacturers of smiles at the movie show" (*fabricanti di sorrisi al Cinematografo*), thereby stressing his commercial rather than artistic significance.[32]

That the only reference to Valentino identified him as "the famous gallant figure of the film world" reveals another dimension of his exclusion in the name of artistry. His connection to a modern commercial enterprise perceived to be the antithesis of artistic craftsmanship was linked to his popularity among women. At issue is the typical gendering of mass culture as

Fig. 3.2b An advertisement for *Camisas negras* (*A noi!*, dir. Umberto Paradisi), *La Película*, December 2, 1926. Courtesy of Fundación Cinemateca Argentina.

feminine versus the granting of masculine features to high art.[33] Argentine culture expressed comparable uneasiness about his popularity among female audiences without necessarily linking his fame to a dystopian view of modern mass entertainments. In the end, as the evidence so far suggests, the nationalistically leaning Italian-Argentine official culture did not recognize Valentino as artist or as immigrant deserving praise.

Hollywood and the Argentine Film Culture

The coverage of the Italian actor in such Spanish-language primary sources as the film journal *La Película: Semanario Cinemátografico Sud-Americano* revealed a similar unassimilability. Over the decades, Argentine film and cultural historians have repeatedly referred to Valentino's films with an approach that has relied on his ex post facto transnational fame, thereby singling out the Italian star through rather familiar tones of mournfulness and praise. Unfortunately, even when describing Valentino and Fairbanks as "imaginary inhabitants of the Pampas," the coverage of "the world's greatest lover," as some of these scholarly accounts referred to him, has failed to indicate specific 1920s sources.[34]

In my research in *La Película*, I did not find many references following the early October 1921 Argentine release of *The Four Horsemen* (first exhibited in the United States in March of the same year), nor about the even more successful *The Sheik* (*La cautiva del caudillo moro*, dir. George Melford, 1921). His name resurfaces only a few weeks before his death, which occurred five years later, on August 23, 1926. The apparent lack of coverage for *The Sheik* is particularly surprising, given that shortly after the actor's passing the same periodical referred to the film as the one "that gave such great fame to the deceased Valentino."[35] Still, scarcity of evidence does not mean total absence. Coincidently, one of the few articles about Valentino appeared when he suddenly fell ill, following the extensive coverage of his sickness in the domestic and international press. The timing coincided also with the much-delayed, but probably opportunistic, Argentine release of *Cobra* (1925) and the more timely one of *A Sainted Devil* (*El Diablo santificado*, 1925), both directed by Joseph Henabery.[36] Specifically, *La Película* discussed the actor's fame in light of the popularity of the cinematic medium more broadly, and specifically of the Hollywood star system's astonishing grip over domestic and foreign spectators alike. The periodical eventually dwelled on the traffic problems and the public disorder surrounding Valentino's Manhattan funeral home; on the much-covered attendance at his New York funeral of such Hollywood stars as Douglas Fairbanks, Mary Pickford, Pola Negri, and Norma Talmadge, and on the extraordinary event of the suicide of a heartbroken London fan. Summarizing these events, the periodical entitled one of its articles with an explicit full sentence: "The death of Valentino has revealed cinema's enormous popularity."[37] Furthermore, after offering snippets of the press coverage from New York City, Italy, Chicago, and Hollywood, *La Película* reported a Rex Ingram interview where the *Four Horsemen* director declared his intention to erect of a monument to Valentino dressed as—what else?—a gaucho.

By the time United Artists released *The Son of the Sheik* (dir. George Fitzmaurice, 1926) about two months later, *La Película* did not mention any

Fig. 3.3 United Artists advertisement for *The Son of the Sheik* (dir. George Fitzmaurice, 1926), *La Película*, October 21, 1926. Courtesy of Fundación Cinemateca Argentina.

public reaction. How to read Argentine film culture's apparent resistance to appropriate the Italian star as a national representative? Comparable cinematic texts may help address the question since tango-related films had been amounting to a recent genre in Argentina cinema.[38] Consider *El tango de la muerte* (*The Tango of Death*, 1917), featuring the famous actor Nelo Cosimi, directed by José Agustín Ferreyra, who later also completed *Mi último tango* (*My Last Tango*, 1925). *El tango de la muerte* was set in the popular quarters of

Buenos Aires. As critics later noted, *El tango de la muerte* sought to avoid any slumming effect and performed an ethnographic account of the city's darkest neighborhoods that did not capitalize on safe voyeurism and exploitative exoticism, but instead aimed at a dramatic but responsible form of cinematic realism.[39] It was a tricky balance, as evidenced a few years later by the controversy surrounding Jorge Luis Borges's association of the humble and plebeian origins of the culture of the tango with brothels, *malevos*, and *guapos*.[40] Compared to Ferreyra's realistic approach, the tango scene in *The Four Horsemen*, where Valentino and his fictional grandfather are shown drinking, seducing women, and sensually tango-dancing in a vice-filled Buenos Aires *tangheria*, had more an air of performative artfulness, and thus of manipulation, than direct appreciation of the local milieu. The Hollywood origins of the film and the sensationalist othering and slumming effect of the tango sequence likely invalidated for Argentine observers any pretense of genuineness. That in turn denied him the possibility of being regarded as a creolizable figure comparable to those of the cocoliche.

Thus, any assumption about the film's apparent cultural inappropriateness ought also to be linked to the ways 1920s Argentine intellectual culture viewed Hollywood and its faux ethnographic intrusions, particularly concerning the much-celebrated national dance. Widespread misgivings about Hollywood hegemony, celebrity culture, and the cosmopolitan popularity of the tango, in fact, raised questions about international mode of address and authentic national identification. Scholars have largely addressed these questions with regard to the fame of Carlos Gardel, especially for the sound period.[41] It was in the context of the same geocultural confrontations that Argentine culture, whether expressing praise or criticism for the Italian actor, found it difficult to view him sympathetically either as a tango-dancing Latin lover or, as we saw, as a struggling Italian immigrant who found success in America.

Porteño intellectuals, in fact, often expressed rather negative views about Hollywood films and stars in general, given their obvious association with US cultural dominion, economic power, and political influence over Argentina. For instance, in his 1920s *Atlántida* columns, Uruguayan Horacio Quiroga captured quite vividly this dystopian position. Quiroga wrote about intellectuals' diffidence for the new medium, not just, and quite expectedly, because of its alienating industrial features vis-à-vis more genuine forms of entertainments but also, and rather surprisingly, because of its democratic appeal.[42] At stake, as Beatriz Sarlo has pointed out, was the critical clash between older versions of national modernity and those originating from a North American and European blend of modern technology and mass-mediated consensus.[43]

Others, such as the iconic writer Roberto Arlt, expressed more ambivalent positions. On the one hand, Arlt maintained that, by fostering the dream for a better life for the masses, cinema held the unique potential of unleashing democratic ideals.[44] On the other hand, he posited that film productions could not deny the representation of social injustices and limit themselves to all-too-easily reconciling resolutions—a phantasmatic projection that he found comparable to the troublesome effects of the tango's international fortunes. Only *after* obtaining a surprising success abroad, in fact, had tango become a source of national identification—a phenomenon that for him indexed the country's profound cultural fragility. Arlt expressed similar dystopian concerns for celebrity culture. Stardom, in his view, fostered forms of utopia and moral irresponsibility and involved both screen stars and powerful figures in general—from political leaders to dictators. Arlt translated his concerns into fiction. In the segment entitled "El discurso del astrólogo" ("The Astrologer's Discourse"), which appeared in Arlt's 1929 novel *Los siete locos* (The Seven Madmen) and was devoted to totalitarian simulations, the main character imagines a messiah who, even while sporting mystical features, bears a strong resemblance to none other than Rudolph Valentino.[45] Nothing could be more dangerous in Arlt's opinion than a literal interpretation of the qualifying term "divo" as short for "divine." In Arlt's admonition, one can hear Bertolt Brecht's famous sentence, "Unhappy is the land that needs a hero," written ten years later in *The Life of Galileo Leben des Galilei*, (1939).

The tango constituted the most explicit terrain for the Argentine rejection of Valentino, caught between the potential of a national authenticity and the reality of his striking cosmopolitan modernity. When *The Four Horsemen* was released on October 2, 1921, several commentators denounced the apocryphal character of Valentino's dancing style—as critic and journalist Roberto Tálice (1902–1999) recounted years later.[46] Tálice reported an article by Helen Ferro who, in the Espectáculo section of *Clarín*, described Valentino's dance as a "hilarious version of Argentine tango invented for the film."[47] Tálice elaborated on the same point by arguing that rather than being the expression of the authentic Argentine style, the actor's bodily moves were a combination of routines from Buenos Aires, Mexico, and Andalucía. Tálice also reported what poet and journalist Carlos de la Púa allegedly told him in

1921, "There is no question that Valentino's tango was a parodic transgression of the authentic one that Casimiro Aín [the famous tango dancer, and tango ambassador to Europe] danced before the Pope and the King of Denmark."[48]

Helen Ferro and Carlos de la Púa were not alone. The cultural attaché at the Argentine Consulate in San Francisco, Santos Goñi, wrote about his experience as a cultural consultant for Hollywood companies, hired during April 1921 to make sure their films did not employ offending stereotypes. Goñi's view about Valentino's Argentine authenticity was also negative. For him, *The Four Horsemen* represented a "bad precedent in terms of 'Argentinidad.'"[49] Specifically, Goñi made reference to an article entitled "Añoranzas de Hollywood" (Longing for Hollywood) that appeared in 1931 in the Spanish-language American film periodical *Cinelandia* (Los Angeles). Its author Agustín Aragón Leiva, a Mexican writer and friend of Sergei Eisenstein, wrote, "When fantasies were not yet taken seriously in the talkies, it was fashionable to pose as Argentine. The most legitimate pride of young film prodigies consisted in having been in the pampas for five or ten years."[50]

The denunciation of the glaring inauthenticity of Valentino's tango moves, part of a broader charge against the inauthenticity of Hollywood performances, was in tune with Argentine intellectuals' denunciation of American imperialistic intrusion into not only their culture but also their society. What further contributed to the exclusion of Valentino from any sort of national-cultural appropriation, in fact, was the star's modern masculinity, prodigiously popular among women, and thus capable of threatening the country's traditional gender balance. More detailed historical research into the film and cultural periodicals of the time is still much needed, but recent readings of his fame, while providing scant original evidence, may point in the right direction. For instance, in a volume devoted to the question of 1920s modernity in the Argentinian capital and entitled *Valentino en Buenos Aires: Los años veinte y el espectáculo* (1994), historian and journalist Sergio Pujol has contended that Valentino was "the great lover," whose masculinity gave rise to either a suspicion of homosexuality or plain envy for his excessive popularity among women. Pujol has described his fame as subversive by virtue of the fact that "his mythical stature as the cinematic Don Juan par excellence was shaped by female enthusiasm and masculine antipathy."[51] The actor's fame sharpened the rivalry between genders—women's enthusiasm versus men's rejection—which ended in women's favor because, in Pujol's view, the 1920s were fundamentally a "feminine decade."[52] Pujol does not support his argument with much primary research; however, his contention addresses the issue of Valentino's gendered reception, which contemporary sources may have brought up, but that film historians in Argentina have rarely developed.

A source that Pujol would have found quite useful is a 1926 short story by journalist and writer Enrique Méndez Calzada, entitled "La enamorada de Rudolfo Valentino" ("The Lover of Rudolph Valentino").[53] The novella tells the story of a couple of young lovers, Leonor and Roberto, whose union initially appears as a "divine communion of two young souls." Over time, however, Roberto grows increasingly insecure. He repeatedly wants Leonor to declare her love for him, and one day he asks whether they could inspect each other's wallets. She agrees. When he discovers a portrait of Rodolfo Valentino instead of a photograph of himself in her wallet, he breaks up their relationship.[54] Leonor is desperate, but Roberto sensed something true. Her love for him spoke the idealizing language of romantic love, but her attraction to Valentino favored the idiom of sheer physical beauty.[55] She may still tell herself that she only *loved* her Roberto, but acknowledges that if her fiancé's "moral qualities were combined with the physical qualities of her favorite actor, her passion for him would be greater."[56] Ultimately, as the title of the novella suggests and as the reader is made to realize, all along Leonor had been in love with Valentino and not with Roberto.

The tone of the novella is humorous and its conclusion even more so. Feeling betrayed, Roberto posts an ad in a newspaper's personals section in which he declares his interest only for women who "had never gone to the movies nor collects portraits of film actors."[57] The passionate following for Hollywood films, perceived to be particularly intense among women, has dramatically altered his approach to romantic life.[58] He has come to equate women's moviegoing habit to a dangerous license to desire screen idols against whom actual men cannot compete.

More research is needed to assess mainstream Argentine culture's uneasiness about Valentino's popularity among women, in terms of both private feelings and public display. What appears certain is that, as in the North American context, gender also played a significant role in the reception of Valentino films in Argentina. There, however, this critical category was correlated to migrant narratives of cross-cultural adaptation that found the Italian actor inadequately solipsistic and to geopolitical aspirations of national pride and cultural sovereignty that resulted in constant critiques of Hollywood's Argentine recreations. Thus, the intertwining of anti-Hollywood condemnation and gender anxiety made it impossible for the Italian actor to find acceptance as either authentic Italian immigrant or genuine Latin lover in Argentina's 1920s mainstream culture. Hollywood made him an international star, but in a country of multiple national cultures that was busy filming its new, composite one, no tango scene could make him a native.

> GIORGIO BERTELLINI is Associate Professor of Screen Arts at the University of Michigan. He is the author and editor of the award-winning books *Italy in Early American Cinema: Race, Landscape, and the Picturesque* (Indiana University Press, 2010) and *Italian Silent Cinema: A Reader* (Indiana University Press/John Libbey Publications, 2013). His recently published monograph *Emir Kusturica* appeared in Italian (Il castoro, 2011), in English (University of Illinois Press, 2015), and is forthcoming in Romanian (IBU Publishing).

NOTES

* I wish to thank the editors for their careful reading of this essay and for their most helpful suggestions about its content and form; all remaining shortcomings are my own. This essay grew out of a conference talk that I gave at the 2012 Latin American Studies Conference in San Francisco. I thank Cynthia M. Tompkins for organizing the panel on Silent Cinema in Latin America, and my fellow copanelists and the attending audience for their feedback. I am grateful to Antonia Lant for lending me her copy of the hard-to-find *Mosaico criollo: Primera antología del cine mudo argentino*, and to Yeidy Rivero for help with some of the original Spanish texts. For my research in Buenos Aires and for permission to use illustration located in their repositories, I am grateful to the archivists and librarians of the Biblioteca Nacional; Centro de Estudios Migratorios Latinoamericanos (CEMLA), particularly Diego Carámbula, Alejandra Porra, and Mónica López; Museo del Cine Pablo Ducrós Hicken; and the Fundación Cinemateca Argentina, particularly Guillermo Fernández Jurado and Marcela Cassinelli. I dedicate this essay to Guillermo Fernández Jurado (1923–2013) who several years ago took the time to screen several silent Argentine films and explain their history to me—a total stranger to him and to the field—with inspiring generosity and enthusiasm.

1. Other regularly mentioned key factors included the infusion of capital from Wall Street, the vertical integration of the American film business, the progressive rationalization of labor division and ensuing high quality and volume of productions, and the multiplication of film periodicals and their links to studios' publicity departments. For Hollywood's popularity in Europe, but also beyond the old continent, one should not ignore the long-term effects of US propaganda activities during World War I, which greatly popularized ideas and practices of modern American lifestyles among non-Americans. See, among others, Richard Koszarski, *An Evening's*

Entertainment: The Age of the Silent Feature Picture 1915–1928 (New York: Charles Scribner's Sons, 1991).

2. One of the most articulated discussions of this hegemony is Victoria De Grazia, *Irresistible Empire: America's Advance through Twentieth-Century Europe* (Cambridge, MA: Belknap Press, 2005), chap. 6. On the expansion of the American film industry's reach, particularly through its public relations, see Ruth Vasey, *The World According to Hollywood, 1918–1939* (Exeter: University of Exeter Press, 1997), esp. chaps. 1 and 2.

3. I have discussed this methodological caution with regard to the question of modernity in Italian American and Italian film cultures. See Giorgio Bertellini, *Italy in Early American Cinema: Race, Landscape, and the Picturesque* (Bloomington: Indiana University Press, 2010), 276–291; Giorgio Bertellini, *Italian Silent Cinema: A Reader* (Bloomington/New Barnet, Herts, UK: Indiana University Press/John Libbey Publications, 2013), 3–13.

4. See the relevant chapters on Valentino in Miriam Hansen, *Babel and Babylon: Spectatorship in American Silent Film* (Cambridge, MA: Harvard University Press, 1991); Gaylyn Studlar, *This Mad Masquerade: Stardom and Masculinity in the Jazz Age* (New York: Columbia University Press, 1996); and Mark Lynn Anderson, *Twilight of the Idols: Male Film Stars, Mass Culture, and the Human Sciences in 1920s America* (Berkeley: University of California Press, 2011). I accessed an earlier version Anderson's discussion of Valentino in his PhD dissertation, *Twilight of the Idols: Male Film Stars, Mass Culture, and the Human Sciences in 1920s America* (University of Rochester, 1999).

5. Giorgio Bertellini, "Duce/Divo: Displaced Rhetorics of Masculinity, Racial Identity, and Politics among Italian-Americans in 1920's New York City," *Journal of Urban History* 31, no. 5 (2005): 685–726.

6. I made this case for early twentieth-century film culture in my volume, *Italy in Early American Cinema: Race, Landscape, and the Picturesque* (Bloomington: Indiana University Press, 2010). On national diversity in early twentieth-century urban and working-class America, see Raymond Mohl, *The New City: Urban America in the Industrial Age, 1860–1920* (Arlington Heights, IL: H. Davidson, 1985); and Herbert G. Gutman (with Ira Berlin) "Class Composition and the Development of the American Working Class, 1840–1890," [1983] in Herbert G. Gutman, *Power and Culture: Essays on the American Working Class*, ed. Ira Berlin (New York: Pantheon Books, 1987), esp. 382–385. I address this issue in Bertellini, *Italy in Early American Cinema*, 238–244.

7. One year later Paramount adapted Ibáñez's 1909 novel *Blood and Sand* into another Valentino vehicle. On American film adaptations of Ibáñez's work, see Sharon Cumberland, "North American Desire for the Spanish Other: Three Film Versions of Blasco Ibáñez's *Blood and Sand*," *Links & Letters* 6 (1999): 43–59.

8. See Nicholas Shumway, *The Invention of Argentina* (Berkeley: University of California Press, 1991), esp. chaps. 3, 9, and 10.

9. Consider such British travelogues as *Dance of the Gauchos* and *The Gauchos' Pericon*, both produced in 1905 by Charles Urban Trading Company; the French *Le Revanche du Gaucho* (*The Gaucho's Revenge*, prod. Pathé, 1909), the Italian films *Il*

Gaucho (prod. Savoia, 1914) and *Amore di Gaucho* (prod. Ambrosio, 1915), and the Brazilian *Coraçao de Gaúcho* (dir. Luiz de Barros, 1920).

10. A possible list would include *My American Wife* (also known as *Mi esposa americana*, dir. Sam Wood, 1922), starring Gloria Swanson and Antonio Moreno; *Good Men and Bad* (dir. Merrill McCormick, 1923); *Argentina Love* (also known as *Amor argentino*, dir. Allan Dwan, 1924), starring Bebe Daniels; *The Temptress* (*La tentadora*, dir. Fred Niblo, 1926), with Greta Garbo, and, of course, *A Sainted Devil*, the other Valentino film set in Argentina, also starring Nita Naldi. For a complete filmography, see Diego Curubeto, *Babilonia gaucha: Hollywood en la Argentina, la Argentina en Hollywood* (Buenos Aires: Planeta, 1993), 171–184.

11. Domingo Di Núbila, *Historia del cine Argentino*, vol. 1: *La época de oro*, rev. ed. (Buenos Aires: Ediciones del Jilguero, 1998), 48–50.

12. For a critical study of the dialectics between autochthonous national narratives vis-à-vis Euro-American cultural hegemony, see Eduardo Romano, *Literatura/Cine Argentinos sobre la(s) frontera(s)* (Buenos Aires: Catálogos Editora, 1991). An interesting case of homage and appropriation is that of comedians Charlie Chaplin and Max Linder. The films of the British-born Chaplin were Hollywood blockbusters distributed all over the world. The French Linder enjoyed a comparable fame. The two comedians inspired two Argentine comedy series, "Carlitos" and "Max and Carlitos," which combined slapstick with tango routines. See Jorge Finkielman, *The Film Industry in Argentina: An Illustrated Cultural History* (Jefferson, NC: McFarland, 2004), 32–33.

13. José Agustín Mahieu, *Breve historia del cine argentino* (Buenos Aires: Editorial Universitaria, 1966).

14. On the film's depiction of the country's landscapes and its debts to photography, see Andrea Cuarterolo, "Imágenes de la Argentina opulenta. Una lectura de *Nobleza gaucha* (1915) desde el proyecto fotográfico de la Sociedad Fotográfica Argentina de Aficionados," in *Civilización y barbarie en el cine argentino y latinoamericano*, ed. Ana Laura Lusnich (Buenos Aires: Editorial Biblos, 2005), esp. 20–25.

15. See Patricia Funes, "Nación, patria, argentinidad: La reflexión intelectual sobre la nación en la década de 1920," in *Representaciones inconclusas: Las clases, los actores, y los discursos de la memoria, 1912–1946*, eds. Waldo Ansaldi and Alfredo R. Pucciarelli, (Buenos Aires: Biblos, 1995), 125–163; and Shumway, *The Invention of Argentina*, passim. For a very helpful comparison, see Rick A. López, *Crafting Mexico: Intellectuals, Artisans, and the State after the Revolution* (Durham, NC: Duke University Press, 2010).

16. The *sainete* was originally a Spanish farcical form, a one-act dramatic vignette, that had become popular in Buenos Aires since the 1880s as a performative genre that showcased immigrants' awkward attempts to imitate such native Argentine figures as the *compadrito*. As such the Argentine sainete made space for the *lunfardo* and all linguistic hybridisms associated with immigrant populations living and arguing in the city's *conventillos*. Commentators on the sainete have raised the same sociocultural questions that have pervaded the debates on the *literatura gauchesca*: whether it was not just a form of literature aligned with the culture of the popular classes, but also, as Borges had famously contended, a cultural production designed and within the urban

culture of Buenos Aires and Montevideo. Jorge Luis Borges, "La poesía gauchesca," *Discusión* [1932] in *Obras completas* (Buenos Aires: Emecé, 1974), 179–197, quoted in Paulo Antonio Paranaguá, *Tradición y modernidad en el cine de América Latina* (Madrid: Fondo 20+1 / Fondo de Cultura Económica de España, 2003), 42. On circo criollo, or Argentine native circus, see Raúl Héctor Castagnino, *El circo criollo: datos y documentos para su historia, 1757–1924* (Buenos Aires: Lajouane, 1953).

17. Derived from the word "lumbardo," which refers to the inhabitants of the Italian region of Lombardy, *lunfardo* is a jargon that emerged among the lower classes, especially Italian immigrants, in Buenos Aires in the second half of the nineteenth century.

18. Eva Golluscio de Montoya, "Le 'cocoliche': une convention du théâtre populaire du Rio de la Plata," *Cahiers du monde hispanique et luso-brésilien* 35 (1980): 11–30; Ana Cara-Walker, "Cocoliche: The Art of Assimilation and Dissimulation among Italians and Argentines," *Latin American Research Review* 22, no. 3 (1987): 37–67; and Micol Seigel, "Cocoliche's Romp: Fun with Nationalism at Argentina's Carnival," *The Drama Review* 44, no. 2 (2000): 56–83.

19. Cara-Walker, "Cocoliche: The Art of Assimilation and Dissimulation," 37.

20. Paranaguá, *Tradición y modernidad*, 43.

21. Fernando J. Devoto, *Historia de los italianos en la Argentina* (Buenos Aires: Biblos, 2006), chap. 5. For an earlier, detailed account, see Jorge F. Sergi, *Historia de los italianos en la Argentina* (Buenos Aires: Editora Italo Argentina, 1940).

22. Several Italian-born figures of Argentine cinema regularly advertised in the pages of the Italian press. They included filmmaker Mario Gallo and the pioneer distributor of newsreel series Federico Valle (*Film Revista*), later followed by Rafael Parodi, who in 1922 founded the *Actualidades Tylca*. On Italian newspapers in Argentina, see Federica Bertagna's well-informed study, *La stampa italiana in Argentina* (Rome: Donzelli, 2009).

23. I have not been able to locate much coverage for the Italian films that film historian Jorge Finkielman describes as particularly successful in the mid-1910s, including the epic-acrobatic *Maciste* (dirs. Vicenzo C. Dénizot and Romano Luigi Borgnetto, 1915) and *Maciste alpino* (*The Warrior*, dir. Giovanni Pastrone, 1916), the melodrama *La Falena* (dir. Carmine Gallone, 1916), starring Lyda Borelli, and the World War I travelogue *La guerra d'Italia a 3000 metri sull'Adamello* (*The War in Italy 3000 Meters Up on Adamello*, dir. Luca Comerio, 1916). Finkielman, *The Film Industry in Argentina*, 34–35.

24. Steeped in nineteenth-century Italian liberalism, *La Patria* came into conflict with such fascist newspapers as *Il Legionario* and *Il Mattino d'Italia*, and was forced to close in 1931. See David Aliano, *Mussolini's National Project in Argentina* (Madison, NJ: Fairleigh Dickinson University Press; Lanham, MD: Rowman & Littlefield, 2012), 67.

25. "Rodolfo Valentino contrattato con United Artists," *La Patria degli Italiani*, April 5, 1925, 11.

26. Aliano, *Mussolini's National Project*, 67.

27. The film consisted of a montage of newsreel footage on the March on Rome of late October 1922.

28. The modern technology of the telegraphic cable, the *Cavo*, is also a major catalyst of patriotic pride, as it allows a direct contact with the homeland. This was also quite similar to what was occurring in the North American ethnic press. I examined its symbolic importance in Bertellini, "Sovereign Consumption: Italian Americans' Film Culture in 1920s New York City," in *Making Italian America: Consumer Culture and the Production of Ethnic Identities*, ed. Simone Cinotto (New York: Fordham University Press, 2014), 83–99.

29. *Patria degli Italiani* starts serializing Verga's *La cavalleria rusticana* on April 2, 1922, 6, and Gabriele D'Annunzio's "Notturno" on January 13, 1922, 3. A posthumous profile of "Giovanni Verga" appeared on January 28, 1922, 3.

30. *Patria degli Italiani*, February 21, 1923, 3. The journalist in charge of this subcolumn went by the name of "Chaplin."

31. "Le attrici e l'amore," *La Patria degli Italiani*, November 1, 1925, 3. This may explain why the *La Patria* failed to discuss the Argentine release of the aforementioned film *La Falena*, starring Lyda Borelli.

32. "La formula comica di Harold Lloyd," *La Patria degli Italiani*, October 12, 1923, 7. Fairbanks remained a favorite star, and his films received extensive coverage.

33. On the history of this gendering practice, see Andreas Huyssen, "Mass Culture as Woman: Modernism's Other," in *After the Great Divide: Modernism, Mass Culture, Postmodernism* (Bloomington: Indiana University Press, 1986), 44–62.

34. Curubeto, *Babilonia gaucha*, 13. See also Alberto Farina, "El mito de Valentino," in *La realidad obstinada: Apuntes sobre el cine italiano*, eds. Claudio España and Luigi Volta (Buenos Aires: Corregidor, 1992), 53–61.

35. "'El hijo del Sheik' mostrará la verdadera fibra artística de Rodolfo Valentino," *La Pelicula*, October 2, 1926, 15.

36. "Valentino y Nita Naldi en 'Cobra,' la venenosa," *La Película*, August 12, 1926, 15, and "La Paramount dió a conocer 'El Diablo santificado,' por Rodolfo Valentino," *La Pelicula*, September 2, 1926, 11.

37. Ibid. See also *La Pelicula*, September 23, 1926, 17.

38. It is worth reminding that the aforementioned stereotypical figures of Argentine popular culture had emerged in different historical periods, from the older, late nineteenth-century gaucho and the turn-of-the-twentieth-century sympathetic Italian immigrant to the early twentieth-century tango dancer whose fame at home was also indebted to intense foreign acclaim.

39. For a discussion of the film, see Jorge Miguel Couselo, *El "Negro" Ferreyra: Un cine por instinto* (Buenos Aires: Grupo Editor Altamira, 2001), 30–34.

40. "Ruffians" and "pimps." For these debates, see "El cine en latinoamérica," in *Historia universal del cine*, no. 103 (Madrid: Planeta, 1982), 238–239. For an example of Borges' view, see his "Historia del tango," in *Evaristo Carriego* (Buenos Aires: Emecé, 1955), 141–164; and his poem, "El tango," in *El otro, el mismo* (Buenos Aires: Emecé, 1969), 53–55.

41. Marvin D'Lugo's work on the reception of Gardel's tango films is quite useful, even though D'Lugo focuses on sound films and the formation of a virtual Hispanic

transnational community through shared auditory culture. See Marvin D'Lugo, "Early Cinematic Tangos: Audiovisual Culture and Transnational Film Aesthetics," *Studies in Hispanic Cinemas* 5, nos. 1–2 (2008): 9–22. On Gardel the literature is not scarce. See also D'Lugo, "Gardel, el film hispano y la construcción de la identidad auditiva," in *Cine, nación y nacionalidad en España*, eds. Nancy Berthier and Jean-Claude Seguin (Madrid: Collection de la Casa de Velázquez, 2007), 147—161; Rielle Navitski, "The Tango on Broadway: Carlos Gardel's International Stardom and the Transition to Sound in Argentina," *Cinema Journal* 51, no. 1 (2011): 26–49; and Nicolas Poppe, "Made in Joinville: Transnational Identitary Aesthetics in Carlos Gardel's Early Paramount Films," *Journal of Latin American Cultural Studies* 21, no. 4 (2012): 481–95.

42. See Horacio Quiroga, "Los intelectuales y el cine," *Atlántida* (Buenos Aires), August 1, 1922; repr. in *Avances de Hollywood: Crítica cinematográfica en Latinoamérica, 1915–1945*, ed. Jason Borge (Rosario: Beatriz Viterbo, 2005), 62–66. For his part, Quiroga expressed a kind of modernist attraction for the medium by publishing short Hollywood-themed stories and more than sixty film columns, which appeared between 1918 and 1931. In his columns, he praised and embraced cinema's nonreal, plastic expression and its privileging of gestures and glances that in turn fueled his own fictional creation. See Lee Williams, "Film Criticism and/or Narrative? Horacio Quiroga's Early Embrace of Cinema," *Studies in Hispanic Cinemas* 1, no. 3 (2004): 181–197.

43. Beatriz Sarlo, *Una modernidad periferica: Buenos Aires, 1920 y 1930* (Buenos Aires: Nueva Vision, 1996), chaps. 1 and 2. A systematic study of the film discourse informing such newspapers as *El Mundo* and *Crítica*, as well as such key periodicals as *Caras y Caretas, Mundo Argentino*, and *El Hogar*, would be helpful here. A cursory examination of *Caras y Caretas* reveals that most references to Valentino appeared in a column entitled "Teatro del Silencio" written by Narciso Robledal. The column mentions Valentino's own concerns about the realism of his interpretation as tango dancer (following Robledal's alleged interview with the actor) and the financial troubles linked to his marital status and his disagreements with the studios. See Narciso Robledal, "Teatro del Silencio," *Caras y Caretas* (Buenos Aires), January 27, 1923, 41, and April 21, 1923, 48. *Caras y Caretas* is available in digital format from the Hemeroteca Digital of the Biblioteca Nacional de España.

44. Maureen Spillane McKenna, "Entre el tango y Hollywood: Hacia una geopolítica argentina en la obra de Roberto Arlt," *Romance Quarterly* 49, no. 4 (2002): 310–311, 304.

45. Roberto Arlt, "Discurso del astrólogo," in *Los siete locos*, ed. Flora Guzmán (Madrid: Cátedra, [1929] 1992), 206–221, 213. Arlt was generally quite concerned about political celebrities: in his 1936 stage play, *Saverio el cruel*, the title character evokes the example of Mussolini, who overnight turned a country of operetta into "el mastín del Mediterráneo" ("mastiff of the Mediterranean").

46. Enrique H. Puccia, *Intimidades de Buenos Aires* (Buenos Aires: Corregidor, 1990), 203.

47. Roberto Tálice, *100,000 ejemplares por hora: memorias de un redactor de "Critica" el diario de Botana* (Buenos Aires: Corregidor, 1977), 290. Years later, film historian Jorge Miguel Couselo referred to the opinion of Italian Argentine filmmaker Roberto

Guidi (1890–1958) to describe Valentino's tango as "product of fantasy," namely "a combination of rumba, paso doble, cueca and apache dance." Quoted in Finkielman, *The Film Industry in Argentina*, 39.

48. Tálice, *100,000 Ejemplares*, 290. For this point, I am indebted to Sergio Pujol, *Valentino en Buenos Aires: Los años veinte y el espectáculo* (Buenos Aires: Emecé Editores, 1994), 108.

49. Santos Goñi, with Carlos A. Goñi Demarchi, "Lo argentino en el Hollywood del cine mudo," *Todo es historia* (1991): 8–36, 14.

50. Agustín Aragón Leiva, "Añoranzas de Hollywood," *Cinelandia* (Los Angeles), June 1931, 39, 66–69, quote on 69.

51. Pujol, *Valentino en Buenos Aires*, 107. Pujol often makes reference to a number of American biographies on Valentino, as well as to a Spanish one that appears unconcerned with the star's reception in Argentina or Latin America in general: Antonio Tello and Gonzalo Otero Pizarro, *Valentino: La seducción manipulada* (Barcelona: Editorial Bruguera, 1978).

52. Pujol, *Valentino en Buenos Aires*, 108.

53. The short story is included in Enrique Méndez Calzada's *Y volvió Jesús a Buenos Aires*, 2nd ed. (Buenos Aires: Editorial America Unida, 1926), 137–145. I am indebted to Nicolas Poppe for locating this source; I wish to thank him and Rielle Navitski for sharing it with me.

54. Enrique Méndez Calzada, "La enamorada de Rudolfo Valentino," 139–144.

55. Ibid., 144–145.

56. Ibid., 145.

57. Ibid., 146.

58. As Laura Isabel Serna notes, in 1920s Mexico audiences and reviewers referred to such cinephilic enthusiasm as "muvimania." Serna, *Making Cinelandia: American Films and Mexican Film Culture before the Golden Age* (Durham, NC: Duke University Press, 2014), 136.

PART II

The Interwar Period:
Between Hollywood and the Avant-Garde

Felipe de Leiva, "Memoirs of an Extra," *Cinelandia* (Hollywood), November–December 1927

> *The pseudonym used to sign this text suggests it was penned by Agustín Aragón Leiva, a frequent contributor to* Cinelandia *and a key figure in early twentieth-century Mexican film culture who moved to Los Angeles in 1926. He participated actively in the formation of the Cine Club de México in 1931 and acted as an assistant for Sergei Eisenstein during the filming of* ¡Que Viva México! *"Memoirs of an Extra" playfully and poetically describes Mexican film labor in Hollywood and the social inequalities it embodied.*

THE FILM STUDIOS, MAGNETIC north for the ships of ambition, a dream for the days and nights of youth; an ocean into which rivers of longings flow.

I never thought I would be Sinbad the sailor, a navigator seeking the opportunities offered by Hollywood. If I went to the movies, there in my Latin land, it was to conceal my flirtation with Leonor in the propitious darkness of neighborhood movie theaters. When a storm of bad luck tossed me up in California, I set my sights on a job as a dishwasher or floor scrubber. That way, I'd have a sure meal at least.

They are thousands, those who arrive feverish with delusions of being extras, first possible step in the golden evolution of the star—note that the star is nothing more than the elaborate evolution of an extra—and they scrub plates and wash floors. I soon joined the ranks of film industry proletarians.

* * *

Charles Stevens, a Mexican from Arizona, *Planchet* in "The Three Musketeers" with Fairbanks and the right-hand man of "Don Q." in the business, gave me a "chance."[1] For "The Gaucho," Douglas Fairbanks' 1927 film, a superproduction, three publicity campaigns, a million-dollar budget.

* * *

Los Angeles, a vast city. An hour and a half on a fast trolley to arrive at United Artists. There I found, blocking the doors, an anxious multitude:

"Charles!..."
"Carlitos!..."
"Charlecitos!..."
"Won't I do?..."
"I'm just the type!..."
"Carlitos!"

Many are called and few are chosen. Stevens, stupified by the din of entreaties. The faces of those who failed to cross the fence!

* * *

The wardrobe: outfits rented from the Costume Company. Outfits that audiences have seen once, twice, five times. Yet still unrecognized. Who can be their incompetent publicity agent? Washed, disinfected, ironed; the unpleasant smell of sweat removed in a pasteurizer. Collars and shirts of a soft pink, very romantic. Charles took pity on my fatness and chose me as a rich man. Very few were offered this bait; the rest are beggars in filthy rags, feigning ten years of grime, fetid pustules, buboes, marks of shameful illnesses, or nearly invalid, with the sores of leprosy, one-eyed. The types for a pilgrimage to Lourdes.

* * *

One boot is larger than the other, a malicious error: the left, from north to south, or rather from point to heel, as if the entire range of the Andes were inside; the peak of Aconcagua, a nail not hammered down. A cinched pant, the cut: from the dawn of time, made of a flannel very much in style for beach cover-ups. A brown frock coat, the lining frayed by the teeth of the washing machine. A lilac sash of raw percale, falling apart. A tie stolen from a shoeshine, rendering him unable to polish the shoes of his clients. "Rich man,"[2] influential, bourgeois... but fallen on hard times, by the grace of some revolution. The hat... a Panama with a plaid band and a chinstrap made of the sash of a bathrobe.

* * *

They stuck a mustache for a Parisian gendarme on me; my skin, never touched by glue, rebelled against the tightness. Sneezing strictly forbidden. The dictator, a youth who, greasing faces and sticking on hair, earns two hundred dollars a week.

* * *

La Aldea del Milagro [Miracle Village], the steepest corner of the Andes. It is made known that the art director has traveled in Central America, with a Kodak. A splendid reconstruction. Would that many cities in Latin America looked this clean and new. Since it is a miraculous city, the streets are not paved with gravel from the river; it has smooth, magnificent concrete pavement, as fine as the best avenue in Los Angeles. In the background, set into the mountain, the shrine where the Virgin of the Rock is worshipped. To reach it, a sumptuous stairway that descends through a tropical orchard of palms and banana trees, leafy thickets of trees that are supposed to be *ombús*.[3] A well-fed lawn grows, and is beginning to flourish. Sparrows sing, for free.

* * *

The conquest of Hollywood by Latinos is a fact. California was Mexican and is becoming so again. Their triumph in the cinema is indisputable. They are the ones who work cheaply, they are the ones who provide greater efficiency, they are the ones who make directors shout less. The use of Mexicans means a savings of hundreds of thousands of dollars for the producers, year after year. Argentines, Chileans, Colombians, fill out the ranks. They are proletarians, they are the masses and they are unredeemed. They await the coming of a socialist redeemer. Between a Tom Mix who earns $17,000 a week and an extra who goes hungry, there is a horrific inequality. Upton Sinclair, who has spoken out against oil, the railroads, and the butchers of Chicago, has not yet spoken out against film stars, all those stars who because of the capricious whims of circumstance, without any real merit, earn upwards of a hundred dollars a week. An extra sweats, endures the sun, the irritating purple lights, the garments that were not made to fit his measurements and have already been used. The extra gives life to a film, given that in an aesthetic evaluation of the best pictures, crowd scenes almost always have a positive value. The extra is a pariah, who has to beg for his supper seeking work from studio to studio.

"¡Carlitos! . . . ¡Charles! . . . ¡Carlos! . . . ¡Charlecito! . . . *viejo* . . . Charles! . . . listen up. . . . *ché!*"[4]

Four hundred bit players are used, at five dollars a head. Four hundred men who have needs and longings are given less significance than a Tom Mix who, in one day, whether he works or not, receives two thousand five hundred dollars. In the cinema, nineteenth-century melodrama flourishes vigorously; the romantic vulgarity of the majority of films contrasts with the refinement of contemporary literature. Capitalism from the point of the view of extras considered as a class has an oppressive backwardness, of two thousand years. This suffering class impatiently awaits the arrival of a Messiah who will come to redeem them.

* * *

Work, never certain. The extra is an idler. Those who have failed in action, those with no profession, the good-for-nothings, are extras. The elderly, children, women who never learned to cook a stew, are extras. Beautiful young people, of both sexes, who aspire to attach themselves through an accident of fortune to the growing caste of Hollywood aristocrats. A democratic caste for which there are no requirements. Valentino, who was the sun of this solar system, even took on disgraceful jobs before his elevation to dandy. This caste shows off its low, improvised origins. It behaves like the "nouveau riches" that appear after wars and crises. The great effort exerted by extras is to wait, hours and hours. Divine patience, the first and essential virtue needed to triumph in the cinema. Sometimes, the extra risks his neck. When he breaks a leg, to silence the protests, they give him room and board while he recovers.

* * *

The boredom, immense. A tangle of figures has formed. Rich men alongside beggars, the exploiters alongside the exploited. The miracle of the Virgin of the Rock. All of them, suffering pilgrims who have traveled to give thanks. They were attempting to capture the scene of the crowd leaving the shrine. For this, complicated scaffolding maintaining the camera at a convenient height and on rails to pull back. Three minutes of action, to be repeated fifteen times, five with the camera and ten for rehearsal. If they had been Yankees, Jews, or Germans, it would have been at least thirty trips back and forth. Under an unfriendly August sun, with an outfit suited for the time when I was thin, a high four-inch collar, starched, and treading on the instrument of torture inserted in my left foot, I cursed the destiny that made me an extra. Annoyance was visible on every countenance. Admiration for Charles Stevens who shouted and shouted, in English and Spanish, without going hoarse.

* * *

Lunch hour arrived, blessed among all hours. A happy stampede towards the canteen. A delightful hunger that longed for delectable delicacies. I forgot my thick mustache. Faced with a fragrant plate of barbecued meat and buttered bread, the repugnant obstacle of a disintegrating mustache. Resignation and recovering my strength drinking a malted milk, with a straw.

* * *

Jack Dempsey arrives accompanied by the madman D. W. Griffith. Two hours of the afternoon had passed rehearsing the scene. Jack is a pretext for a break, taken up by cheering him. His right eye, still black from Tunney's fists.[5] The secret of the force of Jack's right hook is number of handshakes the man has received. Four hundred bit players from *The Gaucho*, with the exception of me, had the honor of strengthening the fists of the ex-champion, jovial, victorious in a recent fight. Charles shouts:

"Here are Mr. Dempsey and Mr. Griffith, the cinematic genius. Let's see if the scene comes out well now. . . . You know who Mr. Griffith is . . . well . . . action!"

The scene came out stupendous because the extras are foolish. If they had done it badly, it would be back to rehearsals and then, after eight hours of work, overtime at twice the price. But their weakness in adoring Jack Dempsey and believing Mr. Griffith a genius has deprived us this afternoon of receiving a few dollars more.

Finally, in the dressing rooms. The unbearable stench of sweaty bodies, the throng hurry to return home quickly. How comfortable one's clothes are, already adapted to the body. To the devil with the infernal, dirty, horrible boots. Still, an hour in a well-disciplined line, to arrive at the cashier's window.

(End of the first day.)

Second Day

"You know it, boys, tomorrow at six . . . don't be lazy . . . get up early," said Charles Stevens to the extras when they were amassed awaiting their pay.

"At six," I thought, "well, I'm not coming. I'd have to get up at the crack of dawn."

In my humble hovel, bathed, in pajamas, I felt the delight of no longer wearing borrowed clothes. And the bottoms of my "paws" were destroyed. On the other hand, the possibility of working as an elevator operator in a hotel had presented itself. So I decided not to go back to United Artists and to desist completely from all cinematic efforts.

But five dollars in Los Angeles, when you're "broke," earned just by filling out the ranks and sunning yourself a bit, are not to be sneezed at.

The next day, at six in the morning, I was at the studio door.

Now the crowd was impressive. The fence didn't buckle only because it is pure steel. Poor Charles was physically flattened by the shouting.

"¡Carlitos! ¡Charles! ¡Stevens! ¡cuate! ¡compadre! Don't forget me, viejo! Look at my hunchback, Mr. Charles! Carlos! . . ." There was also shouting in Yiddish, Turkish, German, English, Russian. But suffocated by the hubbub in Spanish.

* * *

My frock coat, my boots, my sash, my tie stolen from a shoeshine. Now mine. Already impregnated with my personality and my sweat. My collar unstarched by the humidity of my humours. The only thing I was missing was my mustache. It had been a Frenchman's, and now they put on a Tartar's, and also tripled the thickness of my eyebrows. My friends from the previous day failed to recognize me. And now the multitude was a massive wave.

* * *

The Aldea del Milagro is made up of a wide street that extends the straight stairway leading to the Shrine. On either side, palaces in Hispanic colonial style, well reproduced. Arches, portals, roofs of tile not oxidized by time and rain. Windows with lattices. An appearance that is decent, to say the least, clean, and instead of being denigrating, it will be great publicity for tourists to Central America, in tours with two hours to stroll in each port and stuff one's pockets with postcards.

In the middle of the thoroughfare, stalls and tents, put up by merchants. A tropical effect, showing off the touch of expensive fruits: pineapples, watermelons, oranges, bunches of bananas, gourds, avocados, etc. Fans of palm leaves, pots and utensils of Tolucan clay, from Mexico; rosaries and crucifixes, colored beads, missals. Thick candles of unmeltable wax, to resist the sun. The atmosphere of a *tianguis*,[6] on a high holiday, a big market day, a day in the plaza. The most varied types. Spanish peasant woman from a Goya-esque running of the bulls, showy and attractive; bachelors from sentimental novels, from Lamartine and Chateaubriand; lace collars and ties, shirts with cuffs of the same material. Vagabonds from all the countries of the Americas. Dirty, stinking, ugly, unkempt. Without a doubt, in all the film these scenes will be those of picturesque intensity, because this multitude has suddenly taken on a true soul, a soul that can be felt to the point of making one forget California and the studios.

The vigorous emanation of this spirit has its origin in the quality of the extras, the majority of whom are Mexicans. The highest manifestation of genuinely Mexican life is in the *tianguis*, the day all the inhabitants of an entire region go into the city. They come to stock up, they come to treat themselves to bonbons, to fulfill vows, to visit friends, to greet the priest. Anyone who has experienced the popular existence of Mexicans knows the significance of a day in the plaza. Furthermore, the shrine to the Virgin of the Miracle revives a tradition that is the backbone of Mexico; the twelfth of December, day of the Virgin of Guadalupe, patron saint of the Americas.

Mexicans, subconsciously, experience, in their bitter exile, these dear emotions of the life of their country, so full of vernacular color, so vibrant with a unanimous exaltation, in which all the lively and picturesque energies of nationality converge.

Mr. Fairbanks, without realizing it, had provided the occasion for the temperament of the multitude to manifest itself in a stupendous fashion. That of the *Gaucho* had, at least on this day, a soul, a keen personality, that managed to attract and vindicate the camera's lens, and will shake up the emotions of the audience, like the multitudes in the great Russian film *Potemkin*, which Douglas has been one of the first in the United States to warmly praise.

Recognizable cries from the yard, the enchanting cries of native merchants; more than cries, promotional chants: pork skins from Toluca! Good cheeses from Barca! Buy these artichokes, my girl! Come have some *atole*![7] Aaaaa... sorbet of milk and lemon! Here, sweet oranges! Quench your thirst, beauty! A growing clamor, that drowns out the noise of carpenters, the voices of those directing, the screeching of the purple reflectors placed to assist the sun. Charles, Douglas, and friends who have come with him to watch the scene, are moved by the plastic immensity of the moment.

A pity that the camera is deaf, that it has only eyes!

* * *

The moment has come when the village with its river of pilgrims is going to be filmed from the distance, up on the roof of some shacks, where there is an ingenious version in miniature of the immense elevation of the mountains and the location of the buildings in the very heart of the Andes. The details are lost in the distance, and for this reason, all kinds of nonsense are permitted.

Mary [Pickford] has arrived, as enchanting as ever with the perennial freshness of her face. With her, thirteen girls from different capitals of the Union, guests of honor in the Pickfair mansion, the nest of Hollywood's best marriage, according to the magazines.[8] Behind Mary, a group of the curious, onlookers, intruders. The director invites all them all to join the crowd; he distributes sarapes and Mexican sombreros. The Jew who conducts the orchestra that plays for the filming of *The Gaucho*, steps up on a carriage with three lovely costumed women and hides his long nose under the shadow of the aforementioned hat. The thirteen girls position themselves strategically, anxious to be taken into account by the camera so as to be recognized by their friends.

"Ready! . . . Action!" thirty megaphones vomit simultaneously, hidden in the eaves.

Then, the movement, the clamor: pilgrims who move, dying, towards the Virgin . . . some on their knees, others dragging themselves; all lifting their arms in the Muslim manner (Oh, the ignorance of directors!); pilgrims who descend cured, happy. Color, an extraordinary quantity of real life . . . the scene is coming out stupendously.

But Douglas ruins it, making a fool of himself. He wears knickers, white socks, beach shoes, a blindingly white shirt. In the climactic moment, when all this was the liveliness of the Plaza Mayor at the doors to the Cathedral, he took a wicker basket, placed it on his head in the manner of Don Quixote with Mambrino's helmet, and furnished himself with merchandise; hats, baskets, rush matting. Then, in the most grotesque, most irrational, most ostentatious fashion, he set off running through the crowd, leaping like a madman escaped from his cell, believing that he was doing a marvelous imitation of the way humble Indian and mestizo traders offer their wares. Douglas is the type of man who, if he loses a tooth, there are ten people who do the same; such that behind him, his seconds, his monkey-like imitators began giving similar leaps . . . in such a clown-like way . . . that the crowd forgot its role ... solemn ... and laughed at Douglas with the same cordiality as one often laughs at Chaplin, in movie theaters.

The soul of the multitude dispersed, stunned. Douglas, so sensible in many aspects, such an artist in others ... tossed the best of his film on the trash heap. Ah, but he, a man of fortune, good luck's favored son, relied on the complicity of a camera more than a hundred meters away!

* * *

Nigel de Brulier is without a doubt the character most immersed in his role in *The Gaucho*. His monk is a true monk; in his gestures, in his humble gaze, in his slow rocking walk, in his hands worn by counting rosary beads. Now he distributes the coins he has collected among the rich. He gives them to the poor. The most miserable, the most pitiable I have seen. ... They clamor ... beg ... plead ... moan ... weep ... and as they receive, they give thanks, bless, kiss the habit of the Franciscan. The scene turns out to be one of profound grandeur, one of those that make swell up from the soul a wave of emotion that sometimes reaches the eyes. Charles Stevens, who has conceived and directed it, also finds himself trembling, with joy, with sentiment. With a voice that does not hide his admiration but which tries to seem joking, he exclaims:

"Truly, fellows, you must be beggars, because you've done it very well ... divinely well."

When audiences see the hands of the disinherited that rise like stalks in a field, that intertwine like the branches of ash trees and shake like waves in a thick sea of sorrow and anguish, they will think that those who managed to give an intense indication of dramatic sentiment were poor extras, anonymous artists, whose pay is miserable, whose profession is almost disgraceful ... they will think that the majority of them ... are Latinos ... speak Spanish ... reach such extremes because within them is a flame that nourishes and animates ... the temperament of the race ... that triumphs, definitively, in Cinelandia, already in individuals, now in multitudes, in a decisive, undeniable manner, with the approval and delight of producers, as an unsurpassable, highly select, element of production and aesthetic use.

* * *

Spanish America has a diversity of types that is like a scale of a thousand notes. There are women among my comrades in arms, whose beauty and grace is equal to that sung of by poets, in all the rhythms of light and sound; there are gallants who have, in addition to harmony of features, distinction in manners and the dignity of great men; alongside them, young girls with figures deformed as if by a joking whim; old women who seem like witches lifted from old almanacs, boys, mature men, children, who inspire pity for the few physical gifts granted to them by Nature, often a cruel mother. Blondes and brunettes, adorable pinched features of girls from Jalisco or Colima, mulattos, *zambos*, redheads.[9] A conjunction of all the racial forces of the Americas. English, almost displaced. Spanish, in many accents. From the sing-song of the Mexicans to the devourers of letters, Cubans and those from the coast; the *elle* and the *ya 'stá* of the Argentines and Chileans: *ché... compadre... chico... vale...*[10]

In the afternoon, at one point, they lifted up the scaffold. They put the monk in one vise, the virginal Eve Southern, rival of Lupe Vélez in the heart of the Gaucho, in the other. They half-undressed them. Nigel de Brulier was pale. Eve, frightened. Their tormentors, naked from the waist up, showing their solid torsos, covered with abundant hair. The tormenters, with whips. The tormentors, two monsters, frightful, horrendous. The two ugliest beings in California, with colossal jawbones, with noses resembling a mask to frighten children, with enormous mouths, with very thick lips, with ogre-like jaws. Mexicans? ... Perhaps ... because they speak Spanish ... with a Mexican timbre. What a contrast with the handsome young man, a genuine Mexican who gazes from the edge of the platform, with caressing flashes, at the extraordinarily large and green eyes of poor Eve Southern!

Finally, the beating was administered by order of the director by the considerate tormentors—a real beating, though with strips of old rags. Nevertheless, Nigel, perhaps because of his age, fainted, while ... from the eyes of Eve Southern ... beautiful eyes ... beautiful ... though cold ... fell two tears ... that I doubt were of glycerin.

* * *

The idleness of the extras struck me as amusing and I decided to join their ranks. Day after day, with the tenacity praised by Marden, I begged for another "chance"; Charles smiled sadly:

—There's no work for today ... come tomorrow.

I got annoyed ... and here you have me at your service, ladies and gentlemen, as a lettuce seller in one of the clean Broadway markets, in this pleasant city of Los Angeles.

Translated by Rielle Navitski

RIELLE NAVITSKI is Assistant Professor of Theater and Film Studies at the University of Georgia. She is the author of *Public Spectacles of Violence: Sensational Cinema and Journalism in Early Twentieth-Century Mexico and Brazil* (Duke University Press, 2017).

NOTES

1. (Unless otherwise indicated all notes are from the editors.) In English in the original. "Don Q." was a pseudonym used by one of *Cinelandia*'s regular contributors.

2. In English in the original.

3. An *ombú* is a variety of tree native to Argentina.

4. Variations of "Charles/Carlos" in English and Spanish interspersed with terms indicating familiarity and friendship.

5. Boxer Jack Dempsey faced off against world champion Gene Tunney in an attempt to reclaim the title in 1926.

6. A *tianguis* is a term meaning "open-air market," used in Mexico.

7. *Atole* is a sweet, starchy drink made with corn.

8. A reference to Fairbanks's wife, actress Mary Pickford.

9. The term *zambo* refers to a person of mixed race, usually indigenous and African heritage.

10. A list of pronunciations and slang terms used in a range of regional and national dialects of Spanish.

Chapter 4

Mediating the "Conquering and Cosmopolitan Cinema": US Spanish-Language Film Magazines and Latin American Audiences, 1916–1948

Rielle Navitski

IN 1918, A COLUMNIST from Santiago de Chile writing for the US Spanish-language magazine *Cine-Mundial* observed that the "feverish activity in the cinematic circles of this capital have had repercussions all over the country, where the empire of the screen is rapidly expanding."[1] Four years later, a correspondent in Caracas noted that "the conquering and cosmopolitan cinema" now overshadowed live entertainment.[2] While they make no explicit mention of Hollywood film, the imperial metaphors used by these local correspondents strongly evoke the North American industry's self-declared "invasion" of South American markets during World War I, a territory that "would become a major factor in the USA's takeover of world markets and later in its retention of control."[3] The growing importance of Latin American markets for US studios is signaled by the founding of *Cine-Mundial* and later *Cinelandia*, Spanish-language film magazines published in the United States that became heralds of North America's growing "empire of the screen." Yet as these early commentaries suggest, these magazines also linked the expansion of film culture with desires for cultural modernity that were at once cosmopolitan and local, demanding further revision of scholarly accounts that equate the global circulation of Hollywood films with cultural colonization.

During lengthy runs that coincide closely with the golden age of the classical Hollywood studio system, *Cine-Mundial* (1916–1948) and *Cinelandia* (1926–1948) acted as highly ambiguous markers of the presence of US cinema in Spanish and Latin American film markets. They tirelessly promoted not only Hollywood products but also models of distribution, exhibition, and fan consumption that were dominant in the United States, while occasionally publishing criticism of Hollywood's representational and labor practices from both contributors and readers. Featuring mostly original articles in Spanish (*Cine-Mundial* also included columns in Portuguese), the two magazines took pride in the fact that they were published in centers of US film distribution and production. *Cine-Mundial*, whose title translates to "world" or "global cinema," was printed in New York by Chalmers, publishers of the influential trade magazine *Moving Picture World*. Like its sister publication, *Cine-Mundial* was originally targeted toward distributors and exhibitors; its first three years coincided with New York's emergence as the new center of Hollywood's export business, as London's importance to the global film trade declined because of wartime conditions and customs regulations.[4] *Cinelandia*—which literally means "Filmland," and was commonly used to refer to Hollywood in Spanish—was fittingly published in the Los Angeles area for most of its run.[5] It began its life as a fan magazine, capitalizing on audience interest in the star system that had been consolidated in the previous decade.

Although they commanded only a fraction of the readership enjoyed by massively popular English-language film magazines (at its peak circulation between 1929 and 1931, *Cine-Mundial*'s readership was 10 percent that of *Photoplay*), both publications enjoyed broad popularity in Spain and Latin America, as advertisements and letters from readers across the Spanish-speaking world attest.[6] The three decades spanned by *Cine-Mundial*'s and *Cinelandia*'s runs would see a series of rapprochements between the US film industry and Latin American markets, conditioned by a broader rhetoric of Pan-Americanism in trade and politics.[7] Both magazines persisted only briefly after World War II, a moment marked by the restructuring of the US studio system and the rise of Mexico's film industry as a competitor for Hollywood.[8]

As foreign-language publications pitched mostly to overseas audiences in multiple countries, *Cine-Mundial* and *Cinelandia* are curious cultural objects. Although they were published in cities where Spanish-language journalism flourished in the early twentieth century, they are only tangentially linked to the most significant currents of the Spanish-language press in the United States as identified by Nicolás Kanellos: the "exile press" intended to shape politics in the journalists' homelands, the "immigrant press" designed to address the concerns of recent arrivals, and the "native Hispanic" publications that cultivate a sense of shared cultural identity and political agency within established Spanish-speaking communities.[9] *Cine-Mundial* and *Cinelandia* are closer to the trade publications printed in Spanish in the United States beginning in the mid-nineteenth century that advocated for North American commercial interests in Latin America.[10] Predating the division of film markets by language during the transition to sound, *Cine-Mundial* and *Cinelandia* collectively addressed groups of geographically dispersed readers as "*latino*" or "*hispano*" (Spanish-speaking), with the aim of facilitating and reinforcing an asymmetrical flow of cultural goods.

Yet these magazines also opened their pages to locally specific, spatially dispersed, and ideologically contradictory discourses. While they promoted the international expansion of North American film, *Cine-Mundial* and *Cinelandia* also encouraged readers linked by a common language to imagine themselves as part of a cosmopolitan film culture mediated by, but not limited to, the consumption of Hollywood cinema. Explicitly acting as intermediaries between Hollywood studios and distributors, exhibitors, and fans in Latin America, the two magazines highlighted multiple sites of film production and consumption. Evoking language-based cultural kinship between readers and producers, the magazines foregrounded Spanish-speaking communities' contribution to the cultural life of New York and Los Angeles, and rhetorically linked these cities with entertainment culture in the diverse sites where the publications were consumed.

This tendency is most evident in *Cine-Mundial's* practice of publishing *crónicas*:[11] here, reports on local entertainment scenes by correspondents in metropolises such as Buenos Aires, Havana, Mexico City, and Madrid and smaller cities such as Guatemala City, San José in Costa Rica, Camagüey in Cuba, and the Balearic Islands in Spain, which worked to create a sense of simultaneity between far-flung locations. Present in the magazine from its inception through the end of the twenties, these columns covered not only local film exhibition but also theater, opera, sports, and current events. After the transition to sound facilitated the rise of film production in Argentina, Mexico, and Spain, the crónicas reappeared in a more limited form, covering Spanish-language industries in the thirties and forties. In comparison, *Cinelandia* devoted limited space to contributors writing outside Hollywood. Yet it enthusiastically adopted the dialogic structure of the fan magazine, actively soliciting and publishing letters from readers, who commented on films, stars, and the politics of Latin American representation in Hollywood. Conversely, New York and Los Angeles emerge in the magazines' pages not only as sites where US films were produced or dispatched to global markets but also as cities whose large Spanish-speaking communities contributed to their cosmopolitan character. The magazines often evoked the intellectual life and quotidian experiences of local immigrant populations in articles, short stories, and cartoons.

While both *Cinelandia* and *Cine-Mundial* published texts by English-language contributors, most of their columnists were themselves immigrants of Spanish or Latin American origin, who positioned themselves as ideal intermediaries between North American production companies and Spanish-speaking readers in the United States and abroad. Francisco García Ortega, who acted as *Cine-Mundial*'s editor-in-chief for its entire run, was a Cuban national who also wrote for English-language publications and (according to a collaborator) was accepted by North American journalists as "one of their own."[12] Mexican journalist José María Sánchez García, who became the magazine's Hollywood correspondent in May 1922, contributed to a number of periodicals in his home country.[13] Not surprisingly, given the recent influx of immigrants to Los Angeles during and after the Mexican Revolution, *Cinelandia* had a large contingent of writers of Mexican origin. These included journalist Armando Vargas de la Maza, who also published in the popular Mexico City magazine *El Universal Ilustrado*, and Agustín Aragón Leiva, who later worked as Sergei Eisenstein's assistant during the production of *¡Que Viva México!*[14] Alluding to their experience as exiles and expatriates, these journalists framed themselves as cultural translators for readers curious about the film business.

As a consequence of the economic and political imbalances between their sites of publication and their sites of consumption, *Cinelandia* and *Cine-Mundial* intensified the dialectics of proximity and distance, access and remoteness, and consumption and desire that characterize film magazines and the star system they support. In her influential essay "Early Cinema and Modernity in Latin America," Ana M. López argues that "cinema fed the national self-confidence that its own modernity was in progress by enabling viewers to share and participate in the experience of modernity as developed elsewhere," yet at the same time, local "viewers had to assume the position of spectators and become voyeurs of, rather than participants in, modernity."[15]

Beginning in the early 1990s, Anglo-American film scholars have reevaluated the assumed passivity of the film spectator through close attention to Hollywood fan magazines, generating approaches that can shed light on the dynamics of film culture in early twentieth-century Latin America.[16] Laura Isabel Serna has argued that Spanish-language film magazines published on both sides of the US-Mexico border played a key role in fostering new forms of consumer and entertainment culture that were framed as signs of national progress. She notes that in *Cine-Mundial*'s Mexico City crónicas, "critics and journalists positioned participation in a national film culture, built around the consumption of films produced elsewhere, as part of a set of desirable social practices that demonstrated Mexico's modernity."[17] According to *Cine-Mundial*, cultural progress was to be achieved by the "modernization" of film exhibition and fandom, rather than through local production. Although *Cine-Mundial* regularly reported on filmmaking in Latin America through the end of the 1920s, especially in Argentina, the magazine's editorials often subtly discouraged these homegrown efforts or recommended that it occur under tutelage from US or European experts.

With the exception of Serna, who has analyzed *Cinelandia* and *Cine-Mundial* within a broader panorama of Spanish-language periodicals that circulated in Mexico, these long-running magazines have received almost no scholarly attention, although their recent digitization may spur further research. Used occasionally as sources, their transnational character has rendered them marginal to histories of both Hollywood and Latin American "national cinemas." Attending to the exchanges with Spanish-speaking audiences brokered by North American magazines allows for the partial recovery of local meanings and uses of Hollywood films for these publics. Highlighting film production and consumption as local practices, and fostering affinities between a far-flung group of spectators, *Cine-Mundial* and *Cinelandia* constructed North American cinema as a shared point of reference in processes of cultural modernization whose horizons were intercontinental.

In both magazines, readers dispersed across the Americas were called to participate in the construction of a film culture that reconciled the imagined desires of Spanish-speaking markets with the practices of the Hollywood studio system. Analyzing *Cine-Mundial* and *Cinelandia*'s structures of reader address, I suggest that their discursive orientation toward their readership can be divided into three broad phases, determined by shifting economies of production and distribution and broader political discourses on inter-American relations. First, in its early years, *Cine-Mundial* sought to enlist the participation of Latin American spectators in the advancement of cultural "progress" through the distribution and exhibition of Hollywood film. Crónicas express local ambitions for an entertainment culture that would be both up to date and edifying, often echoing the discourse of uplift cultivated by *Moving Picture World* and other US film magazines that sought to make cinema a respectable middle-class diversion.[18] *Cine-Mundial* solicited allies in every aspect of the film business, from US producers and distributors to exhibitors, projectionists, and spectators overseas. Second, beginning in the late 1920s, both *Cine-Mundial* and the newly founded *Cinelandia* turned their attention to the relationship between star and viewer, cultivating fan consumption of stars and associated commodities. By the end of the decade, the transition to sound and the emergence of film industries in Argentina, Mexico, and Spain led to a provisional renegotiation of Hollywood's hegemonic status and its representations of the Spanish-speaking world, with *Cine-Mundial* and to a lesser extent *Cinelandia* providing coverage of film production in Spanish overseas, giving rise to a third phase in the magazines' relationship to their readership. In a development that paralleled the staging of national folklore for export in these industries, reader contributions solicited by the magazines signal the emergence of a touristic and autoethnographic mode during the Good Neighbor era, marked by Hollywood's renewed reliance in Latin American film markets in wartime and a shift within Hollywood toward ostensibly "positive," if no less stereotyped, representations of Latin Americans and Latinos.[19]

Highlighting the prominent place of cinema in the advancement of US political and economic interests in Latin America, *Cinelandia* and *Cine-Mundial* aligned themselves selectively with local desires for a modern and cosmopolitan entertainment culture, encouraging the consumption of imported films and consumer goods while devoting relatively little attention to production abroad. Yet at the same time, their reliance on fan participation and their focus on the creative labor of immigrant populations of Los Angeles and New York tentatively reverse the roles of producer and consumer. As popular and long-running US film magazines published in a foreign language, these publications shed new light on the transnational imaginaries of modernity linked to Hollywood's global presence.

Hemispheric Cooperation and Local Modernization: Cine-Mundial in the Silent Era

Two decades after the inaugural January 1916 issue of *Cine-Mundial* was published, editor-in-chief García Ortega recalled that the "first issue nearly went out with the name Cinematic Pan-America [*Pan-América Cinematográfica*] on a terrestrial globe."[20] While the editors ultimately chose a title that was more geographically expansive, the magazine's explicitly hemispheric orientation is evident in the cartographic image that did appear on the cover: a map of the Americas that identified major urban centers. In a statement outlining its editorial program, *Cine-Mundial* stressed that the "European war . . . has demonstrated *ad nauseum* that we peoples of the Americas, from North to South, from Tierra del Fuego to the North Pole, can live with complete independence in economic matters from the influences of the old continent."[21] This rhetoric of hemispheric cooperation is clearly linked to the wartime conditions that hampered both imports to and exports from Europe, leading North American film producers to turn to Latin America to replace lost revenues.

In September 1916, *Moving Picture World* recommended its sister publication as a guide for companies looking to expand into the "nearly virgin territory" of the Latin American film market.[22] To further this goal, *Cine-Mundial* aimed to "convince the intelligent audience of the Latin republics of this continent of the indisputable merits of American [film] manufacturers, with the end of gaining in those communities the prestige, renown, popularity, and acceptance that they richly deserve."[23] This statement from the magazine's opening editorial frames the commercial success of US cinema in the region not only as a mutually beneficial development but also as a foregone conclusion, attributable to Latin American spectators' discerning tastes. This tautological rhetoric that recurs frequently in the magazine's early years: if the aesthetic superiority of Hollywood cinema to its European competitors was accepted as a given, North American films' growing dominance in a particular market could be construed both as proof of local audiences' already refined sensibilities and as a measure of cultural progress.

These attempts to flatter Latin American audiences were transparently self-serving, and *Moving Picture World* leaves little doubt as to the attractiveness of Latin American markets for film producers and distributors. In June 1916, the magazine quoted a studio representative's declaration that "we find that the people of South America are the best patrons of motion pictures

Fig. 4.1 The inaugural cover of *Cine-Mundial*, January 1916. Billy Rose Theater Division, the New York Public Library for the Performing Arts, Astor, Lenox and Tilden Foundations.

anywhere in the world, we find that they have money and are willing to spend it, we find that they appreciate quality whenever they are allowed to get a glimpse of it. I tell you that we are going into this market with a vengeance and we are going to exploit it according to our own plans."[24] According to the same article, film prices in the region had been depressed by local monopolies that dealt in secondhand stock that was often heavily damaged. Irregularities in distribution, including piracy and difficulties in enforcing exclusive contracts, undercut studios' attempts to maximize profits, as did exhibition practices such as frequent changes in film programs and poor-quality projection.[25] Expansion into Latin American markets became one of the causes that regular contributor W. Stephen Bush relentlessly championed in *Moving Picture World*, where he became well known for urging producers and exhibitors to cultivate the "aesthetic and educational function of film."[26]

Like *Moving Picture World*, *Cine-Mundial* was initially targeted toward professionals in the film business, as its visual design and content suggest. Offering a heavy dose of news and information relating to the business side of cinema, as well as more occasional articles about educational film and aesthetics, *Cine-Mundial* was composed of dense columns of small print broken up by relatively small photographs. Beginning in the twenties, photographic reproductions would become more plentiful in the magazine, as an increased use of white space allowed them to become the focal points of visually striking page layouts. Increasingly, issues featured one or more interviews with actors, as well as large numbers of glamorous star portraits. Although early issues featured a single actress or actor, by 1922 each might contain as many as fifteen photographs of stars. That year, *Cine-Mundial* claimed a 100 percent increase in circulation over the previous one.[27] Across this shift, the magazine's varied content implied that distributors, exhibitors, projectionists, and fans alike had a shared responsibility to foster practices of film distribution, exhibition, and consumption that were modern, efficient, and edifying. *Cine-Mundial* used this notion of "modern" film culture to advocate for business practices that benefited US producers and distributors, such as exclusive booking contracts and the importation of new releases directly from studio offices in New York or the local branch offices established in a number of Latin American countries between 1915 and 1917.[28]

Recurring sections that focused on the practical aspects of film exhibition exemplified this pedagogical mode of address. In his column El Arte de la Proyección, F. H. Richardson fielded questions from Latin American projectionists seeking help for locally specific conditions, such as venues not wired for electricity and the heavy damage to films prevalent in exhibition venues in areas more remote from transportation hubs.[29] At the same time, he urged his readers to cultivate "respect for the profession" and continually reminded them of their role in the smooth functioning of the film industry.[30] Edward Kinsilia's El Teatro Moderno offered recommendations regarding movie theater architecture, which film scholar Aurelio de los Reyes has credited with inspiring Mexico City's first "movie palace," the Olimpia.[31] Brief notices singled out individual US movie theaters as "model" for their spaciousness or releases of recent films.[32] In turn, the progress of exhibition culture in Latin America was showcased in a smaller number of news items that praised specific movie theaters, such as the Cinema Central in São Paulo.[33] Making the connection between up-to-date exhibition venues and cultural modernity explicit, an April 1918 editorial declared, "The state of advancement of a city or country is made evident by its movie theaters." In order to drive home the point, the editor contrasts two towns of similar size located in Chile: Chillán, with a "single movie theater that opens its doors barely twice a week," and nearby Antofagasta, which supported nine venues that screened films nightly; then he asks rhetorically, "Does any sign occur to the reader that would more clearly indicate the relative progress of the two cities?"[34] Implying that even smaller cities not necessarily familiar to most readers contributed to the modernization of film exhibition, the editor sketches an intercontinental frame of reference, suggesting a kinship between widely dispersed locations in the Spanish-speaking world.

Within this geographical imaginary, New York appears as a privileged site of film commerce, and at the same time, as a space of cultural consumption and production in Spanish. In its first two years, when New York was swiftly displacing London as the export center for North American production companies, *Cine-Mundial* emphasized New York's status as "the heart of the cinema world" and "the logical center of the film business."[35] Beginning in 1917, the column Baturillo Neoyorquino (New York Mishmash), provided readers with a sense of the local entertainment scene, which was presented separately from general film industry news. Furthermore, a sense of shared intellectual community—and a perception of the cinema's cultural legitimacy—was generated through interviews with Spanish writers who passed through New York, including Ramón del Valle Inclán and Vicente Blasco Ibáñez, whose novels were adapted both in Spain and in Hollywood, most famously as the Valentino vehicles *Four Horsemen of the Apocalypse* (dir. Rex Ingram, 1921) and *Blood and Sand* (dir. Fred Niblo, 1922). In addition to sharing their pronouncements on film aesthetics, these authors occasionally contributed literary texts.[36] In a more humorous register, in 1922 *Cine-Mundial* introduced Aventuras de la Familia Pérez en Nueva York, a series of stories about a womanizing immigrant and his social-climbing wife and daughters by Costa Rican journalist Modesto Martínez, which García Ortega would later attempt to turn into a film.[37] Crónicas, cartoons, and photographs relating to New York's "Little Spain" began to appear more frequently in the magazine in the late twenties and early thirties.

Quotidian details of immigrant life in New York appeared in *Cine-Mundial*'s pages alongside crónicas from diverse locations in the Spanish- and Portuguese-speaking world. Reporting on the dynamics of exhibition and distribution and the reception of individual films, the crónicas also discussed sports, current events, and even the weather, inasmuch as it affected film attendance. As the chronicles dwindled in number throughout the twenties, some were converted into *crónicas gráficas*, or "photo-chronicles," which, rather than generating a verbal account of local entertainment culture, juxtaposed candid photographs of current events. While the crónicas focused on the imported fare that dominated Latin American screens, they also charted the intraregional circulation of Latin American and Spanish films and the growth of local film journalism with interest. In 1916, the Argentine film *Nobleza gaucha* (*Gaucho Nobility*, dir. Humberto Cairo, Eduardo Martínez de la Pera, and Ernesto Gunche, 1915) was greeted with enthusiasm in Barcelona, while Spanish productions like *Barcelona y sus misterios* (*Barcelona and Its Mysteries*, dir. Albert Marro, 1916) and the 1917 version of Vicente Blasco Ibáñez's *Blood and Sand*, (*Sangre y arena*, dir. Ricardo de Baños) found success in Cuba, Argentina, and Uruguay.[38]

Furthermore, the chronicles observed the expansion of local film journalism and *Cine-Mundial*'s influence on these new publications and columns. Both correspondents and editors complained about newspapers and magazines that repr. content from *Cine-Mundial* without attribution. In an article written by García Ortega for *Moving Picture World*, he cites an American film agent in Buenos Aires who claimed that *Cine-Mundial*'s "reviews, special articles and news items of the American film world are copied so repeatedly by the local press, that it is playing the leading role in popularizing American [photo]plays, actors, and directors."[39] While seeking to create audience recognition of, and demand for, Hollywood films and stars, *Cine-Mundial* may have also helped foster the local development of specialized film publications.

As newspapers and magazines overseas appropriated *Cine-Mundial*'s contents without authorization, correspondents echoed back the cosmopolitan rhetoric central to the magazine's editorial program, linking its goals

Fig. 4.2a (*overleaf*) and Fig. 4.2b The exterior of a *Cine-Mundial* agency in São Paulo; agents Eduardo and Pedro Caruggi at work inside the agency. *Cine-Mundial*, November 1919. Billy Rose Theater Division, the New York Public Library for the Performing Arts, Astor, Lenox and Tilden Foundations.

to local desires for cultural modernization. (It should be noted that correspondents appear to have acted both as contributors and subscription agents, receiving a flat fee for their articles and a commission for the subscriptions, and thus had a financial incentive to praise *Cine-Mundial*'s positive qualities and align themselves with its aims.)[40] A first-time correspondent from Bogotá enthusiastically described *Cine-Mundial* as a "publication . . . that brings to all the corners of the world the exact knowledge of all the magnificence of the cinematic art . . . enlightens the masses and brings the audience and the impresarios knowledge of the goodness and merit of the films that are commercialized."[41] Similarly, a correspondent in Camagüey, Cuba suggests *Cine-Mundial*'s role in a broader current of cultural uplift, declaring, "The influence of the cinematograph in the artistic world is powerful, and so irresistible that it penetrates even in regions where civilization is still in swaddling clothes. Our city demonstrates this by the revolution produced in the elegant, modernized high society, which advances by giant steps. . . . Although Camagüey's society has always been distinguished, it is impossible to deny that the cinema has influenced its evolution."[42] Echoing the rhetorical strategies of the magazine's editorials, the correspondent links the expansion of American-style film culture to a path of artistic progress already charted by locals' elevated tastes.

Cine-Mundial's suggestion that discerning Latin American audiences would welcome any high-quality films was strategic, given the absence of productions specifically designed to appeal to Spanish-speaking audiences. Although Cine-Mundial claimed that studios were recruiting Latin American personnel to better cater to the tastes of their readership, only rarely did the magazine highlight films with Latin American or Spanish settings.[43] This was a prudent stance, given the highly stereotyped treatment of Latin American characters, especially Mexicans, in Hollywood films. Although Cine-Mundial claimed in March 1917 editorial that the "few films of this nature produced today in the United States have no other object than to exploit the credulity of that ignorant element that exists everywhere," this was belied by growing frustration with offensive films, especially in Mexico, where mounting tensions with Hollywood studios culminated in a 1922 boycott of the entire output of several US production companies, decreed by president Álvaro Obregón.[44] In fact, García Ortega wrote in Moving Picture World, also in March 1917, that "films where every Mexican or South American is a bandit or a 'desperado,' whatever that means, should be kept in this country or shipped to Europe, Africa or the North Pole—they are not appreciated in Latin America."[45] Disingenuously claiming that stereotypical representations were on the wane, Cine-Mundial could likewise produce little evidence that Hollywood studios were making serious attempts to cater to Latin American spectators. Instead, a cosmopolitan detachment from national or regional specificity in film production was praised by both editors and correspondents, in contrast with the cultivation of nationalist themes for export that would make Mexican and Argentine film industries profitable after the transition to sound. Building on discourses that framed cinema as a "universal language," an October 1916 editorial praised Hollywood features that "not only have international interest, but have also managed to eliminate, almost completely, those provincialisms that become incomprehensible as soon as the border of the country of origin in crossed."[46] Filmmakers were discouraged from cultivating specifically local audiences and urged to compete with Hollywood on the global market, despite the structural imbalances that characterized it.

Along with its regular, if somewhat skeptical, coverage of film production in the Spanish-speaking world, *Cine-Mundial*'s editors made a modest attempt to highlight Latin American and Spanish performers with the creation of the section Favoritos del Cine (Movie Favorites), in which small photographs and capsule biographies of actors of all nationalities were published. Yet these profiles could not compete with the growing number of interviews and star photographs that filled the magazines' pages. The forging of a Hollywood-oriented fan culture in *Cine-Mundial* is most evident in the Preguntas y Respuestas (Questions and Answers) section, which was introduced in June 1918. The section's editor answered fan queries, provided stars' addresses, and gave basic English translations for use in letters, facilitating interaction with the emerging Hollywood star system, as Serna has observed.[47] In 1925, the columnist in charge of Preguntas y Respuestas estimated he had received sixty thousand letters since the creation of the section, or an average of eighty-five hundred a year.[48] Although this figure is impossible to verify, it suggests considerable engagement from the magazine's readership, reported as 38,103 the same year.[49] Marsha Orgeron has argued that the interactive aspects of movie magazines enact a "discourse of empowerment" that at once highlights and undoes the divide between stars and fans, and thus producers and consumers, of film culture.[50] In the case of *Cine-Mundial*, this participatory mode of engagement sought to bridge geographic divides as well, enlisting the participation of Latin American spectators in American-style practices of fan consumption.

Indeed, many correspondents reported on emerging fan practices, which were claimed as markers of cultural progress. In 1917, Argentine contributor Emilio Chapperon observed young women's particular affinity for film fandom, noting that they "collect portraits, biographies, anecdotes, following with the scrupulousness of a scholar the artistic path traversed by their favorite actors and actresses. . . . The cinematograph is called upon to serve as an extension of school, it is already the extension of the home in this manifestation by the most sensitive and intuitively impressionable [spectators]."[51] Drawing parallels between formal study and film fandom, Chapperon presents cinema as a pedagogical force, whose appeal to young women is proof of its power to foster loftier sentiments. In a less lyrical tone, Havana correspondent Eduardo Quiñones describes the growing affection of local audiences for North American actors: "We treat Grace Cunard and Francis Ford with informality"—that is, using *tú*, the second person pronoun reserved for social equals—and "we have baptized Billie Ritchie ... with the picturesque name Canillita," meaning newsboy.⁵² Such linguistic strategies worked to domesticate Hollywood stars, demonstrating that fan culture involved as much transculturation as it did cultural colonization. Presenting fan practices as a means of aesthetic education or of facilitating a more casual and personal relationship with an emergent star system, these early discussions of fan culture are suggestive of a broader shift in North American discourses on cinema, from a rhetoric of uplift and progress, to a focus on stars and consumer desire. In *Cinelandia*, these elements took center stage as the magazine worked to solicit readers' collective identification with Spanish-speaking actors of varying origins and to navigate Hollywood's troubling representations of Latin America and Spain while foregrounding overlooked forms of immigrant cultural labor.

Star Commodities and Latino/a Labor: *Cinelandia* in the Twenties

Upon *Cinelandia*'s initial launch in September 1926, editor-in-chief Lucío Villegas invoked the pedagogical function of the medium of film while emphasizing the magazine's key advantage: its geographic position at the heart of the US film industry. According to Villegas, a Chilean national who later became the head of dubbing at RKO, *Cinelandia* "proposes to fill a gap that is felt profoundly in the Spanish-speaking countries, by establishing coverage of the screen in Hollywood itself, the world's most important center for the production of this educational agent that we call film."⁵³ He also highlighted the magazine's sponsorship by prominent industry figures such as King Vidor, Ernst Lubitsch, and J. Stuart Blackton.⁵⁴ Perhaps in part because Villegas's tenure at the magazine was short-lived, this explicit discourse of progress, reminiscent of the early years of *Cine-Mundial*, was quickly deemphasized in favor of the play of erotic and consumer desire fostered by the star system.⁵⁵

Cinelandia leveraged its location rather aggressively, commenting, for example, in answer to a reader's query, "New York, as far as cinema goes, is nothing; 95 [percent] is produced in Hollywood; what's published there is peanuts [*tortas y pan pintado*]; they've never gotten a whiff of Hollywood in their life."⁵⁶ Between 1928 and 1929, the magazine's circulation increased more than tenfold from 3,090 to 41,798, quickly coming to rival *Cine-Mundial*'s print run of 53,297 in 1929.⁵⁷ This popularity was almost certainly linked to *Cinelandia*'s photo-heavy, visually appealing layout and its ability to provide a greater number of star interviews. Beyond a single monthly profile by its

Hollywood correspondent, *Cine-Mundial* was largely limited to interviewing actors and other entertainers who passed through New York. As an imagined space in *Cinelandia*, Hollywood overshadows Latin America and Spain, which hardly appear as geographic locations. Instead, they are effectively reduced to sites of individual fan consumption, only glimpsed in the portions of the magazine generated by readers. During the silent era, production in Latin America is the subject of only two articles—a report on the making of the Peruvian film *La Perricholi* (dir. Enzo Longhi, 1929) and a photo spread devoted to the Brazilian feature *Barro humano* (*Human Filth*, dir. Adhemar Gonzaga, 1929)—and local exhibition is rarely covered.[58]

Similarly, *Cinelandia* did not initially make a concerted effort to feature actors of Latin American or Spanish origin or descent; it seems to have assumed, like *Cine-Mundial*, the "universal" appeal of Euro-American stars and themes. During the first two years of its run, the magazine only occasionally profiled Latino/a stars, including Mexican Ramón Novarro, a Brazilian newcomer who went by the stage name of Mario Marano, and Mexican American Gilbert Roland (né Luis Alonso). A shift in editorial policy is evident in January 1929, when *Cinelandia* announced a new editor-in-chief, Juan J. Moreno. At this stage, Hollywood studios were beginning to promote the stars of Latin American origin that appeared in its Spanish language productions, although sound cinema would not have its debut in Latin America until later that year.[59] *Cinelandia* began to feature interviews with Latino/a stars, including Lupita Tovar, Raquel Torres, Mona Rico, Lupe Vélez, and Gilbert Roland at the rate of two per issue, before seemingly running out of popular actors to cover in July.

Given that most of these stars were Mexican or Mexican American, while the magazine circulated in many other Spanish-speaking nations, *Cinelandia* worked to foster a pan-Latino mode of reader engagement. The magazine continually refers to expansive categories such as *raza hispana* (Hispanic race) and *elemento latino* (Latino element), soliciting a sense of affiliation from Spanish-speakers readers whose nationalities were rarely, if ever, represented among the ranks of Hollywood stars. Similarly, by using the possessive *nuestro* (our) to refer to stars of diverse origins, including the Spanish actor Antonio Moreno and the Mexican star Dolores del Río, the magazine fostered a collective sense of ownership over stars among its geographically dispersed readership.[60] The vague, undifferentiated "Latin" identity evoked in Hollywood productions is echoed by *Cinelandia* in its attempts to appeal to the widest possible readership.[61]

A wide array of articles and advertisements sought to capitalize on this imagined identification with stars, using their images to promote consumer goods. The monthly section La Moda en Hollywood (Fashion in Hollywood) featured female stars of varying ethnicities in elegant outfits, and actors of both sexes posing in front of automobiles. *Cinelandia* also included many advertisements for beauty products designed to flatter or conceal elements of physical appearance that were racially marked, including skin-whitening creams and hair-straightening products. An ad for Max Factor featuring Lupe Vélez and Raquel Torres promised to put "the secret of make-up within the reach of all Latina women," while Ramón Novarro appeared in an ad for Stacomb hair cream that promised to tame an unruly hair texture appropriate to his villainous roles, but not his elegant off-screen persona.[62]

In *Cinelandia*'s coverage of stars of Latin American origin, the familiar tension between a star's presumed essence and the labor of their self-fashioning took on a special resonance with regard to ethnic and national identity. A comprehensive discussion of the racial politics of Latino/a star images in the classical Hollywood era, from "Latin lovers" such as Novarro to "spitfires" such as Vélez and "exotic" beauties such as Dolores del Río is beyond the scope of this essay.[63] I limit myself to signaling how the magazine oscillated between criticism of Hollywood's representational practices and material that perpetuated many of their problematic aspects: essentialized notions of "Latin" identity that associated it with stereotyped traits, such as violence or sexual passion, and a fondness for "ethnic masquerade."[64] In a context where white actors could generally play characters of any race, while actors of color were limited—and indiscriminately assigned—to various "exotic" roles, the dissonance between actor and role, especially when subversively highlighted by the performer him/herself, had the potential to highlight ethnicity itself as a performance. Although "ethnic masquerade" might generate a degree of ambivalence, contributors and readers expressed profound dissatisfaction with Hollywood's casting and representational practices, even though *Cinelandia* also perpetuated these practices in its pages.

This delicate navigation of contradictory discourses is evident in a July 1927 article that mocks the studios' practice of deflecting criticism of denigrating representations, especially of Mexicans, by setting the action in an imaginary country.[65] In "Where Is Costa Roja?" journalist Gil Alvear narrates a day spent on the set of the film *La Paloma* (*The Dove*, dir. Roland West, 1927) attempting to locate the film's setting. He finally gets a straight answer from Manuel Reachi, a Mexican attaché present on the set, who explains that Costa Roja was invented to "absolve Mexico of the sins attributed to it by the drama 'La Paloma.' . . . They wanted to take advantage of the picturesqueness of our race. . . . But what is taken from our peoples is so modified and mixed with other capricious elements, that one cannot reasonably take Costa Roja even as an allusion to any of the countries where our language is spoken."[66] Another article protested Hollywood's "odious falsification of types and settings," attributing it to the fact that "the basis of the film business consists of the movie theaters that can be filled with the hundred and ten million inhabitants of the United States. The foreign market is completely secondary."[67] By contrast with the Pan-American discourse of *Cine-Mundial*'s early years, which foregrounded the economic interdependency of the Americas, *Cinelandia* openly acknowledged the significant but ultimately secondary place of Spanish-speaking audiences in the studios' economic calculations.

Despite criticisms of Hollywood productions set in Latin American and Spain, *Cinelandia* often perpetuated the stereotypes ubiquitous in Hollywood films and American fan magazines. Reporting on the studios' search for a replacement for the late Rudolph Valentino in 1927, Villegas writes, "We will discard all the Scandinavian and German combinations, whose masculine element does not lend itself to characterizing Romeos or Don Juans. We are left to examine only the three Latino actors, the three with Spanish blood, Antonio Moreno, Ramón Novarro and Luis Alon[s]o (Gilbert Roland)."[68] *Cinelandia* also availed itself of images (likely furnished by studio publicity departments) that reduced national and ethnic identity to a set of stereotyped signifiers. Monthly photo spreads featured actors in different "national" costumes: for example, the blonde Dorothy Dalton appears dressed as a "Charra gringa" (Gringa cowgirl), while a caption admonishes her to "take off that sombrero and sarape, Dorothy, and don't try to pass for Mexican!"[69] Conversely, in the photo spread México Oriental, Dolores del Río poses in ostensibly Chinese, Egyptian, and Russian outfits that resonate with her film roles, which were characterized by "a vague upper-class exoticism articulated within a general category of foreign/other tragic sensuality."[70] These seductive photo spreads highlight a fluid play with identity, ironically made possible by an indifference to cultural specificity.

The cross-national masquerades highlighted in *Cinelandia* had obvious echoes in English-language discourses that cast the studios as a veritable Babel where actors, characters, and scenery from all over the globe could

Fig. 4.3 Dolores del Río performs a series of "ethnic masquerades" in a photo spread in *Cinelandia*, July 1929. Billy Rose Theater Division, the New York Public Library for the Performing Arts, Astor, Lenox and Tilden Foundations.

be found (or faked).[71] Not surprisingly, the magazine emphasized that "in this cosmopolitan group [of actors] Spanish-speaking elements . . . are noteworthy."[72] Less expected is *Cinelandia*'s practice of foregrounding the presence of Spanish-speaking immigrants in Los Angeles, making visible forms of racialized labor that were elided in most fan-magazine discourse about

Hollywood.⁷³ *Cinelandia* often alluded to the work of Mexican and other Latin American extras, as well as the menial work done by those who tried and failed to find employment in the studios. In 1927, Vargas de la Maza observes that he had "seen arrive in the restless cinematic colony many men and women of our race, with a few coins in their pocket and their minds filled with rich illusions and hopes. The eternal illusions and hopes of the Latinos! They came to lengthen that interminable caravan of old and young, beautiful and ugly, who made the journey from the remotest latitudes, hypnotized by the marvelous mirage of Cinelandia."⁷⁴ De la Maza draws on well-worn narratives that frame Hollywood as a city of (broken) dreams; yet at the same time, he sketches an international imaginary of migration that aligns Hollywood's illusions with Latin American immigrants' desires for economic and geographic mobility.

Beyond superimposing narratives of Hollywood ambition with immigrants' pursuit of the "American dream," *Cinelandia*'s contributors also evoke a rhetoric of reconquest, ironically framing Mexican labor in Hollywood as a means of rewriting the terms of US-Mexico relations. Positioning the work of extras and crew alongside the Latino/a stars featured in the magazine, Cornelio Diricio writes in 1929, "As California was Mexican territory until 1847, it's not surprising that one fine day, there was a Mexican invasion to reconquer it. So it has been and soon, all of Hollywood will be an extension of Mexico. Already, 75 percent of the extras are Mexican; they abound among technical personnel; some are assistant directors or assistants."⁷⁵ Less optimistically, Felipe de Leiva (likely a pseudonym of Agustín Aragón Leiva) comments in "Memoirs of an Extra," "The conquest of Hollywood by Latinos is a fact. . . . Their triumph in the cinema is indisputable. They are the ones who work cheaply, they are the ones who provide greater efficiency. . . . The use of Mexicans means a savings of hundreds of thousands of dollars for producers, year after year."⁷⁶

As Serna has observed, in the late twenties the English-language press in Los Angeles used fears of a foreign "invasion" of Hollywood to stir up xenophobic sentiment against emigré actors and Mexican extras, provoking a strong reaction from the Spanish-language paper *La Opinión*.⁷⁷ Here, Leiva inverts the metaphor of invasion to extend this critique of racially stratified labor. *Cinelandia* thus highlighted the degree to which Mexican migrants, in Serna's words, were ultimately "excluded from the possibilities for social mobility

Los extras son empleados por un día y pagados al terminar su trabajo. Aquí aparece la masa de extras de la película "Carmen," de Dolores del Río, alineados para pasar ante la ventanilla del cajero y cobrar sus siete dólares y medio.

Fig. 4.4 Extras in the film *The Loves of Carmen* (dir. Raoul Walsh, 1927), starring Dolores del Río, wait in line to receive their pay. *Cinelandia*, November 1927. Billy Rose Theater Division, the New York Public Library for the Performing Arts, Astor, Lenox and Tilden Foundations.

promoted by the popular, and indeed international, discourse on Hollywood as a land of promise and possibility."[78] Criticizing the exploitation of immigrant labor and the stereotypical representations deeply ingrained in studio practices, *Cinelandia* also cultivated a collective fascination with Latin American and Latino/a stars and the construction of their ethnically marked personas as it rhetorically instituted a pan-Latino readership. The economic and political terms of Hollywood's relationship to Spanish-speaking markets would shift during the transition to sound and the era of the Good Neighbor policy. Yet in *Cine-Mundial* and *Cinelandia*, Hollywood's star system would remain the locus that connected geographically dispersed readers, while Argentine, Mexican, and Spanish film was granted only a marginal space in their pages.

Remapping Film Production in *Cine-Mundial* and *Cinelandia*: From the Transition to Sound to the Good Neighbor Era

In the pages of *Cine-Mundial* and *Cinelandia*, the transition to sound sparked heated debates without leading to a significant refocusing of either publication toward the incipient sound film industries of Argentina, Mexico, and Spain. Special sections devoted to these developments, especially in Mexico, were introduced in *Cine-Mundial* in the early thirties and made occasional appearances in *Cinelandia* later in the decade. Yet despite contributions by overseas correspondents, reviews of Spanish-language films and profiles of Latin American or Latino/a stars again became fairly rare after the early thirties. Given that they remained closely aligned with the studios, it is logical that *Cine-Mundial* and *Cinelandia* would cover Hollywood stars and films, even at the risk of failing to cater to Spanish-speaking readers' interest in production in their native language.

More puzzling, perhaps, is the magazines' relative inattention to the films produced under the so-called Good Neighbor policy. Expanding on his 1933 declaration of a policy of nonintervention in Latin America, Franklin D. Roosevelt created the Office of the Coordinator of Inter-American Affairs (OCIAA) under the direction of Nelson Rockefeller in 1940. In this spirit of hemispheric cooperation and in conjunction with Hollywood's renewed reliance on Latin American audiences at a moment when European markets were difficult to access, OCIAA's film branch strived to eliminate the most egregious stereotypes of Latin American characters. In keeping with the irreverent tone cultivated by *Cine-Mundial* beginning in the late 1920s, the term *buen vecino* (good neighbor) often appears in a less than serious light. For example, a caption accompanying a publicity photo of Paulette Goddard at a bullfight in Mexico lends "good neighbor" the connotation of a sexual rather than a political approximation between the United States and Latin America.[79] More occasionally, it is used in connection with social events in New York organized to foster Pan-American solidarity. Aside from publicity photos of icons of the Good Neighbor policy, such as Walt Disney and Carmen Miranda, who appears in a photo signing war bonds for the National Defense League, the magazines dedicated little column space to emblematic films produced under its mandate, such as the Disney production *Saludos Amigos* (1942) or *The Gang's All Here* (Busby Berkeley, 1943), starring Miranda.[80] Neither the transition to sound nor the Good Neighbor era led to a lasting

Fig. 4.5 *Cine-Mundial* editor Francisco García Ortega (far left) and Walt Disney (fourth from left) socialize with journalists from Argentina, Brazil, and Mexico at a cocktail party organized by RKO to commemorate Disney's return from his South American trip. *Cine-Mundial*, January 1942. Billy Rose Theater Division, the New York Public Library for the Performing Arts, Astor, Lenox and Tilden Foundations.

realignment of the magazines' geographic horizons, which in *Cine-Mundial*'s case had greatly narrowed since the silent era.

The transition to sound, as a number of scholars have explored, marked a renegotiation of the relationship between Hollywood studios and international markets, which they struggled to retain through experimenting with dubbing, subtitling, foreign-language versions of English-language films, and occasional foreign-language features with original scripts, such as the series of Paramount films starring tango singer Carlos Gardel.[81] As commentators in Spain and Latin America expressed concerns that North American talkies would accelerate cultural Americanization, studio executives feared that foreign-language markets would reject films with dialogue in English. *Cinelandia*'s audience weighed in on both questions: for example, in one issue a reader in Panama observed a marked decline in film attendance that she attributed to a rejection of English-language talkies, while a Mexico City resident scoffed at the "exaggerated use of tired concepts of Mexicanism and the loss of language" in local objections to sound cinema.[82]

The short-lived practice of producing Spanish-language films in Hollywood to cater to Latin American and Spanish markets was also highly contentious, sparking a "War of the Accents" in which "the issue of spoken language (pronunciation, regional slang, and diction) assumed a central position, whereby issues of class, generational conflict, nationality, and cultural integrity were collapsed into a discussion of cinematic dialogue and the proper use of Spanish," even as long-standing criticisms of Hollywood's representation of Spanish-speaking nations flared up with renewed intensity.[83] Some proposed that the Peninsular Spanish used internationally by theater troupes be adopted in sound cinema, a suggestion that reinforced existing cultural hierarchies and sparked protests by spectators and journalists from Mexico, Central and South America, and the Caribbean.

Although a detailed assessment of the politics of Hollywood's Spanish-language productions is beyond the scope of this essay, I want to highlight how the transition to sound briefly reconfigured the positioning of *Cine-Mundial* and *Cinelandia* with respect to the Hollywood studios and the industries that began to establish themselves in earnest in Spanish-speaking nations. The promotion of affiliated sound technologies was quickly integrated into the magazines: illustrated advertisements used the images of stars to promote radios and gramophone records recorded by popular performers, including the Mexican tenor José Mojica, star of several Spanish-language productions, and Argentine tango singer Libertad Lamarque, an RCA Victor recording artist who became a key figure of early Argentine sound cinema and later worked extensively in Mexico.[84] During the transition, several contributors were offered studio positions, suggesting Hollywood's urgent need for cultural advisers. In addition to Villegas's work at RKO, a number of *Cine-Mundial* contributors were contracted by studios: Miguel de Zárraga wrote Spanish-language adaptations for MGM, and his wife Elena de la Torre was employed by Fox to review books by Latin American authors for optioning.[85]

Beyond the impact of individual journalists as consultants, the magazines also presented themselves as intermediaries between Hollywood and

Spanish-speaking viewers. In a January 1930 editorial, editor-in-chief Juan J. Moreno emphasized *Cinelandia*'s role as an advocate for Spanish-language production, addressing himself directly to both spectators and studios: "*To the Spanish-speaking audience*: CINELANDIA will continue fighting for the interests of Spanish-speaking fans, dedicating itself to the task [of insuring] that the films produced here will be worthy of the Latin public. *To the producers*: our position in the industry allows us to serve as interpreters of the desires of the fans in Spanish-speaking countries and our knowledge of these countries, which entails advantages that you can well imagine and that we offer with good will."[86]

Thus Moreno positions *Cinelandia* as a mediator, capable of shaping a program of production that will be satisfactory for both studios and Spanish-speaking audiences. During the silent era, *Cinelandia* had confined itself to criticizing "denigrating" films without presuming to exert pressure on the studios themselves; the introduction of sound cinema prompted the magazine to envision a more substantial role as a power broker within Hollywood. Furthermore, the publication suggested that its film reviews could help shape a desirable product by critiquing Spanish-language films made in Hollywood or abroad and by Anglo or Latino producers. For example, in the case of *Sombras de Gloria*, the Spanish-language version of *Blaze O' Glory* (dir. Renaud Hoffman, 1930), which starred the Chilean José Bohr, a reviewer resists the temptation to be swayed by his sympathy for the director's efforts. He affirms, "What the reader-fan in our countries desires is that talking films be produced in Spanish, of the same quality as the North American [films], and is depending on the honorable criticism of this magazine to deduce their merit."[87]

By January 1932, *Cinelandia*'s hopes for good-quality production in Hollywood were largely frustrated: foreign-language production had been mostly abandoned by the studios because of disappointing return on investment, although smaller numbers of Spanish-language films would continue to be produced, most notably at Fox and Paramount, throughout the thirties. While still presenting itself as the arbiter of Spanish-speaking fans' opinions and desires, *Cinelandia* saw itself obliged to solicit their help in convincing the studios that Spanish-language production was a worthwhile venture. Moreno wrote in an editorial, "The practical thing in this case would be for the fans of Latin America and Spain to resolve to express their authorized opinion about this important matter, by means of letters directed to the office of CINELANDIA, in such extraordinary numbers, and of such a convincing logic, that the producers cannot ignore the force of a desire so unanimously expressed."[88] While the letter-writing campaign seems not to have materialized or in any case, had little impact on studios' production strategies, Moreno's call to action reinforced a sense of fan agency made possible by the economic upheaval of the transition.

Despite a resurgence of film production in New York during the period, brought about by Broadway's supply of playwrights and theatrical talent, *Cine-Mundial* did not claim to have any particular clout with the studios. However, the magazine cosponsored a script-writing contest with Fox in 1934, stressing the importance of facilitating quality Spanish-language production in Hollywood despite the emergence of Spanish-language filmmaking overseas.[89] Addressing these developments, the magazine added columns on the entertainment world in Spain and Mexico in late 1935. The latter, written by pioneering film journalist Marco Aurelio Galindo, offered industry gossip and commentary on Mexican films (which were rarely reviewed by the regular staff) in terms that were more blunt than patriotic. Although these columns were short-lived—the magazine announced that they would be suspended in September 1936, supposedly because of filmmakers' complaints—*Cine-Mundial* incorporated intermittent coverage of the Mexican film industry through the rest of its run.[90] Well-known playwright José Francisco "Pepe" Elizondo penned a series of Mexico City crónicas and other articles for the magazine between 1939 and his death in 1943. Elizondo incorporated occasional discussions of nationalist aesthetics into his reports on the Mexican film industry, which included a behind-the-scenes look at a local film set and an appropriately nonsensical interview with the comedian Mario Moreno (Cantinflas).[91] In early 1944, *Cine-Mundial* inaugurated the columns De Plateros a la Quinta Avenida (From Plateros Street [a central thoroughfare in Mexico City] to Fifth Avenue) and Ventana de Buenos Aires (Window on Buenos Aires) to cover film production in Mexico and Argentina.

For its part, *Cinelandia* briefly experimented with the column Por Otras Tierras (In Other Lands) in 1937, and intermittently published Notas Panamericanas and Notas Hispanoamericanas in 1942 and 1943. In January 1943, the magazine issued a call for articles on "film reviews of the production of Hollywood and Latin America. Pan Americanism. Literature and folklore of our countries. Art. Tourism. Interviews of international importance," for which they offered to pay ten dollars.[92] In addition to the typical subjects of fan letters—opinions of both Hollywood productions and Latin American films—*Cinelandia* solicited contributions that reinforced official discourses of Pan-Americanism or encouraged readers to turn a touristic gaze on their home countries. However, the invitation seems to have had little effect on the content of *Cinelandia*, which largely overlooked Argentine, Mexican, and Spanish film production. Instead, the magazine limited itself to profiles of stars like Mona Maris, who had starred in Hollywood Spanish-language films in the thirties and worked in Argentina before returning to the United States, and Carmen Miranda, perhaps the most emblematic figure of the Good Neighbor policy.

While reader collaboration with *Cinelandia* seems to have been of limited importance, *Cine-Mundial* inaugurated a more successful initiative in April 1937: a monthly *foto concurso* (photo competition), in which readers rather than professional photographers would furnish images of the varied locations in which the magazine was consumed. Each month, eight winners received a prize of one dollar and had their entries published in the magazine. Inheriting the logic of the *crónicas gráficas* of the 1920s, the magazine's preferred subjects were "curious notes about local life; street scenes, [scenes] of action, or on a subject that constitutes a novelty for other American countries. Lastly, the contestant should not forget that the purpose of the Photo Competition is to increase intercontinental interest, showing each other the good things we have in our respective countries."[93] Enlisting readers to perform acts of autoethnography that facilitated the intercontinental circulation of "positive" images, each foto concurso yielded a miscellany of picturesque scenes and contemporary events that renewed *Cine-Mundial*'s role as a mediator between multiple sites in Latin America, here by selecting and juxtaposing graphic content. Yet while the Pan-American rhetoric that marked *Cine-Mundial*'s debut persists, the discursive links between entertainment culture and national or local progress are conspicuously absent. With the growing consolidation of national culture industries, a North American magazine was a less and less relevant space for such discourses to be aired.

From the transition to sound through World War II, the economic importance of Spanish-speaking markets loomed large for Hollywood studios, even as sound film industries in Argentina, Mexico, and Spain successfully exploited the new opportunities offered by talking pictures. Rather than aligning themselves directly with the studios' attempts to recapture international markets during the transition or the Good Neighbor initiatives of the 1940s, *Cine-Mundial* and *Cinelandia* positioned themselves as intermediaries between fans and film producers, soliciting direct engagement from readers in constructing a desirable Spanish-language film culture both onscreen and in their own pages. Yet by the mid-forties, the expansion of both film production and print culture in Spanish-speaking nations was noticeably displacing the US fan magazines from their role as Hollywood's mediators.

Conclusion

In January 1945, *Cine-Mundial* celebrated thirty years of publication, which, by its own reckoning, made it the world's oldest continuously published Spanish-language film magazine.[94] Yet only three years later, it noted, "All the popular magazines published in New York to circulate in Hispano-America are losing money," including *Cinelandia*, which had moved there in 1946, and "most painfully," *Cine-Mundial* itself.[95] While the article does not venture an explanation for the decline, it mentions substantial losses by all of the international divisions of *Reader's Digest*, suggesting waning overseas interest in US publications in a post–World War II geopolitical landscape. After Latin America had served its strategic purpose during the conflict, the rapprochement of the Good Neighbor years shifted toward a much more ambivalent relationship in the Cold War period. Significantly, as Mexican cinema became a more formidable rival in Spanish-speaking markets, Hollywood began to compete more aggressively for market share in these territories, ending the cooperation between the two industries.[96]

The most immediate cause for *Cine-Mundial* and *Cinelandia*'s disappearance may have been the ascendance of competitors such as Mexico City's *Cinema Repórter*, which had been published since 1932, and Buenos Aires's popular *Radiolandia*, which also covered film-related topics.[97] Like *Cinelandia* and *Cine-Mundial*, *Cinema Repórter*'s content spanned the Americas, combining coverage of Hollywood with more substantive reporting on production in Mexico and Argentina. With Argentine, Mexican, and Spanish film magazines founded in the thirties coming of age, *Cine-Mundial* and *Cinelandia*'s roles as intermediaries were of waning relevance. It is also suggestive that both magazines ceased publication in 1948, the year of the Paramount decision, which ruled that Hollywood studios' vertical integration of production, distribution, and exhibition was an antitrust violation, forcing them to divest themselves of their movie theater chains. While Hollywood dominance of Latin American screens would persist long after the golden age of the studio system, by the 1950s its printed emissaries were relics of the past.

In the pages of *Cine-Mundial* and *Cinelandia*, the logic of the fan magazine, which hails its readers as both spectators of and participants in the construction of film culture, took on an intercontinental scope. In their attempts to forge a pan-Latino readership and viewing public, the magazines emphasized linguistic and cultural affinities across national borders (often in essentializing terms) while granting space to local images and discourses and competing claims to *latinidad*. Positioning their contributors as inter-American mediators, much like the immigrants and travelers who shaped the cultural life of Los Angeles and New York, *Cine-Mundial* and *Cinelandia* positioned Spanish-speaking readers as an integral rather than peripheral audience for films and as allies in the construction of a specifically cinematic brand of consumer-capitalist modernity.

> RIELLE NAVITSKI is Assistant Professor of Theater and Film Studies at the University of Georgia. She is the author of *Public Spectacles of Violence: Sensational Cinema and Journalism in Early Twentieth-Century Mexico and Brazil* (Duke University Press, 2017).

NOTES

1. M. Hernández, "Crónica de Chile," *Cine-Mundial*, September 1918, 581. All translations from the Spanish are mine.
2. "Crónica de Venezuela," *Cine-Mundial*, June 1922, 324.
3. Kristin Thompson, *Exporting Entertainment: America in the World Film Market, 1907–1934* (London: British Film Institute, 1985), 41. Invasion was a favored metaphor of *Moving Picture World*. See W. Stephen Bush, "A Note of Warning to Producers," *Moving Picture World*, May 13, 1916, 1136; W. Stephen Bush, "Light Breaking in South America," *Moving Picture World*, June 10, 1916, 1872; J. H. C., "American Film Invasion of Brazil," *Moving Picture World*, December 30, 1916, 1936.
4. Thompson notes that Britain's close trade ties with South America, including frequent coal shipments, facilitated the distribution of films from London. *Exporting Entertainment*, 41, 63, 68.
5. For unknown reasons, *Cinelandia*'s offices moved to New York in 1946, shortly before the publication shuttered in 1948. See Laura Isabel Serna, *Making Cinelandia: American Films and Mexican Film Culture before the Golden Age* (Durham, NC: Duke University Press, 2014), for a detailed discussion of the term "Cinelandia" as a means of reenvisioning Hollywood in the context of Mexican experience.

6. According to *N. W. Ayers and Sons' Directory of Newspapers and Periodicals*, *Cine-Mundial*'s circulation as reported to the Audit Bureau of Circulation was 53,297 in 1929; 57,848 in 1930; and 62,023 in 1931 when it reached its peak, versus *Photoplay*'s circulation of 547,605; 575,625; and 620,331 during the same years. Information on geographic distribution is scarce; I have found sources only for *Cine-Mundial* in the year 1922, which indicate the magazine was particularly popular in Mexico and Cuba and cite paid circulations of 7,000 in Argentina and 3,000 in Spain. See "Effective Publicity in Latin America," *Chicago Commerce*, October 7, 1922, 45; *Printer's Ink*, June 29, 1922, 111.

7. The emergence of Pan-Americanism as political strategy and discourse, which peaked during the two World Wars, can be traced to the International Conference of American States organized by James G. Blaine in 1889–1890.

8. See Seth Fein, "From Collaboration to Containment: Hollywood and the International Political Economy of Mexican Cinema after World War II," in *Mexico's Cinema: A Century of Film and Filmmakers*, eds. Joanne Hershfield and David R. Maciel (Wilmington, DE: Scholarly Resources, 1999), 123–163.

9. Nicolás Kanellos, *Hispanic Periodicals in the United States: Origins to 1960* (Houston, TX: Arte Público Press, 2000).

10. Kanellos, *Hispanic Periodicals*, 73–76.

11. A characteristically Latin American journalistic genre, a *crónica* is short, topical, and often essayistic in style.

12. Miguel de Zárraga, *ABC* (Madrid), May 15, 1924, 5.

13. Ángel Miquel, *Por las pantallas de la Ciudad de México: Periodistas del cine mudo* (Guadalajara: Universidad de Guadalajara, 1995), 103.

14. Armando Vargas de la Maza, "La Vida de Cinelandia," *Cinelandia*, August 1927, 29; Miquel, *Por las pantallas*, 105; Isabel Arredondo, "Sergei Eisenstein's ¡Que Viva México! in the Light of Mexico's Post-Revolutionary Politics," *Colorado Review of Hispanic Studies* 8 (2010): 143–164.

15. Ana M. López, "Early Cinema and Modernity in Latin America." *Cinema Journal* 40, no. 1 (2000): 53.

16. See Gaylyn Studlar, "The Perils of Pleasure? Fan Magazine Discourse as Women's Commodified Culture in the 1920s," *Wide Angle* 13, no. 1 (1991): 6–33; Miriam Hansen, "The Return of Babylon: Valentino and Female Spectatorship," in *Babel and Babylon: Spectatorship in American Silent Film* (Cambridge, MA: Harvard University Press, 1991).

17. Serna, *Making Cinelandia*, 94.

18. Richard L. Stomgren, "*Moving Picture World* of W. Stephen Bush," *Film History* 2, no. 1 (1988): 13–22.

19. For the policy's impact on film, see Allen L. Woll, "The Good Neighbor Policy: The Latin Image in American Film," *Journal of Popular Film* 3, no. 4 (1974): 278–293; Ana M. López, "Are All Latins from Manhattan? Hollywood, Ethnography and Cultural Colonialism," in *Mediating Two Worlds: Cinematic Encounters in the Americas*, eds. John King, Ana M. López, and Manuel Alvarado (London: British Film Institute,

1994), 67–80; Julianne Burton-Carvajal, "'Surprise Package': Looking Southward with Disney," in *Disney Discourse: Producing the Magic Kingdom*, ed. Eric Smoodin (New York: Routledge, 1994), 131–147.

20. Jorge Hermida [pseud. Francisco García Ortega], "En Broadway," *Cine-Mundial*, January 1935, 46.

21. "Nuestro Programa," *Cine-Mundial*, January 1916, 10.

22. "Facts and Comments," *Moving Picture World*, September 23, 1916, 1509.

23. "Nuestro programa," *Cine-Mundial*, January 1916, 10.

24. Bush, "Light Breaking in South America," 1871.

25. W. Stephen Bush, "Hungry for American Pictures," *Moving Picture World*, November 11, 1916, 829. On *Cine-Mundial* and Hollywood's expansion into Mexico, which proved more problematic—and more urgent—than in many South American markets because of widespread piracy, see Serna, *Making Cinelandia*, 29–34.

26. Richard L. Stomgren, "*Moving Picture World*," 15.

27. "Effective Publicity in Latin America," *Chicago Commerce*, October 7, 1922, 45.

28. Thompson notes the establishment of branch offices of Fox in Argentina and Brazil in December 1915 and in Uruguay and Paraguay in early 1917. *Exporting Entertainment*, 72–73. José Inácio de Melo Souza indicates that Universal and Paramount opened branch offices in Rio de Janeiro in 1915 and 1916, respectively, in *Imagens do passado: São Paulo e Rio de Janeiro nos primórdios do cinema* (São Paulo: Editora Senac, 2003), 328.

29. F. H. Richardson, "El arte de la proyección," *Cine-Mundial*, February 1917, 80; ibid., October 1918, 645.

30. F. H. Richardson, "Respeto a la profesión," *Cine-Mundial*, January 1918, 32.

31. Aurelio de los Reyes, *Cine y sociedad en México*, Vol. 2: *Bajo el cielo de México (1920–1924)* (Mexico City: Filmoteca de la Universidad Nacional Autónoma de México, 1994), 310.

32. "Gacetilla—Un cine modelo," *Cine-Mundial*, February 1916, 80; "Gacetilla—Un cine modelo," *Cine-Mundial*, June 1916, 259.

33. "Gacetilla—El Cinema Central," *Cine-Mundial*, August 1917, 412.

34. "Notas," *Cine-Mundial*, April 1918, 181.

35. Juan Rivero, "Los cinematógrafos privados," *Cine-Mundial*, March 1918, 126; "Notas," *Cine-Mundial* February 1917, 61.

36. Francisco José Ariza, "El Cinematógrafo es la Novela de las Imágenes: Vicente Blasco Ibáñez," *Cine-Mundial*, January 1920, 86–89; "Don Ramón el Único nos Habla, en el Metrópoli del Arte Mudo, de la Formidable Equivocación del Cinematógrafo," *Cine-Mundial*, January 1922, 14–15, 44. Blasco Ibáñez also contributed the story "La vieja del cinema," *Cine-Mundial*, September 1920, 783–785.

37. Rogelio Sotela, *Escritores de Costa Rica* (San José, Costa Rica: Imprenta Lehmann, 1942), 412.

38. "Crónica de Barcelona," *Cine-Mundial*, September 1916, 395; "Crónica de Barcelona," *Cine-Mundial*, September 1917, 84; "Crónica de Barcelona," *Cine-Mundial*, May 1917, 241; "Crónica de la Habana," *Cine-Mundia*, May 1917, 244; "Crónica del Uruguay," *Cine-Mundial*, November 1917, 575.

39. F[rancisco] G[arcía] Ortega, "Foreign Trade News," *Moving Picture World*, May 4, 1918, 703.

40. Advertisement, *Cine-Mundial*, February 1917, 95.

41. Luis Martínez Casado, "Crónica de Colombia," *Cine-Mundial*, November 1917, 572.

42. Manuel Rodríguez Artiles, "Crónica de Camagüey (Cuba)," *Cine-Mundial*, 211.

43. See, e.g., "Notas," *Cine-Mundial*, February 1916, 53.

44. "Notas," *Cine-Mundial*, March 1917, 113. See Laura Isabel Serna, "As a Mexican I Feel It's My Duty: Citizenship, Censorship and the Campaign against Derogatory Films in Mexico, 1922–1930," *The Americas* 63, no. 2 (2006): 225–244; Ruth Vasey, *The World according to Hollywood* (Madison: University of Wisconsin Press, 1999), 93–94, 119–120, 170–176; Aurelio de los Reyes, "El gobierno mexicano y las películas denigrantes, 1920–1931," in *México-Estados Unidos: Encuentros y desencuentros en el cine*, ed. Ignacio Durán, Iván Trujillo, and Mónica Verea (Mexico City: Instituto Mexicano de Cinematografía, 1996), 23–35.

45. Francisco García Ortega, "Random Shots about Export," *Moving Picture World*, March 10, 1917, 1545.

46. "Notas," *Cine-Mundial*, October 1916, 413. On the discourse of film as a universal language, see Miriam Hansen, *Babel and Babylon: Spectatorship in American Silent Film* (Cambridge, MA: Harvard University Press, 1991), esp. 173–198; Laura Isabel Serna, "Translations and Transportation: Towards a Transnational History of the Intertitle," in *Silent Cinema and the Politics of Space*, eds. Jennifer M. Bean, Anupama Kapse, and Laura Horak (Bloomington: Indiana University Press, 2014), 124.

47. Serna, *Making Cinelandia*, 95–96.

48. "Preguntas y Respuestas," *Cine-Mundial*, June 1925, 345.

49. *N. W. Ayers and Sons' Directory of Newspapers and Periodicals*.

50. Marsha Orgeron, "You Are Invited to Participate," *Journal of Film and Video* 61, no. 3 (2009): 4.

51. Emilio Chapperon, "Crónica de la Argentina: Las gentiles propagandistas del cine," *Cine-Mundial*, September 1917, 454.

52. Eduardo Quiñones, "Crónica de la Habana," *Cine-Mundial*, February 1918, 89.

53. Colin Gunckel, "The War of the Accents: Spanish Language Hollywood Films in Mexican Los Angeles," *Film History* 20, no. 3 (2008): 331; Lucío Villegas, editorial, *Cinelandia*, September 1926, 4.

54. Lucío Villegas, editorial, *Cinelandia*, September 1926, 4.

55. He was replaced by Eduardo Payá in January 1928, and later by Juan J. Moreno.

56. "El Correo de Hollywood," *Cinelandia*, November 1927, 71.

57. Circulation figures refer to sworn Audit Bureau of Circulation statements drawn from *N. W. Ayers and Sons' Directory of Newspapers and Periodicals*.

58. "La Perricholi: Una cinta peruana," *Cinelandia*, January 1929, 25; "Barro Humano," *Cinelandia*, June 1930, 10. For a rare article on local exhibition, see Dario Varona, "El cine en Cuba," *Cinelandia*, December 1930, 14.

59. The first exhibitions of synchronized sound features in Latin America occurred in São Paulo and Mexico City in April and May of 1929; talking pictures were shown in Buenos Aires in July of the same year.

60. Dario Varona, "Maridos y mujeres," *Cinelandia*, January 1930, 60; Virginia Lane, "Dolores del Río," *Cinelandia*, April 1930, 46.

61. This development prefigures the later institution of a Hispanic media and consumer market examined by Arlene M. Dávila in *Latinos, Inc: The Marketing and Making of a People* (Berkeley: University of California Press, 2001). See also G. Christina Mora, *Making Hispanics: How Activists, Bureaucrats and Media Constructed a New American* (Chicago: University of Chicago Press, 2014), on the construction of Hispanic pan-ethnicity.

62. Advertisement, *Cinelandia*, December 1929, 5; Advertisement, *Cinelandia*, March 1929, 58.

63. For an overview, see Charles Ramírez Berg, *Latino Images in Film: Stereotypes, Subversion, Resistance* (Austin: University of Texas Press, 2002). See also López, "Are All Latins from Manhattan?"; Shari Roberts, "The Lady in the Tutti-Frutti Hat: Carmen Miranda, A Spectacle of Ethnicity," *Cinema Journal* 32, no. 2 (1993): 3–23; Victoria Sturtevant, "Spitfire: Lupe Vélez and the Ambivalent Pleasures of Ethnic Masquerade," *Velvet Light Trap* 55 (2005): 19–32; Ana M. López, "From Hollywood and Back: Dolores del Río, a Trans(National) Star," *Studies in Latin American Popular Culture* 17 (1998): 5–31; Joanne Hershfield, *The Invention of Dolores del Río* (Minneapolis: University of Minnesota Press, 2000).

64. Roberts, "The Lady in the Tutti-Frutti Hat," 15. See also Sturtevant, "Spitfire."

65. See Vasey, *The World according to Hollywood*, 115–122.

66. Gil Alvear, "Dónde se encuentra Costa Roja? *Cinelandia*, July 1927, 29, 70.

67. Agustín Aragón Jr., "Crónicas de Cinelandia," *Cinelandia*, November 1927, 39. The byline may be another of Agustín Aragón Leiva's pseudonyms.

68. Lucío Villegas, editorial, *Cinelandia*, April 1927, 4.

69. "Una charra gringa," *Cinelandia*, August 1929, 28.

70. "México Oriental," *Cinelandia*, July 1929, 28; López, "Are All Latins from Manhattan?," 71.

71. See Mark B. Sandberg, "Location, Location: On the Plausibility of Place Substitution," in *Silent Cinema and the Politics of Space*, ed. Jennifer M. Bean, Anupama Kapse, and Laura Horak (Bloomington: Indiana University Press, 2014); Jennifer M. Bean, "A Horizon Gone Mad: Mapping Hollywood's Universal Geography," keynote address, Berkeley Conference on Silent Cinema, February 21, 2013.

72. Lucío Villegas, editorial, *Cinelandia*, August 1927, 3.

73. This invisibility parallels the erasure of other types of labor, especially male labor, in the discourses about the "extra girl" that proliferated in press discourse on Hollywood. Denise McKenna, "The Photoplay or the Pickaxe: Extras, Gender, and Labor in Early Hollywood," *Film History* 23, no. 1 (2011): 5–19. See also Shelley Stamp, "'It's a Long Way to Filmland': Starlets, Screen Hopefuls and Extras in Hollywood," in *American Cinema's Transitional Era*, ed. Charles Keil and Shelley Stamp (Berkeley: University of California Press, 2004), 332–352.

74. Armando Vargas de la Maza, "La Vida de Cinelandia," *Cinelandia*, August 1927, 29.

75. Cornelio Dircio, "Notas e impresiones," *Cinelandia*, February 1929, 16.

76. Felipe de Leiva, "Memorias de un extra," *Cinelandia*, November 1927, 54.

77. Serna, *Making Cinelandia*, 209–212.
78. Ibid., 212.
79. *Cine-Mundial*, March 1942, 136.
80. "Carmen Miranda en Hollywood," *Cine-Mundial*, September 1942, 448.
81. See especially Nataša Durovicová, "Translating America: The Hollywood Multilinguals 1929–1933," in *Sound Theory/Sound Practice*, ed. Rick Altman (New York: Routledge, 1992), 138–153; Vasey, *The World According to Hollywood*, 63–99; Lisa Jarvinen, *The Rise of Spanish Language Filmmaking: Out from Hollywood's Shadow, 1929–1939* (New Brunswick, NJ: Rutgers University Press, 2012).
82. Letters from Leticia Justiniani in Panama City and Luis Orozco G. in Mexico City, "Cartas al Director," *Cinelandia*, April 1930, 4.
83. Gunckel, "War of the Accents," 330.
84. Advertisement, *Cine-Mundial*, February 1929, 1; Advertisement, *Cine-Mundial*, September 1930, 2.
85. Gunckel, "War of the Accents," 337–338; Jarvinen, *The Rise of Spanish-Language Filmmaking*, 128.
86. Juan J. Moreno, "Cinelándicas," *Cinelandia*, January 1930, 7.
87. "Parlante en Español: *Sombras de Gloria*," *Cinelandia*, March 1930, 42.
88. Juan J. Moreno, "Cinelándicas," *Cinelandia*, January 1932, 7.
89. "En el umbral de la fama," *Cine-Mundial*, January 1934, 26.
90. Hermida, "En Broadway," *Cine-Mundial*, September 1936, 510.
91. Pepe Elizondo, "De Visita en un Estudio de Méjico," *Cine-Mundial*, February 1940, 88–89; Pepe Elizondo, "Cantinflas me Miraba Perflejo . . . Preguntas y Respuestas," *Cine-Mundial*, September 1941, 405.
92. *Cinelandia*, January 1943, 50.
93. "Para los que colaboran en Fotoconcurso," *Cine-Mundial*, May 1942, 241.
94. Hermida, "En Broadway," *Cine-Mundial*, January 1945, 19.
95. Hermida, "En Broadway," *Cine-Mundial*, January 1948, 7.
96. See Fein, "From Collaboration to Containment."
97. *Radiolandia*, a continuation of *La canción moderna* (which was renamed in 1934), boasted a circulation of 450,000 by the mid-1940s. Matthew Karush, *Culture of Class: Radio and Cinema in the Making of a Divided Argentina* (Durham, NC: Duke University Press, 2012), 138.

Octávio de Faria, "Russian Cinema and Brazilian Cinema," *O Fan* (Rio de Janeiro), October 1928

> *Co-founder of the Chaplin-Club and the magazine* O Fan, *Octávio de Faria is an key figure in the establishment of film criticism in Brazil. Eschewing the political activism of Soviet cinema in favor of praising its directors' artistry, "Russian Cinema and Brazilian Cinema" hails the achievements of filmmakers like Eisenstein and Pudovkin. It appeared in* O Fan's *second issue.*

Of all the art forms, the most important for Russia is the cinematographic.

—Lenin

IT IS WITH THIS epigraph that Mr. Léon Moussinac opens his new book, *Le Cinéma Soviétique*. An impassioned manifesto of cinematographic Communism, this work is of great interest not only as a declaration of enthusiastic support but also as a faithful documentation.

It's not even worth clarifying that I'm not a Communist. Such a statement would go beyond the limits of this publication, which is not preoccupied with politics or sociology.

Nevertheless, it would be impossible to hold back tremendous applause for the entire cinematographic movement being developed in the new Russia.

To discuss individual works in and of themselves would be, in our case, frivolous. The great examples have not yet arrived to our shores. Of those that have—as in *Ivan the Terrible*—a public verdict has not been forthcoming, although this film did clarify for me the value of the new Russian theories. (As for *Harem of Death*, I did not have the opportunity to see it when it was exhibited here.)[1]

So we will be guided by what has been proclaimed, by the near unanimous applause. Or, better stated, we will abstract from individual productions in order to focus on the effort employed in this endeavor.

On this matter, everyone who brings us news from Russia speaks with great enthusiasm. Two books in particular are devoted to this question. The first, by R. Marchand and P. Weinstein, dealt with the issue from the perspective of organization and of sustenance. It stressed the economic, and to too great an extent. The second, the above-mentioned work by Léon Moussinac, confirming all that we already knew, has arrived to explain the entire organization of Russian cinema—its achievements, its possibilities. It is truly interesting.

The book's epigraph is quite significant. It transmits the heightened importance that cinema acquired for the leaders of the Soviet republics.

They have understood that the cinema is a worthy weapon to educate a people, all of its possibilities as the propagator of ideas. Yet did they not have, right in front of their very eyes, the example of the United States, which is imposing little by little its ethos on the world, in large part through its influence on the younger generations? It was simply a question of learning, of following this example.

The government wants to make cinema in Russia. And cinema is being made in Russia. The results they have achieved during these ten years of crisis are nothing short of unbelievable. Extraordinary, indeed, that the government has not only created a cinema capable of competing with the great film-producing countries of the world but that it has organized around this cinema an entire theoretical program to teach and foment the art. The program of the Institute of the History of Arts is decisive in this respect. From these new courses, technicians will emerge—the new Eisensteins, the new Pudovkins...

One objection, however, always appears on the lips of detractors of Russian cinema. They proclaim with contempt: propaganda films.

Propaganda films, undoubtedly. But let us not shout so loud so soon. Nor should we go to the extremes of Mr. Moussinac, who agitates for "social expression" cinema. Instead, let us keep calm and consider the question without ill will. Let's hear the arguments in its defense, firm in our commitment to be fair to those who are deserving. Two of these arguments are particularly compelling. The first reminds us that American cinema has done nothing but propagate *its* ideas. A sociology entirely opposed to the Communist one. In the eyes of Moscow, then, it is New York that is the unrestrained propagandist. And since I am neither Moscow, nor New York...

The second argument comes courtesy of Eisenstein himself and seems to me to be even more decisive. According to Moussinac, responding to someone who accused him of propaganda, Eisenstein responded that, according to this logic, as a true Communist he could not have found a different mode of expression. He would have to voice with enthusiasm what he enthusiastically felt. He was sincere...

Let us abstain from a more profound verdict that would necessarily involve discussing Communism itself. Let us retain only the lesson of a government that, during a moment of crisis, understands the importance of cinema as an educational force, as an artistic one. And that employs this vision in the face of all sorts of difficulties.

Other governments should—indeed, must—pay close attention to Moscow. Perhaps, instead of plowing highways so that capitalists might drive by in their Packards, or calling a French urban planner to come and play at making doll-like gardens on the beaches of our capital city of Rio de Janeiro, they should look more seriously at other necessities of our country, at the Brazilian film industry, tooting our own horn for once.

Does our government realize that cinema in the United States is the third or fourth largest industry there? And that all we need are funding and protection against the exhibitor who does not want to put national cinema on the marquee because he already knows that the public won't buy it, preferring to go and see any other thing with a foreign label? (Incidentally, the public is partially correct. What is exhibited in terms of national cinema? It's *Vice and Beauty*. It's *Morphine*.[2] Meanwhile, we all know there are other films out there.... But then why aren't they shown to the public? I would be a false friend to our national cinema if I defended it with these films.)

If our government is aware of this, it does not show it. Officially, it ignores the problem.

However, those few who are trying to create anything in Brazilian cinema are certain that, as soon as they achieve it, the government will come knocking, with a hefty levy, placing a garland of forget-me-nots around one of our local monuments... to see if Rio will look like Paris...

Translated by Sarah Ann Wells

SARAH ANN WELLS is Assistant Professor of Comparative Literature and Folklore Studies at the University of Wisconsin–Madison. She is the author of *Media Laboratories: Late Modernism in South America* (Northwestern University Press, 2017), the coeditor of *Simultaneous Worlds: Global Science Fiction Cinema* (University of Minnesota, 2015), and the translator of Gonzalo Aguilar's *New Argentine Film: Other Worlds* (Palgrave, 2008; 2011).

Notes

1. *Editors' Note*: The first film mentioned is likely most likely *Wings of a Serf* (*Krylya kholopa*, dir. Yuri Tarich, 1926); the second is the Turkmen film *Minaret of Death* (*Minaret smerti*, dir. Viacheslav Viskovskii, 1925). We thank Alexander Spektor for identifying these films.

2. *Translator's Note*: *Vício e beleza* (dir. Antônio Tibiriçá, 1926); *Morfina* (dir. Nino Ponti and Francisco Madrigano, 1928).

Chapter 5

Parallel Modernities?: The First Reception of Soviet Cinema in Latin America

Sarah Ann Wells

IN 1930, THE BRITISH avant-garde film journal *Close Up* published a paean to Buenos Aires' film culture. In "Cinema in the Argentine," H. P. Tew writes, "Though the Argentine is, comparatively speaking, a non-producer, it must be one of the world's greatest consumers." Rendering Argentina's film production invisible, Tew defines its reception in terms of an "impartial" receptivity. The heterogeneity of the population—what Tew deems its "cosmopolitan mass"—mirrors its access to, and appreciation of, foreign films.[1]

For Tew, Buenos Aires' cosmopolitan spectatorship has one clear sign: the surprising frequency with which Soviet films are screened there. Not surprisingly, Sergei Eisenstein's *Battleship Potemkin* (*Bronenosets Potyomkin*, 1925) was the first big success.[2] Fiercely debated, the film circulated widely in all kinds of cinemas: "It must have been seen by workers of every nationality," but also enjoyed by "impartial [i.e., nonleftist] observers," Tew writes. Located in England where Eisenstein's films had been banned—as they were in France, Spain, and elsewhere—he praises the fact that *October* (*Oktyabr'*, 1928) was screened in Buenos Aires "in practically uncut form."[3] The transatlantic, Madrid-basis periodical *La Gaceta Literaria* likewise stressed Buenos Aires' cosmopolitan reception of Soviet films. The Spanish modernist Guillermo de Torre published a piece that proclaimed the most striking element of Cine Club of the Amigos del Arte was its screenings of Soviet films— including *The Battleship Potemkin*, *October*, and Dziga Vertov's *The Sixth Part of the World* (*Shestaia chast' mira*, 1926)—"publicly without causing much shock' in this city 'overflowing with movie theaters and spectators."[4] One

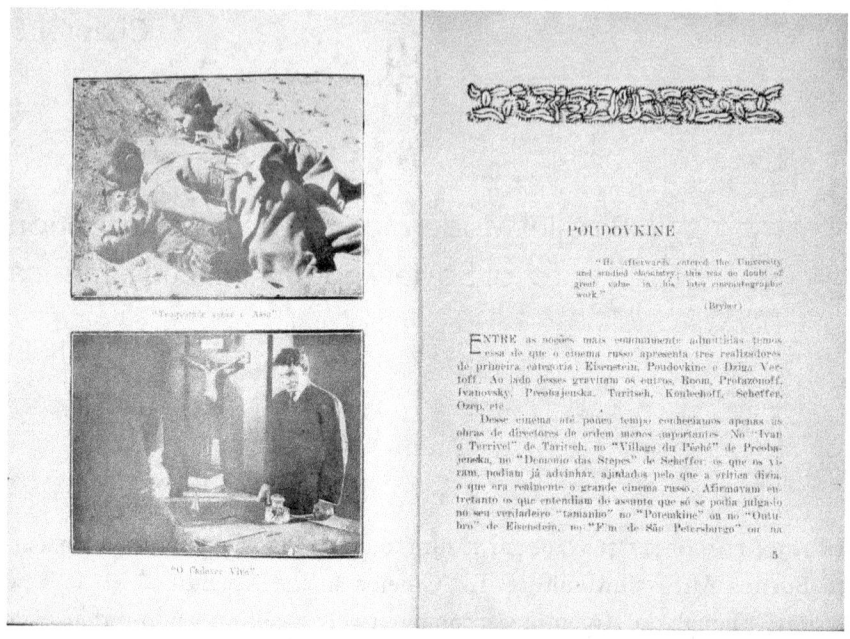

Fig. 5.1 An article dedicated to Pudovkin in *O Fan* (Rio de Janeiro), June 1930.

year before, *La Gaceta Literaria* had published an article by Juan Piqueras entitled "Veinte películas soviéticas en Suramérica" (Twenty Soviet Films in South America), contrasting this reception to the censorship currently experienced in Spain.[5] The large title, film stills, and relatively lengthy text of Piqueras's piece situates South America (or Argentina) at the vanguard of cinema because of its Soviet screenings.

In concluding "Buenos Aires is the perfect cinema cosmopolitan town," Tew, like his Spanish contemporaries, desired a culture of film reception that would transcend the stark polarizations of the 1930s, including nationalism itself.[6] These European observers were correct to see in Soviet cinema an opportunity for Latin American readers and writers to self-fashion themselves as worldly viewers. However, this self-fashioning did not abandon the hope for, or anxiety over, national cinema production. In fact, a multiplication of national cinemas was central to the development of a culture of world film.[7] What is more, it was often in print culture—from mainstream periodicals to the limited circulation of periodicals from incipient film clubs—where

Soviet cinema's role as mediator of a modern, cosmopolitan culture of film spectatorship was located. While access to Soviet films was limited throughout the world by political and economic imperatives, I show here that in Latin America this limitation is compensated for in particularly fraught and compelling ways in the itineraries and remediation of Soviet cinema through print.

This essay explores Soviet cinema as a horizon of expectation during its first reception in Latin America (roughly, 1926–1945). Despite the relative paucity of its actual distribution, Soviet cinema has a striking discursive prominence during this period.[8] Scholars have tended to overlook this prominence, with the key exception of the Mexican context, where Eisenstein's influence was directly felt in the realm of film production.[9] My research shows that Latin American artists' and intellectuals' responses to Soviet films were prismatic, and that the concept of Soviet/Russian cinema functioned in a flexible way in Latin America—traveling and adapting itself, even when the films themselves could only circulate precariously. Here, I will focus on four such iterations: as an expression of cinema as an eminently aesthetic and specific medium; as a vivid, sensorial experience of a mass or collective historical agent that supersedes the individual; as evidence of a cosmopolitan or "worldly" filmgoing experience; and as a model for the construction of national cinemas. As we shall see, none of these responses are mutually exclusive and, in fact, often worked in tandem in the particularly embedded or nested relationships between the national and the global during this period. This is a story of the strange and unexpected uses to which Soviet films were put in Latin America: uses that were also, implicitly, debates about the region's place in the world through the most modern of lenses.

Evidently, Latin American film culture is marked by a vast heterogeneity, and the reception of Soviet film is no exception. Mexico's experience of revolution, for example, more closely paralleled the Soviet case than other Latin American countries; moreover, Eisenstein's influence on national film production was experienced directly and immediately there. Argentina was the first to screen Soviet films and would do so more frequently than many of its neighbors in the late 1920s and early 1930s; the Soviet Union opened a distribution center in Buenos Aires, URSS Films.[10] In contrast, censorship circumscribed the showing of films such as the celebrated *Potemkin* in Brazil and Cuba, leaving writers to imagine the film with the aid of foreign periodicals or to travel to other countries to report back to their readers.[11] Moreover, the regional frame

"Latin America" seldom appears during this period, with writers focusing on either the national or the global in their reflections on cinema. However, while nothing like a Third Cinema Latin Americanist stance—explicitly politicizing film production in the subcontinent as distinct from Euro-American film production and linking it to other Global South contexts—as yet existed, multiple points of intersection link these different national contexts of reception, warranting a transnational Latin Americanist frame.

As Ana M. López has argued, cinema functioned as a metonymy for modernity in early twentieth-century Latin America: as simultaneously a promise, lived reality, and phantasmatic apparition.[12] In this context, Soviet cinema offered a unique point of inflection. As the only foreign film industry not part of western Europe or the US that circulated in Latin America during the modernist period, it represented an important possibility for an alternative cinematic modernity; tracing its earliest iterations allows a glimpse of a counternarrative to the fascination with Hollywood in the region. My interest therefore lies less in Soviet cinema's influence on Latin American cinemas (which would come later, with Third Cinema) than in a broader discursive sphere that sought to locate Soviet cinema, urgently and at times contradictorily, when it first arrived to the region. I argue that Latin Americans negotiated the benefits and limitations of the cosmopolitan when they watched, read about, and debated the value of Soviet cinema, employing "Soviet cinema" as a *tactic* to construct a virtual cosmopolitan film spectatorship that did not preclude a preoccupation with the national, even when—or perhaps precisely when—Soviet films themselves were less available. Soviet cinema was thus a promise, one that became more prominent on the page even as it receded as a lived experience on the screen.

The Contours of Soviet Cinema in Latin America

Soviet films were screened sporadically during the late 1920s through the 1940s in Latin America. As in many parts of Europe, they were frequently banned, cut, or had their circulation limited for commercial reasons.[13] Yet even countries where Soviet cinema was screened relatively rarely—the case of Peru, for example, or Brazil (where censorship played a role in its reception in both the 1920s–1930s and in the 1960s–1970s)—print culture allowed for a prominent conversation about Soviet cinema.[14] Through marginalia, film reviews, *crónicas/crônicas*,[15] and even novels (and borrowing from books and periodicals in Europe and the United States) writers interpreted cinema for those readers who had limited access to the films themselves, exposing them to central debates surrounding Soviet cinema that circulated globally during the 1920s and 1930s—debates that Soviet cinema made possible. These include the use of nonactors; the problem of synchronized sound; and concepts such as intellectual montage, the Kino-Eye, and simultaneity.

As in the United States and western Europe, Eisenstein was both protagonist and metonymic figure for this reception, especially his *Potemkin*, followed by *October* (1928) and *The General Line/Old and New* (*Staroye i novoye*, 1929). Other frequently cited figures are Vsevolod Pudovkin (*Mother* [*Mat'*], 1926; and, in particular, *Storm over Asia* [*Potomok Chingis-Khana*], 1928), Abram Room (*Bed and Sofa* [*Tretya meshchanskaya*], 1927), as well as the names Dziga Vertov, Fedor Ozep, and Yuri Tarich. Because they did not have full access to the debates surrounding these filmmakers—in particular, surrounding montage—Latin American writers located Soviet cinema as a single phenomenon, conflated under the rubric of "Russian" or "Soviet cinema" and, at times, as "Soviet montage," freely interweaving Eisenstein and Pudovkin in ways that would have been anathema to both.

In this context, French intellectuals played a major role in this fragmentary reception, exposing Latin American artists and intellectuals to both the films and the programmatic writings associated with the major figures, decades before the more extensive circulation that Masha Salazkina has identified with the 1960s.[16] Léon Moussinac's enthusiastic monograph *Le Cinéma Soviétique* (Paris, 1928) was frequently cited by intellectuals who employed it as pedagogy for themselves and for their readers in Cuba, Peru, Uruguay, Argentina, and Brazil. In addition, the Spanish writer Julio Álvarez del Vayo wrote on Soviet cinema in the concluding chapter of his book, *Rusia a los doce años* (1929, Madrid Espasa-Calpe). The work was reviewed in the *Revista de Avance* in 1929 by José Manuel Valdés-Rodríguez, Cuba's staunchest early supporter of Soviet film, who calls Eisenstein and Pudovkin "cloudy marvels for our Creole retinas."[17] A few years later, in an article published in the Cuban journal *Social*, Valdés-Rodríguez would sketch out Eisenstein's dialectical processes of cinematography and film projection, the conflict basis of art through montage, and the idea of rhythmic montage, among other concepts of his *cinedialéctica*.[18] He would later travel to the Soviet Union in 1934 and meet with Eisenstein, as his compatriot Alejo Carpentier had done in Paris in 1930. To a lesser extent, German, US, and British periodicals (such as

Close Up) and intellectuals also mediated this first contact. Rio de Janeiro's *O Fan*, for example, includes lengthy transcriptions from French, British, and US journals, as well as excerpts from book-length studies such as René Marchand and Pierre Weinstein's *L'art dans la Russie nouvelle: le cinéma* (Paris, 1927) and Bryher's (pen name; Annie Winifred Ellerman's) *Film Problems of Soviet Russia* (London, 1929), the first English-language book to be published on Soviet cinema.[19]

The emergent phenomenon of film clubs offered a mode of access to Soviet cinema and connects the first reception of Soviet cinema to the later reception of the 1960s. Of particular note is the Cine Club of the Amigos del Arte, which functioned from the late 1920s to the early 1930s in Buenos Aires and which caught Tew's and de Torre's attention.[20] It offered public screenings of films by Eisenstein and Pudovkin, along with lectures by intellectuals such as the Argentine historian José Luis Romero and Arturo Mom's "Masters of Russian Cinematography," accompanied by *Old and New* in a 1931 screening. Consistent with the position of Victoria Ocampo's seminal modernist journal *Sur*, launched in 1931 (and with many of the same participants), the Cine Club screened Soviet films by deemphasizing their political goals. A fragment from an Eisenstein film was projected, for example, accompanied by music by the (avowedly anticommunist) Igor Stravinsky: a literal example of a more broadly "fragmentary" reception, a practice that undoubtedly curtailed the explicitly political diegesis.

Another key example is the Chaplin-Club, founded in Rio de Janeiro in 1928, which projected only two Soviet films, Pudovkin's *Storm over Asia* and Ozep's *Living Corpse* (*Zhivoy trup*, 1929), but covered the problem of Soviet cinema much more substantially in its periodical, *O Fan* (1928–1930), Brazil's first forum dedicated to cinema as an art form.[21] Like the Amigos del Arte, *O Fan* was put together by writers, several of them right-leaning, who wanted to create a forum "above" national politics or the nation as a frame. Its pages cite *auteurs* of international circulation, as well as dialoguing directly with film and general periodicals from Argentina, France, England, Germany, and the United States. In the second issue of *O Fan*, an article by the conservative writer Octávio de Faria, "Cinema russo e cinema brasileiro" appears with an epigraph from Lenin (via Moussinac); de Faria states that despite his political differences with Soviet filmmakers, he has nothing but "great applause" for their efforts. "Let us be guided," he writes, "by what is said, by this applause that is nearly unanimous" in international press accounts of Soviet cinema.[22] *O Fan* positions the Soviet filmmakers/theorists as something like incipient

Fig. 5.2 An advertisement for Sergei Eisenstein's *Battleship Potemkin*, *El Universal* (Mexico City), April 19, 1927. Courtesy of the Biblioteca Miguel Lerdo de Tejada, Secretaría de la Hacienda y Crédito Público.

auteurs, rather than as activists, as tortured artists with unique aesthetic programs rather than representatives of a regime. It will go on to feature excerpts of translations of the theories of Pudovkin, Vertov, and Eisenstein, originally published in French and English-language periodicals.[23] The commentaries that accompany these translations, as well as the fact that many were given as talks in the Chaplin-Club's gatherings, function as modes of intervening in the present, acts of reception in the absence of access to the films themselves (as the authors frequently note).[24]

Soviet Cinema, World Cinema

As we saw in the case of H. P. Tew, the construction of a Latin American cosmopolitan film culture during this period often depended on an outside figure: the traveler, witness, or intellectual, who would triangulate—or, in some cases, "quadrilate"—Latin Americans' approaches to Soviet cinema. That is, Soviet cinema does not appear unmediated to the Latin American reader or writer but is routed through a conversation taking place in Europe and/or the United States. Part of having a cosmopolitan film culture, evidently, was

Fig. 5.3 A discussion of Buenos Aires' Cine Club of the Amigos del Arte in Juan Piqueras, "Veinte Películas Sovieticas en Suramérica"(Twenty Soviet Films in South America), *La Gaceta Literaria* (Madrid), September 15, 1929. Courtesy of the Biblioteca Nacional de España.

being recognized by figures from abroad. Yet it was also the ability to recognize those figures in turn, "hailing" them in multiple ways. If Buenos Aires was cosmopolitan because it screened Soviet films, then Soviet films were, inversely, a mark of cosmopolitanism; as they traveled, periodicals eagerly

Fig. 5.4 L. S Marinho, the film correspondent in Hollywood for Brazil's *Cinearte*, reports on "Eisenstein em Hollywood," *Cinearte* (Rio de Janeiro), August 5, 1930. Hemeroteca Digital Brasileira.

traced their itineraries. Citations from world newspapers accompanied marginalia on them; the adjectives and adverbs "mundial" and "mundialmente" abound. These texts frequently emphasize how far the films had to journey, ticking off their successes along the way, as well as featuring citations from global newspapers that present them to the Latin American public: *Man with a Movie Camera* (*Chelovek s kino-apparatom*, dir. Dziga Vertov, 1929), for example, is the film that "inspired and scandalized Europe."[25] An ad from 1927 in the Mexican newspaper *El Universal* describes, almost poetically, the different cities that *Potemkin* has "conquered": Vienna, Berlin, Paris, New York, Buenos Aires. Playing with the film's narrative of the heroic battleship, this ad also evokes how film canisters in general traveled by ship.[26] Here, Eisenstein's film is literally a way of transporting viewers to a virtual cosmopolitan community of artistic innovation.

In turn, Latin American journalists frequently captured the energy that surrounded these traveling films by traveling themselves, as film correspondents in Berlin, Paris, Hollywood, and New York.[27] For example, L. S. Marinho, a Hollywood correspondent for Brazil's most widely circulated cinema journal, *Cinearte* (1926–1942), declared himself to be one of the first journalists to interview Eisenstein when the filmmaker arrived in the United States. The accompanying photograph situates both Marinho, *Cinearte*, and Eisenstein on the same plane: as worldly travelers in the realm of Hollywood. Eisenstein opens the pages of *Cinearte*, inscribing an image of Brazilian film culture into a global context.[28] Among the most noteworthy traveler-writers on Eisenstein was Alejo Carpentier, writing for the Cuban press from Paris in the late 1920s and early 1930s. In one piece, Carpentier describes the tour of Paris he and the surrealist filmmaker and poet Robert Desnos gave Eisenstein. Providing his Cuban readers with a brief account of Eisenstein's filmography, he also renders palpable key scenes from his films in a technique that itself approaches montage with its "rhythm, intensity, paroxysm."[29]

In this sense, the discourse about Soviet cinema often exceeded material experience with the films themselves. In a note published in the *Correio da Manhã*, for example, the fact that *Potemkin* had been censored by the authorities in Brazil means that viewers were doubly enthusiastic to view *Storm over Asia*.[30] A review of this same film—the first Soviet work to be screened in Brazil—published in Recife in 1930 describes the film as "completely different from all that had been done thus far in celluloid . . . filled with details that will elude the grasp of those unaware that cinema has nuance."[31] The eager embrace of even minor Soviet productions (such as Ozep's *Living Corpse*) reflects a desire to be up to date with a group of films that had been repeatedly out of reach for Brazilian audiences. As in the case of the articles published in *O Fan*, this reception is structured by a horizon of expectation that exceeds the author's experience: he wants to find in the film what he has already read about Soviet cinema. And Soviet cinema is presented as an invitation to the viewer to participate in a heterogeneous community of film producers and spectators. In fact, I would argue that the very lack of material circulation of the films themselves ended up being itself generative, for it produces an opening that allows the author—and, by extension, the periodical or national context in which he writes—to self-fashion a cosmopolitan identity.

Soviet Cinema, *Cinéma Pur*

In the context of the gradual appearance, filtered through the Euro-American press, of a distinction between art-house and commercial cinema, Soviet cinema plays a prominent appearance. Indeed, with Kristin Thompson on the US case, we could say that the precarious circulation of Soviet cinema, and the response to it, was instrumental in facilitating the emergence of a discourse of art-based cinema in the late 1920s and early 1930s in Latin America.[32] As we have seen in the case of the film exhibition practices of the Amigos del Arte and Chaplin-Club, the leftist thrust of Soviet cinema was often disavowed in favor of an emphasis on its aesthetic novelty. First and foremost, then, Latin American artists and intellectuals mobilized Soviet cinema as an example or even definition of *cinéma pur* ("pure cinema"). The discourse of *cinéma pur* entered Latin American periodicals through Jean Epstein's 1923 essay, "On Some Aspects of *Photogénie*," cited throughout the 1920s and early 1930s. Epstein describes cinema as Siamese twins, harboring two simultaneous tendencies, art and industry. This division became more pronounced for Latin Americans as the decade continued, and they began to see these twins as embodied in two powers: the "hegemonía cinematográfica" of the US (which functioned as industry) versus Soviet cinema, impoverished by comparison (equated with art). Inverting the adscriptions put forth by the mainstream US press—in which Hollywood cinema was a bastion of capitalist freedom and Soviet cinema the prison house of politicized, bad art—Latin Americans characterized Soviet cinema as art and Hollywood cinema as political and rapaciously capitalistic. "In the eyes of Moscow, it is New York that is the rampant propagandist. And as I'm neither Moscow nor New York..." writes de Faria.[33] Thus, an article in the Uruguayan modernist journal *La Pluma* from 1930 announces Eisenstein's latest film, *Old and New (Antes y ahora)*, and writes that a tractor could be a "a heavy-handed element of propaganda" in the hands of another director, but Eisenstein raises it to the level of a "a magnificent poem."[34] Writers also bracketed or ignored Soviet filmmakers' deep, if ambivalent, admiration for US filmmaking, including the Taylorist principles undergirding the studio model.[35] Their interests lay elsewhere.

Writers frequently lament the "Americanization" of Latin American viewing publics, expressing the hope that Soviet cinema will counteract the dominance of the US at the box office in an imminent future. In fact, it is rare to find a *crónica* that references Soviet cinema without immediately calling up its heroic struggle against the Goliath of the US film industry. *Cronistas* and periodicals of varying political orientations share this propensity for juxtaposing film industries. The Brazilian writer and filmmaker Olympio Guilherme, contributing to *Cinearte* in 1930, pits "misunderstood" films like *Potemkin*, *Old and New*, and *October* against US "standardization."[36] Another mainstream journal, the Argentine *Caras y Caretas*, claims that "Russian film has eliminated . . . all that pernicious superficiality and standardized conventionalism of the films coming from North America."[37] Soviet films did not make the cover of distributor journals or specialized film periodicals, nor were the ads taken out to support them of the same elaborate visual appeal—none were in color, and the photographs included were generally fewer. They lacked Hollywood's fancy "dressing rooms"—in the words of César Vallejo—but many writers claimed that they possessed something else: a raw, vital appeal that seemed to get at the (vaguely defined) heart of the medium. *O Fan* associates Soviet films above all with the problem of *rhythm*, as a cinema-specific attribute, which produces a strange energy and conviction that never ceases to "surprise" or "upset"—but ultimately convince—writers.[38] Over and over again, Soviet cinema is positioned as a bastion for cinema's aesthetic virtues and the idea of the *new*, an epithet frequently associated with it. Yet this *new* is of a very specific sort: one that depends upon the prowess of technological modernity, as in the case of the United States, but through film form itself.

These crónicas often exhibit a slippage from the defense of Soviet cinema's aesthetics to a more specific problem of the period. In the debates surrounding synchronized sound, Soviet cinema stands in as a proxy for the opposition, denigrating what writers repeatedly position as sound cinema's crass commercialism, with Hollywood as a metonymy for this consolidation. If sound film would quickly be characterized as "an old novelty" (*velha novidade*), then the Soviet filmmaker's commitment to sound film constitutes the opposite: a commitment to the development of pure cinema, a paradoxically new tradition.[39]

This position is particularly marked in the case of *O Fan*, a staunch defender until its death of silent cinema, as embodied by its beloved Chaplin and the Soviet filmmakers and their programmatic writings. (Eisenstein and Pudovkin's ventures into sound territory were thus seen as a betrayal.)[40] In a comment echoed in various contexts, José María Podestá, writing in *La Pluma* in 1930, declares that sound can add nothing to the "admirable framing of antennas, cables and spoke that the Russians composed in *Potemkin*"; nor to the "immobile scenes of *Mother* . . . in which it is light, shadow, all images that speak."[41] This defense of Soviet cinema as representative of silent film continued well after the apex of the experimental film debates of the late 1920s and early 1930s and the consolidation of synchronized sound. In the film column Vinícius de Moraes wrote for the mainstream Rio de Janeiro publication *A Manhã* from 1941 to 1945, Soviet silent film emerges as the highest example of cinema's development as an art form. Influenced by the earlier writings of Octávio de Faria, Vinícius offers a piecemeal pedagogy for the large body of readers with little cinematic education outside of the Hollywood-centric periodicals such as *Cinearte*. At the same time, the untimeliness of Vinícius's position suggests Soviet cinema's capacity to activate, as if it were a chemical agent, long-running discussions about the status of cinema as art. In Latin America as elsewhere, Soviet avant-garde films will indeed have an intense half-life, persisting well after the eclipse of the experimental film of the early 1930s. In this way, it constitutes a prominent example of what Dudley Andrew has called cinematic *décalage*, the "temporal loops, delays, and slippages" that mark the different locations of film's production, distribution, circulation, and reception.[42]

Montage, to the Left

Leftist writers also offered up Soviet cinema as an example of how art might apprehend the increasingly volatile figure of the masses, as well as reflect upon capitalism's production of uneven modernities. Attempts to capture or produce the masses through cinema would become increasingly prominent in Latin American film and film theory in the 1960s and 1970s, but we find an incipient approximation during this earlier period, in which the masses are crystallized as a figure across the political and aesthetic spectra and an incipient discourse of underdevelopment appears. Although censorship and lack of access to the films also limited leftist reception, these discussions are particularly valuable for their reflections on the relationship between cinema and the laboring body.[43] One of the most detailed reflections on Soviet cinema comes courtesy of the Marxist avant-garde poet César Vallejo, living in poverty and relative obscurity in Paris. A screening with Vladimir Mayakovsky of Eisenstein's *Old and New* promises an antidote to bourgeois cinema, as well as an opportunity to explore labor in all of its dynamic capacities. In the crónica "Cinema: Russia Inaugurates a New Era on Screen," Vallejo argues that Soviet cinema's vision of a socialist world produces an entirely new subjectivity. One of the most detailed and lengthy of the early approaches to Soviet film by a Latin American from this period, Vallejo's is also one of the few accounts to link the mass experience of cinema spectatorship with other forms of the *masas* that were becoming increasingly urgent in the late 1920s and early 1930s. Here, the laboring body finds its homology in the spectating one, giving off sparks through its contact with other bodies both in and beyond the discrete space of the movie theater. We can see here how Vallejo's exposure to Eisenstein's films also resonated with a project he had begun to work on: *Tungsten* (1931), an attempt to create a novel whose protagonist is not an individual but that instead registers the forces of capitalist production and exploitation.[44]

Indeed, the multiple proletarian novels that emerged in Latin America during the 1930s often appear inspired by Eisenstein's shift away from the individual as the locus of libidinal investment to create a new form for the genre. How might literature adopt the corporeal and collective potential of the Soviet cinema? Like Vallejo, Brazilian writer and activist Patrícia Galvão suggests that Soviet cinema is the only art form capable of embodying the effects of the contradictions of capitalism on a collective. With her coeditor Oswald de Andrade, Galvão praises "The formidable directors . . . the cinema of the masses . . . Russian cinema" in their avant-garde leftist journal *O homem do povo* (The Man of the People).[45] Along with her contemporaneous novel *Parque Industrial* (Industrial Park)—subtitled "a proletarian novel"—*O homem do povo* presents the clash between Hollywood and Soviet cinema as a provocation: Will "the people" be able to recognize the revolutionary potential of Soviet film? The novel's investment in fragments of the relationship between cinema and daily life in São Paulo registers the tensions of filmgoing during early 1930s Brazil:

"Did you see today's *Cinearte*? It talks about Russian cinema . . ."

"Listen! Do you know what communism is?"

"I don't know and I don't want to know."[46]

In this contingent slice of adolescent girl speech, censorship and bourgeois norms envelop and supersede their alternative, Soviet cinema. It is clear from this fragment that cinema constitutes a choreography of clashing forces: different publics come into view under its distinct orbits. In the chapter "Proletarianization," two characters loosely based on Galvão and Oswald de Andrade attend a Soviet film together, in a scene pregnant with affective, corporeal, and political energies, suggesting Pudovkin's adage that "film is the greatest teacher because it teaches not only through the brain but through the whole body."⁴⁷ A later scene grounds cinematic spectatorship in a similar clash of images, including a movie poster on the façade of the Colombo Theater that:

> opaque and illuminated, indifferent to empty stomachs, receives Braz's aristocratic petty bourgeoisie that still have money for the cinema. At the door, the pale enigma of Greta Garbo, in the poorly drawn colors of a poster. Disarrayed hair. Bitter smile. A prostitute feeding the imperialist pimp of America to distract the masses.⁴⁸

Here, the novel's "shot" of Garbo attempts to provide an x-ray of the violent processes that sustain globalization, while the subsequent shot of the Communist mimeographs reframes the Garbo image through contrast. As Eisenstein states in his "Montage as Conflict," the encounter between opposites is a generative locus. And, as in his films, two contrasting images of the same kind of object throw class difference into relief and urge the reader/viewer to connect them.

In this sense, what at first appear as opposing discourses—that of *cinéma pur* and that of leftist activism—cannot be neatly separated. For in both, as we have seen, the United States frequently appears as the intermediary term that defines what Soviet cinema was not, and vice versa. In fact, there is rarely a reference to Soviet cinema without an immediate allusion to its US counterparts (if not the inverse). Thus, an early review of *Ivan the Terrible* (most likely *Wings of a Serf* [*Krylya kholopa*, dir. Yuri Tarich, 1926]) could call Soviet cinema "*lejos*" (distant) in a double sense—at once geographical and aesthetic—from North American films.⁴⁹ In one of his first film reviews, even Jorge Luis Borges begrudgingly recognized Soviet cinema's importance. After describing certain images in what he deems the best Soviet films—*Ivan the Terrible, Battleship Potemkin*, "and perhaps *October*"—Borges observes that Soviet cinema could produce great impact through efficient, inexpensive devices, such as the oblique angles of certain objects. It therefore brought a breath of fresh air in the saturated worlds of Hollywood films, crammed with objects and extras. However, he goes on to read these as fundamentally contextual in their value: a palate cleanser of Hollywood excess, rather than enduring works of art in and of themselves: "the greatest virtue of the Russian film was its interruption of a continual California regime."⁵⁰ Once acknowledged by "the world," Soviet films no longer hold particular value. In fact, he writes, Hollywood improved the aesthetic quality of its shots, and continued its imperial march, having at its fingertips an infinitely vaster repertoire.

We can see here how Borges, like many of the writers examined thus far, adopts a technique that itself approximates montage: the confrontation of oppositions to produce a new meaning. These texts employ Eisenstein's staging of oppositions through relational composition, suggesting that it might have been Latin American print culture, rather than film itself, that was the first to be impacted by the particular form of Soviet cinema. In them, a common discursive strategy—defining Hollywood and Soviet cinema as antagonistic—becomes a tactic that approximates Eisenstein's own film technique: "How far we are from Hollywood and all its schmaltzy, decadent *dressing rooms* [in English]!" Vallejo writes in the last line of his account of *Old and New*, the presence of Hollywood erupting suddenly into his meditation on Soviet cinema.[51] This kind of strategy responds to the logic of an increasingly globalized world, in which cinema does not travel as free circulation but, at times, as aggressive superimposition. Moreover, it is precisely this confrontation among different film idioms that produces a cosmopolitan spectator.

National Cinema as Cosmopolitan Project

A cosmopolitan spectator, however, is not one devoid of national desires but rather one who actively foments them through an appeal to a multilingual, transnational cinema culture. During this moment, the national was neither "above" nor "below" the global scale but its twin, its other face. For, while it functioned as a calling card into a cosmopolitan film community, the reception of Soviet cinema was also lived and attached, prompting, as in a boomerang effect, viewers' own questions about local alternatives. In an early article, "El cine en la nueva Rusia" (Cinema in the New Russia, 1928), Carpentier wrote of *Potemkin*'s first screenings: "It was surprising to see emerging from the new Russian film industry—an industry without tradition, one which encountered every imaginable difficulty—a production so perfect, a film which, in a flash, situated itself among the twenty master works that the art of moving shadows has given us since the beginning of the century."[52] Indeed, the emergence of a Soviet style, despite the vast differences that existed among its films, was continually noted by both distributors and incipient film critics in Latin America. Soviet cinema's ability to imprint its specific national consciousness on a global community of spectators in light of its relative lack of resources was particularly impressive. In the repetition of adjectives and adverbs that indicate the rapid, astonishing progress without precedent of Soviet cinema that run through many different accounts from the period, it is not hard to see a hope for the particular national cinemas of Latin America, precarious as they might have been. For example, in 1932 *Cinearte* published a talk for the Radio Educadora written by Humberto Mauro, Brazil's most prominent director in both the silent and early sound periods, that simultaneously underscores the difference between Russia and Brazil and praises Soviet cinema for its founding of "a new and original national essence."[53] Mauro thus argues that what Soviet cinema can offer is the very obligation of a search for the national through cinema. For countries and regions that found themselves on the outskirts of global capitalism—such as Russia and Brazil—national cinema could, in some instances, have the force of a vanguard, constructing virtual identities with arguably more power than the newspaper or novel, Benedict Anderson's privileged sites of nineteenth-century nation formation.

On a more explicitly political plane, the assertion of a national cinema is undergirded by calls for protectionist strategies by the state, in which the Soviet Union served as a model. Praising the rapid progress of its film production, an article that spans two issues of *Cinearte* describes in detail—from party directives to funding sources—the Soviet Union's legal and political measures to protect it. The editors "wish to remind our political leaders that, with State support, any cinema is possible," citing post-revolutionary Soviet cinema as "a source of inspiration for the adoption of protectionist measures in the Brazilian marketplace."[54] Nearly a decade later, *Cinearte* continued to make such claims: the Soviets have "adapted the cinema to their ends and creating in a short amount of time, in a country which still has much to organize, a production which awes the greatest German and US technicians."[55] Such assertions are particularly striking in a periodical such as *Cinearte*, dedicated to fomenting national film production by positing Hollywood cinema as its principal model. In 1930, the magazine published a lengthy excerpt from an interview with Eisenstein taken from a foreign periodical under the title "Messiah or Threat?" The article was prefaced with a paragraph on Eisenstein's international reputation: "an interesting figure: magnetic, dynamic, revealer of new horizons," excerpting many of his chief ideas: that cinema should be in the hands of the state, for and about the masses (in contrast to US cinema); cinema's pedagogical function; and the ever-present anxiety surrounding synchronized sound.[56] "In Russia, we are forming a new world, with the help of Cinema," Eisenstein is quoted as stating. But for the writer (or editor) of this article, Russian cinema sounds more national than international. He ends by underscoring the backwardness of the Soviet Union when compared to the United States; a country just discovering the power of tractors, which have existed for years in "America."[57] The people want beauty, not tractors and unshaven masses; King Vidor's *The Crowd* (1928), he/she concludes, is "healthy, attractive, and uses a 'Gilette.'"[58] Still, the model of state-based cinema for national production is underscored.

This crônica reveals how Eisenstein—not just his films but his auteur-figure—had become a sign that Latin American artists and intellectuals were eager to embrace in order to locate a place for their own cinemas within world cinema debates. Intellectuals and filmmakers thus sought out Eisenstein as a stamp of approval for the health of their respective national film industries. Although the Mexican case has been examined in some detail, what is perhaps less known is that other Latin Americans also vied for Eisenstein's attention as an arbiter in their project to construct a national film industry. These include, for example, Victoria Ocampo, the crucial broker of Argentine modernism. Eisenstein and Ocampo met in New York and corresponded extensively. Ocampo recounts telling him, "You can show our people how to make good cinema," and fervently believed that his presence would lead to the creation of a national film school in Argentina. But the project fell through because of funding problems.[59]

A striking and revealing ventriloquism of Eisenstein took place in Brazil at a later moment. Mário Peixoto's *Limite* (1930) looms large in the history of Latin American films of the historical avant-gardes. In 1953, the film/theater journal *A Scena Muda* cited Eisenstein's earlier, vociferous praise of this film, based on a screening he had apparently attended in Paris and later registered in a lengthy, detailed article ostensibly entitled "Um filme da América do Sul" in the British journal *The Tattler*.[60] A decade later, the filmmaker Carlos Diegues would publish a "complete" version of Eisenstein's account in a dossier. But in the 1990s, in an interview with a very elderly Peixoto, an article in *Folha de São Paulo* made public the fact that the article was apocryphal and written by Peixoto himself. (A faux French translation of the English version contributed to the authenticity effect.[61])

Notably, Peixoto's apocryphal article eschews the national frame for a broader regional identity. "Eisenstein" (or Peixoto) writes, "South America, at first unknown to me, came alive to me that night [at the screening of *Limite*] . . . in this perturbing capture of universal [film] language." The article also locates an affinity between the Brazilian location and Eisenstein's beloved "ancestral Steppes."[62] In its extensive pages, it shuttles between an intensely personal, very un-Eisensteinian vision of *Limite* and an assertion of the film's importance for an international film culture, one of which Peixoto was well aware from his travels to Europe and his friendship with the members of the Chaplin-Club. Like Eisenstein's Mexico project and his failed Argentine one, the Peixoto anecdote makes clear the extent to which the support of a foreign auteur was mobilized to consecrate a Brazilian one. This Peixoto example does not hinge on a question of influence on the level of film form (his poetics are quite different, and in some senses, opposed, to those of Eisenstein).[63] Its value for my purposes is in its particularly pointed and poignant attempt to inscribe, retrospectively, Brazilian film production into a broader map of cosmopolitan film spectatorship. It transposes the lengthy half-life of Soviet films themselves onto Peixoto's own film, locating as another "instant classic," in an act of ventriloquism that attempts to participate in a dialogue that persisted on disavowing its existence.

Conclusion

In this way, the first Latin American reception of Soviet cinema enacts a counterpoint to Miriam Hansen's seminal concept of vernacular modernism. In "The Mass Production of the Senses" and "Vernacular Modernism: Tracking Cinema on a Global Scale," Hansen puts forth a powerful model for scholars of the modernist period, including those who more recently have sought to challenge the national paradigm in Latin American film studies. My interest here has been to press on the avenues she opens up by tracing a different itinerary of global cinema during this same period. Writers and filmmakers quite ideologically opposed were invested in Soviet cinema, I suggest, because they perceived it as an alternative to the cinematic modernities they encountered in western Europe and the United States. In this sense, Soviet modernity was parallel but not equivalent to their own. I take the phrase "parallel modernities" from Brian Larkin's analysis of the Nigerian reception of cinema from India, in which the parallel modernity of Hindi cinema creates alternative ways of imagining daily life in contemporary Nigeria.[64] Larkin argues that Hindi cinema's prominence in this context derives from the ways in which its films constitute an alternative world for Nigerian viewers—similar but not equivalent to their own—to imagine forms of daily life in a postcolonial context in a way that eschews the Hollywood hegemon.[65] This similarity without equivalence, Larkin shows, affords a gap. And this gap allows viewers to fill in their own experiences of modernity.

Although the viewing practices I have explored here differ from the popular reception described by Larkin (and Hansen), I would argue that Soviet cinema supplied that same interpretive gap. We see this not only in the emphasis on its fierce national character, but also in the frequent observation about Soviet cinema's strikingly swift progress: the triumph over its own "backward" past and its closing in on the colossus of Hollywood on some sort of racetrack of world cinema. In this sense, Soviet cinema offered up a promise for nations and regions struggling with questions of literacy, the tension between rural and urban masses, and the experience of being on the hither side of Euro-American modernity. It is for this reason, too, that Soviet films, despite the relatively short period of their international prowess, have an intense half-life in Latin America, as they also would later in other parts of the Global South: they represent the possibility of a cinema that does not fit neatly onto a consolidating geopolitical map but instead posits a potential itinerary.[66] Long before Latin American filmmakers would dialogue with Soviet cinemas through film form, Latin American artists and intellectuals grappled with the possibility of Soviet cinema on the page.

Thus, I have emphasized not how cinemas from Hollywood were vernacularized in local cultures of film production—a process that has been explored through various concepts, including *transculturation, indigenization,* and *vernacularization*—but the very process of staging confrontations between a variety of sites of the cinema/modernity nexus. And the more such confrontations, the better. This was a way for Latin American audiences to reconfigure their sense of themselves as "voyeurs of, rather than participants in" cinematic modernity.[67] At this moment, being of the world, or cosmopolitan, meant adopting *tactics*—when *strategies* proved unsuccessful—to participate in a conversation that threatened to convert itself into a monologue: what Latin Americans were beginning to perceive as the monotonous roar of globalization.[68]

> SARAH ANN Wells is Assistant Professor of Comparative Literature and Folklore Studies at the University of Wisconsin, Madison. She is the author of *Media Laboratories: Late Modernism in South America* (Northwestern University Press, 2017), the coeditor of *Simultaneous*

Worlds: Global Science Fiction Cinema (University of Minnesota, 2015), and the translator of Gonzalo Aguilar's *New Argentine Film: Other Worlds* (Palgrave, 2008; 2011).

NOTES

1. Thanks to Rielle Navitski, Andrea Cuarterolo, Gonzalo Aguilar, and Luciana Sá Leitão Corrêa de Araújo for bibliographic advice and materials and Perin Gurel and Jesse Constantino for comments on an early draft. A very special thanks to Saulo Pereira de Mello and the Arquivo Mário Peixoto in Rio de Janeiro. H. P. Tew. "Cinema in the Argentine," *Close Up* (Territet, Switzerland), February 1930, 140–145.

2. *Potemkin* was first screened at the Cine Opera, where it was shown twenty-two times before opening in other theaters in the city center. It is not clear which of the film's censored versions was shown in Buenos Aires, but since Probst worked with a German branch of Soviet distributors, it was probably the same cut version. See Kristin Thompson, "Eisenstein's Early Films Abroad," in *Eisenstein Rediscovered*, ed. Ian Christie and Richard Taylor (New York: Routledge, 1993), 52–62.

3. Tew, "Cinema in the Argentine," 142. I also briefly address aspects of this reception in *Media Laboratories: Late Modernist Authorship in South America* (Evanston: Northwestern University Press), 29–30; 43–44; and 51–52.

4. Guillermo de Torre, "El 'cineclub' de Buenos Aires," *La Gaceta Literaria*, April 1, 1930, 5. (The article is signed from Buenos Aires, 1929.) Spain would have to wait until 1930 to publicly screen a Soviet film, *Ivan the Terrible* (most likely *Krylya kholopa* [*Wings of a Serf*, dir. Yuri Tarich, 1926]). Thanks to Alexander Spektor for his assistance with the identification. The film screened alongside *Baby ryazanskie* [*Peasant Women of Ryazan*, dir. Olga Preobrazhenskaya, 1927] in Spanish cineclubs. See *La Época* (Madrid), January 21, 1930, 1; *Popular Film* (Barcelona), February 2, 1930, 2.

5. Juan Piqueras, "Veinte películas sovieticas en Suramérica," *La Gaceta Literaria* (Madrid), September 15, 1929, 2.

6. Tew, "Cinema in the Argentine," 145.

7. Thus, this context troubles what Lúcia Nagib has critiqued as "adversarial transnationalism"—the reading that transnationalism is necessarily a subversive critique of the nation. Lúcia Nagib, introduction to *Theorizing World Cinema*, ed. Lúcia Nagib (London: I. B. Tauris, 2012), xxiv–xv. Revisions of cosmopolitanisms have countered earlier definitions as universal, detached, or unhooked from the nation, and described cosmopolitanism instead as plural/multiple, local, inflected, lived. See Peng Cheah and Bruce Robbins, *Cosmopolitics: Thinking and Feeling Beyond the Nation* (Minneapolis: University of Minnesota Press, 1998).

8. On the concept of "horizon of expectations," see Hans Robert Jauss, *Toward an Aesthetic of Reception*, trans. Timothy Bahti (Minneapolis: University of Minnesota Press, 1982). Soviet film of the 1920s would have an impact on film production in Latin America in the work of auteurs of the 1960s–1970s, including Glauber Rocha, Tomás Gutiérrez Alea, Fernando Solanas, and Leon Hirszman. Beginning in the early 1950s, the first book-length translations by Sergei Eisenstein, Vsevolod Pudovkin, and others

would begin to be published in Latin America by diverse presses, including Sur (Buenos Aires) and the leftist Editôra Iris (São Paulo) that published, for example, a translation of Pudovkin's writings on montage in 1954.

9. Eisenstein's fascination with Mexico can be read back into his later films in various ways, both formal and philosophical. In turn, Eisenstein and his cinematographer Eduard Tisse influenced a generation of key Mexican filmmakers. See Masha Salazkina, *In Excess: Sergei Eisenstein's Mexico* (Chicago: University of Chicago Press, 2009). See also Laura Podalsky, "Patterns of the Primitive: Sergei Eisenstein's ¡Que Viva México!" in *Mediating Two Worlds: Cinematic Encounters in the Americas*, eds. John King, Ana M. López, and Manuel Alvarado (London: British Film Institute, 1993), 25–39.

10. Berlin was the first city outside of the Soviet Union to show *Battleship Potemkin*, which first screened in the United States on December 5, 1926, slightly later than its debut in Buenos Aires. See Thompson, "Eisenstein's Early Films Abroad," 54.

11. I have consulted periodicals from Uruguay, Cuba, Mexico, Brazil, Argentina, Peru, and Spain, focusing mostly on periodicals published in the national capitals.

12. Ana M. López, "Early Cinema and Modernity in Latin America," *Cinema Journal* 40, no. 1 (2000): 48–78.

13. See, e.g., *Revista de Avance*, October 15, 1927, 4, 28. The article cites the Comisión Revisora de Películas as stating that *Potemkin* was shut down after an initial screening because it "enflamed the public's passion" (28).

14. For example, a screening of *Potemkin* at the Cine Opera in Rio de Janeiro was shut down in medias res by the military police during the dictatorship of the 1960s–1970s. (Author's personal conversation with Saulo Pereira de Mello, August 2014.)

15. A literary-journalistic genre.

16. See Masha Salazkina, "Moscow-Rome-Havana: A Film-Theory Road Map," *October* 139 (2012): 97–116.

17. José Manuel Valdés-Rodríguez, "Letras: Rusia a los doce años," *Revista de Avance* (Havana), January 15, 1929, 152.

18. José Manuel Valdés-Rodríguez, "El montaje cinematográfico y Eisenstein," *Social* (Havana), May 1932; repr. in *Avances de Hollywood: Crítica cinematográfica en América Latina, 1915–1945*, ed. Jason Borge (Rosario, AN: Beatriz Viterbo, 2005).

19. These books also appear in the library of Mário Peixoto. Peixoto and Octávio de Faria's travels to Europe made possible their exposure to these and many other works on international film culture (Arquivo Mário Peixoto, Rio de Janeiro).

20. The Cine Club of the Amigos del Arte anticipates the cosmopolitan film culture of the *cineclubismo* of the 1950s–1960s and key institutions for screening Soviet films such as Cine Cosmos in Buenos Aires, where many intellectuals of the next generation would first see them. On this pioneering Cine Club, see *Amigos del Arte, 1924–1942*, eds. Patricia Artundo and Marcelo Eduardo Pacheco (Buenos Aires: Museo de Arte Latinoamericano de Buenos Aires / Fundación Constantini, 2008), esp. the articles by Fernando Martín Pena and Gonzalo Aguilar. See also Jorge Miguel Consuelo, "Los origines del cineclubismo en la Argentina y 'La Gaceta Literaria,'" (Alicante, ES:

Biblioteca Virtual Miguel de Cervantes, 2000), http://www.cervantesvirtual.com/nd/ark:/59851/bmcf76b3.

21. *O Fan* and the Chaplin-Club were codirected by Plínio Süssekind Rocha, Almir Castro, Octávio de Faria, and Cláudio Mello. Over a decade later in Rio, the Faculdade Nacional de Filosofia's Clube de Cinema, organized by Süssekind Rocha, offered a public screening of *Potemkin*, along with fragments of *Alexander Nevsky* (dir. Sergei Eisenstein, 1938), advertised in *A Manhã* by a columnist who signed himself "Long-Shot" (in English). Other issues of *A Manhã* published fragments of Eisenstein's filmography and translated excerpts of his *Film Sense*. See the column "Cortes de Cámara," *A Manhã* (Rio de Janeiro), July 14, 1945, 6; July 18, 1946, 9; November 24, 1946, 6; and July 27, 1947, 6.

22. Octávio de Faria, "Cinema russo e cinema brasileiro," *O Fan* (Rio de Janeiro), October 1928, 2, 3.

23. See "Transcrevendo... O Cinema Sonoro e os Manifestos dos Tres Cineastas Russos," *O Fan*, June 1930, 10–14; "Transcrevendo: Dziga Vertof e o 'Cine-Olho,'" *O Fan* 9, December 1930, 21–25.

24. See also Ismael Xavier, *Sétima arte: Um culto moderno* (Rio de Janeiro: Editora Perspectiva, 1978), 207.

25. Aluízio Bezerra Coutinho, "Uma orientaçao fecunda na arte do cinema," *O Fan*, September 1929, 1.

26. Advertisement, *El Universal* (Mexico City), April 15, 1927, 5.

27. See, e.g., Mario de Campos, "De Hollywood a Leningrado: O film americano e o film europeo," *A Manhã*, March 17, 1928, 1 (reporting from New York City). Jason Borge's *Latin American Writers and the Rise of Hollywood Cinema* (New York: Routledge, 2008) analyzes the importance of these figures during the same period.

28. L. S Marinho, "Eisenstein em Hollywood," *Cinearte* (Rio de Janeiro), August 5, 1930, 12.

29. "Con el Creador del *Acorazado Potemkin*," *Social*, March 1930, quoted in Alejo Carpentier, *El cine, décima musa*, ed. Salvador Arias (Havana: Instituto Cubano de Artes e Industria Cinematográficos, 2011), 53.

30. "No Mundo da Téla," *Correio da Manhã* (Rio de Janeiro), April 12, 1930, 9.

31. Evaldo Coutinho, "Tempestades sobre a Ásia," *Jornal do Commercio* (Recife, BR), October 2, 1930, 12.

32. On the Brazilian case, see Xavier, *Sétima arte*, esp. 125–130. On the US case, see Thompson, "Eisenstein's Early Films Abroad."

33. De Faria, "Cinema russo e cinema brasileiro," 3.

34. "Una nueva producción cinemática de Eisenstein: 'Antes y ahora,'" *La Pluma* (Montevideo), April 1, 1930, 143. A version of *Potemkin*—edited and with sound added in Buenos Aires in 1943—was not screened in Montevideo until 1944. The screening was funded by the periodical *Cine Radio Actualidad*. Earlier, in 1938, Eisenstein's *Alexander Nevsky* was screened in Montevideo. See http://www.uruguaytotal.com/estrenos.

35. See Peter Wollen, "Cinema/Americanism/The Robot," *New Formations* 8 (1989): 7–34.

36. Olympio Guilherme, "Questão de gosto..." *Cinearte*, January 8, 1930, 10.
37. "5 minutos de intervalo," *Caras y Caretas* (Buenos Aires), October 13, 1934, 130.
38. See, e.g., Octávio de Faria, "O scenario e o futuro do cinema," *O Fan*, August 1928, 2; Octávio de Faria, "A Cinematographica de Poudovkine," *O Fan*, June 1929, 4.
39. See "A imagem e o som," *O Fan*, June 1930, 37.
40. See Octávio de Faria, "Transformações do mundo pelo cinema sonoro," *O Fan*, December 1930, 64.
41. "Notas de cine: El film hablado," *La Pluma*, June 1, 1929, 34–35.
42. Dudley Andrew, "Time Zones and Jetlag: The Flows and Phases of World Cinema," in *World Cinemas, Transnational Perspectives*, eds. Nataša Ďurovičová and Kathleen Newman (New York: Routledge, 2010), 59–89.
43. In general, Soviet cinema is not as popular among the leftist press as we might expect. Argentina's most experimental leftist journal, *Contra* (1933), for example, never mentions it, and Peru's *Amauta* (1926–1930) only mentions it briefly in passing.
44. César Vallejo, "La pantalla: Rusia inaugura un nuevo cine," in *Ensayos y reportajes completos*, ed. Manuel Miguel de Priego (Lima: Pontífica Universidad Católica del Peru, 2002), 46–56. (First published in *Rusia en 1931* [Madrid: Ediciones Ulises, 1931]). In this sense, *Tungsten* recalls one of Eisenstein's rich failures, his project to make a film of *Capital*, referenced in this crónica.
45. "Palco tela e picadeiro," *O homem do povo*, April 13, 1931, 4. *O homem do povo* was published in São Paulo from 1931 to 1932, following Oswald and Galvão's recent affiliation with the Communist Party and her trip to Argentina, where she likely first saw Soviet films.
46. Patrícia Galvão, *Industrial Park*, trans. Elizabeth and K. David Jackson (Lincoln: University of Nebraska Press, 1993), 28.
47. Quoted in Siegfried Kracauer, *Theory of Film: The Redemption of Physical Reality* (Princeton, NJ: Princeton University Press, 1997), 160. Given the description, the film they watch appears to be Pudovkin's *Mother*.
48. Galvão, *Parque industrial* (Porto Alegre: Editora da Universidade Federal de São Carlos, 1994), 78.
49. This article from *La Prensa* was repr. in the distributor journal *La Película* (Buenos Aires), July 28, 1927, 15.
50. Jorge Luis Borges, "Street Scene," *Sur*, Summer 1932, 198–199. My translation.
51. Vallejo, "La pantalla," 156.
52. Alejo Carpentier, *Carteles* (Havana), October 7, 1928; repr. in Alejo Carpentier, *El cine, décima musa* in Arias 2011, 22–23.
53. Humberto Mauro, "Cinema falado no Brasil [pt. 1]," *Cinearte*, May 11, 1932, 10.
54. Humberto Mauro, "Cinema falado no Brasil [pt. 2], *Cinearte*, July 27, 1929, 3. See also Cláudio Aguiar Almeida, "O Cinema Brasileiro no Estado Novo: O diálogo com a Itália, Alemanha e URSS," *Revista de Sociologia e Política* 12 (1999): 121–129. Similar claims were made in an article published in the distributor journal *La Película*, September 2, 1926, 23; November 25, 1926, 21; August 4, 1927, 1.
55. *Cinearte*, July 23, 1937, 3.

56. *Cinearte*, October 15, 1935, 12.
57. Ibid., 32.
58. Ibid., 35.
59. Victoria Ocampo describes her meeting and spending time with Eisenstein in New York in *Autobiografía III* (Buenos Aires: Ediciones Fundación Victoria Ocampo, 2006), 191–198, where she also publishes correspondence with him regarding his potential contribution to her journal *Sur*. *Testimonios, 1920–1934* (Buenos Aires: Ediciones Fundación Sur) describes her experience meeting Eisenstein in New York.
60. Earlier, *O Fan* had compared *Limite* to Soviet films; see Xavier, *Sétima arte*, 217. The Clube de Cinema of the 1940s would also screen *Limite* with Soviet films, suggesting a link between them.
61. The article in *A Scena Muda* features an unattributed quote by Eisenstein praising effusively the new cinema from South America that would give the world a "message." See Paulo Brandão, "Uma Lenda (*Limite*) e un Nome (Mário Peixoto), *A Scena Muda*, January 14, 1953, 7. The complete version of the apocryphal article was first published in Portuguese in an issue of the journal *Arquitetura*, edited by Carlos Diegues (August 1965): 21–24. During the dictatorship, *Limite* was also recalled for six months by censors, along with early Soviet films, before being released; *Potemkin* did not have the same luck. See Saulo Pereira de Mello, "Peixoto escreveu artigo que atribuiu a Eisenstein," *Folha de São Paulo*, May 17, 1993, 3. For an in-depth account of the apocryphal article as a statement of Peixoto's own poetics, see Pereira de Mello, "Introdução," in *Mário Peixoto: Escritos sobre cinema*, ed. Saulo Pereira de Mello (Rio de Janeiro: Aeroplano Editora, 2000), 11–41; Pereira de Mello, "Um filme da América do Sul," in ibid., 155–203.
62. I cite from the version of the apocryphal article published in *Arquitetura* (August 1965), 22.
63. See Pereira de Mello, *Mário Peixoto*, 38.
64. "Indian Films and Nigerian Lovers: Media and the Creation of Parallel Modernities," *Africa* 67, no. 3 (1997): 406–440.
65. In the later article, Hansen notes, in passing, "the alternative modernity offered by the Soviet Union and communism." See "Vernacular Modernism: Tracking Cinema on a Global Scale," in Ďurovičová and Newman, *World Cinemas, Transnational Perspectives*, 293.
66. See, for example, Jessica Ka Yee Chan, "Translating 'Montage': The Discreet Attractions of Soviet Montage for Chinese Revolutionary Cinema," *Journal of Chinese Cinemas* 5, no. 3 (2011): 197–218; Josephine Woll, "The Russian Connection: Soviet Cinema and the Cinema of Francophone Africa," in *Focus on African Films*, ed. Françoise Pfaff (Bloomington: Indiana University Press, 2004), 223–240.
67. López, "Early Cinema and Modernity," 53.
68. On tactics versus strategies, see Michel de Certeau, *The Practice of Everyday Life* (Berkeley: University of California Press, 1984), 29–42.

Guillermo de Torre, "The 'Cineclub' of Buenos Aires," *La Gaceta Literaria* (Madrid), April 1, 1930

> *Intimately connected to both European and Latin American avant-gardes, writer and critic Guillermo de Torre (1900–1971) moved between his native Madrid, Paris, and Buenos Aires. He was closely linked to the Ultraísta poetry movement and the author of early critical works on avant-garde literature. In this piece, which was published alongside an article on the cineclub of Madrid, de Torre traces the emergence of cosmopolitan cinephilia in Argentina's capital.*

BUENOS AIRES, TOO, NOW has its own Cineclub, which has just concluded its first series after having held fifteen very interesting sessions. The only strange thing is that in this city, overflowing with movie theaters and spectators—without a doubt, the largest consumer of films of any Spanish-speaking market—the formation of such a society had not taken place earlier. But multitudinous environments leave little space for the gathering of select groups. Thus the Cineclub of Buenos Aires emerged, perhaps a bit precipitously, without the support of any artistic entity to back it, without being able to count among its organizers persons of truly wide renown, who would have attracted the attention of a more extensive and cultivated audience. In spite of this, given impetus as it was by competent youths of true good will, holding its sessions in the prestigious auditorium of the Amigos del Arte, the Cineclub was able to conclude its first season with the sympathy and full confidence of its numerous spectators.

Here is a brief overview of its programs. What has been lacking in them is the almost total absence of modern novelties, of authentically new works, such as those that tend to receive preferential exhibition in European cineclubs or specialized venues.

Economic difficulties, the lack of organization, and of contact with similar organizations, impeded this. But, in the absence of such incentives, the sessions of the Cineclub of Buenos Aires—in a manner similar to Madrid's Cineclub—were structured around goals that were historical, retrospective and, in short, didactic. There was, as here, an Anthology of the Comic Film, very complete and well organized, with the inclusion, not only of well-known prewar clowns of the Mack Sennett school but also less well-remembered actors like Charles Bowers, Larry Semon, and the once-again-popular Harry Langdon. Additionally, we also had a retrospective session, The Evolution of Cinema, very representative if necessarily schematic. There were other less predictable sessions: An Homage to Paul Leni and the Mystery Film, Sports and the Cinema, Documentary Films, Anthology of the Animated Film, etc.

It was not only in the genre-based or retrospective sessions that the projected works revived before our retinas the touchingly puerile stages of cinema's childhood—such as, in general, all the so-called prewar films—but also others that represent more evolved moments; to wit, the little-known and highly expressive work by [Josef von Sternberg], *The Salvation Hunters*; the famous [*Cabinet of Dr.*] *Caligari*, by Robert Wiene; *The Saga of Gosta Berling*, by [Mauritz] Stiller; and others.[1]

Masterpieces that, despite having been shown in ordinary theaters, only received true consideration in the Cineclub: [*The Passion of*] *Joan of Arc*, by [Carl Theodor] Dreyer; *Metropolitan Symphony* [*Berlin: Symphony of a Great City*], by [Walter Ruttmann]; *St. Sylvester's Night* [*New Year's Eve*], by Lupu Pick. With regard to the purely and specifically avant-garde films, the Cineclub could only show those imported by French filmmaker Benjamin Fondane for the Amigos del Arte. Among them: *L'étoile de mer* by Man Ray and the famous, furious *Un chien andalou* by Luis Buñuel, screened in Buenos Aires not without some scandal, but before being shown in Madrid and only two months after its premiere in Paris. (Buenos Aires breaks all "records"[2] concerning the speed of its theatrical and cinematic imports. It's a pity it can't maintain the same position with regard to the vitality of its own film production.)

But the most significant novelty that the Cineclub de Buenos Aires can offer in comparison with similar clubs in Europe is the abundance of films from Soviet Russia, which are prohibited by the censors in Europe, and which are shown here publicly without causing much shock. So we have had the good fortune to view a good group of Russian works that have placed the cinematic art of this country at the forefront of Europe. Such as: the highly celebrated *Battleship Potemkin*, and later, *October*, by [Sergei] Eisenstein; *The Sixth Part of the World*, by Dziga [Vertov]; *The End of St. Petersburg*, by [Vsevolod] Pudovkin; *The Village of Sin [Peasant Women of Ryazan]*, by Olga [Preobrazhenskaya].

The simple and rapid enumeration of these films gives a sufficient idea of the appeal held by the first season of the Cineclub's screenings, which will resume at the beginning of next autumn. I should note that, as a complement, all the screenings were accompanied by introductory lectures by young writers and cinephiles. I note, firstly among these, the names of some of the founders of the Cineclub of Buenos Aires: León Klimovsky, Felipe Debernardi, Horacio Coppola, and José Luis Romero. There were also lectures by Néstor Ibarra, Romero Brest, Héctor Eandi, and the author of these lines.

From the foregoing it should be clear that the Cineclub of Buenos Aires, well oriented from its beginnings and on the correct course, now only needs to avail itself of better resources, with the goal of incorporating into its programs works of absolute and essential novelty. It must establish relationships with European cineclubs, and especially with Madrid's, which will contribute to refining its guiding principles and to enriching its screenings, obtaining films that would otherwise be impossible to obtain here. We must cultivate the vitality of organizations like the Cineclub, indispensable in milieus where the artistic hierarchy of cinema is exposed to a thousand corrupting influences, where the best-intentioned spectators feel their taste threatened by the miscellany offered by common movie theaters. The Cineclub will be the only refuge for this art as such, as long as specialized venues do not emerge, as long as the typical movie theaters of the city center (and in Buenos Aires there are no fewer than ten within four blocks) indiscriminately lavish the excellent and the detestable on a public that is more addicted than cinephilic.

Translated by Rielle Navitski

RIELLE NAVITSKI is Assistant Professor of Theater and Film Studies at the University of Georgia. She is the author of *Public Spectacles of Violence: Sensational Cinema and Journalism in Early Twentieth-Century Mexico and Brazil* (Duke University Press, 2017).

Notes

1. (Unless otherwise indicated all notes are from the editors.) Throughout, we have replaced de Torre's nonstandard versions of directors' names with standard spellings or transliterations in brackets. English-language release titles, where substantially different from the titles given by de Torre, are provided in brackets.

2. In English in original.

Chapter 6

A Gaze Turned toward Europe: Modernity and Tradition in the Work of Horacio Coppola

Andrea Cuarterolo

> From my window. . . . I see the real illuminated: I find—from a determined point of view—an image, one could say, of my own world. When from the infinite possible points of view from my window, I choose the one that is for me the most essential and revealing of the presence of the real—my image is an *imagema*. . . .[1] My work is an optical image of the real, transcribed by the camera and contained in the final image is the testimony of my identity as author: testimony, apparent fragment of reality, creature of my vision, now liberated to live its own life according to its nature.
>
> —Horacio Coppola, *Imagema*[2]

THE PERIOD OF AVANT-GARDE movements in the 1920s marks the beginning of a singular moment, in which, for the first time, one can speak of a certain parallelism between modernity in the visual arts—above all, painting and photography—and filmic modernity. This is also, aside from cinema's earliest years, the phase where one most often encounters photographers who are simultaneously dedicated to or experimenting with the seventh art.

The still images and films of these new artists should not be studied in isolation, but must be inserted in the broader context of their indisputably intermedial works. Furthermore, this is perhaps the last period in the history of cinema that demands a historiographic approach that necessarily links the two media. In this essay, I analyze the emergence during the interwar years of a series of artistic movements that introduced, in film and photography, an innovative and novel gaze toward the reality of their time. Although the majority of these avant-garde movements arose in Europe, their influence had a much wider scope, including in Latin America, where they confronted and eventually displaced the first wave of modernism. I analyze how the new ideas introduced by these innovative movements were adopted and reformulated in the Argentine context in the specific work of an artist who to some extent introduced visual modernism to this country's photography and cinema: Horacio Coppola.

In Argentina, as in most of Latin America, the influences of the avant-garde did not touch photography or cinema until the 1930s, and in general they did so in a short-lived and diffuse fashion. Furthermore, in the cinema, this process of formal experimentation was almost immediately interrupted by the coming of sound, which initiated an accelerated period of industrialization that was ever more driven by market imperatives and populist politics. However, although in general this production is scant and isolated, these films must be inscribed within a broader context, with a regional scope, where auteurs like Mário Peixoto (*Limite*, 1930), Humberto Mauro (*Ganga bruta*, 1933), Rodolfo Rex Lustig and Adalberto Kemeny (*São Paulo, A Sinfonia da metrópole/São Paulo, Symphony of the Metropolis*, 1929) in Brazil; Emilio Amero (*777*, 1929), Sergei Eisenstein, (*¡Que Viva México!* 1931), Paul Strand (*Redes*, 1934), and Manuel Álvarez Bravo (*Disparos en el Istmo/Shots Fired on the Isthmus*, 1935) in Mexico; or Armando Rojas Castro (*Santiago*, 1933) in Chile, were giving shape to a true process of modernization in cinematic language which, although brief, served to present alternative models of filmmaking, which would later function as antecedents for a second avant-garde in the 1960s. As Paul Schroeder Rodríguez suggests, these films are manifestations of a global avant-garde rhizome, which shared aspirations of rupture "in relation to the visual and narrative conventions of cinema that predominated in this period, and in some cases, of rupture with the dominant *criollo*[3] values, whether these were liberal or conservative, positivist or no."[4]

The majority of these auteurs who brought avant-garde trends to Latin America were European or had been educated in the Old World. In Argentina, the emblematic example is Coppola who, like many young people of favorable economic position, had experienced an important coming-of-age voyage to Europe. There, he attended courses in the Photography Department at the Bauhaus, at this time directed by the photographer and mathematician Walter Peterhans, where he met other *Neues Sehen* (New Vision) artists such as Ellen Auerbach and his future wife, Grete Stern.

Although Lázló Moholy-Nagy was no longer at Bauhaus when Coppola arrived in Berlin and although the Argentine photographer would some years later express a certain antipathy for him and his photographic work—probably because of the Hungarian's tendency toward experimentation and the nonfigurative—the work of Moholy-Nagy perhaps has the closest affinities to Coppola's later photography. As Natalia Brizuela argues, it is "impossible not to see the resonances of *7am New Year's Day* (1930) and *From the Radio Tower of Berlin* (1929), both by Moholy-Nagy . . . —to name only a few examples—in *Victoria esquina Bolívar* (*Corner of Victoria and Bolívar*, 1936), *Mateo y su victoria* (*Mateo and His Victory*, 1931), *Calle Corrientes* (*Corrientes Street*, 1936), and so many other works by Coppola."[5] Like Moholy-Nagy, Coppola would make a simultaneous passage through photography and cinema, translating to his work many of the ideas and objectives of the New Vision. However, this was not a case of an imitative or purely mechanical translation. Even without local points of reference, Coppola was able to appropriate this avant-garde language and reformulate it in an absolutely personal manner, managing to reflect in his images an innovative synthesis between modernity and tradition, completely absent in the European movements of the interwar years, but particularly appropriate for a city where modernity still had the character of an unfinished project.

New Photography for New Societies: The *Film und Foto* Exhibition and the Advance of the Avant-Gardes

Perhaps the first great effort to put film and photography in dialogue and to attempt a definition of both media through their connections emerged in this moment with *Film und Foto* (FiFo), an ambitious avant-garde exposition held in the German city of Stuttgart between May 18 and July 7, 1929. It was organized by the Deutscher Werkbund (DWB), an association inspired by the Arts and Crafts movement, which gathered together architects, artists and businessmen to seek a reconciliation between art and technology. Founded in Munich in 1907, the principal goal of this organization was to improve the quality of professional work through cooperation between art, industry, and handicrafts, with the aim of allowing Germany to compete with powers such as Great Britain or the United States.

In this period, art photography was emerging from a stage where it had imitated painting—a tendency at its height with movements such as pictorialism in the immediately preceding years—to seek its independence, aligning itself with newer artistic disciplines such as cinema or graphic design. The exhibition *Film und Foto* brought together close to twelve hundred images by a hundred and fifty photographers and some sixty films, which represented the most recent trends in European, American, and Soviet photography and cinema.[6] The photographic sections of *Film und Foto* embraced a wide spectrum of content, with techniques and genres as diverse as photojournalism, photomontage, photocollage, aerial photography, X-ray photography, rayogrammes,[7] graphic compositions, texts and images, and even microphotography. The selection of artists was as varied as the range of techniques, and included works by key figures of the pantheon of international photography, such as Eugène Atget, Andreas Feininger, Umbo, El Lissitzky, Germain Krull, Aenne Biermann, John Heartfield, Man Ray, Moholy-Nagy, Edward and Brett Weston, Walter Peterhans, Albert Renger-Patzsch, Hannah Höch, Piet Zwart, and Karel Teige, together with works by anonymous news photographers and students of the principal European photography schools, including the Bauhaus in Dessau and the Folkwang School in Essen. In parallel with the photographic exhibition, a film festival was organized, programmed by the experimental filmmaker Hans Richter, in which the latest avant-garde cinema from Russia, Europe, and the United States was exhibited. More than sixty films were shown, including landmarks of filmic vanguards such as the *Cabinet of Dr. Caligari* (*Das Kabinett des Dr. Caligari*, dir. Robert Wiene, 1919), *Battleship Potemkin* (*Bronenosets Potyomkin*, dir. Sergei Eisenstein, 1925), *Diagonal Symphony* (*Diagonal-Symphonie*, dir. Viking Eggeling, 1925), *Ballet mécanique* (dir. Fernand Leger, 1925), *Berlin, Symphony of a Great City* (*Berlin, die Symphonie der Großstadt*, dir. Walter Ruttmann, 1926), *The Passion of Joan of Arc* (*La Passion de Jeanne d'Arc*, dir. Carl Dreyer, 1928), *L'etoile de mer* (dir. Man Ray, 1928), *Inflation* (dir. Hans Richter, 1928), *The Man with a Movie Camera* (*Chelovek s kino-apparatom*, dir. Dziga Vertov, 1929), *The Bridge* (*De brug*, dir. Joris Ivens, 1929), and even *The Circus* (dir. Charles Chaplin, 1925). During this exhibition Richter proposed an early taxonomy of avant-garde film, making a distinction between pure or documentary film and narrative art film.

One of the objectives of this exhibition was to highlight the importance of new trends in photography in the development of avant-garde cinema of the period, and for this reason some artists such as Man Ray even showed their photographic and filmic works simultaneously, initiating a tendency that would have prestigious adherents such as Helmar Lerski, Paul Strand, and Lázló Moholy-Nagy himself, who, influenced by these screenings, shot his first film the same year.

Film und Foto was the first exhibition to emphasize the informative and educational power of the new modes of mechanical reproduction and mass dissemination, and also the first attempt to connect film and photography by means of an intermedial comparison of themes, applications, and aesthetic resources. Yet perhaps its greatest contribution was to serve as a showcase for the artistic ideas of the New Vision, an avant-garde movement that emerged at the beginning of the 1920s, based on a structuralist vision of reality, which emphasized the specifically photographic character of the image, breaking definitively with the traditional movements of art photography.

The Rejection of Pictorialism: The Neues Sehen and the Estrangement of the Real

As previously noted, during the interwar period a significant shift occurred within the photographic medium, which consisted essentially of a fierce rejection of the pictorialist tendencies dominant up to that period, in which photography sought to emulate painting. At this moment, three main movements emerged that proposed to work exclusively with the specificity, or singular characteristics, of the photographic medium: the New Vision, the *Neues Sachlichkeit* (New Objectivity), and Direct Photography. These three movements coincided in their opposition to the pictorial models that, according to their point of view, only resulted in images with little appeal, distanced from reality. They proposed that photography be considered an autonomous artistic practice, with its own laws of composition and lighting. Although agreeing on their basic principles, the New Vision—perhaps the most revolutionary of the three movements—advocated for experimentation and the use of different technical procedures for photographic expression, an attribute that provoked various criticisms from other sectors of the art world, who accused its practitioners of excessive experimentalism and an inability to produce results of uniform technical quality.

The New Vision movement initially emerged in Germany, but toward the end of the 1920s it had taken on international proportions, with adherents in various European countries, the United States, and even Japan. Essentially, this movement proposed to look through the camera lens in a way that was new and unprecedented, deforming the real, tightening its framing to make the frame a basic element of the composition. They sought in photography a degree of social and political commitment, and to fulfill this commitment it was necessary to revolutionize visual thought and disrupt conventional ways of looking at things. They proposed to use the camera to discover, more than to register, creating with it disconcerting sensations and achieving in images an estrangement of the real or the quotidian. This principal goal translated to a preference for innovative compositions, such as overhead and extreme low angles, which were the formal opposites of those used by pictorialism and which sought to generate an impact on the spectator, revealing extraordinary aspects of everyday objects. The majority of these avant-garde photographers also cultivated what has been called the "aesthetic of the fragment," making use of extreme close-ups or an excessive fragmentation that made faces and objects almost unrecognizable. Oblique vanishing points were also common, which allowed photographers to work with a more dynamic visual plane, in addition to marked contrasts of light and shadow, which at times produced large dark areas in the image. There were active experiments with photomontage—a technique very favorable to sociopolitical commentary, which additionally permitted these photographers to move beyond the limits of abstraction, without having to return to fully figurative images—but also with collage, graphic design and visual techniques from science, such as x-rays, microphotography, and aerial and astronomical photography. In this period, Alexander Rodchenko wrote a manifesto that perfectly summarizes some of the principles and objectives of this movement: "By showing common things in an uncommon light, artistic techniques should contribute to raising man's awareness of his relationship to the universe. Close-ups and unexpected and dynamic angles of vision must break with the automatism of perception and expand the field of consciousness. If I present a tree seen from below, like an industrial object—a chimney, for example—this will be seen as constituting a revolution for the bourgeois eye."[8]

The New Vision movement was composed principally of young photographers from the Russian and German Constructivist movements, such as Rodchenko, El Lissitzky, and Walter Peterhans. But the central figure of this movement was, without a doubt, Moholy-Nagy, who in parallel to his work as a painter, sculptor and set designer, dedicated himself actively to photography and cinema and also produced a series of pioneering theoretical studies of the relationship between the two media, including his polemical book *Malerei, Photographie, Film* (Painting, Photography, Film, 1925), which influenced multiple generations of German photographers. In tune with the ideas of the New Vision movement, Moholy-Nagy maintained that, in comparison with painting and other legitimized arts, the camera was much less marked by ideological precepts and could approach reality in a much more objective way, and for this reason he was especially interested in photography and cinema, media that he considered much less contaminated by capitalist ideology. In this sense, the Renaissance perspective disseminated by traditional painting was for Moholy-Nagy the principal manifestation of a bourgeois mentality, because it transformed space in order to present a unifying and monolithic vision of the objects in the frame. The photographer proposed to combat and destabilize this type of perspective in order to help liberate the spectator's consciousness and stimulate him or her to construct a more objective vision in the act of perception.

Moholy-Nagy was one of those principally responsible for introducing photography into the influential Bauhaus school, where he worked as director of the metalworking workshop and the course Material and Space. This important German school of design, art, and architecture, founded in Weimar in 1919 by the architect Walter Gropius, had as its principal goal to create a closer relationship between art and life. For this purpose, he proposed to organize a new type of education that, on one hand, taught the fine arts as if they were artisanal crafts—avoiding the radical technologization of the work of art—and, on the other, incorporated into its programs the greatest possible number of arts and trades, eliminating specialization in its students.[9] This profound reform in artistic instruction should serve, in the end, as a basis for the transformation of bourgeois society in the period, the ultimate goal of the school's founders. With the arrival of Moholy-Nagy at the Bauhaus in 1923, photography quickly gained relevance in the curriculum and contributed to the gradual displacement of the expressionist and romantic style that had characterized the school in its first years of existence in favor of the ideas of the New Vision.

Although Moholy-Nagy is best known for his photographic works, the recent discovery of many of his films, considered lost for years, has permitted us to begin studying the important role of his cinematic pieces in the history of avant-garde cinema as well. These works are, furthermore, absolutely indispensable for analyzing the photographer's coherent visual and theoretical project.

His first cinematic work, *Impressions of the Old Port of Marseille* (*Impressionen vom alten Marseiller Hafen*) was shot in 1929, the same year he acted as curator of the *Film und Foto* exhibition, where he was doubtless highly influenced by the avant-garde films exhibited there. In addition, 1929 was the year of the transition to sound in Europe, an event that had a great impact on the cinematic experimentation of the avant-gardes. The high cost of sound productions, monopolies on sound film patents, and the great temptation that commercial cinema presented for filmmakers ultimately modified and slowly annihilated experimental cinema, which was obliged to depend on private initiatives or state support. For this reason, we encounter the paradox that the silent shorts that Moholy-Nagy began to film in this period were at once aesthetically revolutionary for the time and completely anachronistic in technical terms. In *Impressions of the Old Port of Marseille*, Moholy-Nagy rejected any attempt at narrative editing and instead recurred to a type of montage based on associative principles. The result is a film that is almost impressionist in its attempt to capture the atmosphere of the port neighborhood, at that time not only Marseille's poorest but also little known because of its dangerous reputation.

In terms of composition, Moholy-Nagy takes up many of the choices we see reflected in his photographs during this period. Extreme camera angles, oblique framings that slant the horizon creating distortions and deformations, or the strong contrasts between light and shadow are only some of the elements that we see constantly repeated in his film work. In fact, there are shots in the film that are practically identical to images captured by his camera on the same trip. However, Moholy-Nagy makes an innovative contribution in this film through his specific work with movement, which forces the spectator to constantly revise his/her perception of space and the relationship between objects in the frame.

The Influence of Cinema in the Gaze of Horacio Coppola

From his beginnings as a photographer at the end of the 1920s, Horacio Coppola shows a marked tendency toward the modern. However, this phenomenon is not part of a gradual process but rather that, as many scholars have affirmed, as a photographer Coppola was born modern. According to Jorge Schwartz,

> A large number of celebrated artists of the modernist period moved through a trajectory that begins with the figurative to culminate in the abstract and the geometric. With Coppola, a phenomenon occurs that is nothing less than extraordinary: the "evolutionary" line is absent. The thesis that Coppola is modern before the Bauhaus, in addition to being affirmed by the artist himself, is confirmed by critics. . . . Before the 1920s, Horacio Coppola

had assimilated, at a distance, in a fragmentary fashion, the idiom of European modernity, of the Neue Sachlichkeit or New Objectivity, of a New Vision that in his case is already compatible with the daily life of a *mysterious Buenos Aires*.[10]

Before traveling to Europe, Coppola had not had any type of formal education in the field of photography. Undoubtedly, the influence of his older brother Armando—an established photographer with a style that was also unusually modern for the time—was decisive in his almost intuitive formation. Yet without a doubt, his cinephilia and his vast knowledge of experimental cinema of the period were what truly molded his particular approach. As we have seen, the new photographic movements of the 1920s and 1930s had forged strong connections with the seventh art that become particularly obvious in the case of photographer-filmmakers such as Moholy-Nagy, Manuel Álvarez Bravo, and Coppola himself. In 1934, the Spanish writer and art critic Guillermo de Torre, then married to Norah Borges, and closely linked to the literary magazine *Sur*, wrote a significant and illuminating article in which he highlighted the influence of cinema on the photographic movements of the time.[11] The author maintains that

> it is not photography—as is so often thought—whose evolution gave rise to the *cinema*. It is the *cinema* that has given birth to photography, at least the new photography with its unprecedented angles of vision, with its unexpected perspectives. Why? Because it is the cinema—and not in its beginnings either, but already approaching its maturity and setting in motion the camera that previously was still—that made visible, for the first *time*, the graphic and plastic value of unconnected images, the beauty, drama, humor or super-reality of certain shreds of reality that we previously did not perceive. . . .With the example of the *travelling* [shot][12] . . . which perhaps achieves its first truly magnificent expression in Dupont's *Variétés*, the discoveries begin. Simultaneously, the employment of the *close-up*,[13] whose systematic use initially corresponds to the Russian filmmakers—Eisenstein, Pudovkin, Dziga Vertov—contributes to the underlining of purely photographic values and qualities.[14]

Although Coppola is better known today for his photographic work, his first contact with avant-garde movements was in fact through the cinema, which he himself recognizes as the basis for his own autodidactic training.[15] In 1927, León Klimovsky, who at this time worked as a film and jazz critic, organized the first exhibitions of "artistic cinema" at the Anatole France Library in Buenos

Aires. Encouraged by the success of these screenings, the following year he called on a group of artists and intellectuals to create the city's first cineclub, which was baptized the Cine Club de Buenos Aires.[16] Barely twenty-two years old, Coppola was part of the directorial board, which was made up of various young figures in the artistic and cultural milieu of Buenos Aires, including the art critic Jorge Romero Brest, the historian José Luis Romero, and Klimovsky himself. It could count among its members even more distinguished personalities, such as the writers Jorge Luis Borges, César Tiempo, Nicolás Olivari, Sixto Pondal Ríos, Victoria Ocampo, and Ulises Petit de Murat and the visual artists Horacio Butler, Juan Carlos Castagnino, and Lino Spilimbergo, among others. The screenings took place at the Asociación Amigos del Arte, an institution that brought together a group of artists and intellectuals interested in disseminating avant-garde art and which, among other important activities, would sponsor Federico García Lorca's visit to Argentina in 1933, as well as the celebrated lectures of Le Corbusier in 1929, which would be seared into Coppola's young mind.[17] On August 7, 1929, the newspaper *La Nación* published an article announcing the preliminary formation of the group along with its program of action, which would be set in motion with the season of exhibitions that took place between August 21 and November 27 of this year:

> This organization, like its European counterparts, proposes to bring together all those interested in the cinematograph in terms of the knowledge, study and research of cinematic works—especially those that are out of the public's reach because of commercial factors—and also literature related to the seventh art.
>
> The Cine Club, founded by writers, artists and fans of all tendencies and sectors, concretized their goals in this program of action:
>
> (a) An illustrative series or review of films from 1905 to today that suffice to give an idea of the evolution of technique, of directors' conceptions and of artistic unity in the cinematic work.
> (b) Introductions and lectures by poets, critics, essayists and fans, who will attempt to orient the spectator in the discernment of cinematic qualities.
> (c) The importation of films of the French and German vanguards, as well as all those works that for their boldness, because they are ahead of today's tastes or for another reason hold no interest in terms of commercial exploitation.
> (d) The founding of a magazine in which to publish essays by foreign and domestic filmmakers.

(e) Organization of the first cinematic library.
(f) Organization of the first cinémathèque in the country.[18]

This pioneering initiative, which involved the revalorization and study of films at the margins of commercial film circuits but also of industry films with mass appeal that were distinguished by its unusual formal characteristics, was in itself an avant-garde project, which granted cinema an autonomous place in the cultural and intellectual field of the period. In this milieu, Coppola had access to an eclectic variety of films, from works by silent comedians such as Chaplin and Buster Keaton and classic American cinema, to the latest from the French, German, and Soviet avant-gardes. As Fernando Martín Peña suggests,

> The principles of programming seem to have arisen from a combination of specialized readings in French and English, with the added experience of local cinephilia. During these years, the discussions were less about cinema as an artistic entity and more about its expressive autonomy. Klimovsky and Horacio Coppola, in contemporary and later texts, cite Louis Delluc and his postulates regarding *Photogénie*, which constituted the first serious effort to approach a definition of the specifically cinematic, those aspects of cinema not indebted to other arts. From this discussion were derived terms such as "visualism," which would soon become obsolete, but which in this moment served to articulate the desire to approach an "absolute cinema."[19]

Among the most emblematic films shown by the Cine Club of Buenos Aires during its two years of life were *Battleship Potemkin*; *L'étoile de mer*; *Entr'acte*; *Shoulder Arms* (dir. Charles Chaplin, 1918); *The Cabinet of Dr. Caligari*; *Berlin, Symphony of a Great City*; *The Passion of Joan of Arc*; *Moana* (dir. Robert Flaherty, 1926); *Rain* (*Regen*, dir. Joris Ivens and Mannus Franken, 1929); *Destiny* (dir. Fritz Lang, 1921); *The Fall of the House of Usher* (*La chute de la Maison Usher*, dir. Jean Epstein, 1928); *The Student of Prague* (*Der Student von Prag*, dir. Henrik Galeen, 1926); *The Sixth Part of the World* (*Shestaia chast' mira*, dir. Dziga Vertov, 1926); and *À propos de Nice* (dir. Jean Vigo, 1930). If one considers that most of these films were being presented as novelties in a revolutionary exhibition like *Film und foto* in 1929, it should be noted that the same avant-garde films seen in Europe arrived almost simultaneously in Argentina. Indeed, in another article published in *La Gaceta Literaria* in April 1930, the aforementioned Guillermo de Torre, at that time also closely linked to the Cine Club of Buenos Aires, gives a detailed commentary about the films exhibited in the previous year, noting that the most "significant novelty" offered by the association "in comparison with similar clubs in Europe is the abundance of films from Soviet Russia, which are prohibited by the censors in Europe, and which are shown here publicly without causing much shock."[20] After specifically praising the exhibition of *Un chien andalou* (Luis Buñuel, 1929), which premiered in the cineclub two months after screening in Paris and before it was shown in Madrid, "not without some scandal," De Torre concludes his summary affirming that "Buenos Aires beats all 'records' concerning the speed of theatrical and cinematic imports. It's a pity it can't maintain the same position with regard to the vitality of its own film production."[21] The founders of the Cine Club of Buenos Aires were, however, quite conscious of this lack, and for this reason in 1931 they decided to hold their final screening in order to dedicate themselves to a goal they considered much more significant: the production of their own films.[22] Three filmmaking groups were formed, led respectively by Jorge Luis Borges, León Klimovsky, and Néstor Ibarra; albeit, as David Oubiña notes, there is no concrete evidence today regarding whether these efforts came to fruition, Coppola, at least, would concretize this objective slightly later and on his own initiative, when he shot his first three films during his European sojourn.[23] Although some of these films precede the advent of sound cinema by a few years, they are artisanal films that, like those of Moholy-Nagy, are advanced in aesthetic terms, but still respond to the technical and narrative canons of the silent era.

Between 1931 and 1932, Coppola published in numbers four and five of *Sur* a photo-essay in two parts entitled "Seven Themes: Buenos Aires."[24] The thirteen images of the city included in the magazine show a fragmented city, with striking shots from low and high angles and extreme segmentations, which render figures geometric and, in some cases, almost abstract. Definitively, one finds in these photographs all the formal characteristics of the European New Vision, with which Coppola had thus far had no contact.[25] Although the lectures Le Corbusier gave in Buenos Aires in 1929 had had an important influence on the young photographer's approach, it is evident that the avant-garde films shown in the Cine Club of Buenos Aires and the diverse bibliography on cinema—which, we will see, he acquired in Europe—shaped his gaze toward the city. The fact that Coppola's initial points of reference were filmic and not photographic is in no way coincidental, but rather is related to the specific characteristics of the Argentine cultural field. In contrast with the situation in the cinematic milieu, where the circulation of foreign avant-garde films was varied and constant, local photography suffered from a marked isolation from European and North American modernist movements. As Luis Príamo notes,

> This isolation, however, was not exclusive to our country. The works of avant-garde photographers had difficulty circulating even in their own countries, and one of the reasons for this was the firm implantation of pictorialism as a widely dominant model in the photographic activity showcased in the context of the traditional photo-clubs. In fact, the photography magazines exported by central nations were precisely those published by the photo-clubs. On the other hand, the only photographic club active in Argentina at that moment was the Sociedad Fotográfica Argentina de Aficionados, which was already in decline. This lack of photographic references from the world outside his own home in some ways spared Horacio from all aesthetic confrontations and eventually, from any misguided influences, leaving his sensibility, shaped by his enthusiastic familiarity with modern art and avant-garde cinema, free and disposed to soak up his modern photographic experiences in Europe.[26]

Horacio Coppola and His European Initiation

Coppola took two trips to Europe, a brief one between December 1930 and May 1931, and another of almost three years between October 1932 and August 1935. In the second of these sojourns, doubtless the more important, the photographer moved to Berlin with the goal of studying aesthetics and art history. There he bought a great quantity of books, soon submerging himself in the major film theories of the period. Rudolph Arnheim, Béla Balázs, Paul Rotha, Vsevolod Pudovkin, Jean Epstein, Henri Diamant-Berger, Léon Moussinac, and Raymond Spottiswoode, as well as the magazines *Close Up*, *L'Art Cinématographique*, *Cinema Quarterly*, and *Film Art* were some of the readings that determined, at this time, his particular approach.[27] His objective at this moment was not to dedicate himself to photographic or filmic production, but rather to educate himself in art criticism and develop a theoretical language within this field. However, when he arrived in Berlin, he learned that the Department of Photography in Richard Hamann's Art History program at the University of Marburg (where he had planned to carry out his studies at the suggestion of his teacher, the philosopher Luis Juan Guerrero) had closed. At this point, Fritz Heller, a friend of Guerrero's and the first contact made by Coppola in the city, mentioned the Bauhaus and the photography courses given there by Walter Peterhans, then director of the Photography Department of this school.[28] In this workshop, Coppola had his first contact with the photographers of the New Vision, and particularly with Grete Stern, who would shortly after become his wife.

Peterhans dedicated himself, above all, to the still life, which he constructed meticulously using abstract textures, with an approach often close to that of surrealism. The first images that Coppola made in Europe were in fact studies for Peterhans's course at the Bauhaus. These are shots where nothing is random; instead, objects are carefully analyzed with the end of transfiguring them or making them strange. His *Study No. 2* for the Bauhaus is an emblematic example. In this photograph, Coppola captures a doll from a completely distorted and fragmented angle. What is essentially proposed in this image, in which the inert body becomes almost invisible beneath the infinite folds of the dress, is to generate the estrangement of an utterly domestic object. There is no documentary vocation, but rather an effort to cast a new gaze at the real, making the familiar strange and the quotidian absolutely surprising.

As previously discussed, during his stay in Europe and in parallel with his photographic work, Coppola developed an interest, similar to that of Moholy-Nagy and other avant-garde photographers of the time, in cinema. It was no longer a cinephilic fascination, but rather a true will to creativity. This accounts for the fact that, at the same time he was studying at Bauhaus, he enrolled in a course given at Karl Marx University by the Bulgarian director Slatan Dudow—who had worked as an assistant director on *Metropolis* (dir. Fritz Lang, 1927)—and attended the shooting of the film *Second Youth* (*Reifende Jugend*, 1933) by Carl Froelich. Excited by these experiences, in 1933 Coppola finally bought a sixteen-millimeter Siemens camera, with which he would shoot three films during his travels in Berlin, Paris, and London.

In a trajectory similar to that traced by the New Vision photographers in reaction to the pictorialist tendencies dominant at the beginning of the twentieth century, the filmic avant-garde of the period was fighting to impose an aesthetic alternative to the "cinema of narrative integration" widely exploited by the entertainment industry and still closely linked to traditional arts such as theater or literature. The goal was, instead, to use film language as a pure artistic form, which would produce strong sensations in the spectator and distance cinema from its predominantly narrative aspects. With this objective in mind, these new movements followed two trends that, in spite of their marked differences, coincide in their strong opposition to the dominant cinema: the experimental tendency and the documentary tendency. Like many other artists of his time, Coppola engaged with both tendencies. He began by making experimental film and later definitively turned toward documentary cinema, where he was able to much more fully develop the ideas of the New Vision and the New Objectivity that he was simultaneously putting into practice in his photographic work.

His first film, shot in Berlin in 1933 and entitled *Dream* (*Traum*), is basically an aesthetic study that explores a number of the principles of avant-garde cinema of the interwar period. Realized in an absolutely artisanal fashion, with the help of the photographer Ellen Rosenberg (a business partner of Grete's) and her husband Walter Auerbach, who volunteered themselves as actors, the film was inspired by the poetic and psychological explorations of the surrealist cinema of Luis Buñuel, Germaine Dulac, and René Clair. The cinema, according to Buñuel, was "the best instrument for expressing the world of dreams, emotions, instinct . . . among all the means of human expression, the one most similar to the mind of man, or even better, the one that best imitates the functioning of the mind in a dream state."[29] *Traum* begins with an image of a man slumped on a tabletop, asleep, and the entire absurd story that begins there can be interpreted as the character's oneiric imaginings. For the surrealists, the artwork arose from pure automatism, that is, any form of expression over which the conscious mind did not exert any type of control. These artists attempted to capture, by means of abstract forms or symbolic figures, images of the deeper reality of the human subconscious. To achieve this objective, the surrealist filmmakers made use of a variety of expressive resources, such as the animation of inert objects, metamorphoses, and empty landscapes. *Traum* exploits many of these resources, even as it takes up some of the favored subjects of this movement such as *amour fou*, the theme of the double, irrational impulses and the fusion between fantasy and reality. However, as David Oubiña argues, the film does not have the destructive and anarchic character of *Un chien andalou*, or the somber atmosphere of the films of Dulac or Antonin Artaud. *Traum* brings out, by contrast, the brighter and more ludic side of surrealism, that of films such as *Entr'acte* "with its wild chases, its humorous characters and its absurd disappearing (and appearing) acts or like *Ghosts before Breakfast* (*Vormittagspuk*, Hans Richter, 1928), with its flying shadows, proliferating revolvers, and its little tribe of quotidian objects that rebel before obediently returning to their places when the day starts."[30]

On an aesthetic level, Coppola keeps formal experimentation to a minimum. He uses only a few simple special effects, stopping the camera to make

Fig. 6.1 Still from *Traum* (*Dream*, 1933).

people or objects appear and disappear, and he does not allow himself to be tempted by optical distortions or geometric abstractions that fascinated other photographers of the time who turned to cinema, such as Man Ray or Moholy-Nagy himself. *Traum* is the first and only experimental film by Coppola, who upon his arrival in Paris put aside the subjective experiments characteristic of surrealism to turn definitively to the documentary genre.

In 1934, a trip along the Seine and "the dynamic vision of a black cat submerged in waters disturbed by the passage of a barge," inspired him to film some sequences in sixteen millimeter from the Pont Neuf and the Pont des Arts.[31] Coppola describes this film as "an elemental exercise of camera and montage ... completed on an autumn day in 1934, ... an intent to capture the expression of a determined place, visually analyzing the physical aspects of things and people and presenting the images edited in a simple succession."[32] Indeed, this short, which he titled *Un muelle del Sena* (*A Dock on the Seine*), deliberately avoids postcard images and attempts to present itself as a personal look at this space and the different characters that inhabit it, in a manner similar to the majority of the photographs that he simultaneously took on the same trip and in which he even repeated some motifs and subjects. Like Moholy-Nagy in *Impressions of the Old Port of Marseilles*, Coppola manifests in this film a marked interest in capturing social abandonment in the great metropolis, with images of beggars and homeless people that become an integral part of the Parisian landscape. As we have seen, the will to use the camera as a tool for social criticism was a relevant characteristic of these new photographic movements, which sought to disrupt the traditional bourgeois gaze at reality. Coppola would continue to explore his interest in the images created in London the following year, and even in Argentina, where in 1936 he captures images of life in a slum next to the Riachuelo.

Un muelle del Sena begins with a photograph of a sign of the Pont des Arts and ends with an inverted negative of the same photo. Between these two opposing images, which function as two sides of a single coin, an agglomeration of short, descriptive shots appear in succession almost without continuity and without any kind of hierarchy, as if they were an animated series of photographs. Tramps, some graffiti, garbage floating in the river, excrement, trees, more tramps, the stones of the dock, passersby, boats, smoke from chimneys, fishermen; Coppola constructs with these motifs the "presence without time" that impacted him so deeply upon his arrival in Paris.[33] According to the precepts of the New Vision, the camera is used as a tool of exploration, attempting to reveal what cannot be seen at first glance. The artist has recourse to overhead shots, oblique framings, contrasts of light and shadow, and, above all, extreme fragmentation that allows a play with textures and the denaturing of objects, which renders them generic or unrecognizable.

In the spring of 1935, Coppola traveled to the Ardèche, a municipality halfway between Lyon and Marseille. For a month, he undertook an extensive project of photographic documentation in this rural region as a study for a documentary film that ultimately was never made. His camera would prove to be more attracted to urban motifs, as would be evident in his next short, produced in London this same year, which brings to a close this particular European trilogy. In this brief documentary, entitled *Un domingo en Hampstead Heath* (*A Sunday on Hampstead Heath*), Coppola captures the different events that take place on a single Sunday in this famous London park. As in *Un muelle del Sena*, the film repeats motifs that can be observed in the photographs he simultaneously created in the same period. It is almost as if Coppola worked with a still camera in one hand and a film camera in the other. However, by contrast with his Parisian documentary, here the

Fig. 6.2a and Fig. 6.2b Stills from *Un muelle del Sena* (*A Dock on the Seine*, 1934).

Fig. 6.3 Still from *Un domingo en Hampstead Heath* (*A Sunday on Hampstead Heath*, 1935).

different fragments that make up the film no longer have a cumulative and apparently aleatory function, but rather are part of a carefully constructed narrative that attempts to synthesize the course of a day in this space of leisure, from the early morning, when the visitors begin to arrive, until sundown, when the passersby lose themselves among the frenetic and hypnotic lights of an amusement park. In this film Coppola perfects and refines his more purely cinematic language. Montage becomes a key element, but the camera also takes on greater movement and significance. As David Oubiña highlights, "From *Traum* to *Un domingo en Hampstead Heath*, Coppola constructs his own experience of passage from the avant-gardes to high modernism."[34] This is the longest of his films and also the last he made in Europe. Near the end of 1935, the advance of Nazism and the overall intensification of the social and political situation accelerated Coppola's return to Argentina, shortly after his marriage to the German Jewish Stern. This was the conclusion of his European sojourn and the beginning of his fruitful career in Argentina.

Horacio Coppola and the Modernist Pampa

Coppola and Stern's stay in Buenos Aires was to last only three months, but ended up being definitive. Not long after their arrival, Victoria Ocampo offered them a space at the offices of *Sur* magazine for both to present their photographic work. Although it is not known precisely what photographs were exhibited by the couple in this exposition, we do know, thanks to the reviews published in the period, that it was not an exhibition with a defined thematic structure and that the majority of the material shown in it had been created by the artists in Europe.[35] As Veronica Tell notes, "Coppola and Stern debut on the local photography scene with themes and modes of execution that manifest, in different ways and degrees, innovative characteristics that distance established photographic subjects, like landscapes and portraits, from the conventional or pictorial treatments common up to this point."[36] The notion of photography not as fortuitous capture but as careful construction, the product of a minute observation and study of the object, was present in most of the exhibited works. In this sense, the text that Coppola published for the presentation of the show, based on a piece by Walter Peterhans, had the radicality of a manifesto and to some extent summarized the characteristics of his photographic work up to this point:[37]

> The photographic image is the result of two acts: the preparation of the shot . . . and the photographic process. The first is conditioned and orchestrated by the free and subjective activity of the photographer from an exact consciousness of the photographic process. In this first stage the photographer makes a selection of the object's photogenic values. This selection is not mechanical. The photographer expresses in it his intuition about the object and his comprehension, his knowledge of the object. . . . This free and subjective act ends at the moment of making the exposure; photographic technique is an optical-chemical process. Annulling this process or modifying it with a later manual treatment, would be to deprive photographic technique of its specific properties.[38]

This show, which as the art critic Jorge Romero Brest noted, was "the first serious manifestation of photographic art we have been privileged to see," initiated the era of modern photography in the country.[39] After visiting the exhibition, Mariano de Vedia y Mitre, at this time mayor of Buenos Aires, and Atilio Dell'Oro Maini, secretary of culture, entrusted Coppola with the creation of a book about Buenos Aires to commemorate the city's four hundredth anniversary. Although it was essentially a commissioned work of official publicity, Coppola managed to mark this project, which finally materialized in the book *Buenos Aires 1936. Una visión fotográfica* (Buenos Aires 1936: A Photographic Vision), with his creative and artistic stamp, and his place was assured as the emblematic photographer of modern Buenos Aires.[40] The images created by Coppola in this work were a complete departure from the photographs that were usually used to represent the city in this moment. More than capturing the real Buenos Aires, the artist constructed an avant-garde urban imaginary for a city where modernity was still more a seductive promise than a reality. The photographer gathers together "a series of images, in existence but dispersed and not yet constituting a meaning, and he constructs them in a very personal manner, creating in a double movement an invented imaginary and his aesthetic matrix."[41] In this way, his camera registers with fascination the geometry and abstraction of the brand-new obelisk, but at the same time, it obsessively captures the landscape of the city suburbs, challenging the hegemonic vision of a Buenos Aires that had been defined up to that point in terms of the modernity of its center. In the simple geometric designs of the new houses that populate these margins, where the city still mingled with the pampas, Coppola recognizes a spontaneous Cubism, almost modernist, and at the same time he recuperates vestiges of an archaic temporality in the parts of the city that were the most booming and up to date.

If at the beginning of the twentieth century, in the first Argentine films, and in photographic projects such as those of the Sociedad Fotográfica Argentina de Aficionados, modernity and tradition coexisted and were superimposed as if they were antagonistic and contradictory discourses, Coppola's work, by contrast, seeks out atemporal motifs that manage to concretize a synthesis, typical of a sector of the Buenos Aires avant-garde that combined the innovative with the popular, the present with the past, the city with the pampa.[42] Adrián Gorelik notes that the worst error that can be made in interpreting the images of the photographer's work "is to observe them as a generator of nostalgia for the Buenos Aires that was disappearing in the moment they were taken."[43] On the contrary, as is suggested in an article by Coppola himself published in the magazine *Clave del Sol*, where he proposes to supersede the bellicose and rupture-oriented character of the "avant-garde field," the artist's work manages to present an approach to Buenos Aires that combines modernity and tradition harmoniously.[44] Faced with the question articulated by local avant-garde—from where to situate the essence of a city that was constantly changing and agonizingly monotonous, flat, and without natural or historical beauty, Coppola responds with a classicism that "seeks to anchor itself in what remains after time passes: an essential order."[45] This is, as Gorelik suggests, an antiprogressivist aspiration, which the photographer shares with Borges and other contemporary artists, which seeks to represent the city as a mirror of a mythic pampa that has already disappeared but is still present in various urban spaces. Thus one of the principal motifs that runs through the work of Coppola is the setting of the suburbs, the landscape of the outskirts, of a traditional Buenos Aires at a moment of accelerated modernization.[46] In this space, the photographer captures the simple, working-class homes erected by urban expansion, separated by sidewalls, and with even roofs that contribute to an image of a flat, horizontal city. It is also in these margins, where the city meets the pampa, that Coppola encounters the prism, the structure through which he will later view all of Buenos Aires: the grid.

> In general, in the Western tradition the grid has been identified with capitalist rationality, or more crudely, with the radical modernization of a territory without cultural mediation, that takes as its parameters the North American city. . . . But the principal tradition in Buenos Aires was an acculturated interpretation of the grid, which rejects it not because it represents that which is most modern but rather that which is most traditional: in this version the grid suffers the ignominious destiny imposed by the Spanish tradition and by nature, the pampa. . . . The classicist sector of the avant-garde places itself in confrontation with this tradition, maintaining the cultural relationship of grid/pampa but inverting its conclusions. For this reason Borges will present the mythological foundation of Buenos Aires in terms of a city block, "an entire block but in the middle of the plains," provocatively uniting these two rejected symbols.[47]

Coppola discovers the essence of Buenos Aires in these suburban houses that he takes as a modernist motif and in the straight and standardized streets of the grid, which conform to the vision of a metropolis that is flat and extended like the pampa. In these images that celebrate horizontality, typical of development through the parceling out of lots in an immense and empty territory, the photographer highlights in particular the skies, which recuperate the traces of a rural *criollismo* still very proximate in time. In *Avenida Juan B. Justo*, for example, Coppola occupies more than two-thirds of the frame with a rendering of this subject, barely anchored by a faint horizon line, an approach that is close to certain paintings by Pedro Figari, the traditional painter admired by the local avant-garde. In the urban photos, by contrast, the skies become geometric through framings that reproduce the architectures of modern constructions. As Beatriz Sarlo notes, in these images "Coppola renders the skies geometric in such an extraordinarily deliberate way that it is as if he did not accept them as referential and wished to transform them, formalizing their abstract indeterminacy."[48]

But the synthesis of tradition and modernity that characterizes Coppola's work is not only manifest in his suburban photos, but also in the images that capture the very center of the city, where the geometry of the new constructions coexists harmoniously with elements of the nineteenth-century village. For example, in *Bartolomé Mitre, esquina Maipú* (*Corner of Bartolomé Mitré and Maipú*), the tall building of the Muro & Cia department store, symbol of modern consumer goods, coexists with an anachronistic horse-drawn cart, which appears almost immobile in front of the frenetic traffic of out-of-focus automobiles, trolleys, and pedestrians. In a similar way, *Iglesia de Nuestra Señora de Monserrat* (*The Church of Our Lady of Montserrat*), the almost abstract geometry of the new urban buildings is superimposed almost without conflict on traces of the city of yesteryear.

As Coppola was working on the book *Buenos Aires 1936*, the obelisk was being constructed in the city, and the photographer decided to make, on his own initiative and parallel to his photographic commission, a film documenting the construction of the structure, at this time the tallest in the Argentine capital. His fourth film, the first made in the country, was entitled *Así nació el obelisco* (*Thus the Obelisk Was Born*). This film, in a fashion, brings to a close his brief period of film production initiated in Europe and condenses all that Coppola had learned as a photographer and filmmaker.[49] The subject was ideal for the filmmaker to put into practice all the resources of the New Vision, which, as we have seen, had a special predilection for documenting modern architecture. The photographer takes maximum advantage of overhead and extreme low angles to communicate the monumentality of the structure, uses oblique vanishing points to film the city from a height, and devotes careful attention to the workers and, above all, to the materials used, attending obsessively to textures and details to the point of rendering them abstract and unrecognizable. Near the end of the film, he places the camera on a crane and films an extended travelling shot that moves from the dark earth to the sky. Once above, the shot shows how the speed and frenzy of the city contrast with the immobility of the structure.

Fig. 6.4a and Fig. 6.4b Stills from *Así nació el obelisco* (*Thus the Obelisk Was Born*, 1936).

Fig. 6.5 Still from *Así nació el obelisco* (*Thus the Obelisk was Born*, 1936).

One of the most notable characteristics of the film is the way Coppola connects this new and emblematic monument in construction with the city that received it. In 1955, the photographer commented about the short: "After seeing wood, wires, iron, we find a landscape where we experience emotions, recognize views of our city, pieces of sky, perhaps the river, in the background. We construct the obelisk. Then, we reconstruct the city that surrounds it."[50] Indeed, *Así nació el obelisco* perfectly condenses this synthesis between classicism, criollismo, and modernity that, as we have seen, dominates the urban images of Coppola. In this sense, the film is closer to some of the earliest "city symphonies" such as *Manhatta* (dir. Charles Sheller and Paul Strand, 1920) than other films that are closer in chronological terms, such as *Berlin, Symphony of a Great City*; *Man with a Movie Camera*; *À propos de Nice*; and *A Bronx Morning* (dir. Jay Leyda, 1931), among others. *Manhatta*, an emblematic documentary made by painter/photographer Charles Sheeler and the photographer/filmmaker Paul Strand, is now considered by many historians to be the first genuinely avant-garde film made in the United States, and the first "city symphony" in film history. Like many of the first works of the

North American avant-garde, *Manhatta* is at once modernist and romantic in its search for a mythic synthesis between city and country, technology and nature, a subtext that, as Jan-Christopher Horak notes, is absolutely absent in European modernism.[51] On one hand, as in the case of *Así nació el obelisco*, the filmmakers deconstruct Renaissance perspective in favor of multiple, reflexive points of view imposed by the photographer rather than by the subject. In this way, the film elaborates an urban imaginary through oblique vanishing points and extreme angles that enlarge the already enormous New York skyscrapers and transform the urban masses into an almost imperceptible human swarm. At the same time, the film emphasizes the abstract elements of visual design, just as Coppola does with the various construction materials used in the obelisk. However, on the other hand, the film attempts to present a romantic vision of technology in tune with the environment, in which the poetry of Walt Whitman (included in a number of the intertitles) and the imposing images of the sunset on the Hudson River that conclude the film, coexist harmoniously with the modernist perspective of the skyscrapers. In this sense, this film is intimately connected with Strand's celebrated essay, "Photography and the New God," where the author proposes the search for a synthesis between nature and technology, using the camera as a catalyzing force.[52] This synthesis is also present in the images of *Así nació el obelisco*, where the high-angle shots from the heights show a city that is horizontal and extended like the pampa, which loses itself in the distance in the mythic Río de la Plata and in the immense sky beyond the horizon. As Brizuela argues, the respect for the object and for the specific characteristics of the medium that define the work of Strand and Coppola, "produced visual works about their respective cities—New York and Buenos Aires—at once documentary and fantastic, realistic and avant-garde."[53]

As we have seen, at the height of the (early twentieth-century) avant-gardes, photography and cinema exerted strong reciprocal influences that were highly productive for the development of new artistic currents in both media. As Jan-Christopher Horak notes, "The establishment of a modernist, avant-garde movement in cinema, both in Europe and America"—and, in isolated cases and with its own characteristics, in Latin America as well—"is unthinkable without the participation of photographers."[54] The work of these photographers is, in turn, inseparable from the novel and transformative approach of modernist film movements of the interwar period. This was particularly true in the case of Argentina, where avant-garde cinema circulated in a much more constant and heterogeneous manner than photography—whose dissemination was greatly diminished by the persistent dominance of the pictorialist model. Although Coppola's film work was of brief duration and was rapidly displaced in significance by his vast photographic work, cinema was undoubtedly fundamental in the forging of his fresh and innovative gaze at the realities of his time.

Translated by Rielle Navitski

ANDREA CUARTEROLO is a researcher at the Consejo Nacional de Investigaciones Científicas y Técnicas (CONICET) in Buenos Aires, where she specializes in the history of Argentine photography and silent cinema. She is the author of *De la foto al fotograma. Relaciones entre cine y fotografía en la Argentina, 1840–1933* (CdF Ediciones, 2013), and she coedits the journal *Vivomatografías. Revista de estudios sobre precine y cine silente en Latinoamérica*.

RIELLE NAVITSKI is Assistant Professor of Theater and Film Studies at the University of Georgia. She is the author of *Public Spectacles of Violence: Sensational Cinema and Journalism in Early Twentieth-Century Mexico and Brazil* (Duke University Press, 2017).

NOTES

1. *Editors' Note*: The word *imagema* is a play on words, incorporating the Spanish terms for "image" and "gem." It was also the name given to a group of photographers to which Coppola belonged in the 1980s.

2. Horacio Coppola, *Imagema. Antología fotográfica, 1927–1994* (Buenos Aires: Fondo Nacional de las Artes, 1994), 19.

3. *Editors' Note*: Often referring to a person of European descent born in the Spanish colonies, the term *criollo* implies a hybrid cultural position, informed by nationalism but also by cultural affiliation with colonizers or neocolonial powers.

4. Paul A. Schroeder Rodríguez, "La primera vanguardia del cine latinoamericano," paper presented at the international colloquium Cine Mudo en Iberoamérica, Instituto de Investigaciones Estéticas, Universidad Nacional Autónoma de México, Mexico City, April 21 and 22, 2010, accessed July 17, 2011, http://cinemudoiberoamericano.blogspot.com/2010/06/la-primera-vanguardia-del-cine.html.

5. Natalia Brizuela, "Horacio Coppola y el extrañamiento de lo real," in *Horacio Coppola. Los viajes* (Buenos Aires: Galería Jorge Mara / La Ruche, 2009), 183.

6. The photographic exposition was composed of various sections, each with its own individual curator. The photographers Edward Weston and Edward Steichen were responsible for the United States section, the editor Christian Zervos organized the French exhibition hall and the architect, graphic designer and photographer Piet Zwart was in charge of the Dutch and Belgian section. El Lissitzky selected works to represent the Soviet Union, while the photographers László Moholy-Nagy and Gustav Stotz were the stewards of the German section. Moholy-Nagy also conceived and designed the entrance hall where the history and technique of photography were presented, and in another room outlined the principles and materials for his *Malerei, Photographie, Film* (Painting, Photography, Film), published as a book by Bauhaus in 1925.

7. *Editors' Note*: Photographs created without a camera, for example, by placing objects on photosensitive paper and exposing it to light.

8. Quoted in Rosalind Sartori, "La fotografía y el Estado en el período entre las dos guerras: La Unión Soviética," in *Historia de la fotografía*, eds. Jean Claude Lemagny and Andre Rouillé (Madrid: Alcor / Ediciones Martín Roca, 1988), 128.

9. See Brizuela, "Horacio Coppola," 182.

10. Jorge Schwartz, "Fundación de Buenos Aires: La mirada de Horacio Coppola," in *Horacio Coppola, Fotografía* (Madrid: Fundación Telefónica, 2008), 22.

11. *Editors' Note*: Sister of writer Jorge Luis Borges.

12. *Editors' Note*: In English in original.

13. *Editors' Note*: In English in original.

14. Guillermo de Torre, "Nueva visión del mundo: La fotografía animista," *Gaceta de Arte: Revista Internacional de Cultura*, March 1934, 1–2.

15. Coppola, *Imagema*, 9.

16. For more information about the creation of this cine club, see Miguel Couselo, "Orígenes del cineclubismo," in *Cine argentino en capítulos sueltos* (Buenos Aires: Festival Internacional de Cine de Mar del Plata, 2008), 95–99.

17. For more information about this association, see Patricia M. Artundo and Marcelo E. Pacheco, eds., *Amigos del arte, 1924–1942* (Buenos Aires: Museo de Arte Latinoamericano de Buenos Aires, 2008).

18. "El 21 del actual iniciará su actividad el Cine Club," *La Nación*, August 7, 1929, 11.

19. Fernando Martín Peña, "Amigos del cine," in *Amigos del arte, 1924–1942*, eds. Patricia M. Artundo and Marcelo E. Pacheco (Buenos Aires: Museo de Arte Latinoamericano de Buenos Aires, 2008).

20. Guillermo de Torre participated in a number of the informative lectures that accompanied the screenings of the Cine Club de Buenos Aires, among them one about German cinema that accompanied Walter Ruttmann's *Berlin, Symphony of a Great City*. Some of these activities were organized outside of Buenos Aires, in La Plata and Paraná, with the objective of disseminating these films in other cultural centers in the country. In addition, de Torre wrote various articles that promoted and supported the work of the group, including the one cited here. Guillermo de Torre, "El Cineclub de Buenos Aires," *La Gaceta Literaria*, April 1, 1930, 5.

21. Ibid., 5. *Editors' Note*: "records" appears in English in the original.

22. Perhaps foreseeing this decision, on May 15, 1931, the Cineclub de Buenos Aires dedicated a screening to cinema in sixteen millimeter, in which foreign film and reductions from thirty-five millimeter were shown together with documentaries by Argentine amateur filmmakers filmed in this format. Among the Argentine films shown in this program, Jorge Miguel Couselo highlights *Palomas* (*Doves*) by J. M. Méndez, *Imágenes urbanas* (*Urban Images*) by Carlos Connio, and *Experiencia de montaje* by Marino Cassano and León Klimovsky. See Couselo, "Orígines del cineclubismo," 97.

23. David Oubiña, "La piel del mundo: Horacio Coppola y el cine," in *Horacio Coppola. Los viajes* (Buenos Aires: Galería Jorge Mara / La Ruche, 2009), 193.

24. Horacio Coppola, "Siete temas: Buenos Aires." *Sur*, Spring 1931–Summer 1932.

25. In his first visit to Europe in the winter of 1930–1931, Coppola concentrates his interest in the artistic avant-gardes, meeting or visiting expositions by artists like Paul Klee, Marc Chagall, and Ernst Ludwig Kirchner. However, as Natalia Brizuela notes, he did not have contact with the photographers of the New Vision during this first trip. Nor did he purchase photography books that could have influenced his approach in this direction. See Brizuela, "Horacio Coppola," 187.

26. Luis Príamo, "El joven Coppola," in *Horacio Coppola. Los viajes* (Buenos Aires: Galería Jorge Mara / La Ruche, 2009), 10.

27. See Oubiña, "La piel del mundo," 193.

28. At the beginning of the 1930s, the arrival of the Nazis in Dessau and the growing political instability, combined with the precarious financial state of the Bauhaus, which was considered a socialist, internationalist, and Jewish institution and had ceased to receive aid from the state, prompted its then director Ludwig Mies der Rohe to move the prestigious school to Berlin. There it functioned in a limited way until 1933, when it was definitively closed by the Nazi party.

29. Luis Buñuel, quoted in Juan Francisco Aranda, *Luis Buñuel. Biografía crítica* (Barcelona: Lumen, 1975), 389.

30. Oubiña, "La piel del mundo," 196.

31. Coppola, *Imagema*, 14.

32. Quoted in the introductory text for the film series *Horacio Coppola–3 Films*, which took place at the Museo de Arte Latinoamericano de Buenos Aires between August 3 and September 3, 2006, accessed January 2011, www.malba.org.ar/web/cine_pelicula.php?id=1900&idciclo=314&subseccion=programacion_pasada.

33. Coppola, *Imagema*, 14.

34. Oubiña, "La piel del mundo," 206.

35. Among the most relevant are two long articles published in the illustrated supplements of the newspapers *La Prensa* and *La Nación* on October 6, 1935, with various images of the show and reviews published by Jorge Rinaldini in *El Mundo* and Jorge Romero Brest in *Sur* (both Spring 1935).

36. Verónica Tell, "Entre el arte y la reproducción. El lugar de la fotografía," in *Arte de posguerra. Jorge Romero Brest y la revista Ver y Estimar*, eds. Andrea Giunta and Laura Malosetti Costa (Buenos Aires: Paidós, 2005), 244.

37. As Coppola himself recognizes in "Horacio Coppola. Testimonios," in Adrián Gorelik, "Imágenes para una fundación mitológica. Apuntes sobre las fotografías de Horacio Coppola," *Punto de Vista* 53 (1995): 25.

38. Horacio Coppola, "Exposición de fotografías de Horacio Coppola y Grete Stern," brochure/invitation published in *Sur*, October 1935; repr. in Schwartz, *Horacio Coppola*.

39. See Jorge Romero Brest, "Fotografías de Horacio Coppola y Grete Stern," *Sur*, Spring 1935.

40. Horacio Coppola, *Buenos Aires 1936. Visión fotográfica* (Buenos Aires: Municipalidad de Buenos Aires, 1936).

41. Adrían Gorelik, "Vanguardia y clasicismo. Los Buenos Aires de Horacio Coppola y Facundo de Zuviría," in *Buenos Aires [Coppola + Zuviría]* (Buenos Aires: Ediciones Larivière, 2006), 11.

42. On this subject, see Gorelik, "Imágenes para una fundación mitológica."

43. Ibid., 20.

44. The short-lived but influential magazine *Clave de Sol* was founded in 1930 by Horacio Coppola, Jorge Romero Brest, José Luis Romero, and Isidro Maiztegui. Although only two issues of this publication appeared, they incorporated important discussions about notions of modernity and the avant-garde in painting, music, literature, and cinema of the period. Horacio Coppola, "Superación de la polémica," *Clave del sol* 1 (1930).

45. Gorelik, "Imágenes para una fundación mitológica," 22.

46. The suburb emerges as a literary, political, and artistic theme in the 1920s. At this moment, the traditional country-city dichotomy is displaced by a new debate that opposes the center to the suburb, represented by the tango and urban reform. This dichotomy irrupts forcefully in the cinema of the period, above all in melodramas of the suburbs by José Agustín Ferreyra, where this new frontier will install itself systematically as a marker of class. Coppola's first images of Buenos Aires date from this period; they will later serve as illustrations for Borges's *Evaristo Carriego* (1930), the text with which the writer brings to a close his period of "avant-garde urban criollismo," dedicated to forging the "epic" of Buenos Aires. In the two photographs that illustrate this book, taken in 1929, Coppola introduces in his photography for the first time the motif of the suburb, which Borges had been exploring in his texts during the 1920s and which would profoundly mark the photographer's approach.

47. Gorelik, "Imágenes para una fundación mitológica," 23.

48. Beatriz Sarlo, quoted in Schwartz, *Horacio Coppola*, 29.

49. In fact, Coppola would film two more shorts in the country for the Dirección de Maternidad e Infancia (Department of Motherhood and Childhood): *Vestir al bebé* (*Dressing Baby*, 1937) and *Do de pecho* (*Falsetto Note*, 1943), "a film on nursing whose title plays on the musical term's use of *pecho* (breast or chest)". This title translation is a literal one, and the contributor has pointed out that it doesn't address how the title is a play on words with the subject of the film, breastfeeding. However, these are commissioned films, shot without the creative freedom that characterizes his earlier works, and for this reason are beyond the scope of this essay.

50. Quoted in the introductory text of the film series *Horacio Coppola–3 films*.

51. See Jan-Christopher Horak, *Making Images Move: Photographers and Avant-Garde Cinema*. (Washington, DC: Smithsonian Institution Press, 1997), 80.

52. Paul Strand, "Photography and the New God," *Broom* 3 (1922); repr. in *Photography 1900 to the Present*, eds. Diana Emery Hulik and Joseph Marshall (Upper Saddle River, NJ: Prentice Hall, 1998).

53. Brizuela, "Horacio Coppola," 188.

54. Horak, *Making Images Move*, 5.

PART III

The Golden Age of Latin American Film Industries: *Negotiating the Popular and the Cosmopolitan*

Jack Alton, "Motion Picture Production in South America," *The International Photographer* (Hollywood), May 1934

> *Winner of the 1951 Academy Award for color cinematography for his work with Alfred Gilks on Vincente Minnelli's* An American in Paris, *John Alton is principally remembered as the visual stylist of film noir. Before shooting films noirs like* The Big Combo *(dir. Lewis. 1955),* He Walked by Night *(dirs. Werker and Mann, 1948), and* T-Men *(dir. Mann, 1947), he lived and worked in Argentina. During this period (1932–1939), he contributed frequently to* International Photographer. *In the following piece, which appeared in the May 1934 issue, Alton opines on the state of Spanish-speaking markets in the Americas in the early sound period.*

THE SPANISH MARKET, AS you know, is the second after the English. I believe there are about one hundred and sixty-three million Spanish-speaking people, although many of different accents, but always Spanish. During the silent era of motion pictures this market was controlled entirely by Hollywood. Here and there appeared a few pictures of German origin, or a few French comedies, but the Latins preferred the quick tempo of American cutting.

There were no so-called Spanish productions. There was no need for them, for a picture could be interpreted in various ways. A Spaniard saw it in Spanish. Then the talkies came and here the difficulties began. Subtitles, a strange language, misinterpretations, wrong translations, half of the screen covered with titles—one did not know where to look or what to listen to. And on top of all never in history has Hollywood sent out so many pictures of inferior quality. And so we arrive at the year 1933.

People in the Spanish-speaking countries are getting tired of the gaba-gaba they do not understand. Pictures are too much nationalistic. Problems, that little interest the public of South America. Managers of local exchanges of American firms beginning to complain. Box office dropped considerably. So the producers got their heads together and soon Hollywood sent out a few so-called Spanish talkies.

A well-known Spanish studio began to manufacture them like sausages. The result? Tragi-comic. Tragic for the box office and comic for the public. It so happened that the man in charge of Spanish productions in Hollywood sent out an SOS for Spanish-speaking authors, actors, etc. He had no idea of the different accents; during the most serious dramatic scenes the public burst out laughing. Why? Because one of the actors would speak in Mexican and the other would answer him in a Cuban accent. Soon appears a Spanish policeman and yells out in pure Chilean accent until the final result was that the picture flopped. Or, in another production, the leading man would make love to his señorita in pure Castillian that, to the Argentinian, is something like if they would show an Englishman making love in good old Cockney accent. Wouldn't you all laugh at it in Hollywood?

Then again producers in Hollywood have little or no idea of local costumes and customs. Whenever the tango appears on the screen even in an English talkie people get a kick out of it and they love to see girls dressed up in Spanish shawls and high combs.

True, here and there some of the American companies send the inspector down here to study conditions. He arrives with the Pan-American Airways, for he is in an awful hurry. The reporters await his arrival and ask him how he likes the country. He looks around on the flying field and answers in Spanish, "fantastico." They get him in a car and it being a hot day, the local manager takes him to the nearby seaside resort, where the press is invited. The Mogul announces the friendship between the United States and Argentina and his next year's program. Big applause and, while others still enjoy the imported French champagne he is on his way to the flying field with the detailed report that some stenographer has, in the meantime, prepared for him. He arrives in the States and reports his "studies." The next Spanish productions are even worse.

The most phonetic of all Spanish accents and the most generally accepted in the Spanish world is the Argentine. Also the most motion picture minded of all are the Argentinians. As may be seen from the annual report of a Buenos Aires trade paper published during the season of 1933, 404 films were shown and only a small percentage of them in Spanish. Five of them were produced in the Argentine. Two of the five, the only two that can be accepted as pictures, were produced by myself. At least, technically they were OK and are making money. One of the other two for a local studio and the other two on my own account, even released by myself, which for a foreigner is no easy task.

When I was in Paris (at that time in the post of chief cameraman of the Paris Paramount studios) I asked the president of the company about equipment, especially about lights. He took a deep breath and with the air of a "Thinkheknows" around him, answered: "Lamps! Ha! Ha!—we have more than enough!" Imagine my embarrassment when, upon my arrival in Buenos Aires, I found the ceiling of the new studio full of reflectors of the kind they use to illuminate a tennis court at night, or a huge ballroom. I died instantly.

The other day I asked a local exhibitor his opinion about last year's Hollywood product. He took as an example "The Sign of the Cross," a De Mille production. "H'mm," said he, "very poor, empty theaters. People down here don't like artistic pictures. My customers in the neighborhood like Spanish pictures," and he mentioned a local made picture. When I heard that I almost fainted. Six times he re-booked it, a picture or rather a calamity of film strips on which the patches sound like huge guns; without a story, no sets, underexposed negatives, actors barking like dogs, something that never would have been accepted in the States as far back as 1800; the director of which would have been shot at sunrise in Soviet Russia—in other words, a crime against good taste and civilization. And this they liked.

At the same time pictures like "A Kiss Before the Mirror," "The Rebel," with its gorgeous photography, "Cavalcade," the picture that went over like a million in England; all these and others of similar quality flopped down here. They have a peculiar taste. Only ten percent of the population have or form their own opinions; of the others I can only answer with the following incident that actually happened to me.

I asked a local yokel why he did not like a certain picture that was quite a success in Europe. "Read in the paper that it was no good," was the answer, and when he reads in the paper that a picture is good he swears it is marvelous. Building on my experience I produced my picture for the *masses* and not for the *ten per cent*. True, it was called everything by members of society, but in the neighborhood they are enjoying it and it makes money. After all that's what counts.

There is no company at present that is equipped to produce pictures of the required quality. The company I was with before has an old Bell & Howell camera and a Debrie developing machine, but has no technicians and needs badly to be reorganized.

Several local people are experimenting in an effort to invent a sound recording machine. This would be the same as if I went out tomorrow on some deserted island trying to invent a vehicle that will run without horses. And they still spend thousands of dollars on tests and tests and tests, instead of wiring ARTREEVES for a complete set. But they will not listen.

The country is beautiful, has the well known Tango and is rich in old legends which could easily be adapted for screen purposes. The possibilities are enormous, but not until foreign technicians will take the matter in their hands and with foreign organization will there be local industry.

The gorgeous countryside lends itself wonderfully to background of even a Hollywood made picture. Some of these days some smart producer will realize the gold mine that no camera has touched as yet. Production cost[s] would be considerably lower than in the States. Of a fairly good picture, Buenos Aires and its province would and should cover the negative cost. Then there is all of South America, Spain, Mexico, Central America, the West Indies, etc.

Chapter 7

John Alton in Argentina, 1932–1939

Nicolas Poppe

CAUGHT WITHIN TRANSNATIONAL FLOWS between the United States and Latin America in the early-to-mid-1930s, which would lead to the development of national film industries in Argentina, Brazil, and Mexico, were a set of production, distribution, and exhibition practices and processes. Even though several film historians have detailed how some of these distinct influences helped to shape emergent film industries in the region, little work has been done on the aesthetic, economic, social, and technological contributions and labors of specific individuals. Unable to easily fit into national film histories, these individuals often served a familiar role within the context of developing Latin American economies of the early twentieth century: as intermediaries between foreign capital—whether it be cultural, economic, or human—and local markets. Seizing new opportunities abroad and/or contracted for their expertise, an assortment of individuals like the producer Wallace Downey in Brazil and the directors John Auer, Robert Curwood, and Robert O'Quigley in Mexico contributed to fledgling national film industries.[1] Precisely because of their intermediary roles, their in-betweenness, these film practitioners often slip through the cracks, not only within national film histories but also in film criticism exploring the global reach of Hollywood.

So as to approach the influence of Euro-American film labor within the framework of the rise of a particular national film industry, as well as within the broader context of Latin American film history of the early sound period, in this essay I explore much of the work that the cinematographer John Alton completed in Argentina in the 1930s. In many ways, Alton's early career is indicative of the cosmopolitanism, as well as transnationalism, of cinema in the period. Part of a Jewish family who spoke Viennese German, Alton grew up between Austro-Hungarian cities in present-day Hungary, Austria, and Romania. Soon after arriving in New York in 1919 at the age of eighteen, he would begin to apply his childhood love of photography to the moving image.[2] Starting his career as a film technician with Paramount in their Long Island lab, Alton later moved to Hollywood and worked at MGM. Given his cosmopolitan background, Alton spent the late 1920s shooting for MGM and Paramount in Europe and the Middle East.[3] While working in Paramount's studios in Joinville on the outskirts of Paris, Alton was offered the opportunity by an assemblage of Argentine radio pioneers nicknamed *los locos de la azotea* ("the fools on the roof")—consisting of Luis Romero Carranza, César José Guerrico, Miguel Mugica, and Enrique Telémaco Susini—to participate in the creation of Lumiton, which became one of the first studios in the country along with Argentina Sono Film. A brief report in the June 1932 issue of *International Photographer* underlines the significance of Alton's international experience in its development: "Present plans also include the erection of a studio about thirty miles from Buenos Aires, in which project Mr. Alton will take part, proffering the benefit of his experience of years in the industry which has taken him to various interesting parts of the globe."[4] Contracted by Lumiton for an initial period of six months beginning in late April 1932, which had been envisioned to be extended to a year, Alton would work with several other emerging studios before joining rival Argentina Sono Film as technical director in 1935.[5] Together with his Argentine wife, Rozalia Kiss, he would leave the country in 1939, returning permanently to Hollywood.

Not only does his work in various labs and locations in the 1920s and 1930s on several continents make Alton an interesting case study into the transnational flows of the late silent and early sound periods, impacting factors ranging from film style to labor, but Alton's later centrality to the aesthetics of film noir, which underlines the in-betweenness of postwar sentiment in the United States, makes his Argentine films important objects of study. Much like European antecedents traced by scholars such as Thomas Elsaesser, Janice Morgan, Jonathan Munby, Charles O'Brien, and Ginette Vincendeau, Alton's overlooked Argentine films must be recovered and incorporated into the genealogy of film noir.[6] Even though he would later somewhat curiously win an Academy Award for Color Cinematography for his work with Alfred Gliks on the 1951 picture *An American in Paris* (dir. Vicente Minelli), Alton is best known for visually framing film noir. Photographing film noirs like *The

Big Combo (dir. Joseph H. Lewis, 1955), *Border Incident* (dir. Anthony Mann, 1949), *He Walked by Night* (dir. Alfred L. Werker and Anthony Mann, 1948), and *T-Men* (dir. Anthony Mann, 1947), Alton painted the *chiaroscuro* tones now associated with film noir. As Todd McCarthy argues, "In the definitive noir period, roughly 1946–1951, no one's blacks were blacker, shadows longer, contrasts stronger, or focus deeper than John Alton's. In fashioning the nocturnal world inhabited by noir's desperate characters, Alton was ever consistent and imaginative in forging his signature, illuminating scenes with single lamps, slanted and fragmented beams and pools of light, all separated by intense darkness in which the source of all fear could fester and finally thrive."[7] Along with others like Burnett Guffey, Nicholas Musuraca, and John F. Seitz, Alton photographed the alienation and anxiety of film noir. Allowing viewers access through the image to otherwise inaccessible psychological states of the films' characters, Alton's cinematography is vital in shaping film noir.

In this essay, I examine John Alton's work in the early sound period through brief formal analyses of nearly all of the films in which he is credited in Argentina, only omitting those films that are presumed to be lost. Credited as cameraman, director of lighting, and cinematographer in these movies, which I review in chronological order according to their premieres in Buenos Aires, Alton was a central figure to the Argentine national film industry in the 1930s.[8] Alton, in fact, understood his role as a foreign technician to be vital to its development. In a 1934 article of the *International Photographer* entitled "Motion Picture Production in South America," Alton argues of Argentina: "The country is beautiful, has the well known Tango and is rich in old legends which could easily be adapted for screen purposes. The possibilities are enormous, but not until foreign technicians will take the matter in their hands and with foreign organization will there be local industry."[9] Seemingly contradictory, but intelligible given the industrial, stylistic, and technological context, Alton held that only outside expertise would make possible the kinds of cinematic experiences that already captivated local spectators. In a similarly divergent line, Alton is also representative of the implicit tension facing foreign technicians like cinematographers vis-à-vis questions of authorship and production: while serving the demands of narrative intelligibility, often borrowed from Hollywood and twisted to suit local genres and tastes, they also lend their own style and vision to a film and its production.[10] Pulled in different directions, even within the same picture, these technicians mediate tendencies that may be contradictory, but are not necessarily mutually exclusive.

My analysis focuses on two distinct moments in Alton's career in Argentina: an experimental phase in which he collaborated on projects with several different incipient studios, and a second, more conventional period in which he worked for what might be considered the first major local studio, Argentina Sono Film. Beginning with his contract with Lumiton, which culminated in the second Argentine sound film, *Los tres berretines* (*The Three Whims*, dir. Equipo Lumiton, 1933), the first moment is indicative of the stuttering first steps of an emerging national cinema.[11] In this period, film style is inextricably enmeshed with cinematic, economic, experiential, ideological, and technological issues confronting new studios, especially independent ones in a city whose inhabitants express what Beatriz Sarlo calls *una modernidad periférica* (a peripheral modernity). The second—concluding with the premiere of his last Argentine film, *Caminito de gloria* (*Little Path to Glory*, dir. Luis César Amadori, 1939)—treads a different path. Even more constrained by industrial limitations, especially rushed shooting schedules, Alton's personal style and vision was restricted to specific scenes. Consequently, Alton's pictures for Argentina Sono Film demonstrate the cinematographer's flexible application of Hollywood lighting conventions in order to fit an appropriate mood within the story, while foreshadowing lighting techniques he would later use in his film noir pictures and describe in his seminal book *Painting with Light* (1949). Focusing primarily on the use of light, while also touching upon novel ways of framing his shots, I trace the ways in which genre films from comedies to historical dramas are connected to the conventions and style of classical Hollywood cinema. So as to draw attention to emerging elements of Alton's cinematic aesthetics that anticipate his later work in film noir, I also closely analyze important sequences in these Argentina Sono Film pictures. Through analyzing nearly all of Alton's pictures in these two distinct periods in Argentina of the 1930s, I attempt to recover their importance not only in establishing the visual aesthetics of early Argentine sound cinema, but also in developing a film style that continues to shape what we think the moving image can look like to this day.

EXPERIMENTATION AND EXPRESSION FOR VARIOUS STUDIOS (1932–1936)

Drawn to Argentina to establish Lumiton, Alton continued his work as a director of photography for numerous studios in a creatively generative period of his career. After working on *Los tres berretines*, Alton then directed the comedy *El hijo de papá* (*Father's Son*, 1933), whose star (and fellow coproducer)

Luis Sandrini famously enlisted Alton to help destroy its negatives. Having been unable to launch his own motion picture company, Alton photographed two pictures for Luis Saslavsky and Alberto de Zavalía's fleeting studio Sociedad Industrial Fotográfica Argentina Limitada (SIFAL) that premiered in 1935. Perhaps unsurprisingly because of its lack of initial commercial success, Saslavsky's first talkie *Crimen a las 3* (*Crime at Three O'Clock*) is presumed lost. SIFAL's second production, Zavalía's debut *Escala en la ciudad* (*Layover in the City*), has been largely overlooked, but nonetheless marks an important moment in Argentine film history as an initial attempt at art cinema. This period of experimentation and expression concluded with films for short-lived independents, both of which are presumed lost: *Tararira* (also known as *La bohemia de hoy*/*The Bohemia of Today*, dir. Benjamin Fondane, 1936) and *Compañeros* (*Mates*, dir. Gerardo Húttula, 1936).[12] In the article "Motion Picture Production in South America," which was published in the January 1936 issue of *International Photographer*, Alton argues that "Argentina's motion picture production business as yet cannot be called an industry. It is still in its experimental stage, but judging by the talent of its pioneers and the enormous progress it has made in such a short time, it may soon turn out to be one."[13] Abandoning somewhat the experimentalism of these ephemeral film companies when he joined Argentina Sono Film, the first major national studio, Alton also developed visual strategies in this more expressionist period that he would continue to implement throughout his career.

Beginning with a kind of city siteseeing tour, to borrow theoretical neologism that Guiliana Bruno explores in her seminal essay "Siteseeing: Architecture and the Moving Image," the opening scene of *Los tres berretines* leads spectators through modern, cosmopolitan Buenos Aires to the soundtrack of jazz (more specifically, Duke Ellington's "The Mooch").[14] Rather than a phantom ride situating us in the very front of the moving vehicle, our gaze is allowed to wander the streets, sidewalks, and parks of *porteño* spaces and places. The overall production value of *Los tres berretines* makes it notable not only in comparison to *Tango!* (dir. Luis Moglia Barth, 1933), whose release some three weeks earlier made it the first Argentine sound film, but also to other Argentine films of the early-to-mid 1930s. Of particular distinction in the film is Alton's cinematography. Unlike most Argentine pictures of the period, which never really overcome the canned theater style of the early sound period that Nastaša Ďurovičová describes as possessing "minimal camera movement, predominately theatrical rather than analytical space, conversational rather than action-oriented dramaturgy," *Los tres berretines* is a frequently artful adaptation of the *sainete* written by Arnaldo Malfatti and Nicolás de las Llanderas.[15] McCarthy likens the film to "Renoir's early 1930s naturalistic human dramas and the speedy, topical, common-people quickies Warner Brothers was turning out at the same time."[16] Perhaps McCarthy is a little eulogistic, especially in the comparison to a picture such as *Boudu Saved from Drowning* (*Boudu sauvé des eaux*, dir. Jean Renoir, 1932). Ultimately, Alton's photography adjusts to the demands of the story through balancing style conventions and more expressive effect lighting.

Although the exteriors of *Los tres berretines* have drawn much attention, Alton's adaptability is particularly evident in its interiors.[17] Take, for example, the evocative sequence in which Eusebio (Luis Sandrini) initially "composes" the tango "Araca la cana" through whistling a tune to an Italian pianist, only later to realize at a friend's house that it was transcribed poorly. After an initial scene in which the bright and clear illumination parallels the light diegetic music, the scene marks the passage of time through two shots of a burning cigar. In the next scene, Alton uses extra light on the background of a darkened room to create depth, while centering attention on the slightly comical conversation between the stutterer and the Italian through the use of a lamp sitting next to the piano. This effect lighting draws attention to Eusebio's amusing facial expressions while he rather absurdly whistles the ditty and to the attentive Italian's unkempt mustache. Cutting to an even darker corridor, whose sole faint light casts the shadows of a ladder and the banister onto the back wall, Eusebio walks up the stairs. Before entering an apartment in which ten or so men sing the tango "Ventanita florida," a barely lit shot lingers on Eusebio's hesitant feet. The subsequent scene remains dark, which allows Alton to use the contrast of front-cross key lighting to suggest the characters' masculinity through modeling the distinctiveness of their faces. The high-key lighting used with Eusebio, however, is much more reminiscent of how female characters were shot at the time. In this sequence, as well as others throughout the film, Alton shies away from implementing the flatter lighting associated with classical cinema. Rather, he adapts lighting expressively and adopts darkness to fit the mood of the story.

The relatively unknown 1935 film *Escala en la ciudad*, effectively forgotten in Argentine film history, marks a point of departure for Alton. Produced by SIFAL, it is an attempt at a kind of art cinema that would not exist in Argentina until the late 1940s and early 1950s. After two flops in a row (*El hijo de papá* and *Crimen a las 3*), *Escala en la ciudad* is a technical achievement, albeit a rather uneven one.[18] Its critical reception was as irregular as the film itself: while *La Vanguardia* panned it, *La Prensa* and *Heraldo del Cinematografista* noted that its artistic ambitions and effort to express something new rose above its faults.[19] Much like a review in *Imparcial Film*, *Cinegraf* praises the cinematography of *Escala en la ciudad*.[20] Alton, for his part, describes the film in an article published in *International Photographer* in the following manner: "Alberto Zavalia, a young director with his picture entitled 'Escala en la Ciudad,' and whose photography won the highest merits in 1935, deplores the misunderstanding of most of the world about the Argentine. He proves that Buenos Aires is as modern a city as London, New York, Paris or Los Angeles and the Indians are not running around on the streets and that the only gaucho in B.A. is one working in pictures."[21] Rejecting *criollista* representations of Argentina in (often, but not always, foreign) films like *The Four Horsemen of the Apocalypse* (dir. Rex Ingram, 1921) and *Las luces de Buenos Aires* (*The Lights of Buenos Aires*, dir. Louis Gasnier, 1931), Alton highlights Buenos Aires' cosmopolitanism and modernity.

As alluded to previously, SIFAL's attempt in *Escala en la ciudad* at a more experimental, aesthetically creative cinema is conveyed through Alton's cinematography. One particularly salient example is the film's closing sequence. Beginning with a stylized image of a skyscraper shrouded in smoke, which recalls Fritz Lang's 1927 *Metropolis*, the film returns to where it started: the dock and its social outcasts and marginalized bohemians. After a series of medium shots traverse spaces explored by Jaime Lara (Héctor Cataruza)—a brothel, an Italian restaurant, a jazz bar, and the bar "El capitán sirena"—the camera returns to Isa (Ester Vani), the film's jilted protagonist. Arms crossed and leaning slightly against a heavy wooden beam, Isa recalls her love interest Jaime's earlier lines through voiceover. Drawing attention to Isa and casting shadows upon the side of a building, Alton lights her rather harshly from her left side (i.e., camera right). As the camera draws nearer to the disillusioned young prostitute, the sheen of her dress and blouse becomes more apparent through hard lighting from overhead, as do her facial features and the blonde of her hair. Dissolving into a close-up, Alton utilizes three-point lighting on Isa's face. The use of more severe lighting here contrasts with the more classical lighting implemented at the beginning of the film. Using the key to create shadows on her expressionless face, especially hiding her eyes, Alton also uses a strong backlight to emphasize the wind blowing through her blonde hair. Fading slowly to black, the film ends.

Balancing Convention and Individual Style for Argentina Sono Film (1936–1939)

Alton worked directly on at least twelve pictures for Argentina Sono Film before returning to the United States three years later. According to numerous film historians, he was contracted to work as the studio's principal cinematographer. Emphasizing the multiple roles he played at the studio, however, Claudio España suggests that "Alton entered Argentina Sono Film more as a kind of art director (technical manager of the studios) than a mere lighting technician."[22] In his 1936 article for *International Photographer*, "News Letter from South America," Alton describes his role in the following way: "The Argentine Sono Film Company, under the technical direction of 'yours truly,' John J. Alton. According to my contract I am to supervise all production, but, as I am a born cameraman, I am not going to trust anyone else with the lighting. It remains a hobby."[23]

Job titles aside, his time with the studio would prove to be a formative period in his career. Though relatively brief, it is important not only in terms of active production but also because it represents a shift in the way in which he practiced his craft. No longer functioning within the more experimental confines (or, perhaps fringes) of independent, new, or small studios, but rather within a much more industrial system, Alton was forced to balance artistry and convention (much like George Barnes, James Wong Howe, Rudolph Maté, and Leon Shamroy in Hollywood).[24] Following discourse being shaped in *American Cinematographer*, which Patrick Keating examines in his excellent *Hollywood Lighting from the Silent Era to Film Noir*, Alton seems to have welcomed this shift toward coding genre. When, as noted above, Alton stated in *International Photographer* in 1936, "Argentina's motion picture production business as yet cannot be called an industry," he stressed "That local production has not progressed more is partly due to the fact that local producers do not *as yet realize the importance of a good story as the base of a successful film*" (my emphasis).[25] Much of the failure of these films is their inability to develop story within genre codes. Even though specific scenes in each of his Argentina Sono Film pictures might considered to be quintessentially Alton, including a few that prefigure the visual stylistics of film noir, their film style is closely tied to specific, and sometimes contradictory or incompatible, generic conventions.

The first film Alton shot for Argentina Sono Film to premiere was the Luis Sandrini comedy *Loco lindo* (*Crazy Dandy*, 1936). Directed by Arturo Mom, *Loco lindo* generally functions within the cinematographic conventions of comedy, albeit with slight tinges of a crime film.[26] Its bright and generally flat lighting not only maintains the positive mood of comedy, but it also allows the viewer to clearly follow the film's gags, particularly close-ups of the daft reactions of Sandrini's Miguelito. Brightness is also associated in the film with sylvan exteriors of the gauchesque countryside.[27] The comedic language of visual storytelling that the film employs is interrupted, however, when Miguelito attempts to save his love interest Carmencita (Anita Jordán) from a villain's gang. The darker tones of these scenes—some of which, such as a shot-counter-shot of a shadowy criminal standing imposingly in a doorway, are rather excellent—use techniques from crime films that would later recur in film noir. Given the dichotomous representation of city and country in Argentine cinema of the 1930s, it is little surprising that the city is visually linked to higher contrast dark tones in *Loco lindo*.[28] Ultimately, humor is drawn out of immediate or eventual contrast between these scenes and brighter ones. This is perhaps most obvious in a short scene in which Miguelito is shown reading "Manual del perfecto detective" on a country fence. Heavy lighting slightly from the front right, as well as the very brief shot, nearly conceal the barns in the background.[29] Brightness, comedy, and Miguelito eventually win out in *Loco lindo*.

Alton then worked on two films with the prolific director Luis Moglia Barth: *Amalia* (1936) and *¡Goal!*, which is presumed lost.[30] A "superproduction" and "'prestige' picture" in Alton's words, *Amalia* is the second on-screen adaptation of José Mármol's 1855 romantic novel.[31] Set in 1840 in the midst of the oppressive dictatorship of Juan Manuel de Rosas, *Amalia* recounts the doomed love story of the eponymous protagonist (Herminia Franco) and the dissident Eduardo Belgrano (Floren Delbene). Following the dichotomous needs of a historical costume drama, *Amalia* oscillates between flatter frontal illumination to highlight its detailed mise-en-scène and higher contrast melodramatic lighting to underline mood. Even though much of the film's photography is conventional, there are moments in which "Juan Alton," as he is credited, pays special attention to establishing heightened emotionality. McCarthy argues, "if one were given only one guess as to who photographed the dazzlingly dark night scenes that open the picture, one would have to venture Alton's name."[32] The first sequence features several sinister-looking caped figures skulking out of a minimally lit doorway. They then head into a forest, where, in some extremely dark high-contrast images, most of them are killed in a violent sword fight with some soldiers. Juxtaposed with the action scenes, whose more flat and luminous light evokes fog, is the particularly forceful use of key lighting of Belgrano as he is felled by two swordsmen. In three separate shots, a single, faint key light is used: first to focus attention on Belgrano receiving a painful blow, then to his friend Daniel Bello's successful attempt to save him. Even though these shots break with realist lighting conventions, as the light sources do not seem to match, it draws the viewer into the film's emotional gravity much like the similarly brief, albeit impactful, scene in *Loco lindo*.

After *¡Goal!* Alton continued with comedy in his first direct collaboration with Luis César Amadori in *El pobre Pérez* (*Poor Pérez*, dir. Luis César Amadori, 1937).[33] So as to feature the comedic talents of Pepe Arias, who plays the eponymous protagonist, bright, even, and low-contrast lighting is used throughout the film. In two contemporary articles in *American Cinematographer*, comedy lighting is described as "more conventional" by Victor Milner because, as John Arnold proposes, it aims to "simply reveal a stage for the comics."[34] Even though this convention allows light to be spread evenly throughout space, thus focusing the viewer's attention on the film's jokes, it allows the cinematographer little artistic license. As Keating notes, "D.P.s may have referred to cinematography as 'painting with light,' but the artistry was more accurately found in the shadows."[35] Furthermore, as production schedules were generally tight (*El pobre Pérez* was "filmed between August and September of 1936," according to España), only a few key scenes could employ more complex lighting techniques.[36] In *El pobre Pérez*, two exterior sequences allow Alton to express himself through shadow: the first, which follows the film's opening in a *boîte*, places Pérez in a situation of mistaken identity, while the second serves as the film's romantic denouement. In both, light and shadow are used to dynamically assemble temporary feelings of uncertainty. Given cinematographic and diegetic conventions, the viewer knows that happiness is to come.

Helmed by the prolific director Mario Soffici, whose films in the 1930s are tied to what Domingo Di Núbila and later Ana Laura Lusnich describes as the social folkloric drama, *Cadetes de San Martín* (*Cadets of San Martín*,

Fig. 7.1 Alton's lighting on the film *Amalia* (dir. Luis Moglia Barth, 1936). Courtesy of the Museo del Cine Pablo Ducrós Hicken.

1937) was the next of Alton's pictures for Argentina Sono Film to premiere.[37] In it, Alton worked on interiors, while Antonio Merayo took care of exteriors.[38] Given their framing of the military, Merayo's epically scaled exteriors frequently overshadow Alton's work. As the film's patriarch, Julio Ortega (Enrique Muiño), descends into a public health scandal that completely overcomes him, Alton employs increasingly melodramatic light. In doing so, he continues a trend that can be seen throughout his work for the studio: the use of different, and often conventional, lighting styles to fit the right mood for the story at hand. If the interior scenes at the beginning of *Cadetes de San Martín* are bathed in light, the film's final interiors are marked by the heavier contrasts of melodramatic lighting. This is most evident in the use of effect lighting in sequence in which Julio commits suicide. Leaving his family in the next room, Julio enters a darkened room ostensibly lit by the flashing bursts of lightening outside. Turning on a lamp, which illuminates the entire room, he then composes his suicide note. The scene then cuts to a close-up that helps draw attention to Julio's disquietude through lightly shadowing his

Fig. 7.2 Nedda Francy on the set of *Palermo* (dir. Arturo Mom, 1937). Courtesy of the Museo del Cine Pablo Ducrós Hicken.

face, especially his eyes. This is accomplished through using soft light with a key slightly above Julio's right (i.e., camera left) and fill to his left (i.e., camera right). Coupled with increasingly frenetic string music, Julio's hand is shown to rifle through a desk drawer in which he finds a pistol. The camera then pans up to show the window, which is brightened through the flashes of lighting. After a shot of the gun rings out, the sequence returns next door. Shadows are again central in showing the close-up reactions of Filomeno (Elías Alippi) and Juan Carlos (Ángel Magaña). Through obscuring much of their faces, their horror and surprise is intensified.

Moving away from the flatter lighting of the social drama *Cadetes de San Martín*, in his next film for Argentina Sono Film Alton would play with a different set of lighting conventions: the crime drama. *Palermo* (dir. Arturo Mom, 1937) allows Alton to be much more expressive—not necessarily in the sense of drawing from German expressionism—in his use both of light and shadow. As well representing a darkening of its cinematographic geography, *Palermo* also marks a foray into glamor lighting. Central to this somewhat contradictory aesthetic is Ana María Nielsen, played by the strikingly blonde Nedda Francy. Ultimately, Ana María is not only revealed to be on an undercover police assignment, but her true love interest Adolfo Villanueva (José Gola)—rather than the villain Conrado Schweitzer (Orestes Caviglia)—implores her, "Venga a mis brazos para siempre" (Come to my arms forever). As Elena Goity argues, "the figure of Nedda Francy, like that of all of those that performed roles of '*devoradoras*' ['man eaters'], lives on in the memory of spectators more for its devious journey—transgressive, immoral, and criminal—than for the hurried vindications of their normative endings."[39] Enmeshed within her role as a femme fatale are the ways in which Alton lights Francy in the film. Exploiting the tension between the shadows and mystery of the crime drama with the glitter and luster of glamor lighting, Alton both draws us to and repels us from Ana María in such scenes as the one in which she returns two thousand pesos she had borrowed from Schweitzer. In it, she wears a shiny coat with a hood, to which Alton draws our attention in both close-up and medium shots. In a sense, certain other elements like profile shadows, lattice lighting, and inky blacks prefigure Alton's work in film noir. While the film's strategies are best understood within their own context, Alton experiments with particular techniques for which he would later become renowned. William Stull, a Hollywood cameraman and contemporary of Alton's, argued that "today's trend among Hollywood's outstanding exponents of cinematographic lighting is toward the use of fewer light-sources and more actual lighting effects."[40] Even though evident throughout his experimental first period in Argentina, generic and Argentina Sono Film house-style conventions limited Alton's ability to employ effect lighting more freely. In spite of these restrictions, there are moments in which Alton is allowed to express himself by painting with light in *Palermo*.[41]

In his next project, *El último encuentro* (*The Last Encounter*, 1938), Alton reunited with Moglia Barth for the third time. Drawing from Hollywood crime films, as well as being reminiscent of the 1935 Mexican film *Luponini (el terror de Chicago)* (*Luponini* [*The Terror of Chicago*]) directed by José Bohr, *El último encuentro* can be understood to be a kind of *comedia policial*.[42] Pairing Floren Delbene and Amanda Ledesma as unlikely lovers Carlos Martínez and Marta Zapiola Bermúdez, "The story sentimentally reunites a delinquent and a millionaire, who ignores his social position. The affective bond already secured, when the suitor is about to confess the truth, he is killed by the police. She learns of the truth through newspaper headlines."[43] Given the amalgamation of genres, it is little surprising that the picture fails to use specific genre lighting conventions. In preferring to fit the story's shifting mood, rather than utilizing the more realistic lighting that came into vogue in the late 1930s, *El último encuentro* is in many ways past its time. However, there are several scenes in which Alton is able to feature his talents, particularly with shadow. Perhaps the most notable is a sequence at the beginning of the film in which Carlos watches Marta sing the waltz "¿Cuándo llegarás a mí?" from a distance. Juxtaposed with flatter, brighter lighting used with interior spaces—both the previous scene in the gang's hideout and subsequent cuts to Marta in her house—those shots of Carlos arriving and taking cover in order not be seen by his love interest use light to puncture a canvass of darkness. This strategy not only calls attention to the disparate backgrounds of its protagonists but also anticipates the film's tragic, albeit morally fitting (at least given its normative logic), climax.

Continuing his work in melodrama, Alton's next picture would have him working alongside Luis César Amadori in *Madreselva* (*Honeysuckle*, 1938). The film marked the return of Libertad Lamarque to Argentina Sono Film after she completed a highly successful trilogy of films with the director José Agustín Ferreyra for the Sociedad Impresora de Discos Electrofónicos (SIDE).[44] A story of a convoluted love triangle involving Mario del Solar (Hugo del Carril), Blanca (Lamarque), and her sister Delia (Malisa Zini), "The film displays a solid narrative structure and a concern for its visual style, thanks to the work of Raul Soldi's scenery, John Alton's accomplished photography, and Amadori's mature direction."[45] Like many pictures of the 1930s, particularly those featuring famous female leads, its visual style is marked by tension between the needs of glamor lighting and those of melodrama. Nevertheless, its opening scene foreshadows what we see in Alton's films after he returned to the United States.

Madreselva begins mysteriously. Foregrounding opaque figures silhouetting a shipyard and textures of distant cumulus clouds, dawn peaks out of

Fig. 7.3 Initial scene of *Madreselva* (*Honeysuckle*, dir. Luis César Amadori, 1938). Courtesy of the Museo del Cine Pablo Ducrós Hicken.

the horizon. Cutting to the darkness of the waterside, evoking the infamous Buenos Aires neighborhood of La Boca, the scene transitions to a street not yet lit by the morning sun. After furtively exiting a building, a man slinks along its exterior wall and peeks around the corner. Satisfied with his safety, his posture relaxes and he calmly crosses a street. Followed by the panning camera, the man is surprised by a figure lurking in darkness that knocks him to the ground and puts three bullets into him. Illuminated by two beams of light in the foreground and flatter lighting showing buildings and ships in the background, the wide shot shows the silhouette of the shooter, including the contours of his hat and his crumpled-up victim. Piercing the resulting silence, an off-screen voice declares "Corte, corte" ("Cut, Cut") and four lights quickly illuminate the scene from the background. Placing the viewer not at the scene of a mysterious murder at the hand of a malevolent *compadrito* but rather under a canopy of lights and boom microphones, the opening metafictional scene of *Madreselva* may not fully set the visual tone for the film, whose glamor lighting (especially of Lamarque's Blanca) and melodramatic high contrasts take the viewer through a much different set of emotions, but it does foreshadow some of the uses of darkness audiences would later see in Alton's work in film noir. It is certainly less sharp and mysterious than his film noir cinematography, but we can see how Alton is building toward it. The rest of *Madreselva* is shot using similar the sometimes expressive, sometimes flatter melodramatic lighting typical of the films Alton shot for Argentina Sono Film.

The first two films of Alton's to hit porteño screens in 1939 were melodramas: *Puerta cerrada* (*Closed Door*, dir. Luis Saslavsky) and *12 mujeres* (*12 Women*, dir. Luis Moglia Barth).[46] *Puerta cerrada* is told largely through flashback. In it, Libertad Lamarque plays Nina Miranda, a young singer who falls in love with Raúl (Agustín Irusta). The pair marry and have a son. Because their marriage is not accepted by Raúl's wealthy aunts, the young family slides into poverty. Nina is then coerced by her manipulative brother Antonio (Sebastián Chiola) to return to the stage. In a tragic accident, Nina accidentally and fatally shoots her husband. Separated from her son, who was taken in by Raúl's family, during her twenty years in jail, Nina returns. In the film's finale, Nina saves her son's life; having been shot, she is carried into the family's elegant mansion, whose doors were previously closed to her. *Puerta cerrada* marks a point of departure for Lamarque as it shows her transition from a youthful love interest into a more mature, graceful woman. Lamarque is reshaped in *Puerta cerrada*, evoking praise from the Chilean writer María Luisa Bombal in her February 1939 review of the film for influential magazine *Sur* as she argues that "we see her act and move for the first time with skill, grace, and dignity."[47] Transformation is as visual as it is diegetic in *Puerta cerrada*. McCarthy notes an important moment in the first half of the film: "One highlight is a flashback to the singer's love affair in which the visuals strikingly resemble Lee Garmes' gorgeously romantic work in Henry Hathaway's 1935 *Peter Ibbetson*, with the characters in a park or forest surrounded by petals and trees, all appearing within images that have their edges smudged to heighten the intoxicated atmosphere."[48]

A previous collaborator, the actor and director Orestes Caviglia, directed Alton's next project for Argentina Sono Film: *El matrero* (*The Outlaw*, 1939). *El matrero* forms part of a trajectory of Argentine films that aims to translate the gauchesque imaginary to the big screen. Based on Felipe Boero's opera of the same name, which debuted in the Teatro Colón in 1929, *El matrero* was shot in part on location in the northwestern province of Tucumán. Though perhaps unsuccessful—critic Domingo Di Núbila, among many others, points out acting and directorial flaws—it is an ambitious film that deviates from norms established by Argentina Sono Film in the period.[49] Portraying the doomed love affair of place-bound Pontezuela (Amelia Bence) and the singing outlaw Pedro Cruz (Agustín Irusta), *El matrero* attempts to visually balance melodramatic conventions with a stylized representation of the Argentine countryside. Shot with the aid of the cameraman Merayo, the film's exteriors depict the pastoral lives of gauchos. Not always well integrated into its interiors, which tend toward higher contrast, they capture the expansiveness of landscape. The nocturnal scenes, particularly one in which Pontezuela speaks with her father Don Liborio (Carlos Perelli) that anticipates the denouement, frequently employ shadow and shards of bright light to increase the melodramatic tension. The execution of this effect lighting, however, is more typical of melodramatic films of the previous decade or two as it lacks both the increasing depth and sharper visual style of the late 1930s and early 1940s.

In *Caminito de gloria* (*Little Path to Glory*), his final Argentine picture to be released, Alton paired up again with Amadori on a Libertad Lamarque star vehicle. Much like *Madreselva* and *Puerta cerrada*, the film is a rather convoluted romantic melodrama. Lamarque plays Marta Rinaldi, an aspiring working-class singer. She heads to the train station, where she meets Darío (Roberto Airaldi). After a family dispute, she goes with her uncle (Miguel Gómez Bao) to Buenos Aires to seek work. Having worked as her understudy, Marta assumes the identity of famous singer Luisa Maraval on a trip to Rio de Janeiro with the help of her uncle. Eventually, she is caught by the real Maraval. In order to be able to perform once more in a beautifully recreated Casino Urca and not disappoint her love interest Darío (Roberto Airaldi), Marta locks up Maraval in a dressing room. While Marta performs a song that evokes Carmen Miranda, Maraval accidentally causes a massive fire. Because she was caught in smoke and flames, Marta loses her sight. Darío arranges for a surgery that returns her sight, and the lovers reunite (and a future marriage is implied). Unsurprisingly, given all its diegetic twists and turns, *Caminito de gloria* uses lighting techniques that had become conventional to Argentina Sono Film melodramas in the late 1930s. Maintaining practices established in Hollywood such as glamor and low-key melodramatic lighting, the film is shot competently. In addition to spectacular shots of the Casino Urca, an early sequence in which the Rinaldi family slip out of their lodgings and head to the Lucerito train station is notable. While not realizing the mystery seen in a film like *The Big Combo*, the use of light and shadow through fog in the sequence not only adds emotional tone to it but also shows Alton working through lighting techniques he employed to serve later stories.

As well as being an important period in Alton's growth as a cinematographer, challenging him to remain creative while applying the conventions of film genres from comedy to period melodrama, 1936 to 1939 saw many changes happen to Argentine cinema. If the assemblage of motion picture producers in Argentina could not yet be deemed an industry in 1936, things changed by 1938. In an essay published that year in *International Photographer*, whose title "Motion Picture Production In South America Up to Date" is rather self-explanatory, Alton details important industrial developments. Not only is the application of certain conventions and trends apparent in the photography seen onscreen, but by that time the itinerant production manager Tom White arrived in Argentina with new film equipment ("he has flooded local studios with Hollywood cameras, lenses, sound and photographic material") and established a new, modern laboratory; sound improved with the introduction of RCA pictures equipment; Max Factor makeup came to Argentina with Bruno Boval, an imported makeup artist; and, finally, the period also saw investment: Falma Film was created and US studios such as Paramount and United Artists financially backed local production.[50]

Industrial developments in early Latin American sound film industries may seem outside the individual experiences of film practitioners like Alton; however, they are inextricably enmeshed with their work. In addition to allowing the Argentine national film industry to compete against imported films, especially those from Hollywood, they made possible modes of cinematic expression that were either technically too difficult to realize given industrial limitations or previously inaccessible. Work by technicians like Alton may seem at times to be rustic. Nevertheless, the individuality and inventiveness of their creative efforts can be disentangled and appreciated if properly contextualized.

John Alton's Argentine Photography

In its November 1939 issue, *American Cinematographer* reports "John Alton Returns to Hollywood from Abroad."[51] A largely biographical piece discussing Alton's work abroad, particularly in Europe and Argentina, the article ends with a section in which the cinematographer answers the question

"What is the prospect for American pictures in South America?" In his response, which mirrors what he had previously written for *International Photographer*, Alton argues that "A picture is made by attention to a multiplicity of little things—or it is correspondingly marred. When dealing in a medium other than your own the little things will multiply. That is inescapable."[52] While he is commenting on the cultural failures of movies referencing or representing Argentina, as well as the linguistic deficiencies of the *films hispanos* (Spanish-language features produced by US studios), I contend that we could also apply Alton's thought to his own craft. Not only through his writing for trade publications and his later *Painting with Light*, but also his work on films throughout his career, Alton is shown to have deeply cared about the "multiplicity of little things." In two very distinct periods in Argentina, Alton refined different cinematic techniques that would later apply in his postreturn career in Hollywood. Through the expressiveness of the first period and the balance of the second, Alton equipped himself with visual modes of expression that indelibly marked what early Argentine sound film looks like, while also showing, albeit sometimes subtly, an important and critically overlooked antecedent to film noir. If we are to understand the "multiplicity of little things" constituting early Argentine sound film, or film noir for that matter, more attention needs to be paid to figures like John Alton.

> NICOLAS POPPE is Assistant Professor of Spanish at Middlebury College. His work on Latin American cinema and cultural studies has appeared in several edited volumes, as well as journals such as *Arizona Journal of Hispanic Cultural Studies*, *Cinema Journal*, and *Journal of Latin American Cultural Studies*.

NOTES

1. Of Wallace Downey, Mônica Rugai Bastos states, "Beyond new companies being created in the period, various independent producers functioned in Brazil. Among them was Wallace Downey, an American who, ironically, directed a film named 'Coisas nossas' (*Our Things*), speaking of samba, carnival, and other Brazilian peculiarities with great success." Rugai Bastos, *Tristezas não pagam dívidas: cinema e política nos anos da Atlântida* (São Paulo: Olho d'Agua, 2001), 37.

2. Todd McCarthy, "Through a Lens Darkly: The Life and Films of John Alton," in *Painting with Light*, by John Alton (Berkeley: University of California Press, 1995), xi–xii. Much of this biography is taken from McCarthy, director of the documentary on cinematography *Visions of Light* (1992) and longtime film critic for *Variety*. Written to

accompany the volume's reissue, McCarthy's insightful introduction contains various factual errors regarding Alton's period in Argentina.

3. "John Alton Returns to Hollywood from Abroad," *American Cinematographer*, November 1939, 491–492.

4. "John Alton in Argentine for Making of Productions," *International Photographer*, June 1932, 37. This article preceded by six months the detailed announcement of Lumiton's inauguration in *Revista del exhibidor*, "Nuevos estudios argentinos," December 20, 1932, 5. A frequently cited piece was published in the December 21, 1932, issue of the *porteño* magazine *Heraldo del Cinematografista*. Later, a similar brief note was published in *International Photographer*: "Alton Goes to Argentine," March 1933, 39.

5. An article published in the April 20, 1932 issue of *Revista del exhibidor* announces Alton's arrival that day on the steamship *L'Atlantic*. It states, "He will remain in our country, according to the contract signed to the effect, for a space of six months, if the contract is not extended. He will direct two or three films in said time." "Viene a filmar a nuesto país un operador americano," 11. César Maranghello indicates Alton arrived with Laszlo Kish, citing an article in the film magazine *La Película*, April 21, 1932, 5. Maranghello, *Breve historia del cine argentino* (Barcelona: Laertes, 2005), 68.

6. Of the work done on film noir's European precursors, a 1996 special issue of the film journal *IRIS: European Journal of Philosophy and Public Debate* is particularly useful. Thomas Elsaesser, "A German Ancestry to Film Noir? Film History and Its Imaginary," *IRIS: European Journal of Philosophy and Public Debate* 21 (1996): 129–143; Janice Morgan, "Scarlet Streets: Noir Realism from Berlin to Paris to Hollywood," *IRIS: European Journal of Philosophy and Public Debate* 21 (1996): 31–53; Jonathan Munby, "The 'Un-American' Film Art: Robert Siodmak and the Political Significance of Film Noir's German Connection," *IRIS: European Journal of Philosophy and Public Debate* 21 (1996): 74–88; Charles O'Brien, "Film Noir in France: Before the Liberation," *IRIS: European Journal of Philosophy and Public Debate* 21 (1996): 7–20; Ginette Vincendeau, "Noir Is Also a French Word: The French Antecedents of Film Noir," in *The Book of Film Noir*, ed. Ian Cameron (New York: Continuum, 1993), 49–58.

7. McCarthy, "Through a Lens Darkly," x.

8. Alton claimed to have worked on some twenty-five pictures while in Argentina. While McCarthy (among others) repeats this figure, I have only been able to verify eighteen. It is possible, of course, that he may have collaborated uncredited on a film such as *La fuga* (*The Getaway*, dir. Luis Saslavsky, 1937) as several sources claim. Until definitive evidence proves otherwise, however, it would seem prudent to accept Gerardo Húttula as cinematographer, per the film's credits.

9. Alton, "Motion Picture Production in South America," *International Photographer*, May 1934, 14, 27. In an interview conducted in the run up to the premiere of *El hijo de papá*, Alton discusses similar issues with the Buenos Aires press. "'Estoy entregado en cuerpo y alma a la producción nacional'," *Film*, September 15, 1933, 3.

10. Chris Cagle, "Classical Hollywood, 1928–1946," in *Cinematography*, ed. Patrick Keating (New Brunswick, NJ: Rutgers University Press, 2014), 52–58, discusses the authorship and personal style of cinematographers George Barnes, James Wong Howe, Rudolph Maté, and Leon Shamroy. As Patrick Keating notes, "Any successful work of

Hollywood cinematography is the sum total of countless choices and decisions," many if not most of which lie outside the control of the individual cinematographer. Keating, "Shooting for Selznick: Craft and Collaboration in Hollywood Cinematography," in *The Classic Hollywood Reader*, ed. Steve Neale (New York: Routledge, 2012), 280. Not only has Keating worked on how a producer (i.e., David O. Selznick) affected cinematographic authorship but he has also examined the ways in which institutional forces, primarily through the American Society of Cinematographers (ASC), shape photographers' use of light in a wide range of films in his *Hollywood Lighting from the Silent Era to Film Noir* (New York: Columbia University Press, 2010). Christopher Beach also examines the collaborative relationship between directors and cinematographers. Beach, *A Hidden History of Film Style* (Berkeley: University of California Press, 2015). I do not explicitly explore questions of authorship in this essay, but focus on how Alton interprets the demands of a film's story and implements his own style, often in a specific scene.

11. It is fitting that the first comic superstar of Argentine cinema was Luis Sandrini, whose stuttering character Berretín was featured in several films.

12. Using "From its beginnings, cinema was transnational, diasporic, an invention of exiles" as his point of departure, Gonzalo Aguilar examines the Franco-Romanian surrealist Fondane's lost Argentine film. Aguilar, "*Tararira*," *Imágenes compartidas: cine argentino—cine español*, ed. Ricardo Ramón Jarne (Buenos Aires: CCEBA, 2011), 8–27. A short piece by Olivier Salazar-Ferrer on its filming follows Aguilar's essay. Salazar-Ferrer, "El rodaje de *Tararira*," *Imágenes compartidas: cine argentino—cine español*, ed. Ricardo Ramón Jarne (Buenos Aires: CCEBA, 2011), 28–29.

13. Alton, "Motion Picture Production in South America," *International Photographer*, January 1936, 23.

14. Guiliana Bruno, "Site-seeing: Architecture and the Moving Image," *Wide Angle* 19, no. 4 (1997): 8–24. Drawing on Bruno's notion, see Nicolas Poppe, "Siteseeing Buenos Aires in the Early Argentine Sound Film *Los tres berretines*," *Journal of Cultural Geography* 26, no. 1 (2009): 49–69.

15. Nastaša Ďurovičová, "Translating America: The Hollywood Multilinguals 1929–1933," in *Sound Theory/ Sound Practice*, ed. Rick Altman (New York: Routledge, 1992), 145. Rather tellingly in the film adaptation, cinema replaces the radio as one of the three *berretines*, popular passions or whims. The two that remain the same are soccer and tango.

16. McCarthy, "Through a Lens Darkly," xiv.

17. Adrián Pérez Melgosa puts forward that "The exterior urban night scenes . . . , where there is prominent use of mood lighting, high-contrast cinematography and deep focus mise-en-scène, suggest that during his time in Argentina, Alton was already developing many of the visual traits that would eventually become central to the Hollywood aesthetics of film noir." Pérez Melgosa, *Cinema and Inter-American Relations: Tracking Transnational Affect* (New York: Routledge, 2012), 10.

18. Somewhat curiously, given Alton's own failure as a director, in an article imploring studios to look toward camera departments for directorial talent, he argues that "Many of the few cameramen here have been given a megaphone and failed as directors. But why? They failed because they remained cameramen. They kept on worrying about

the photography, ordering lights, etc., thereby driving both the cameraman and the gaffer absolutely crazy. The result? That the picture was neither photographed nor directed." Alton, "The Cameraman as Director," *International Photographer,* July 1934, 36.

19. Jorge Finkielman notes the reception of *Escala en la ciudad* in the dailies *La Vanguardia* and *La Prensa.* Finkielman, *The Film Industry in Argentina: An Illustrated Cultural History* (Jefferson, NC: McFarland, 2004), 204–205. "Escala en la ciudad," *Heraldo del cinematografista,* November 6, 1935, 1056.

20. A review of a private screening of *Escala en la ciudad* in *Imparcial Film* argues "there are very good takes of the *bajo fondo* (underworld), carried out in a chiaroscuro that expresses an assured understanding of photographic effects" (6). "Producción Nacional. 'Escala en la ciudad.' Producción del Sello Sifal, dirección: Alberto de Zavalía," *Imparcial Film,* October 15, 1935, 6. Unlike *Imparcial Film,* which credits the film's director, *Cinegraf* suggests the following: "The pleasant and harmonious handling of light, reflected in tonalities of expressive and skilled suggestion—which we should attribute to John Alton" (44). "'Escala en la ciudad', de A. de Zavalía," *Cinegraf,* November 1935, 44.

21. Alton, "The Cameraman as Director," 36–37.

22. Claudio España, "John Alton," in *Cine Argentino: Industria y clasicismo, 1933/1956,* vol. 1, ed. Claudio España (Buenos Aires: Fondo Nacional de las Artes, 2000), 220.

23. John Alton, "News Letter from South America," *International Photographer,* May 1936, 16.

24. See note 9.

25. Alton, "Motion Picture Production in South America," 23.

26. Somewhat parenthetical to my discussion of lighting in *Loco lindo* is another important element in the film's cinematography: camera movement. By 1936, as is evident in *Loco lindo* and *Amalia,* the camera is moving extensively in Argentine cinema.

27. In his article "Motion Picture Production In South America Up to Date," Alton states, "'Loco Lindo' won recognition for its authentic exteriors of Patagonia. It was directed by Arturo S. Mom, a director who acquired his 'technique' in Hollywood and Russia. Remember him?" Alton, *International Photographer,* March 1937, 29.

28. An important trope in Argentine cultural production, the city/country dichotomy was first seen and heard in sound film in Carlos Gardel's 1931 film *Las luces de Buenos Aires,* directed by Adelqui Millar in Paramount's studios in Joinville, France.

29. While it was difficult to tell, given the poor state of my copy of the film, it appears that the scene was shot outdoors using sunlight, possibly with an additional spot light on Miguelito.

30. Alton writes in *International Photographer* that "At present we are installing a brand new studio and have to be ready to shoot by the end of February. During the early part of March we start the first of our 1936 productions and it is to be called 'Amalia,' after an historic novel." Alton, "News Letter from South America," May 1936, 16. It is, of course, important to remember that production and release schedules often differ, sometimes greatly and for various reasons.

31. Alton, "Motion Picture Production in South America Up to Date," 29. The previous adaptation of *Amalia* (1914) was the first full-length Argentine feature. Produced

by the media pioneer Max Glücksmann, the silent picture was directed by Enrique García Velloso and photographed by Eugenio Py.

32. McCarthy, "Through a Lens Darkly," xv.

33. As technical director of Argentina Sono Film, Alton previously supervised Amadori and Soffici's codirected film musical *Puerto Nuevo* (1936). Pepe Arias also starred in the film.

34. Victor Milner, "Creating Moods with Light," *American Cinematographer*, January 1935, 14. John Arnold, "Why Is a Cinematographer?" *American Cinematographer*, November 1937, 462. Both are cited in Keating, *Hollywood Lighting from the Silent Era to Film Noir*, 150.

35. Ibid., 150.

36. Claudio España, *Luis César Amadori* (Buenos Aires: Centro Editor de América Latina, 1993), 20.

37. *Cadetes de San Martín* is also the only film in which Alton and Soffici collaborated. In an interview, Soffici claimed, "I got along very poorly with Alton" (quoted in España, "John Alton," 221). Domingo Di Núbila, *La época de oro: Historia del cine argentino*, vol. 1 (Buenos Aires: Jilguero, 1998): 258; Ana Laura Lusnich, *El drama social-folclórico: el universo rural en el cine argentino* (Buenos Aires: Biblos, 2007).

38. With a career spanning six decades, Antonio Merayo is among the most prolific and influential cinematographers in Argentina. In the opening credits, exteriors are attributed to "Antonio M. Utges."

39. Elena Goity, "Claroscuro y política," in *Cine argentino: Industria y clasicismo 1933/1956*, vol. 2, ed. Claudio España (Buenos Aires: Fondo Nacional de las Artes, 2000), 437.

40. William Stull, "Summing Up Modern Studio Lighting Equipment," *American Cinematographer*, October 1935, 424–425, cited in Chris Cagle, "Classical Hollywood, 1928–1946," 45.

41. During "a unique trip to test and purchase technical devices in Hollywood" (España, "John Alton," 220), Alton worked as the cinematographer on the Josef Berne-directed film *La vida bohemia*, which was shot in July 1937 and released in Latin America in 1938 (Juan Heinink and Robert Dickson, *Cita en Hollywood* [Bilbao: Mensajero, 1990], 262). Produced by Jaime del Amo for Cantabria Films and distributed by Columbia Pictures, it was one of the final major Hollywood Spanish-language films of the 1930s. Much like other period love stories, *La vida bohemia* swings between flat frontal illumination and higher contrast melodramatic lighting. Alton's cinematography is particularly notable in two melodramatic scenes involving Mimi (Rosita Díaz Gimeno) and Rodolfo (Gilbert Roland): their initial encounter and the film's final sequence, in which Rodolfo suffers alongside the selfless Mimi as she dies.

42. Goity, "Claroscuro y política," 434.

43. Ibid., 439.

44. The SIDE trilogy consists of *Ayúdame a vivir* (*Help Me to Live*, 1936), *Besos brujos* (*Enchanting Kisses*, 1937), and *La ley que olvidaron* (*The Law They Forgot*, 1938).

45. César Maranghello and Diana Paladino, "*Besos brujos/Enchanting Kisses*," in *The Cinema of Latin America*, ed. Alberto Elena and Marina Díaz López (London: Wallflower, 2003), 42.

46. Even though McCarthy comments on having seen *12 mujeres*, it seems that the film is currently lost. McCarthy, "Through a Lens Darkly," xv.

47. Quoted in Jason Borge, *Avances de Hollywood: crítica cinematográfica en Latinoamérica, 1915–1945* (Rosario: Beatriz Viterbo, 2005), 229.

48. McCarthy, "Through a Lens Darkly," xv.

49. Di Núbila, *La época de oro*, 251.

50. In his pieces for *International Photographer*, Alton often refers to projects on which he worked without disclosing his participation. In this case, he does not mention that he photographed Falma Film's one and only production, *Tararira*. Alton, "Motion Picture Production In South America Up to Date," 29.

51. "John Alton Returns to Hollywood from Abroad," 491–492.

52. Ibid., 492.

Chapter 8

The Golden Age Otherwise: Mexican Cinema and the Mediations of Capitalist Modernity in the 1940s and 1950s

Ignacio M. Sánchez Prado

FEW CRITICAL COMMONPLACES ARE as pervasive and lasting as the connection between Mexican Golden Age cinema and national identity. The link between the two is undeniable, given the well-known catalog of stereotypical characters played by figures such as Cantinflas and Pedro Infante and of carefully crafted landscapes captured by Gabriel Figueroa's legendary lens. However, Mexicanness—or Mexicanidad, the representation of a national self on the silver screen and in other forms of culture—constitutes merely part of a larger and more complex system of cinematic production related to the "Mexican miracle," a process of rapid capitalist modernization that followed the consecration of the pos-trevolutionary regime in the 1940s and 1950s. When looking carefully at the list of films produced in that decade, the diversity in genres and topics seems to be united not by the construction of Mexicanidad, but by the way in which the industry dealt from different ideological and aesthetic stances with the societal and cultural challenges posed by a nation undergoing a rapid process of urbanization and development. In what follows, I propose—through a set of examples from the cinematic production of the 1940s and 1950s—that we need to revise the idea of Mexican Golden Age cinema (or "classical Mexican cinema," as Charles Ramírez Berg calls it in a recent book) through a paradigmatic shift that strategically underplays the role of Mexican national identity and that considers modernization as the core signifier underlying the decade's production.[1] In this, I follow some hints in the work of scholars such as Ernesto R. Acevedo-Muñoz and Dolores Tierney, who have studied two major directors—Luis Buñuel and Emilio Fernández—under a more transnational light, as well as recent work on cabaret films, all of which tie Mexican production to questions of modernity.[2] In doing so, I contend that existing understandings of Golden Age cinema—the ones that place at the center the films of Ismael Rodríguez and Emilio Fernández, Gabriel Figueroa's cinematography, and the characters played by actors such as Pedro Infante and Cantinflas—unjustly exclude from critical attention (and even from commercial reissue) films that show Mexican cinema not only as a machine for the construction of social identities but also as part of the mediation of capitalist modernity. These less discussed films render visible a cultural network that registered and confronted the anxieties of the modernization process that moved Mexican society from revolutionary unrest and nation building to a new era marked by increased cosmopolitanism and uneven yet considerable economic development.[3] In placing the films of directors such as Alejandro Galindo, Julio Bracho, Juan Orol, Emilio Gómez Muriel, and even Luis Buñuel (whose early Mexican work is at times ignored by critics) alongside Rodríguez and Fernández as part of a core tradition of cinema defined by capitalist modernization, one can see the emergence of a "structure of feeling" whose most lasting impact was not the construction of national identity.[4] Rather, the territorialization of social subjectivities developed into a tension between a revolutionary *ethos* that remained central to Mexico's recent historical memory and the cosmopolitanism required to negotiate the country's growing engagement with an international economy. This way, we can more properly discuss the idea of a "global Mexican cinema," as a remarkable recent book calls it, in terms of the heterogeneity of its symbolic economies and cultural languages.[5]

In light of this set of issues, my following analysis asserts the need to rethink the Mexican Golden Age not as a period when Mexican cinema gains some kind of edge vis-á-vis American cinema, but rather as an expansion of the cultural repertoires available to Mexican spectators in relation to the process of modernization that the country underwent in the 1940s and 1950s. As a matter of fact, statistics from the period show an important piece of information: Mexican films were never predominant in the domestic market. In the years typically considered as the height of the Golden Age (the mid-to-late 1940s), Mexican films constituted around 18 to 24 percent of total releases. In fact, American films, which provided around 27 percent of releases in

1940, averaged between 53 and 65 percent of the market in every single year between 1945 and 1959.[6] Box-office figures confirm this diversity. In a sampling of box-office returns from 1948 and 1949, one can see that Hollywood films typically outperformed Mexican productions. Furthermore, alongside classics such as the Pedro Infante vehicle *Nosotros los pobres* (*We the Poor*, dir. Ismael Rodríguez, 1948), one could find at the top of the box office films such as *Café de chinos* (*Chinese Café*, dir. Joselito Rodríguez, 1949), a crime melodrama informed by the growing presence of East Asian immigrants in the city.[7] The experience of going to the movies in Mexico during the Golden Age most certainly included a respectable amount of Mexican alternatives, but audiences did have access to a considerable number of films from the United States and other countries at all times. Under this light, my contention is that we must read the Golden Age not only in terms of the expansion in production but also in terms of the cultural and aesthetic diversification of the film experience in the context of the Mexican Miracle. As I will develop later, this also affects the aesthetics of Mexican cinema. Major figures like Arturo de Córdova, Pedro Armendáriz, Pedro Infante, Jorge Negrete, Cantinflas, and Tin Tan played not only Mexican stereotypical archetypes but also characters facing the challenges of cosmopolitan modernization and even figures that came directly from European literary classics.

A path to rethinking the nature of cinematic culture and representation in the Golden Age is to trace what people were in fact watching in theaters at any given time. If we take a snapshot of the cinematic offerings in Mexico City in the week of June 12–18, 1950, as documented by María Luisa Amador and Jorge Ayala Blanco, a fascinatingly complex picture emerges.[8] According to their *Cartelera cinematográfica, 1950–1959*, twelve movies opened that week.[9] Five of them were American: *Bad Boy* (dir. Kurt Neumann, 1949), about a young delinquent; *Neptune's Daughter* (dir. Edward Buzzell, 1949), a romantic comedy starring synchronized swimmer Esther Williams; *Chinatown at Midnight* (dir. Seymour Friedman, 1949), a thriller about a thief who mistakenly kills two people; and *Shadow on the Wall* (dir. Pat Jackson, 1950), another thriller, this time about a murderer's attempt to suppress a witness. Two were English: *San Demetrio London* (dir. Charles Frend, 1943), a World War II movie about an English supply ship; and *The Fallen Idol* (dir. Carol Reed, 1948), the classic David O. Selznick production, still widely admired by film enthusiasts and the most popular of the lot, given that it showed for three weeks. Two were French: *Not Guilty* (*Non coupable*, dir. Henri Decoine,

1947), a crime drama; and *The Mysteries of Paris* (*Les mystères de Paris*, dir. Jacques de Baroncelli, 1943), one of the many adaptations of Eugène Sue's novel. Finally, four Mexican films were released: *Pasión jarocha* (*Veracruz Passion*, dir. Carlos Véjar, 1949), a drama about the conflict between two Veracruz towns related to labor issues in the sugar cane fields; *Cuando acaba la noche* (*When the Night Ends*, dir. Emilio Gómez Muriel, 1950), a thriller about a crime-fighting reporter; *La marca del zorrillo* (*The Mark of the Skunk*, dir. Gilberto Martínez Solares, 1950), a parody of *The Mark of Zorro* starring comedic star Germán Valdés Tin Tan, which also lasted three weeks in exhibition; and *Una mujer de Oriente* (*A Woman of the East*, dir. Juan Orol, 1946), a convoluted thriller about a secret agents in New York dealing with the death of an inventor.

This landscape of cinematic options available to a Mexican spectator at a specific moment in time provides important clues about the way in which cinema works simultaneously as a site of the nation and as a site of cosmopolitanism, locating Mexico City's audiences into flows of cultural circulation related to capitalism and modernity. In Mexican culture and politics, 1950 is a key year. Mexico was in the middle of President Miguel Alemán's administration, which consolidated a model of development based on industrialization and urbanization and resulted in the country's consequent opening to foreign trade and investment.[10] These radical transformations in Mexico's life and culture impacted culture decisively and the tension between capitalist development and the social and cultural spheres of the country produced some of Mexico's major cultural works, including Octavio Paz's widely read *El laberinto de la soledad* (The labyrinth of solitude), a landmark essay on national identity and modernity, and Luis Buñuel's Mexican masterpiece *Los olvidados*, a scathing critique of the Alemán modernization project from the perspective of those excluded by it. While the late 1940s and early 1950s fall squarely into most accounts of the Golden Age (i.e., the cinematic boom rendered possible by the industry's growth that resulted from the involvement of Europe and the United States in World War II), the fact is that a closer look into the period shows a complex cinematic landscape in which iconic nationalist productions share the urban space with a diversity of nationally produced films that dealt with the new modern realities and with a new flow of productions coming from the United States and Europe. Film historians like Carl J. Mora correctly note that the Golden Age is possible thanks to the emergence of a star system, but the repertoire of topics one finds in mainstream accounts still reflects a preference for icons closely related to topics like *comedia ranchera, barrio* portrayals, and melodramas.[11] Still, even in the most canonical of criticism there is recognition of the effect of foreign influences, mostly as a result of the flows between US and Mexican cinema, and even of open attempts by Hollywood to obstruct the dominance of Mexican productions in both the local market and the Spanish-language market at large.[12]

In a recent study, Andrew Paxman describes well the institutional paradox that underlies the arguments in my analysis. Paxman recognizes that, even though cultural nationalism was alive and well as expressed in some of the most important films by Emilio Fernández and Ismael Rodríguez, "the goal of cultural nationalism—in terms of healthy local output and protection from foreign product—was partly compromised in favor of free market forces, from which Hollywood, the president and his cronies stood to benefit."[13] Beyond the historical details described by Paxman, such as the emergence of the Banco Cinematográfico, the relevant point for my purposes is that the process of cultural modernization rendered a cinematic culture that came into quick tension with the Mexicanist culture promoted by the post-revolutionary regime. This was due to the need of opening culture to the same kind of free-market processes that the rest of the economy was fostering. In these terms, cinematic production in Mexico must be approached not within paradigms that replicate the critical expectations and preferences regarding the productions of the period (i.e., to find the "Mexican" in Mexican cinema) but in terms of the concrete, heterogenous offering that the newly created cinematic market was providing to Mexican spectators.

Going back to June 1950, it is important to note the absence of traditional "Mexicanist" films in the offerings. In this particular week, there were no major Pedro Infante vehicles, no rancheras, not even a Cantinflas comedy. The strategic critical focus on a week where such production is absent allows us to see the true heterogeneity of the period's film culture. Each one of the four Mexican films shown in theaters during that short period represents an interesting set of trends with consequent relevance to the study of productions in preceding and subsequent years. We may start by pointing to the most successful of the four films, *La marca del zorrillo*. The film, as I mentioned earlier, is a parody of *The Mark of Zorro* (dir. Rouben Mamoulian, 1940), which had a successful run in theaters in the Christmas season of 1940. The film resonated with Mexican spectators because of its reference to Spanish culture in California resisting Mexican authoritarianism, a thorny subject in the context of the then upcoming one-hundredth anniversary of the Mexican-American War in 1946. *La marca del zorrillo* is a systematic spoof of the Mamoulian version, operating as a brilliant reductio ad absurdum of the original film's epic discourse into a parody based on deflating the heroic nature of the character. The visual language of the film is thoroughly constructed through an interesting counterpoint. On the one hand, some scenes (such as the one depicted in Figure 8.1), recreate Europeanized imageries through work in art direction that places generic signifiers of the cosmopolitan devoid of meaning, such as a medieval suit of armor that has no historical place in the nineteenth-century world of El Zorro or the random weapons in the back of the room that range from a medieval axe to a couple of rifles (the only historically accurate element) to a Sarracene sword, most likely copied out of some Orientalist Hollywood film. On the other hand (as Figure 8.2 shows), the film also features spaces such as a traditional Mexican kitchen, decorated with craft pottery and utensils. Something similar happens at the level of dress: both of Tin Tan characters in the figures are dressed in a European style, marking their status as aristocrats, while the women in Figure 8.2 are dressed in more traditional Mexican style. This counterpoint between hollowed-out Europeanness and meaningless Mexicanness (as one cannot really derive any consistent identitarian discourse from these elements) deploys cultural parody as a way to enact historical recreation, not through realism, but through a stance able to exercise critical distance from it.

The point of this distance is a depreciation of the cultural density of both cosmopolitan and national signifiers. The word *zorrillo* (skunk) in the title is in itself a deflation of the word *zorro* (fox), an animal that many English-language viewers likely do not identify with the Zorro character. The fact that this was a vehicle for Germán Valdés—known as Tin Tan, one of Mexico's most popular comics—at the height of his fame, is telling precisely because of his usual identification with figures attached to Mexicanness, such as the *pachuco* character of his 1940s films. It may be the case that the iconicity of the character comes in part from the fact that Paz, in his aforementioned *El laberinto de la soledad*, devoted a chapter to the pachuco, and Tin Tan's biographies still privilege this character as his central contribution to the culture.[14] But one must not forget, as Paz himself reminds us, that the pachuco subculture was a Mexican American cultural subjectivity mostly visible in Los Angeles, becoming particularly relevant in the 1943 Zoot Suit riots.[15] Tin Tan's own rendering had important debts to the Mexican American subculture and, as Javier Durán argues, "Tin Tan's linguistic hybridity, his mimicry,

Fig. 8.1 Anachronistic and out-of-place props act as generic signifiers of the cosmopolitan in *La marca del zorillo*.

and his stereotyping (of pochismo) placed him in a liminal position that began unmasking and menacing the homogeneous realm of Mexican nationalism, since the pachuco's cultural survival strategy was not recalcitrance or silence but loudness."[16] In other words, Tin Tan is hardly an icon of Mexican national identity. Rather, he is a cultural negotiator between Mexican urban culture and a repertory of cosmopolitan influences that Mexican audiences were processing through different processes of cultural mediation. However, even his most admiring readers fail to acknowledge the brilliance of his cosmopolitan work. Carlos Monsiváis, for instance, characterizes his parodies of world literature and culture as "poor distortions," showing a clear preference for his work on the pachuco and the barrio.[17] Such dismissals, in my opinion, fail to see that Tin Tan reflected the tensions of modernity and cosmopolitanism in the context of a country that was, simultaneously, conforming an "imagined community" via cultural nationalism and developing symbolic ties to the transnational flows of capitalist modernization.[18]

Fig. 8.2 The décor of the kitchen and the actress's costumes evoke traditional Mexican iconographies, while Tin Tan is dressed in a more European style.

La marca del zorrillo belongs to a genre in which major figures of national cinema adapted works of classic literature and film into the languages predominant in Mexican cinema: *carpa*-style humor and melodrama.[19] The film is remarkable because of the absence of visible elements of the kind of working-class Mexicanness Tin Tan would advance in his more recognized 1950 film, *El rey del barrio* (*The King of the Neighborhood*, dir. Gilberto Martínez Solares), still deemed to be one of his most memorable performances. Nevertheless, in *La marca del zorrillo*, the kind of performative humor located in the liminal spaces of national identity is deployed as an instrument engaging with the cosmopolitan culture of newly urbanized Mexico. The film has elements that would be familiar to working- and middle-class audiences, such as the comedic use of vernacular lower-class speech. Tin Tan's romantic interest in the film, Lupita (Silvia Pinal), speaks with a mock-accent that imitates expressions by Mexicans of lower-class and indigenous origins. Of course, Pinal, the actress who plays her, was in fact a blond, upper-class film star in the making, which emphasizes the ironic nature of her interpretation of Lupita. The protagonist, the son of a member of the local aristocracy who secretly becomes the "Zorrillo," tries to seduce Lupita with the kind of high-cultured register expected from members of nobility. At one point in the film, he asks Lupita to love him "like Francesca loves Paolo or like Juliet loves Romeo," referencing respectively Dante Alighieri and Shakespeare. This kind of reference was not alien to comedy viewers. Tin Tan's film belongs to a series of parodies of Western literary classics by Mexican stars of the day. García Riera mentions that this film was made as a follow-up to the success of Cantinflas with his parodic renderings of Alexandre Dumas's *The Three Musketeers* (dir. Miguel M. Delgado, 1942) and Shakepeare's *Romeo and Juliet* (dir. Miguel M. Delgado, 1943).[20] Tin Tan himself would make, also in 1950, a version of the Sinbad myth from the Arabian nights entitled *Simbad el mareado* (*Simbad the Seasick*, dir. Gilberto Martínez Solares, 1950), parodying the Douglas Fairbanks Jr. vehicle *Sinbad the Sailor* (dir. Richard Wallace, 1947), which enjoyed great success in its four-week run in December 1947. It is not at all coincidental that Cantinflas and Tin Tan were aiming their parody skills not only at stereotypes of urban popular subjects but also at characters from Western literary classics. Adaptations of this kind of work were quite popular in Mexico. In fact, in 1949, Laurence Olivier's *Hamlet* (1948) was in the top three grossing movies for five weeks, a feat few films could match.[21]

Tin Tan also starred in his own parody of Dumas's classic, entitled *Los tres mosqueteros y medio* (*Three and a Half Musketeers*, dir. Gilberto Martínez Solares), in the role of D'Artagnan. Cantinflas was most likely appropriating the 1939 slapstick version of the story directed by Allan Dwan and starring Don Ameche, while Tin Tan's version may have had in mind George Sydney's 1948 version with Gene Kelly and Lana Turner. In this film, it is notable that a musical number, entitled "Pobres gentes de París" (The Poor of Paris), is interpreted by Tin Tan using Spanish with an American accent, closely appropriating styles from American music and referencing the American source of his parody. While the musical generally appears as a site of articulation of national culture (mostly through the work of Pedro Infante and Jorge Negrete in rancheras), Tin Tan's musical repertoire belongs to a wide canon of music imported from slapstick musicals and crooning traditions in the United States. In yet another memorable performance, in the 1948 film *Músico, poeta y loco* (*Musician, Poet, and Madman*, dir. Humberto Gómez Landero), Tin Tan, pretending to be a teacher in a school for foreign women, improvises the supposed history of a series of dance styles (tango, rumba, foxtrot, and others) proceeding to perform each one of them with a female counterpart from the country of origin of the dance. This performance of transnational musical prowess, of course, was far from being the only example in Golden Age cinema. One can remember Pedro Infante's famous crooning version of "Bésame mucho" in *A toda máquina* (*Full Speed Ahead*, dir. Ismael Rodríguez, 1951), which is received, in the context of the film, by adoring American women yelling "Sinatra" at him. The highly performative vocal range deployed by Tin Tan, informed by hemispheric traditions of popular music, along with his embodiment of a worldy set of characters (besides Sinbad, D'Artagnan, Zorro, and the pachuco type, one could recall "Puss without Boots," a pirate and a sultan, all from late 1950s movies), were all instruments that mediated the cultural languages and flows of modernity into the imaginary of Mexican spectators, who, following all of these popular films, would possess a surprisingly diverse literary and transnational culture that had little relationship with the languages of national identity.

Mexican audiences acquired through film significant exposure to literary classics thanks to the extensive distribution of American and French classics, and these adaptions were not the sole territory of comedic stars. In the very same week when *La marca del zorrillo* opened, audiences could also see Jacques de Baroncelli's adaptation of Sue's *Mysteries of Paris*, starring Marcel Herrand and Yolande Laffon. Nineteenth- and twentieth-century fiction and other literary classics received attention from producers and distributors in Mexico, and various adaptations found their way into Mexican theaters. Víctor Hugo's *Les misèrables* constantly played on Mexican screens thanks to the celebrated American versions from 1934 directed by Raymond Bernard, starring Harry Baur as Jean Valjean, and from 1935, directed by Richard Bolewslawski, starring Fredric March.[22] Not surprisingly, a 1943 Mexican version was also released, directed by Fernando Rivero, and with Domingo Soler as Valjean. An even more important, earlier example of this trend is Chano Urueta's *El conde de Montecristo* (*The Count of Monte Cristo*, 1942), which launched Arturo de Córdova's career thanks to his compelling interpretation of Edmond Dantès. The film is a masterful epic adaptation (with a running time of nearly three hours) of Alexandre Dumas's classic. It enjoyed a three-week run in the Cine Palacio in April and May 1942, which, as I have exemplified in other cases, is a mark of success. This movie is noteworthy in the context of my discussion because of its early release date, in the Ávila

Camacho administration, during the World War II years that supposedly privileged Mexican-themed films because of the purported decline of Hollywood and European productions. This grand production, which was, according to García Riera, enthusiastically received by the press as superior to previous French and American versions, is strictly contemporary with many of the films that consecrated major stars of national cinema, such as Cantinflas and Sara García, and it preceded Emilio Fernández's nationalist classic *Flor silvestre* (*Wildflower*, 1943) by one year.[23] *El conde de Montecristo* is a foundational film that has yet to achieve the critical recognition it deserves (it is hardly even mentioned in histories of the period) in part because national-culture frames of interpretation put it under erasure. But the film shows the way in which drama evolved in the first part of the 1940s with the adoption and deployment of an arsenal of narratives that entered the consciousness of Mexican producers and directors through their continuous interactions with the offerings of English- and French-language cinema of the times. This was not mere imitation. It was a recognition that, insofar as the cinematic ecosystem of national production also included the considerable circulation and consumption of foreign films, audiences' tastes were diversified with the cosmopolitan discourses and affects proper to urban culture and to the gradual intersection of Mexico City with global economic and symbolic flows. The story had such cultural presence in filmmaking imaginaries that Tin Tan also shot its parody: *El vizconde de Montecristo* (*The Viscount of Monte Cristo*, dir. Gilberto Martínez Solares, 1954).

An interesting figure within this paradigm is Jorge Negrete, whose standing as the middle-class alternative to Pedro Infante's more populist persona allowed him to interpret more cosmopolitan characters. Even Negrete's role within codes of Mexicanist iconicity had tints of transnationalism, as Mercedes Díaz López has argued in her study of his connections with Spain.[24] Negrete participated in a series of movies that expanded the visual representation of Spanish culture, including *En tiempos de la Inquisición* (*In the Times of the Inquisition*, dir. Juan Bustillo Oro, 1946), a romance based on Christian-Moor relations in Golden Age Spain. Negrete's resume shows participation in the same paradigms of cosmopolitan literary adaptation from the standpoint of drama as those articulated by Tin Tan and Cantinflas in comedy. Negrete starred in *El jorobado* (*The Hunchback*, dir. Jaime Salvador, 1943), a Mexican adaptation of French writer Paul Féval's novel *The Hunchback*, the source of a long tradition of movies about the hunchback of Notre Dame. Negrete was also part of yet another example of links constructed by Mexican cinema's cosmopolitan endeavor: the adaptation of Venezuelan novelist's Rómulo Gallegos's *Canaima* (dir. Juan Bustillo Oro, 1945), which, along with Fernando de Fuentes's adaptation of *Doña Bárbara* (1943), starring María Félix as the title character, incorporated into the discourses of Mexican cinema forms of literary drama that evolved from codes of nineteenth-century global narrative into the portrayal of national and regional realities of the early twentieth century.[25] The point to be made is that Negrete not only embodied his better-known Mexican characters. His cinematic persona became the site for the introduction of an array of global characters and subjectivities that confronted Mexican audiences with cosmopolitanism and with forms of cultural engagement that had less to do with identity formation and more to do with the intersection of affect and the flows of symbolic imaginaries across borders.

Up to this point, considering the role of canonical figures of Mexican cinema such as Cantinflas, Jorge Negrete, Arturo de Córdova, and Tin Tan in the representation of characters from Western traditions of culture, and the constant presence on Mexican screens of domestic and foreign adaptations of a wide array of literary classics, a few preliminary conclusions must be drawn. A cosmopolitan framework of analysis of the Golden Age requires us to rethink the way in which we conceive the iconicity of its main figures and the plurality of imaginaries they embodied across their different roles. The canonization of Cantinflas as the *"peladito,"* (an untraslatable term that refers to lower-class urban subjects), Tin Tan as the *"pachuco,"* (a term generally used by Mexican and Chicana/o participants in the Zoot Suit subculture), and Jorge Negrete as the *"charro,"* (the cowboy-like protagonist of the ranchera film) while not inaccurate, provides an exceedingly limited understanding of their performance in the context of the 1940s and the 1950s. Their embodiments of Zorro, Romeo, or the Hunchback inserted their work into the global paradigms of circulation of culture that cinema enacted in the same period and that also included icons from other traditions, such as Douglas Fairbanks Jr., Tyrone Power, or Jean Gabin. In the marketplace of the star system constructed in Mexico during the Golden Age, their performances allowed audiences to negotiate with the icons brought by Hollywood and French cinema to domestic screens by way of the different strategies through which local productions recast their source materials. In some cases, as in De Córdova's *Count of Montecristo*, the characters embodied transcultural intersections that conveyed the affective frameworks of global melodramatic forms in order to deliver the moral codes of family and honor that national cinema privileged since its early manifestations.

The more subversive comedic presentations, particularly Tin Tan's, provided a deftly carnivalized version of transnational melodramatic affects, precisely by hollowing out the adaptations' emotional loads and constructing humor through a critical distance that allowed audiences to question the very processes of cultural modernization that rendered these films possible. One can speculate, for example, that audience members deciding between *The Mysteries of Paris* and *La marca del zorrillo* were in fact presented with the alternative of either participating affectively in world culture, via the constant reactualization of melodramatic codes in French, American, and Mexican films, or distancing themselves critically from that world culture through the deployment of comedy as a performance of resistance vis-á-vis global affect economies. Of course, my contention here is not that audiences are overdetermined by melodrama and other genres. Rather, a full study of the landscape of cinema options available to Mexican spectators shows that they could develop diverse relationships of distance with genres that perform different degrees of emotional participation. Tin Tan, then, is someone who enlarges the affective archives available to audiences, by formalizing a critical distance from foreign forms of culture that most likely were part of the audience's cultural repertoires. Tin Tan's national nature is not so much his construction of identifiable stereotypes of Mexicanness, but his ability to subvert the increasingly hegemonic codes of import capitalism through a perfect command of worldly cultural repertoires, which he performs in order to methodically hollow out their affective registers. This is particularly obvious in *Simbad el mareado*, where the Orientalist fantasy that allows the effective delivery of Douglas Fairbanks Jr.'s iconic masculinity is thoroughly ridiculed.

Cosmopolitanism is not solely about the incorporation of transnational tropes into the local imaginary. It is also about the integration of bodies and subjectivities into the global flows of transnational capital. Mexico's Golden Age took place in the wake of the parallel construction of a politicized national identity and of social bodies of ideological engagement (such as unions), which were at the base of President Lázaro Cárdenas's project of socialist-oriented modernization. As Alan Knight documents, the late 1930s and early 1940s were a period of political "de-radicalization" in which the social mobilization of Cardenismo was held back both by elites, who started decrying communist ideas, and by workers, whose economic interests were increasingly at odds with the state's ideologies of reform.[26] The increasing process of economic cosmopolitanism found its way into the Mexican screens by turning cinema into a vehicle of confronting local and regional realities with the pressures of capital and the collapse of Cardenista political communities. This is the case of *Pasión jarocha*, a film that, regardless of its title, embodies the violence of labor disruption as much as it does national identity. Out of the four Mexican movies in our June week, *Pasión jarocha* is perhaps the one that articulates the desire for the national in the most intensely contrived way. The film is an allegory of the conflicts that economic competition creates in microregional contexts.[27] It focuses on a problem that arises between cane-field peasant Omar (Víctor Manuel Mendoza), from the rural town of Tlacotalpan, Veracruz, and fisherman Hugo (Rafael Lanzetta), when the latter tries to court the former's sister Rosalinda (Irma Torres). The conflict between Omar and Hugo, which turns violent, mirrors that between the communities, when cane-field workers related to Omar tie up the transportation the Alvarado fishermen need for their commodities. The conflict is resolved when Rosalinda persuades both communities to mend their conflicts, while her love story achieves a happy ending. The movie is famously trite and Garcia Riera offers an unmatched description of the ending: "The moment in which Irma Torres, turned into a champion of the folkloric-trade union-sentimental unity between Alvarado and Tlacotalpan, discovers in herself the oratory virtues necessary to end localist misunderstandings, is one of the most dismaying that any regionalist melodrama had ever proposed."[28]

Behind the trite localist rhetoric, the film is in fact a testament to the anxieties that capitalist modernization was bringing into the myth of national articulation fostered by other more canonical cinematic productions. The use of the adjective *jarocho* (which refers to people from the state of Veracruz) makes it part of a canon of movies that deploy comedy and melodrama to appropriate regional difference into a more unitary national identity. The established example is *Los tres huastecos* (*The Three Huastecans*, dir. Ismael Rodríguez, 1948), in which Pedro Infante famously played triplets who were separated at birth, each one representing both one of the three states that make up the Huasteca region and one of three social sectors: the army, the church, and the people embodied by an outlaw who nonetheless has a good heart and also belongs to the community. *Pasión jarocha*, however, has a crucial difference from the nationalist fantasy of *Los tres huastecos*: labor. The Huasteca's unification symbolically embodied in Infante's playing of the three characters is devoid of economic conflict as none of the three characters is an economic agent: it is an alliance between the state, the church (a powerful entity in the country's interior), and a people that is represented in no relation to the economic chain of production. The conflict between fishermen and *cañeros* (cane-field peasants) is more properly a conflict between two forms of traditional economies that negotiate with each other as modernization disrupts traditional forms of life. In the 1940s and 1950s, a considerable number of melodramas and thrillers reflected the anxieties produced by a modernization process that contradicted the utopian rural scenes constructed by films such as *María Candelaria* (dir. Emilio Fernández, 1944) and *Los tres huastecos*. However, one should note that even the most entrenchedly rural film directors were problematizing the nostalgic construction of small-town life through the adoption of critical languages from abroad. A good example is another 1950 film, *Rosauro Castro*, Roberto Gavaldón's tough critique of the figure of the post-revolutionary cacique. As Fernando Mino García points out, Gavaldón uses the resources of noir cinema and the western, appropriating both stylistic and ideological strategies from both, in order to articulate some of the political and moral messages embedded in the film, while simultaneously introducing idealizing and mythical elements that undid some of the more radical angles of the source materials.[29] Like *Pasión jarocha*, Gavaldón's rural world begins to show, albeit in a somewhat idealized way, the frictions of modernity placed under erasure in Emilio Fernández's more canonical rural melodramas.

Canonical languages of Mexican cinema inherited from the 1930s conceived of the city as a site of vice, a place that perverted the values of rural Mexicans. The cultural myth of the "midnight virgin" was developed in such foundational films as *Santa* (dir. Antonio Moreno, 1932) and *La mujer del puerto* (*The Woman of the Port*, dir. Arcady Boytler, 1934).[30] However, as the 1940s brought the political concerns tied to urbanization and the post-Cárdenas deradicalization previously mentioned, many key works would reframe these inherited paradigms in terms of the social conflicts of the age. A key example of this process is *Distinto amanecer* (*A New Dawn*, dir. Julio Bracho, 1943), in which Octavio (Pedro Armendáriz), a union leader, seeks justice for another leader, murdered at the command of Vidal (Enrique Uthoff), a corrupt politician. The movie evidently represents in its main plotline the breakup between the political class and union structures in the Ávila Camacho regime. However, the political language of the film has strong influences from screenwriter Max Aub, a Spanish exile. Like Buñuel, Aub was part of the left-wing intelligentsia that arrived in Mexico in the late 1930s, and, even though cinema was for him mostly a way to make a living, the way in which this movie inflects a critique of political authoritarianism and the resistant role of activists is yet another cosmopolitan influence. Notably, the film has a disclaimer at the beginning, perhaps to protect itself from censorship, in which it says that its story could happen in any context, even though the film opens with a series of shots identifiably set in downtown Mexico City, portraying a bustling metropolis. This new conception of Mexico appeared across different films in which the struggles of Mexican labor and the perils of industrialization gradually developed a language that translated affective modes of narration into the challenges of economic life. A good example of this is *Prisión de sueños* (*Prison of Dreams*, dir. Victor Urruchúa, 1949), which, after a long shot of Mexico's new industrial landscape, provides a melodramatic vehicle for emerging star Kathy Jurado, focused on the challenges of a family in the new economic reality. Changing social mores are also registered in cinema, most notably in Ismael Rodríguez's melodrama *Borrasca en las almas* (*Stormy Souls*, 1954), which features a worker who loses a hand in an work-related incident and a set of twins, played memorably by María Elena Marqués, one of whom is an economically independent worker. This narrative of union workers appears even in the work of major directors of the period, most notably in Alejandro Galindo's *Dicen que soy comunista* (*They Say I'm a Communist*, 1951) and *Los dineros del diablo* (*The Devil's Money*, 1953), more directly based in the director's personal political views. In Francisco Peredo Castro's words, "the union is for Galindo an autonomous, sovereign world, a paternalistic cloister, which gives workers security, finances their ball games, pays their fines and protects him from an authentic, wider, political life."[31]

Distinto amanecer, which can be considered a precursor in this line of labor-themed cinema, makes reference to 1930s cinema by casting Andrea Palma, the actress who achieved fame as *La mujer del puerto*'s protagonist, in the lead role of Julieta. Bracho's film offers viewers a very distinctively urban and cosmopolitan setting, framed by the type of hard-boiled fiction that was rendered famous by *The Maltese Falcon* (dir. John Huston, 1941), which was released in Mexico a year before *Distinto amanecer*. The performances by Armendáriz and Palma echo those of Humphrey Bogart as the detective figure and Mary Astor as femme fatale. However, their lack of romantic cynicism may put their relationship closer to more properly romantic films like *Casablanca* (dir. Michael Curtiz, 1942), which is a more relevant influence in the type of love story represented in the film. But the appropriation of the noir in Mexico seems to negotiate the genre's embedded cynicism with the type of idealist moral tale favored by Mexican cinema. It is not coincidental that Emilio Gómez Muriel, *Distinto amanecer*'s producer, was the director of the third movie in our June 1950 cinematic week: *Cuando acaba la noche*. This film replicates a similar narrative of the individual detective fighting corrupt structures of power. In this case, the protagonist, Federico (Rafael Baledón) is a news reporter who brings down a drug-trafficking network, while also assisting in liberating Gabriel (David Silva) from a wrongful conviction. García Riera reminds us that this kind of thriller is outdated in its representation of the news reporter as detective, because Hollywood movies of the 1920s and 1930s failed to construct a plausible rendering of the character.[32] The film has unmistakable moral narratives related to female perdition: Gabriel's wife Consuelo (Lilia Prado) is seduced by Enrique (Carlos Múzquiz), and her reconciliation with her husband results in her being wounded in the struggle between Rafael and the gangsters. These familiar melodramatic plots, though, coexist with the anxieties of a Mexico embedded in the dark sides of transnational capitalism. Set in Ciudad Juárez, the film constructs a narrative of social corruption and moral debauchery tied to the emerging role that drug trafficking had in the shaping of capital circulation between Mexico and the United States. Consuelo is portrayed as a woman who is trapped by this new capitalism, as she is forced by Enrique into prostitution, which in turn is an obstacle to her ability to be a good wife to Gabriel. Lilia Prado's stunning screen presence (Figure 8.3a) provides Consuelo traits of sophistication and beauty similar to Andrea Palma's channeling of Marlene Dietrich in late 1930s and early 1940s films. Characterized with a look not too distant from Hollywood stars of the day, Consuelo's blond hair and wealth, expressed in this particular shot by the subtle but obviously luxurious jewelry that frames her visage, is presented to spectators as a fiction financed by Enrique's corrupt labors. In fact, as we can see in Figure 8.3b, when Enrique, the gangster, enters the screen, his menacing presence, reminiscent of famous Hollywood actors of the genre, such as James Cagney, immediately exposes the fiction of Consuelo's beauty, whose face suddenly shows grief and fear. The framework

Fig. 8.3a and Fig. 8.3b Lilia Prado channels glamorous international stars like Marlene Dietrich, while the performance of Carlos Múzquiz evokes the Hollywood gangster.

of the cabaret as the site of this double personality confirms, as it happens in many Mexican films of the period, the relationship between this plethora of characters connected with urban contemporaneity and the feared moral decadence that Mexican cinema, since its origins, represents as a consequence of modernization.

For my purposes, it is worth noting, as Álvaro Fernández Reyes has extensively documented, that both *Distinto amanecer* and *Cuando acaba la noche* belong to a paradigm of representation of mafias and gangsters that rose to prominence, influenced by Hollywood noir cinema and crime journalism, in the late 1940s.[33] Fernández Reyes's study offers a useful example of the deep penetration of the genre. He provides a nonexhaustive list of crime and suspense films, mostly set in urban contexts, in an appendix to his book; it contains 110 films shot between 1946 and 1955, which expands to nearly two hundred titles when including those that go from the earliest films to 1959.[34] Fernández Reyes's framing of this production is symptomatic of the challenges that the Mexican noir in particular, and cinematic cosmopolitanism in general, pose in a critical tradition that still has to grapple with the limitations of the "national cinema" paradigm. He confesses that his first idea was to find a noir cinema that would move beyond melodrama, although he would later echo ideas that noir cinema proper does not exist in Mexico. Instead, rather than studying the noir genre, he identifies the use of crime, suspense, and thriller as elements that become embedded into films that also maintain elements proper to the Mexican film industry.[35] Fernández Reyes, of course, accurately describes the formal elements of the production studied in his book, but the critical judgment decries the films as "an aesthetic crisis and not a production one," and as a phenomenon related to commercialization and to "the modernizing needs of tastes and the habits of the consumer immersed in social restructuration."[36]

I am not convinced that the challenges of Americanization and commercialism can be described as an "aesthetic crisis." I would rather say that the "social restructuration" and "modernizing needs" mentioned by Fernández Reyes relate to the ways in which the affective modernization of cinema audiences via an increasingly global offering in theaters: besides French, Mexican, American, and English movies, films from Spain, Portugal, Germany, and Italy opened in 1950s and productions from places like Eastern Europe, Japan, Brazil, Israel, China, and even Australia would open in the subsequent decade.[37] If anything, the "crisis" was in fact the decreasing relevance of productions espousing rural nostalgia in an exhibition ecosystem that provided spectators films that, regardless of their status as foreign, were more relevant to the cultural tastes and to the mediations of subjectivity that the new industrial, urban society produced. Even as early as 1943, *Distinto amanecer*'s embrace of contemporary political realities and of the dynamic urban experience radically challenged the aesthetic and ideological hegemony of rural productions of the Fernández-Figueroa paradigm. According to Jesús Ibarra, critics considered *Distinto amanecer* the "antithesis" of Fernández's *Flor silvestre*, which also cast Armendáriz as its protagonist.[38] Ibarra also highlights the rivalry and animadversion between them: Bracho considered Fernandez's films a mere postcard and the director of *Flor silvestre* vulgar, while Fernández deemed Bracho to be an elitist, and his camera work (which was influenced by American noir) "useless boasts of technique."[39] What this polemic renders visible is that the tension between nationalist ideology and cosmopolitanism is part of Mexican cinema from the very outset of the Golden Age. Figueroa's contemplative cinematography is widely remembered as the iconic visual regime of the period, but he also shot *Distinto amanecer*, reflecting the social acceleration of urban life and the noir's penchant for closed, claustrophobic spaces, in stark contrast with the open spaces of his nationalist imagery.

If we go back to our week of June 1950, one could point out that *Cuando acaba la noche* was released in competition with a major thriller, *The Fallen Idol*, which in fact was the most successful foreign film of the week, as well as two American and one French film in the genre. *The Fallen Idol* was a tremendously innovative work of cinema, narrating its suspenseful plot from the perspective of a child. The film, the first one of three landmark collaborations between director Carol Reed and writer Graham Greene, also provided audiences with a gender-bending noir that used drama and humor in a highly skillful way.[40] If one contrasts this with the purportedly outdated melodramatic tone and narrative structure of *Cuando acaba la noche*, it would be tempting to conclude that there was indeed an aesthetic crisis. However, when looked at closely, Gómez Muriel's film relates to Reed's work in more or less the same way in which *Distinto amanecer* relates to *The Maltese Falcon*. As the noir develops in the United States and England into a major site of formal innovation and ideological critique (considering, for instance, that the major practitioner of the genre was none other than Alfred Hitchcock), Mexican directors working in the genre (major figures in the domestic industry, as we have seen) develop for the form a surplus signification that allows for the positioning of their commodity vis-á-vis domestic audiences. The melodramatic structure of the love story between the protagonists of both *Distinto amanecer* and *Cuando se acaba la noche*, and the reference that both make to forms of crime specific to modern Mexico (political corruption, drugs, and so on) invests the form with a surplus value that keep the films viable in an expanding cinematic market. Also, the inability of critics to find forms of noir cinema that would strictly correspond with the classic understandings of the genre results from the fact that directors such as Bracho, Galindo, and Gómez Muriel were not in the business of reproducing transnational cinematic forms, but of developing narrative and affective languages that could effectively engage an unprecedentedly heterogeneous consumer taste and the resulting ideological proliferation of urban audiences.

A good way of concluding my analysis is to bring to the fore the fourth film in our June 1950 week, Juan Orol's *Una mujer de Oriente*, one of the most preposterous yet fascinating examples of the cinematic consequences of cosmopolitanism in Mexico. Orol was an exiled Galician filmmaker who made a number of films in Mexico and Cuba, chaotically adopting, with results bordering many times on the surreal, the diverse repertoire of cinematic discourses flowing through Mexico's screens. Regardless of his cult status—which recently fostered a successful carnivalesque biopic/tribute, *El fantástico mundo de Juan Orol* (*The Fantastic World of Juan Orol*, dir. Sebastián del Amo, 2012)—and of his commercial success, Orol's work is usually absent from readings of the period, perhaps because of the questionable quality of his work and the loss of many of his negatives in the Cineteca Nacional fire of 1982.[41] In roughly the same years as the Alemán administration, Orol produced a series of thrillers of films starring himself and his wife and collaborator, Cuban actress Rosa Carmina, who was a major figure of the *rumbera* genre that nationalized cabaret culture into cinema.[42] *Una mujer de Oriente*, shot in 1946, four years before its release, is Carmina's first film with Orol. The film is a hodgepodge of a thriller in which Orol's detective, an American colonel named Randolph Campbell, must research a weapon invented by Japanese count Amaru Saito (Carlos López Moctezuma). Carmina plays Loti, a Japanese woman who helps Campbell with the investigation. The film has many preposterous plot twists, the most notorious of which is the fact that we learn at the end that Loti was Campbell's daughter, pretending to be Japanese, a turn that García Riera interprets as Orol's inability to leave behind the "pathetism of family relations in Spanish-language melodrama."[43]

In its craziness, *Una mujer de Oriente* conceives the thriller as a repository of the different elements of cinema provided by the modern era and adopted in a thoroughly superficial way. Loti is clearly inspired in the work of Asian-American performers like Anna May Wong.[44] The film is also an underdiscussed precursor of the Santo wrestler films, which also negotiated foreign genres (such as James Bond intrigues) with Mexican imaginaries, in its work with the idea of the evil scientist and the development of science-fictional weapons (in this case Saita's ray) that embodied Cold War paranoias.[45] Orol's novelty is precisely his unapologetically commercial approach to the cosmopolitan repertoire in his reach, his surface appropriation of a film culture that audiences enthusiastically received, accepting the critical distance unwittingly generated by the ridiculousness of its plots and the obvious technical errors of his production. But under the mantle of their absurdity, Orol's films created a cinematic language that unapologetically exploited the cultural fears of American-style modernization. A meaningful example is his saga of Johnny Carmenta. In *Gángsters contra charros* (1947), Carmenta (Orol), dressed in Bogartian fashion, fights his nemesis, charro Pancho Domínguez (José Pulido) for control of Mexico City's netherworld. The "charro" here has two interesting meanings. It shifts the stereotypical hero of Mexico's nationalist films into the place of the criminal, running a mafialike ring in the city. "Charro" does have a second meaning that refers to corrupt union leaders at the service of the government, which the film implicitly claims in placing the charro in the location of the criminal. The film hilariously pits the ranchera genre—songs and all—in conflict with the kind of American noir and the rumbera sensibility favored by Orol, upending the symbolic economy of Mexico's national cinema. The film's musical numbers juxtapose the typical Golden Age mariachi scene with Rosa Carmina's sexy rumbera numbers, recording with unexpected success the kinds of cultural struggles embodied in films of the day. The film concludes with a standoff in which the two enemies kill each other and kill Carmina's fictional self (her character shares her name), a scene that suggests, if one could derive meaning from Orol's romps, a reluctance to resolve the conflict between cosmopolitanism and nationalism. The film was very successful and managed to open on three screens, a true feat for films of its kind. Audiences who went to see Orol's film were confronted with a spectrum of cultural modernities, and his kitschy style allowed them to not choose between the values of an emerging nation and the exciting cultures of global capitalism and modernity. In the crossroads between different imaginaries, nations and symbolic economies that could be found in microcosms such as the week that started on June 12, 1950, we find a Mexican cinema that provided a worldly experience that cannot be accounted for with the languages of national culture and identity.

> IGNACIO M. Sánchez Prado is Professor of Spanish and Latin American Studies at Washington University in St. Louis. He is the author of five books, including *Screening Neoliberalism: Transforming Mexican Cinema 1988–2012* (Vanderbilt University Press, 2015), *Intermitencias americanistas: Estudios y ensayos escogidos (2004–2010)* (Universidad Nacional

Autónoma de México, 2012), and *Naciones intelectuales: Las fundaciones de la modernidad literaria mexicana (1917–1959)* (Purdue University Press, 2009), and the editor/coeditor of twelve anthologies, including *A History of Mexican Literature* (Cambridge University Press, 2016).

NOTES

1. See Charles Ramírez Berg, *The Classical Mexican Cinema: The Poetics of the Exceptional Golden Age Films* (Austin: University of Texas Press, 2015). This excellent book represents the most recent iteration of this idea of the Golden Age that this essay seeks not so much to refute, but to revise and discuss.

2. See Ernesto R. Acevedo-Muñoz, *Buñuel and Mexico: The Crisis of Mexican Cinema* (Berkeley: University of California Press, 2003); Dolores Tierney, *Emilio Fernández: Pictures in the Margins* (Manchester: Manchester University Press, 2007); Andrew G. Wood, "Blind Men and Fallen Women: Notes on Modernity and Golden Age Mexican Cinema," *Post Identity* 3, no. 1 (2001): 11–24.

3. When referring to "existing understandings," I do not make reference solely to scholarship but also to the way in which film is distributed in television outlets such as Televisa and the work done in classic books such as Carl J. Mora, *Mexican Cinema: Reflection of a Society, 1896–2004* (Jefferson, NC: McFarland, 2005); Paulo Antonio Paranagua, ed., *Mexican Cinema* (London: British Film Institute, 1995). It is telling that most DVDs of cinema of the period are part of series with nationalistic titles such as *Viva México* or *Nuestro cine nacional*.

4. Raymond Williams, *The Long Revolution* (Peterborough: Broadview Press, 2001 [1961]), 64–67.

5. Robert McKee Irwin and Maricruz Castro Ricalde, *Global Mexican Cinema: Its Golden Age* (London: British Film Institute, 2013).

6. These data come from María Luisa Amador and Jorge Ayala Blanco, *Cartelera cinematográfica, 1940–1949* (Mexico City: Universidad Nacional Autónoma de México, 1982); Amador and Ayala Blanco, *Cartelera cinematográfica, 1950–1959* (Mexico City: Universidad Nacional Autónoma de México, 1985).

7. I am making reference here to box-office figures from the magazine *Cinevoz*, which included the top three domestic and international films for every week. The issues consulted are from 1948 and 1949. I thank Rielle Navitski for providing this information.

8. My argument here is, of course, a microcosm of a larger structural process of penetration of transnational cultural industries into the market of Mexican cinema. For a good study of the larger process in relation to the United Sates, see Seth Fein, "From Collaboration to Containment: Hollywood and the International Political Economy of Mexican Cinema after World War II," in *Mexico's Cinema: A Century of Filmmakers*, eds. Joanne Hershfield and David R. Maciel (Lanham, MD: SR Books, 2005), 123–163.

9. Amador and Ayala Blanco, *Cartelera cinematográfica, 1950–1959*, 23–24.

10. Luis Aboites Aguilar, "El último tramo, 1929–2000," in *Nueva historia mínima de México* (Mexico: El Colegio de México, 2004), 272–273.

11. Mora, *Mexican Cinema*, 71.

12. Emilio García Riera, *Breve historia del cine mexicano: Primer siglo, 1897–1997* (Mexico City: Instituto Mexicano de Cinematografía, 1998), 175–177. A very rich discussion of this matter may be found in Francisco Peredo Castro, "Las intervenciones gubernamentales como estrategia de crecimiento y supervivencia durante la Segunda Guerra Mundial y la posguerra (1940–1952)," in *El Estado y la imagen en movimiento*, ed. Cuauhtémoc Carmona (Mexico City: Instituto Mexicano de Cinematografía / Consejo Nacional para la Cultura y las Artes, 2012), 75–108.

13. Andrew Paxman, "Cooling to Cinema and Warming to Television: State Mass Media Policy, 1940–1964," in *Dictablanda: Politics, Work, and Culture in Mexico, 1938–1968*, eds. Paul Gillingham and Benjamin T. Smith (Durham, NC: Duke University Press, 2014), 306.

14. See, particularly, Rafael Aviña, *Aquí está su pachucote—¡Noooo! Una biografía de Germán Valdés* (Mexico City: Consejo Nacional para la Cultura y las Artes, 2009).

15. Octavio Paz, *El laberinto de la soledad*, ed. Enrico Mario Santí (Madrid: Cátedra, 2008), 148–149.

16. Javier Durán, "Nation and Translation: The *Pachuco* in Mexican Popular Culture; Germán Valdés Tin Tan," *Journal of the Midwest Modern Language Association* 35, no. 2 (2002): 43. The term *"pochismo"* refers in a derogatory way to the hybridization of Mexican and United States culture, and was commonly used to reference things such as Spanglish in mid-century Mexico.

17. See Carlos Monsiváis, "Cantinflas and Tin Tan: Mexico's Greatest Comedians," in Hershfield and Maciel, *Mexico's Cinema*, 123–164.

18. Benedict Anderson, *Imagined Communities: Reflections on the Origin and Spread of Nationalism* (New York: Verso, 1983).

19. *Carpa* is a kind of variety spectacle that was popular in Mexico in the 1930s. The name refers to the circuslike tent in which they took place, and they usually included a mixture of comedy sketches, musical performances, and novelty acts. Many famous comedians in Mexican cinema came from the carpa scene.

20. Emilio García Riera, *Historia documental del cine mexicano*, vol. 4 (Mexico City: Ediciones Era, 1974), 154.

21. This information comes from the *Cinevoz* reference mentioned in note 6.

22. The two film versions of *Les miserables* opened in Mexico in the 1930s. The two-part version by Raymond Bernard, starring Harry Baur as Jean Valjean, opened in June and October 1934. The American version directed by Richard Boleslawski had a two-week run in August 1935. See María Luis Amador and Jorge Ayala Blanco, *Cartelera cinematográfica, 1930–1939* (Mexico City: Universidad Nacional Autónoma de México, 1980).

23. García Riera, *Historia documental del cine mexicano*, vol 2 (Mexico City: Ediciones Era, 1974), 41.

24. Mercedes Díaz López, "Connecting Spain and the Americas in the Cold War: The Transnational Careers of Jorge Negrete and Carmen Sevilla," *Studies in Hispanic Cinemas* 5, nos. 1–2 (2008): 26–31. One can also note Negrete's connection to Argentina,

in films that cast him alongside Argentine stars such as Amanda Ledesma and Libertad Lamarque, and in his visits to the country, which coincided with a rise in interest on Mexican cinema there. See Mónica Szurmuk and Maricruz Castro Ricalde, "Latin American Rivalry: Libertad Lamarque in Mexican Golden Age Cinema," in Irwin and Castro Ricalde, *Global Mexican Cinema*, 115–116.

25. For a discussion of Rómulo Gallegos's adaptations in Mexican cinema, see Robert McKee Irwin, "Mexico's Appropriation of Latin American Cultural Imaginary: Rómulo Gallegos in México," in Irwin and Castro Ricalde, *Global Mexican Cinema*, 107–131. Yet another example was the vast number of adaptations from nineteenth-century Spanish novelist Benito Pérez Galdós. See John H. Sinningen, *Benito Pérez Galdós en el cine mexicano: Literatura y cine* (Mexico City: Universidad Nacional Autónoma de México, 2008).

26. Alan Knight, "The End of the Mexican Revolution? From Cárdenas to Ávila Camacho, 1937–1941," in Gillingham and Smith, *Dictablanda*, 63.

27. An interesting precedent is *Alma jarocha* (*Soul of Veracruz*, dir. Antonio Helú, 1937), which has another story of modernization: Mexico City students reaching Veracruz. The Helú film is set in the port of Veracruz and not in the area where *Pasión jarocha* takes place, though. In focusing on a more rural area, Véjar's film shows the growing reach of modernity in localities of the interior.

28. García Riera, *Historia documental*, 4:129.

29. Fernando Mino García, *La nostalgia de lo inexistente: El cine rural de Roberto Gavaldón* (Mexico City: Consejo Nacional para la Cultura y las Artes, 2011), 104–105.

30. For a discussion of this archetype in major prostitution melodramas, see Sergio de la Mora, *Cinemachismo: Masculinities and Sexualities in Mexican Film* (Austin: University of Texas Press, 2006), 20–67.

31. Francisco Peredo Castro, *Alejandro Galindo, un alma rebelde en el cine mexicano*, (Mexico City: Instituto Mexicano de Cinematografía / Miguel Ángel Porrúa, 2000), 178. I want to thank Raúl Miranda López for helping me to identify some of the films mentioned in this paragraph.

32. García Riera, *Historia documental*, 4:195.

33. Álvaro Fernández Reyes, *Crimen y suspenso en el cine mexicano, 1946–1955* (Zamora: El Colegio de Michoacán, 2007), 100–113.

34. Ibid., 284–294.

35. Ibid., 28–32.

36. Ibid., 100–101.

37. Amador and Ayala Blanco, *Cartelera cinematográfica, 1950–1959*, 355–365.

38. Jesús Ibarra, *Los Bracho: Tres generaciones de cine mexicano* (Mexico City: Universidad Nacional Autónoma de México, 2006), 115. In one of those paradoxes of cinematic marketing, one of the current DVD releases of *Distinto amanecer* is sold as a duo with Fernández's *La perla*, presumably because both have Pedro Armendáriz in the lead role, even though the films are radically different from each other.

39. Ibarra, *Los Bracho*, 116.

40. For a thorough study of the film, see Peter William Evans, *Carol Reed* (Manchester: Manchester University Press, 2005), 81–93. A testament of the film's influence is the fact that it is currently part of the Criterion Collection.

41. For a study of Orol's work, see Eduardo de la Vega Alfaro, *El cine de Juan Orol* (Mexico City: Universidad Nacional Autónoma de México, 1985); De la Vega Alfaro, *Juan Orol* (Guadalajara: Universidad de Guadalajara, 1987).

42. Rumba was an import from Cuba and Juan Orol was one of the main agents of its popularization in Mexico. For an excellent discussion of the topic, see Maricruz Castro Ricalde, "Rumba Caliente Beats Foxtrot: Cinematic Cultural Exchanges between Mexico and Cuba," in Irwin and Castro Ricalde, *Global Mexican Cinema*, 35–64.

43. García Riera, *Historia documental*, 3:117.

44. Wong's figure was a true challenge to ethnic and cultural perceptions in cinema at the time, and Orol is clearly using that as an opportunistic appropriation of the controversy behind her figure. For a study of Wong, see Tim Bergfelder, "Negotiating Exoticism: Hollywood, Film Europe and the Cultural Reception of Anna May Wong," in *Stars: The Film Reader*, eds. Lucy Fischer and Marcia Landy (London: Routledge, 2004), 59–75.

45. In one of the few scholarly pieces to seriously discuss Orol's role in the history of Mexican cinema, Ana M. López places him next to José Bohr and Ramón Peón as a precursor of exploitation cinema. See Ana M. López, "Before Exploitation: Three Men of Cinema in Mexico," in *Latsploitation, Exploitation Cinemas, and Latin America*, ed. Victoria Ruétalo and Dolores Tierney (London: Routledge, 2009), 13–33.

Gabriel García Márquez, "The Mambo,"
El Heraldo (Barranquilla), January 12, 1951

> *This piece by Nobel Prize–winning novelist Gabriel García Márquez (1927–2014), whose career had a long cross-fertilization with cinema, dates from his years working as a journalist in the coastal city of Baranquilla. After moving to Bogotá, García Márquez became a prolific film critic for the newspaper El Espectador, and later worked as a screenwriter in Mexico. While not addressing the mambo's presence in the cinema, the piece captures the genre's anarchic and infectious spirit and its circulation on a global scale.*

WHEN THE SERIOUS, WELL-DRESSED Cuban composer Dámaso Pérez Prado discovered a means of stringing all urban sounds onto a thread of saxophone, there was a coup-d'état against the sovereignty of all known rhythms. Maestro Pérez Prado emerged from anonymity overnight, while the spectacular Daniel Santos took slices of music from of all the typical Havana characters, and Miguelito Valdés died of decadence trying to pay his own orchestra and Orlando Guerra (Cascarita) howled his extraordinary wild *sons*[1] in the nightclubs of Cuba while waving the astonishing red handkerchief that has won him as much renown as his voice.

In the past five years, jukeboxes have become the great mills of musical fashion. Daniel Santos, after three or four run-ins with the police, made his presence felt in the machinery where singers' popularity is made, and for two years could be heard hollering for five cents in any suburb in America. The same thing happened with Orlando Guerra. But one had the impression that if these first two had madness to spare, a little insanity was still lacking to achieve total insanity. So Dámaso Pérez Prado got together twelve musicians, formed an orchestra, and began to evict with saxophone blows all those who had preceded him in the boisterous world of the jukeboxes.

Academics are throwing ashes on their heads and tearing their vestments. Yet vulgarity remains the best barometer. And I have the impression that more than a few academics will be dead and buried before the kid on the corner feels inclined to accept that "Mambo no. 5" is little more than a hodge-podge of barbaric chords, randomly strung together. It's the kid on the corner, as a matter of fact, who told me this morning: "There's nothing like the mambo." And he said it with such conviction, with such sincerity, that there is not the least doubt that Maestro Pérez Prado has found the definitive key to the hearts of all the kids who whistle on all the corners of the world.

Perhaps the mambo is an absurdity. But everyone who sacrifices a nickel in the slot of a jukebox is, in fact, sufficiently absurd to expect to hear something that corresponds to his desire. And perhaps the mambo is also a danceable absurdity. And so what had to happen is really happening: America is almost howling with healthy admiration, while Maestro Pérez Prado mixes slices of trumpets, diced saxophones, a sauce of trumpets and morsels of well-seasoned pianos, to spread this marvelous salad of astonishing absurdities throughout the continent.

I said to the kid on the corner, "Of course, Maestro Pérez Prado is indeed a genius." And he lit up more than if I'd given him a coin. After this, no one could feel even a vague pang of conscience, although there are still those in the neighborhood liable to say that you have stated a personal and certainly very debatable absurdity. This is so natural, so human, that it might even be the ideal subject for a mambo.

Translated by Rielle Navitski

RIELLE NAVITSKI is Assistant Professor of Theater and Film Studies at the University of Georgia. She is the author of *Public Spectacles of Violence: Sensational Cinema and Journalism in Early Twentieth-Century Mexico and Brazil* (Duke University Press, 2017).

NOTES

1. *Editors' Note:* A reference to the Cuban musical genre that combines elements of the melodic Spanish *canción* with Afro-Cuban percussion.

Chapter 9

Bad Neighbors: Pérez Prado, Cinema, and the Politics of Mambo

Jason Borge

IN THE EARLY 1940S, operating through the Office of the Coordinator of Inter-American Affairs (OCIAA) and film industry collaborators, the US government promoted hemispheric "brotherhood" based on an asymmetrical understanding of global politics. As cultural showpieces of the Good Neighbor policy, films such as the Carmen Miranda vehicle *The Gang's All Here* (dir. Busby Berkeley, 1943) and the Disney pictures *Saludos Amigos* (1942) and *The Three Caballeros* (1944) promoted a harmonious relationship that mostly avoided the grossly pernicious stereotypes plaguing Hollywood representations of Latin America in previous decades. Yet the films also lent spectacular form to the fundamental imbalances underpinning newly strategic inter-American alliances. By overtly juxtaposing "modern" North American and "primitive" Latin American characters and settings, the Miranda pictures offered up visually dazzling and seductive justifications for the long-standing economic and symbolic exploitation of south-of-the-border subjects and cultural patrimonies. The Disney films, meanwhile, projected the epistemological and technological mastery of Latin America by way of the paternalistic gaze and authoritative narration of US characters, frequently cast as tourist-ethnographers eager to exploit the tropics for their natural beauty, quaint pastimes, and erotic appeal.

Although the Good Neighbor policy and in particular the OCIAA responded to geopolitical imperatives specific to the Franklin D. Roosevelt administration and World War II, the overarching strategies, goals, and hierarchies of such intrahemispheric identity projects predated and also survived the United States' involvement in the war. It is for this reason, among others, that Aníbal Quijano and Emmanuel Wallerstein's conceptualization of "the deification and reification of newness" as one of the constitutive traits of New World cultural dynamics remains useful as a theoretical lens through which to better grasp the historical conditions underpinning mid-twentieth century attempts to forge—and thwart—inter-American alliances through modern mass culture.[1]

Strongly associated with modernity and coloniality, the theory of "Americanity" posits resistance as a concomitant of the peripheralization and "hierarchical layers" that resulted from the inherent systemic imbalances of the colonial system.[2] However, Quijano and Wallerstein's emphasis on colonial processes largely downplays analogous patterns of exploitation and resistance that have marked relations within the Americas since the nineteenth century. Beginning in the aftermath of the so-called Spanish-American War (1898), the United States not only dawned the mantle of hegemonic chieftain throughout the hemisphere but also routinely monopolized claims to epistemological dominance at the expense of Latin American nations and subjects. Perhaps nowhere is this clearer than in the realm of cultural politics. If the end of World War II saw a retreat from the Good Neighbor policy, the postwar period did not end North America's fascination with south-of-the-border spaces and practices any more that it signaled the quick-and-easy symbolic transfer of "newness" and know-how to Latin American nations. In fact, the potency of Good Neighbor tropes lingered in the regional imaginary for some time.

A very telling response to Hollywood's wartime films came from the Mexican film industry and centered around mambo—a hybrid musical style and associated dance that reigned during the decline of big band jazz but before the rise of rock and roll, briefly challenging the hegemony of the US culture industry and subverting the strategies underlying transhemispheric policies and cultural flows. The style of mambo popularized by Cuban-born bandleader and musician Dámaso Pérez Prado flourished within the transnational matrix of global capitalism. In this essay, I argue that cinematic mambo played a pivotal role in the postwar landscape as an ambiguous, subversive spectacle highly emblematic of the shifting complexities of midcentury inter-American cultural politics. Pérez Prado's numerous Mexican film appearances—from *cabaretera* classics such as *Aventurera* (dir. Alberto Gout, 1950) and *Víctimas del pecado* (*Victims of Sin*, dir. Emilio Fernández, 1951) to

Chano Urueta's comedies *Al son del mambo* (*To the Sound of Mambo*, 1950) and *Del can-can al mambo* (*From the Can-Can to the Mambo*, 1951)—playfully but often explicitly distorted *buen vecino* commonplaces, shunting them into the service of (Mexican) national objectives and preoccupations. Meanwhile, the later Hollywood films *Underwater!* (dir. John Sturges, 1955) and *Cha-Cha-Cha-Boom!* (dir. Fred F. Sears, 1956) brought to a boil the simmering inequities and asymmetries on which midcentury hemispheric projects rested. Mambo films exemplified "Bad Neighborism" not just in the sense that they presented Latin American subjects that did not always adhere to the blueprint of Roosevelt's and Nelson Rockefeller's political orthodoxy but also because the very instability and acrobatic multifunctionality of the mambo sign contested the notion that hemispheric cooperation could be scripted in the first place.

Josh Kun has observed that music performs a "delinquent" act in the sense that it "unsettles . . . the geopolitical boundaries of the nation state." For Kun, the frequently unfettered movement of music across borders in the global era at once transcends and scrambles "fixed" configurations of identity and power.[3] Of course, popular music's globe-trotting mobility has hardly stopped many Latin American states from trying to harness sound cultures for patriotic ends. This was especially true in the mid-twentieth century, when populist regimes in Brazil, Argentina, and Mexico consistently promoted "pedagogical narratives" of national unity, historical exceptionalism, and ideological orthodoxy through the productive overlap of popular music and film.[4]

A heady blend of distinct Cuban forms and certain strands of big-band jazz, mambo presented audiences with an overtly—even aggressively—hybrid sound. Yet its hybridity in itself did not distinguish mambo from contemporaneous musical styles and dances from other regions of Latin America. After all, tango and samba owed a debt not just to other national forms (in the case of tango, the milonga; in the case of samba, maxixe; and so on) but also to international music as well, including jazz. Mambo, however, could not be so easily conscripted into national service. For starters, unlike Mexico, Argentina, and Brazil, pre-revolutionary Cuba did not have a film industry of sufficient strength with which to promote homegrown musical practices as unifying emblems of national identity. And the problem was not just a symbolic one. Thanks to the relatively chaotic state of pre-revolutionary Cuba's cultural institutions, many innovative and ambitious Cuban musicians were compelled to look elsewhere for artistic and commercial fulfillment, namely Mexico and the United States.

There has been considerable debate over the years about mambo's "true" origins. As early as June 1948, in a rebuttal to an essay published days earlier in the weekly *Bohemia*, Odilio Urfé claimed the word first emerged in a musical context with the appearance of an eponymous *danzón* written by Orestes "Cachao" López and performed with the *charanga* orchestra Arcaño y sus Maravillas some eleven years earlier, in the last part of which was added a coda, or "montuno sincopado," that eventually evolved into an autonomous rhythmic style all its own.[5] Another key contributor to mambo's early development, as scholar David F. García has recently demonstrated, was *conjunto* innovator Arsenio Rodríguez, who by 1943 had begun to insert syncopated variations (which he called "diablos") at the end of *son* recordings to challenge dancers into improvising technically difficult maneuvers. By 1947, García writes, such mambo moves had spread to big-band dances as well, becoming popular in both Havana and New York City.[6]

In spite of such important musical antecedents, there remains little doubt that mambo, as it came to be known by 1950, depended primarily on the innovation, showmanship, and sheer good timing of Cuban-born bandleader Dámaso Pérez Prado. One of the main characterizing features of Prado's version of the mambo was the debt it owed to Stan Kenton and his "progressive" big-band sound. Cuban music criticism, especially since the triumph of the Cuban Revolution, has tended to underplay Kenton's influence, perhaps because such an acknowledgment might well diminish the nationalist/Latin American credentials often applied to mambo ex post facto.[7] Ned Sublette has written convincingly of the centrality of Kenton's work to the development of the Pérez Prado sound. Of course, it is commonly assumed that the Cuban bandleader borrowed from Kenton his frontal big-band attack, with blistering saxophones and trumpets on either end of the register. But Pérez Prado also gleaned from Kenton a novel approach to harmony and dissonance that "never sought to banish the tonal center, using dissonance instead as an extension of tonal harmony."[8] His Afro-Cuban sensibility brought to his orchestra a rhythmic intensity relatively absent, at least initially, in Kenton's performances. Over time, the Prado-Kenton exchange would prove mutual. Kenton had been incorporating some Afro-Cuban elements into his big band since 1947, when for the first time he heard Noro Morales's and Machito's orchestras play in Harlem.[9] Pérez Prado released the single "Mambo a la

Kenton" in 1950; Kenton would return the favor a year later with his recording of "Viva Prado!"[10]

Although the Cuban bandleader had begun developing his signature style in Havana in the mid-1940s, Pérez Prado's career would only come to full fruition in Mexico. The move off the island is explainable partly by the Kentonesque "progressive" qualities mentioned earlier—a sound that Cuban producers and even other musicians at the time saw as both technically difficult and eccentric.[11] One person who clearly recognized Pérez Prado's uniqueness was the vedette Ninón Sevilla, who brought her compatriot on board as an arranger just as her star was rising in the Mexican movie industry.[12] Within months of his arrival, Pérez Prado was not only making the records that had eluded him in Cuba but also numerous appearances in radio, live music, and theatrical venues.[13] He found in Mexico City, moreover, a vibrant Cuban expatriate community that included the singers Cascarita (Orlando Guerra) and Benny Moré, both of whom would record for Prado's new orchestra in the years to follow. In March 1949, Pérez Prado recorded "Qué rico el mambo" for RCA Victor's international division, and the song became an instant hit throughout Latin America. Within two years of leaving Cuba, he had gone from making $50 a week to around $5,000.[14] Pérez Prado's sudden popularity north of the border, meanwhile, was partly the product of good fortune. "Qué rico el mambo" was released by RCA just as the American Federation of Musicians went on strike, compelling its members to uphold a temporary ban on recording. RCA took advantage of the situation to push its "Latin" productions in the North American market.[15]

As important as Pérez Prado's budding recording career was to the dissemination of mambo, the Mexican film industry of the late 1940s and 1950s was the crucible through which the music was forged. The widespread collaboration between Cuban dancers and musicians and Mexican directors, actors and technicians made the *rumbera* or *cabaretera* film somewhat of an anomaly in Latin American cultural history. For starters, the rumberas were decidedly more of a transnational spectacle than the *comedias rancheras* and tango melodramas of the 1930s and the samba-fueled *chanchadas* of the 1940s and 1950s.[16] Moreover, the rumbera film was arguably the main vessel of the period through which Spanish Caribbean music and spectacle were rendered international.[17] Specifically, Mexican directors such as Alberto Gout, Emilio Fernández, and Chano Urueta—in films ranging from noir melodramas to light musical comedies—regularly employed mambo, boogie-woogie, and other hybridized forms as emblems of exotic modernity and licentiousness against which normative Mexican/Latin American identities could be elaborated and celebrated, but also thrown into question.

The typical rumbera film combines elements of the Hollywood musical with Mexican melodrama, while adding stylistic and thematic touches of film noir. The centerpiece of the rumbera storyline is the fallen working-class heroine whose sad world invariably revolves around a nightclub or cabaret that often doubles as a bordello. The music heard in such places frequently plays as central a role as the characters themselves. In *Aventurera*, the heroine Elena (Sevilla) literally uses mambo to exact revenge on her former madam and nemesis Rosaura. Elena seduces and weds Rosaura's son Mario out of spite, having discovered that Rosaura leads a double life as the madam of a brothel in Ciudad Juárez and the matriarch of a wealthy family in Guadalajara. At their wedding, to humiliate her new mother-in-law and scandalize her friends and family, Elena dares to dance unaccompanied to a mambo that begins as an innocuous *son*. The orchestra adjusts its sound to her socially inappropriate gyrations; the upper-crust wedding guests begin to complain and then to leave in droves.

The scene is remarkable in the way it removes mambo performance from of its "native" context (the night club or cabaret, typically located in a border or port city) to illustrate the moral intolerance and class bias of Mexican elites during the presidency of Miguel Alemán (1946–1952). For this social milieu, mambo bears a number of negative connotations, associated not just with lower-class prurience but also the kind of life that Elena had been forced to accept once she lost her parents to scandal and suicide: a subculture stripped of the normative rectitude of "correct" Mexican behavior, particularly for women who find themselves without the protection of bourgeois affluence and respectability. Nightclub music and dance—and mambo specifically—thus emerge in films such as *Aventurera* and *Víctimas del pecado* as metonymies of cultural impurity: dirty urban spectacles antithetical to the Mexican pastoral ideal of the comedia ranchera, with its nationalist celebration of traditional values.[18]

Yet mambo in the rumbera films comes off as "dirty" not just because it is urban based. When the story of *Aventurera* switches back to Ciudad Juárez at the end of the film, we witness a nocturnal montage of cars and clubs—Kentucky Bar, Jockey Club, Rio Grande Bar and Café, The Stork Club, and so on. The fact that most of the neon signs are in English and that the scene is

Fig. 9.1 Elena (Ninón Sevilla) seeks revenge on her former madam—now mother-in-law—by using the mambo to scandalize guests at her wedding reception in the film *Aventurera* (dir. Alberto Gout, 1950).

set to jazz brands Ciudad Juárez not just as any Mexican city but rather as an iconic border town whose national character had been visibly compromised by US urban culture—in the same way, the film implies, that mambo is Latin music "compromised" by big-band jazz.

Such issues of morality and national identity cannot be fully understood without unpacking some of mambo's racial baggage. Robin Moore has pointed out that Cuban music of the 1940s and 1950s underwent a "blackening" or "re-Africanizing." Previous Afro-Cuban forms denigrated by the cultural elites (such as the percussion-heavy noncommercial rumba) were recovered in much the same way as jazz underwent a transformation during the same period, as bebop musicians such as Charlie Parker and Dizzy Gillespie attempted to wrest it away from commercial swing bands then dominated by white musicians. "Blackening" therefore followed "whitening" in both Cuban and US contexts.[19] In the Mexican rumbera films, one notices both tendencies at work simultaneously. In *Víctimas del pecado*, for instance,

Fig. 9.2 Neon signs outside the clubs of Ciudad Juárez emphasize the border town's role as a space of vice and musical/cultural mixture.

the Pérez Prado orchestra plays not just mambo and boogie-woogie but also traditional *guaguancó*, establishing the film's white heroine Violeta (once again played by Ninón Sevilla) as a knowledgeable, seductive, and "authentic" dancer of noncommercial rumba and modern hybrid forms alike. Her intimate connection to Afro-Cuban sources is reinforced by her coquettish interplay with the orchestra's various black and mixed-race musicians and, of course, by her self-assured, uninhibited interpretation of "Africanized" Cuban numbers.

The iconic rumbera's performance straddles the line between Afro-Caribbean authenticity and commercial viability of the tourist variety, her "tropical" white body at once belying the former and facilitating the latter. But Sevilla and the Prado orchestra also ultimately bear the mark of US mass culture. Through the deployment of mambo as a symbol of new hybridity, social conflict, and even corruption, the (North) Americanization of Latin American cultural production is not so much embraced as it is accepted—with deep ambivalence—but accepted nonetheless as inevitable fact. Jazzed-up Latin

American musical performance thus serves as a soundtrack and key backdrop to the temptation of transnational modernity: a siren song that often leads to calamity, but also serves as a refuge from the rigidity of conservative, insular models of Mexican identity.

The Mexican film industry's strategic uses of mambo did not end with the rumbera melodramas. Germán Valdés (Tin Tan) was probably the most prominent comedic actor to exploit the early 1950s Mexican mambo craze, most notably in a series of films directed by Gilberto Martínez Solares. While Tin Tan dances to mambo in *El revoltoso* (*The Rebellious One*, 1951) and cha-cha-chá in *Lo que le pasó a Sansón* (*What Happened to Samson*, 1955), the most mambo-intensive of his films is *Simbad el mareado* (*Simbad the Seasick*, 1950), in which he plays an Acapulco tourist tout given to seasickness. During one of his episodes, Tin Tan dreams he is a sultan in a harem populated by an ensemble of characters including his girlfriend, a dwarf, and dancing twins, all clad in extravagant oriental costumes while moving wildly to the sounds of the Pérez Prado orchestra. At one point during the second of two sequences, featuring the song "Mambo bebop," Tin Tan gets so completely carried away with scatting that he ends the number riffing off Pérez Prado's signature grunt: the starting point, as it were, for nonsensical communication.

According to the bandleader himself, the famous grunt was a slurring of the entreaty "*¡dilo!*" ("say it!" or more loosely, "let me hear you!"), one intended to encourage his orchestra to play more emphatically. For Pérez Firmat, Pérez Prado's grunt is an example of *logoclassia*, the reduction of speech to sounds or "vestigial words" through the disarticulation of language.[20] On one level, Tin Tan merely brings such a reduction to its logical conclusion: if the Cuban bandleader insists on producing noises instead of words, Tin Tan turns the noises into notes. The scene from *Simbad el mareado* underscores the mistranslation that often accompanies such slapdash appropriations. Tin Tan's bebop improvisation brings to parodic extremes the frequently incoherent and undifferentiated exoticism of the period's transnational spectacles. Yet it also foregrounds the inherent violence underlying the culture clashes. Instead of achieving erotic satisfaction in his dream harem, Simbad ends up being pummeled by his own subjects. Bruised and harassed, Tin Tan awakens only to confront the equally daunting world of modern beach tourism, with foreign wealth, danger, and erotic temptation to match those of his dreams. Eventually fleeing the *güera* (fair-skinned woman) he had sought for her family fortune, he limps back to the arms of his long-suffering Mexican sweetheart.

A similar pattern of international temptation, recrudescence, and finally settlement for homegrown simplicity defines Chano Urueta's *Al son del mambo*, in many ways the culminating work of Mexico's mambo films. Like another Tin Tan vehicle of the period, *El mariachi desconocido* (Unknown Mariachi, dir. Gilberto Martínez Solares, 1953), Urueta's *Al son del mambo* sets up an erotically charged Cuban scenario with a plane ride from Mexico that doubles as an island escape. A number of scholars have suggested that the gender politics of the rumbera/cabaretera film answered a need in Mexico to fashion otherness that would benefit the emerging middle class beyond the tight moral restrictions of residual Porfirian orthodoxy. "Idealized, independent, and extravagantly sexual," Ana M. López writes, "the exotic *rumbera* was a social fantasy, but one through which other subjectivities could be envisioned, other psychosexual/social identities forged."[21] The cinematic cabaret, though, was also a transnational space that evoked a whole range of intersecting performances, from Argentine tango films of the 1930s to Hollywood musicals of the 1940s and 1950s. Particularly in Carmen Miranda's Good Neighbor films, the cabaret serves as a "framing device" for modern technologies and "the world-views they sponsor."[22]

By assigning Cuban dancers and musicians roles of primitive sensuality in comedies like *Al son del mambo*, Urueta was able not only to cast white Mexican males as conservative apprentices but also to position them as modern, cosmopolitan avatars of Mexicanidad. Another way in which *Al son del mambo* differs from films such as *Aventurera* and *Víctimas del pecado* is in its placement of musicians and musical performance in the foreground, rather than in the background as dance accompaniment. In the rumbera films, Pérez Prado and his orchestra are typically consigned to auxiliary roles, interacting only fleetingly with the films' main characters during the dance numbers. In *Al son del mambo*, mambo itself is moved to the center of the plot. In one of the film's pivotal scenes, Roberto spies on Pérez Prado taking notes as he walks around the hotel late at night. The scene flirts with racial tension, with the white *galán* (leading man) Roberto (Roberto Romaña) suspicious of what the Afro-Cuban bandleader may be doing at such a late in hour in a hotel filled with women. Yet his suspicion quickly turns to fascination when he realizes Pérez Prado is in fact taking notes on the sounds he hears around him—the chirping of a caged bird, the word "negrito" that echoes through the halls. The bandleader explains to Roberto that he is a "collector of sounds," keeping his scribbled notes in a box in his hotel room. When

Fig. 9.3 Roberto (Roberto Romaña), the white Mexican leading man, channels the "primitive" musical genius of Pérez Prado in *Al son del mambo* (*To the Sound of Mambo*, dir. Chano Urueta, 1950).

Roberto suggests that Pérez Prado put the sounds to music, the bandleader responds that he would not know how. The Mexican musician offers to help him; he has found his calling as the enabler, or transcriber, of "native" genius.

On a certain level, of course, the scene is absurd. Pérez Prado was by 1950 already a highly recognizable figure in Mexico, not just as a bandleader but also as a composer and arranger. Yet the film nevertheless frames him as a primitive Cuban artist in need of the mediation (and musical literacy) of a Mexican Creole—in a sense a microcosm of the institutional role served by the Mexican film industry vis-à-vis unlettered Cubans such as Pérez Prado and Ninón Sevilla. The fruit of the collaboration is mambo itself. Passing briskly through the process of transcription and written composition, the camera quickly cuts to the hotel lobby. In a series of close-ups of instruments followed by medium-range shots, the lobby is taken over by Pérez Prado's orchestra, musician by musician. The sequence is easily the most cinematically adventurous of the film, as Urueta visually and aurally "constructs" the mambo from the ground up, displaying the fusion of instruments associated with both Afro-Cuban forms (bongos, tumbadoras) and jazz (the saxophone, the trumpet). The instructional slant of the montage, culminating in a performance of "Mambó José," precedes a didactic soliloquy delivered by Roberto. The mambo, he declares, is "A new rhythm created by Pérez Prado, created for everyone's pleasure. A different rhythm, formed by the simplest and most primitive elements of nature, one that excites and provokes happiness and praise alike. Let's spread it from city to city, town to town, to the remotest places on earth, proclaiming our idea with mambo as the example. And we will see that even the Eskimos will end up happy, dancing to the sound of mambo."

Preceded and followed by a collective shout of "mambo!" the speech assumes messianic proportions. For the purposes of Urueta's film, Pérez Prado's music, even if "discovered" and promulgated by Roberto, serves as an emblem of ideal freedom and idyllic pleasure. In the various musical numbers that follow, the interspersion of mambos ("Elysyel Mambo," "Quién inventó el mambo," "El ruletero") with the occasional Mexican piece ("Malagueña") underscores the ostensible message of Cuban-Mexican fraternity—even if, as I have suggested, the desire and exoticism defining such reciprocity are marked by asymmetry. If the film's musical climax plays out like a party devoted to postwar solidarity, the specter of the United States is never far off. The Mexican film's exploitative use of the Cuban culture and landscape uncannily resembles the Cuba-as-primitive-playground ideology of so many Hollywood films of the 1940s, from the Carmen Miranda vehicle *Week-End in Havana* (dir. Walter Lang, 1941) to *Holiday in Havana* (dir. Jean Yarbrough, 1949), starring Desi Arnaz. The liberating sound of the mambo, meanwhile, with its thick jazz accent, reflects the incorporation of US popular culture into the very mood and fabric of the offshore Mexican fiesta.

Chano Urueta's second mambo comedy, *Del can-can al mambo*, is remarkable for the way it inverts the city-country tensions of *Al son del mambo*, recasting Mexico City and mambo (again symbolized by Pérez Prado and his orchestra) as beacons of freedom and progress against the social conservatism of the nation's heartland. As Carlos Monsiváis observes, at the time of *Del can-can al mambo*'s release, the Mexican film industry was at open war with the Liga de Decencia, an organization that actively sought whenever possible to remove "morally objectionable" films from theaters, and when this was not possible, to intimidate and even humiliate spectators who insisted on watching them. Monsiváis specifically cites *Del can-can al mambo* as an example of

Fig. 9.4 A prim headmistress (Maruja Grifell) is swept up by the rhythm of mambo at the conclusion of *Del can-can al mambo* (*From the Can-Can to the Mambo*, dir. Chano Urueta, 1951).

the film industry's resistance to such measures. Urueta's fictitious provincial city Tompiatillo, he writes, "is liberated by the intercession of the rhythm and arrangements of Pérez Prado which, in stripping bodies of their rigidity, destroys the paralysis imposed by the tyranny of 'decorum.'"[23] The film's final scene, in which even the rigid headmistress of a provincial boarding school gets caught up in the mambo frenzy, shows, however optimistically, that even the most reactionary elements of Mexican society harbor a potential for progress and tolerance.

The moral subtext of *Al son del mambo* and *Del can-can al mambo* touches on ideological tensions that go well beyond the Liga de Decencia. In the late 1940s and early 1950s, when Pérez Prado's groundbreaking sound and spectacle first reached an international audience, a number of Latin American intellectuals stressed the connection between mambo and public morality. As early as 1948, the Cuban critic Manuel Cuéllar Vizcaíno, in an essay published in *Bohemia*, had acknowledged that "the enemies of mambo" dismissed the music for its lack of elegance, a characteristic they attributed to its

US "aggressiveness," introducing "prosaic movements and gestures that can in no way be reconciled to our [national] customs."[24] One such enemy was apparently the cardinal of Lima, Juan Gualberto Guevara, who, according to various reports in the United States ranging from *Newsweek* to the Spanish-language daily *La Prensa* (New York), roundly and publically condemned the mambo, reportedly going so far as to deny absolution to anyone who dared to dance to the music.[25]

In a *crónica* published in the Barranquilla newspaper *El Heraldo* in January 1951, a young Colombian journalist named Gabriel García Márquez ironically dismissed the verdict of erudite critics as elitist, and worse, apocalyptic: "Academics are throwing ashes on their heads and tearing their vestments. Yet vulgarity remains the best barometer. And I have the impression that more than a few academics will be dead and buried before the kid on the corner feels inclined to accept that 'Mambo no. 5' is little more than a hodge-podge of barbaric chords, randomly strung together."[26] García Márquez's biblical overtones jibe perfectly not only with the real-life rhetoric of Latin American religious leaders but also with the language employed by the provincial characters of *Del can-can al mambo*, who consistently refer to both mambo and the medium through which it first reaches local residents (television) as "diabolical" and "modern witchcraft."

For the Colombian writer, as for Urueta's Roberto, one of mambo's true values lay in its raw appeal to youth culture. A second crónica published later the same year chronicles Pérez Prado's celebrated arrival and performance in New York, the first leg of the orchestra's first US tour. García Márquez correctly asserts that "North American girls . . . will [soon] notice that there is something about Coca-Cola, blue jeans and sneakers that proves particularly adaptable to Pérez Prado's devilish musical cataplasms."[27] Yet here García Marquez takes his "vulgarity as social barometer" argument one step further. Such visceral appeal to the North American public, he suggests, is also a "dangerous" one for cultural conservatives and nationalists, in the sense that the unusual hybridity of the new sound poses a threat to the status quo. For US music purists, even if some academics had argued that mambo was "a legitimate, displaced offspring of Harlem rhythms," mambo reappropriated jazz in much the same reckless manner than jazz had often taken liberties with the sacred cows of classical music.[28] Despite the "devilish" menace that Pérez Prado represented, his visit to the US metropolis was bound to leave a mark, García Márquez concludes, since all North Americans, whether or not they approved of his music, "[would] be left with a lasting memory [of his performance], without knowing for certain whether it [was] an homage, or a revenge."[29]

The subtle irony of García Márquez's position spoke both to mambo's formal heterogeneity as a Latin American "rhythm" that drew heavily on jazz harmony and instrumentation and to its deep symbolic ambiguity for US audiences. Interestingly, Alejo Carpentier wrote in a 1951 piece that the menace of mambo was due not to its vernacular inelegance, but rather the opposite. No doubt alluding to the influence of Kenton, Carpentier argued that mambo was the first genre of dance music to owe such a debt to harmonic approaches until recently belonging exclusively to composers considered "modern." For the same reason, he says, such writers had "frightened away a large sector of the public."[30] Carpentier's position was typically iconoclastic in its expansion of what contemporaneous audiences may have perceived as menacing in mambo. Yet, like most Cuban criticism of the period, his essay still treated Pérez Prado largely as an exponent of *national* music traditions. By contrast, García Márquez's crónicas fundamentally broke with debates over mambo's origins—debates that, though useful, tended to treat mambo as a purely musical phenomenon as opposed to a transnational spectacle involving multiple sites of enunciation and mediation.

The Colombian writer was correct in predicting that Pérez Prado's music would eventually leave its mark on the North American public. Alexandra Vásquez has more recently remarked that mambo "dovetailed the last postwar vestiges" of the Good Neighbor policy just as "cold war paranoia turned into policies of containment."[31] It would not be until the middle of the decade, however, that mambo would fully arrive in the US in the sense that García Márquez predicted—and in the way it had already arrived in Mexico and elsewhere in Latin America. Although Pérez Prado was already a recording star, his 1951 tour of the United States did not initially lead to such multimedia success.[32] The Pérez Prado orchestra's second tour in 1954, though, led to a May appearance on NBC's *The Spike Jones Show*, introducing the orchestra's music to tens of thousands of North American television viewers not yet familiar with its RCA Victor recordings or live performances. From the outset of his appearance, the show's host played off Pérez Prado's supposed lack of English. In his "interview," the bandleader responded to Jones's questions in Spanish only. At one point the host implored him to stop his "enchilada" gibberish, provoking the arrival of two "interpreters" (a giant and a dwarf,

Fig. 9.5 *Jet* magazine highlights Pérez Prado's appearance on *The Spike Jones Show*. May 20, 1954. Editor's collection.

Spike Jones's regular Billy Barty), neither of whom spoke Spanish. The linguistic impasse quickly led to a challenge and subsequent battle of the bands: Pérez Prado's orchestra versus Jones's satirical house band, the City Slickers, whose dissonant incompetence made a mockery of the competition itself while poking fun at Pérez Prado's trademark sound. It seems that mambo's flamboyance was not to be taken too seriously.[33]

The *Spike Jones* appearance would set the tone for the second, more decisive period of Pérez Prado's triumph in the United States. Rather than playing the part of the erotic underworld soundtrack as it had in the rumbera films, or serving as an emblem of moral laxity/liberty as in the comedies of Tin Tan and Chano Urueta, mambo in its North American phase would increasingly assume caricaturesque proportions in televised programs that ranged from

The Ed Sullivan Show to *The Dinah Shore Show*. Somewhat disturbingly, the television appearances signaled Hollywood's return to an early tendency to relegate Latin American actors and performers to highly stereotyped, often denigrating roles. While Good Neighbor films hardly put an end to such representations—for proof, one need look no further than Carmen Miranda films such as *Week-End in Havana*—they at least softened their edges, and went to some lengths to avoid pegging cultural bias to overarching narratives of racial inferiority and social backwardness. Breaking with what we might call the Good Neighbor cinematic code of ethics, Hollywood's mid-1950s treatment of Pérez Prado seemed to herald a partial return to the unrestrained stereotyping of the silent and early sound eras.[34]

The bandleader's first appearance in a Hollywood feature was in the drama *Underwater!*, which uses mambo to accentuate the ambience of south-of-the-border adventure and the pursuit of enormous wealth. The film's two main characters, Dominic Quesada and Johnny Gray (played by Gilbert Roland and Richard Egan), seek an elusive Spanish treasure sunken in the Caribbean. Pérez Prado's performance of his smash hit "Cherry Pink and Apple Blossom White" accompanies a key conversation in a Havana bar in which Quesada and Gray, with a timely assist from Theresa Gray (Jayne Russell), secure the means with which to pursue the booty. Unlike Good Neighbor films set in Latin America, *Underwater!*'s wayfaring gringo heroes are affably venal, and its cast of local characters range from vaguely untrustworthy to downright treacherous. Indeed, the film's villains are pirates who evoke the "greaser" stereotypes of early silent pictures. "Cherry Pink" thus furnishes the soundtrack for uncharted depths of tropical greed.

If *Underwater!* ultimately showcases diving footage, exotic locales, and a scantily clad Russell more than mambo, *Cha-Cha-Cha-Boom!* pushes musical performance once again to the forefront. The film's rather thin plot revolves around a US record company executive's quest to find new talent, one that leads him and his wife to Cuba. In spite of the picture's title (a nod to the cha-cha-chá's sudden rise in popularity in the middle of the decade), the musical numbers run the gamut of mambo, rumba, jazz, and even rock and roll. By far the most revealing of the scenes is Pérez Prado's performance of his "Voodoo Suite," an ambitious composition that mingles mambo with bebop and guaguancó. Set outdoors in a way clearly meant to play up the exoticism of the setting, the scene features frenetic collective dancing by locals and tourists alike. For the film's North American characters in particular, the music provokes wild shouts, lewd gyrations, and spastic writhing on the ground. To punctuate the "primitive" quality of the music, the crowd dances barefoot, the spectacle peppered with the approving banter of record executive Bill Haven (Stephen Dunne) and his friends Pedro (José González González) and Álvarez (the dancer Dante DiPaulo):

> Pedro: Man, dig that crazy dance!
>
> Haven: That music has a beat I've never heard before.

Then, a minute later:

> Álvarez: Pérez Prado makes music, *señores*. Native music, right from the heart of Cuba.

In the second, rumba movement of "Voodoo Suite," Álvarez's dance partner Nita (Sylvia Lewis) provocatively rips her tight skirt to expose her long legs; she is joined on stage by Álvarez, who pursues her with lascivious brutality, pushing her to and fro and dragging her by the hair. At one point the two dancers exchange unintelligible shouts and even animal calls—verbal extensions of their savage corporeal expressions.

In a number of ways *Cha-Cha-Cha-Boom!* stands out as a vivid rejoinder to the Mexican mambo comedies of the early 1950s, particularly Urueta's *Al son del mambo*. The Hollywood picture likewise uses Cuba as a licensed and licentious enclave in which white, non-Cuban characters are free to express themselves in ways they would not be inclined or permitted to otherwise.[35] In both *Cha-Cha-Cha-Boom!* and *Al son del mambo*, Pérez Prado is "discovered" by an authoritative judge of local talent, his music championed at once as innovative and close to nature. *Cha-Cha-Cha-Boom!* presents mambo and related forms as synecdoche of urban modernity refreshed by their new contact with the tropics. In the Hollywood film, the sheer corporeal histrionics accompanying Pérez Prado's "Voodoo Suite" draws loosely from the performative vocabulary of guanguancó, pushing the film into a fanciful realm of alterity frequently seen in 1930s Hollywood pictures, such as the Dolores del Río vehicle *Bird of Paradise* (dir. King Vidor, 1932). Robert E. Kent's screenplay offsets Pérez Prado's over-the-top musical hybridity with reassurances from local characters that his orchestra is actually playing "[n]ative music, right from the heart of Cuba." Abandoning any pretense of historical accuracy, *Cha-Cha-Cha-Boom!* places tall, lean non-Latino dancers in the place of curvy rumberas and injects their performance with an erotic violence that reads like an unchecked Northern fantasy of primitive excess.

Like *Underwater!*, *Cha-Cha-Cha-Boom!* revolves around the mercenary interests of North American travelers. When the "Voodoo Suite" number has concluded, discussion quickly revolves around the marketability of the spectacle they have witnessed. "You think this is something we could use, *amigo*?" Pedro asks Haven. "The music may not be new," the record executive responds, "but it sure *sounds* new, the way he plays it. All you have to do is get that message across to the people in our country." To which Pedro remarks slyly, "That Nita . . . she has the best equipment for sending messages I ever seen."

The exchange underscores the primary purpose of Haven's trip to Cuba—to find new talent that will appeal to music consumers back home—while acknowledging both the "newness" and the traditional roots of Pérez Prado's music. Pedro, in this context, serves as an accommodating local agent and an accomplice to Haven's capitalist designs. At the same time, his ironic rejoinder suggests that the erotic spectacle of Nita's dancing—her "equipment"—will help sell the sound to a US public. The "message" of *Cha-Cha-Cha-Boom!* is a far cry from that of *Al son del mambo*, in which Cuba had represented an escape from, rather than a solution to, the demands of modern capitalism. The fundamental disparities between these two odd movies highlight the symbolic versatility of mambo in articulating quite distinct national objectives and epistemological approaches. *Del can-can al mambo* and *Al son del mambo* give voice to México's vacillation in the face of the "deification and reification of newness" even as they suggest an *arribista* claim to an intermediary position within the new inter-American hierarchy—still one rung beneath the United States but one or two above Cuba. Hollywood's embrace—and in many ways its embodiment—of postwar modern capital demanded of mambo an updated auxiliary role of Latin America that augmented the rest-and-relaxation typecasting already present in Good Neighbor films. In *Underwater!* and *Cha-Cha-Cha-Boom!* the Southern tropics are not just sites of kindred cultures and quaint curiosities for the benefit of North American tourists and weekend ethnographers. Rather, they are cast as lurid ways and means to the acquisition of financial fortune and thrills, erotic fulfillment, and creative inspiration (but again with an eye on wealth). The acquisitive impulse lurking in the 1940s films now no longer leans so heavily on Utopian inter-American alliances, as the guiding hand of Roosevelt and Rockefeller has given way to the "invisible hand" of savage commerce during the high anxiety of the Cold War.

Revolutionary Postscript

Although mambo and cha-cha-chá gradually went out of style in the United States, eclipsed by dance forms spurred by the rapid ascent of rock and roll, Pérez Prado enjoyed a long and successful career as a bandleader in Mexico City. He also maintained an active, if sporadic, relationship with his native Cuba well after the triumph of the revolution in January 1959. Pérez Prado's ambiguous association with global capital, having achieved stardom on the basis of highly commercial recordings and decidedly "alienated" film and television appearances in both the United States and Mexico, did not prevent him from contributing to the soundtrack of one of ICAIC's most propagandistic documentary films: *Hasta la victoria siempre* (*Until Victory*, 1967), Santiago Álvarez's ardently anti-imperialist tribute to Ernesto "Che" Guevara shortly after his death. Although Pérez Prado's "Suite de las Américas" is hardly dance music (and is actually based loosely on a composition by Brazilian composer Heitor Villa-Lobos), its foundations in mambo and jazz seemingly place the piece at odds with its subject material—the revolutionary struggle between Bolivian peasants and state- and US Central Intelligence Agency-sponsored terrorism, punctuated by footage of Guevara's later speeches.

In some ways, Pérez Prado's score resembles the Latin and swing-inflected modernist experiments of such arrangers as Gil Evans, Chico O'Farrill, and early Lalo Schifrin. Yet Álvarez manages to capitalize on the echoes of postwar Hollywood and pre-revolutionary Cuba implicit in Pérez Prado's still instantly recognizable sound, using the score's mambo palette as both a metonymy of predatory capitalism and the soundtrack of its undoing. All the while, the Afro-Cuban strains remind the audience of Cuba's importance as a sponsor of peasant uprisings in the hemisphere. Placed at the service of revolutionary resistance, "Suite de las Américas" thus stands as a truly remarkable follow-up to *Cha-Cha-Cha-Boom!*'s "Voodoo Suite." Pérez Prado's score for *Hasta la victoria siempre* illustrates the deftness with which both the Cuban-born composer and Castro's cultural policy, seemingly against all odds, straddled the rift between vernacular authenticity and modern commercialism, Cuba and the world. As we have seen, it was not the first time mambo had shown its ideological malleability as a trope of inter-American relations. Viewed from a certain angle, "Suite de las Américas" was eerily reminiscent of Nelson Rockefeller's government-hatched cultural projects from the early 1940s. Even if the rules had changed somewhat, Pérez Prado's revolutionary foray in the 1960s proved his music's symbolic cachet as a trans-Caribbean cultural practice regardless of political philosophy.

Now safely "deglobalized" and relocated, cocooned in a Latin American nation acceptable to Castro's ideological sensibilities, Pérez Prado was ripe for appropriation as a post-Cuban, postcapitalist performer—what José David Saldívar has termed an "outernational" force—whose sonic storehouse resonated with the sort of pan-hemispheric Latinidad prized by the revolution. In the end, Pérez Prado never fully conformed to the industrial or national agents that sought to exploit him for monetary or ideological gain any more than mambo respected geopolitical borders. Saldívar has rightly questioned Quijano and Wallerstein's somewhat rigid distinction between Anglo and Latin "Americanities" for this very reason, using the US-Mexico borderlands as a case in point.[36] Yet surely the same applies to the cultures of the greater Caribbean. Like Pérez Prado himself, mambo over the course of more than two decades flitted from Havana to New York to Mexico City and beyond, exemplifying not only the unique mobility of music and film but also modern spectacle's unique potential to transgress the limits of national boundaries, and not just to demarcate them.

> JASON BORGE is Associate Professor of Latin American Cultural and Media Studies at the University of Texas at Austin. He is the author of two books documenting and analyzing the early impact of Hollywood on Latin American intellectuals: *Avances de Hollywood: Crítica cinematográfica en Latinoamérica, 1915–1945* (Beatriz Viterbo, 2005), and *Latin American Writers and the Rise of Hollywood Cinema* (Routledge, 2008), and has written extensively on such topics as film, jazz, popular performance, and hemispheric American studies.

NOTES

1. Aníbal Quijano and Immanuel Wallerstein, "Americanity as a Concept, or the Americas in the Modern World-System," *International Social Science Journal* 134 (1992): 551–552.

2. Ibid., 549–550.

3. Josh Kun, "Against Easy Listening: Audiotopic Readings and Transnational Soundings," in *Everynight Life: Culture and Dance in Latin/o America*, eds. Celeste Fraser Delgado and José Esteban Muñoz (Durham, NC: Duke University Press, 1997), 288–289.

4. Ana M. López, "Of Rhythms and Borders," in Delgado and Muñoz, *Everynight Life: Culture and Dance in Latin/o America*, 311. Curiously, Hollywood was never able (or willing) consistently to put jazz to similar use during the apogee of the music's appeal in middle decades of the twentieth century. Eric Hobsbawm has noted the relative paucity of classical Hollywood films about jazz. The subject of jazz, the bemused Hobsbawm remarks, "over most of its history . . . did not appeal to the indeterminate mass public by which the industry lives." Hobsbawm, *The Jazz Scene* (New York: Pantheon Books, 1993), 123. This interpretation simplifies the paradox a bit too neatly and overlooks the sticky issue of race that certainly discouraged the US film industry from capitalizing on the music's popularity.

5. Odilio Urfé, "La verdad sobre el mambo," in *El mambo*, ed. Radamés Giro (Havana: Letras Cubanas, 1993), 31–33. David F. García notes that the generally accepted date for Arcaño y sus Maravillas' performance of "Mambo" is 1938, although it was not actually recorded until 1951. David F. García, "Going Primitive to the Movements and Sounds of Mambo," *Musical Quarterly* 89, no. 4 (2006): 521n.

6. García, "Going Primitive," 507–508.

7. Even the venerable Leonardo Acosta, generally so clear-headed in his analysis, has fallen into this trap. While attempting to repudiate assertions that Pérez Prado was influenced by Stan Kenton, Acosta nonetheless ends up invoking Kenton's name constantly in his discussion of Pérez Prado's style. Acosta, *Elige tú, que canto yo* (Havana: Letras Cubanas, 1993), 32–33.

8. Ned Sublette, *Cuba and Its Music: From the First Drums to the Mambo* (Chicago: Chicago Review Press, 2004), 559.

9. Michael Sparke, *Stan Kenton: This is an Orchestra!* (Denton: University of North Texas Press, 2010), 59.

10. Scott Yanow, *Afro-Cuban Jazz* (San Francisco: Miller Freeman Books, 2000), 60.

11. Pérez Firmat, *Life on the Hyphen: The Cuban-American Way*, rev. ed. (Austin: University of Texas Press, 2012), 77, 209n.

12. Mayra A. Martínez, *Cubanos en la música* (Havana: Editorial Letras Cubanas, 1993), 72.

13. Sublette, *Cuba and Its Music*, 561.

14. Pérez Firmat, *Life on the Hyphen*, 77.

15. Josephine Powell, *Tito Puente: When the Drums Are Dreaming* (Bloomington, IN: AuthorHouse, 2007), 148.

16. The *chanchada* is "Partially modeled on American musicals (and particularly on the 'radio-broadcast' musicals) of the [1930s], but with roots as well in Brazilian comic theater and in the 'sung films' about carnival, the *chanchada* typically features musical and dance numbers often woven around a backstage plot," Randal Johnson and Robert Stam, "The Shape of Brazilian Film History," in *Brazilian Cinema*, eds. Johnson and Stam (New York: Columbia University Press, 1995), 26–27.

17. Again, this is not to say that these other genres were wholly national affairs. The popular Carlos Gardel films of the early 1930s that inspired late 1930s and early 1940s Argentine-made melodramas were in fact Hollywood productions that featured

international casts, often in North American and European settings. And even the relatively insular *chanchadas* frequently mimicked international fashions and musical styles and occasionally showcased foreign performers such as the Cuban rumbera María Antonieta Pons, who appears in Carlos Manga's *Carnaval Atlântida* (1952).

18. Carl J. Mora has argued that the cabaretera film epitomized widespread disenchantment with the corruption associated with the Alemán administration, while also suggesting a breakdown of traditional values expressed in the comedia ranchera. Mora, *Mexican Cinema: Reflections of a Society*, rev. ed. (Berkeley: University of California Press, 1989), 84–85.

19. Robin D. Moore, *Nationalizing Blackness: Afrocubanismo and Artistic Revolution in Havana, 1920–1940* (Pittsburgh: University of Pittsburgh Press, 1997), 110, 178–179.

20. Pérez Firmat, *Life on the Hyphen*, 79. Building on Pérez Firmat's analysis, Alexandra Vázquez has argued that Pérez Prado's signature grunt is indexical of a "a place of dwelling, a place for kinship, a site of mutual release across the Americas." If the grunt is "not limited by access to language or attention to national borders," however, Vázquez suggests that it carries more affective weight within a "shared [Afro-descendant] past." Alexandra T. Vásquez, *Listening in Detail: Performances of Cuban Music* (Durham, NC: Duke University Press, 2013), 153–156.

21. López, "Tears and Desire: Women and Melodrama in the 'Old' Mexican Cinema," in *Mediating Two Worlds: Cinematic Encounters in the Americas*, eds. John King, Ana M. López, and Manuel Alvarado (London: British Film Institute, 1993), 267.

22. Adrián Pérez Melgosa, *Cinema and Inter-American Relations: Tracking Transnational Affect* (New York: Routledge, 2012), 52. It is this transnational intersectionality of the cinematic cabaret that explains the frequent quotation across film industries. Carmen Miranda's patented visual and vocal style was emulated and burlesqued not just by Hollywood but also in Latin American films. Just to give two examples close at hand, Ninón Sevilla borrows from Miranda in one lavish scene from *Aventurera*; and fellow rumbera María Antonieta Pons manages to lampoon both Hollywood and cabaretera musicals in the Brazilian chanchada *Carnaval Atlântida*, a film I have already mentioned.

23. Carlos Monsiváis, "Censura: La eternidad de las costumbres," *El Universal*, November 18, 2001, accessed September 1, 2013, http://www.eluniversal.com.mx/hemeroteca/edicion_impresa_20011118.html.

24. Manuel Cuellar Vizcaíno, "La revolución del mambo," in Radamés Giro, *El mambo*, 24.

25. Don Tyler, *Music of the Postwar Era* (Westport, CT: Greenwood Press, 2008), 63; David F. García, *Arsenio Rodríguez and the Transnational Flows of Latin Popular Music* (Philadelphia: Temple University Press, 2006), 76–77.

26. Gabriel García Márquez, "El mambo," in Radamés Giro, *El mambo*, 19.

27. Gabriel García Márquez, "Mambo de Nueva York," in Radamés Giro, *El mambo*, 22.

28. Ibid., 21–22.

29. Ibid., 22.

30. Quoted in Radamés Giro, "Todo lo que usted quiso saber sobre el mambo...," in Radamés Giro, *El mambo*, 14.

31. Vásquez, *Listening in Detail*, 145–146.

32. See Barbara Squires Adler, "The Mambo and the Mood," *New York Times Magazine*, September 16, 1951.

33. For more criticism in the same vein, see Mrs. Arthur Murray's "What the Heck Is the Mambo?" *Down Beat*, December 1, 1954.

34. For a critical overview of Hollywood's troubled history of Latin American and Latino stereotyping, see Charles Ramírez Berg, *Latino Images in Film: Stereotypes, Subversion and Resistance* (Austin: University of Texas Press, 2002). For a more detailed history of Mexico's particularly fraught relationship with the early US film industry, see Emilio García Riera, *México visto por el cine extranjero*, vol. 1, *1894–1940* (Mexico City: Ediciones Era, 1987).

35. Such national typecasting was employed in other Hollywood pictures of the period, perhaps most notably in *Guys and Dolls* (Joseph Mankiewicz, 1955).

36. José David Saldívar, *Trans-Americanity: Subaltern Modernities, Global Coloniality, and the Cultures of Greater Mexico* (Durham, NC: Duke University Press, 2012), xiii–xiv.

PART IV

The Afterlives of Moving Images:
Cinephilia and Cult Spectatorship

Thomas E. Sibert, "Fox Film de Cuba, S.A.'s Continuing Competition for Scholarships to Summer School at the Universidad de la Habana" (unpublished circular, June 1956)

> *This announcement of a contest sponsored by Fox Film de Cuba, signed by the studio's local branch manager, signals the key role that Hollywood distributors played in shaping postwar cinephilia in Latin America. The company offered scholarships to José Manuel Valdés-Rodríguez's influential film course at the Universidad de La Habana's Summer School to the writers of the best essays on an upcoming Fox release. Fox thus promoted its films and novel widescreen technologies while presenting itself as a supporter of local cultural progress.*

CINEMASCOPE 55, INAUGURATED WITH *Carousel*, is the topic of the competition.

Fox Film de Cuba, S.A. once again offers ten scholarships to the Summer School session of the Universidad de La Habana. As in past years, the president of Fox Film de Cuba, S.A., Mr. Thomas E. Sibert, deeply interested in cultural activities, has decided to sponsor scholarships for the course "Cinema: Industry and Art of Our Times," to be given by Professor José M. Valdés-Rodríguez in the next session of the summer school. With this, Fox will once again join in the labor of artistic and cultural improvement of the Universidad de La Habana.

This contest has as its object to awaken the interest of the public, and in particular of the student body, in the study of cinema, and exemplifies a concern for the problems of culture. All that which encourages broad sectors of society to have occasion to examine manifestations of intelligence and sensibility promotes the elevation of the artistic level of the milieu, which necessarily translates into a movement towards overall improvement.

The summer school of the Universidad de la Habana, since its creation, has given special attention to film as art through the course "Cinema: Industry and Art of Our Times," offered in eighteen theoretical lessons complemented by the screening of films representative of various genres and originating in different centers of production.

The aforementioned course entails the economic, social and aesthetic appreciation of cinema and can be considered an introduction to the criticism of the so-called seventh art. The course attends to the study of the technical and aesthetic antecedents of cinema, to the relationships of the novel and the theater with the cinematograph and to the specific characteristics of the new art.

The incessant progress of cinematic technique, which has significant aesthetic implications, demands constant change in the appreciation of the film. In recent years 20th Century Fox has made a significant contribution to the technical development of cinema: CinemaScope, now CinemaScope 55, and stereophonic sound.

These are the rules of the competition:

Fox Film de Cuba, S.A., in its desire to promote the study of cinema as a social influence and as an art representative of this moment, offers ten scholarships for the course, "Cinema: Industry and Art of Our Times," in the next session of the Summer School of the Universidad de la Habana during the summer of 1956, given by Professor J. M. Valdés-Rodríguez.

These ten scholarships will be granted to the authors of the ten best texts about the CinemaScope 55 film *Carousel*, directed by Henry King, with Shirley Jones, Gordon MacRae and Cameron Mitchell, which will premiere in the Payret and Trianon theaters Wednesday, June 20 to Tuesday, June 26.

1) Students and those who are not journalists, professional writers, or employees of newspapers and magazines, nor have any relationship with the film or theatrical business in any of its manifestations, are eligible.
2) The texts should not exceed four standard letter-size sheets, single-sided, typed, double-spaced.
3) The texts may be sent to the offices of Fox Film de Cuba, S.A., Almendares no. 155, Havana, beginning on the day following the first exhibition of the film in the aforementioned theaters until three days after the final exhibition of *Carousel* in the same.

4) The jury designated by Fox Film de Cuba, S.A., will consist of Professor J. M. Valdés-Rodríguez, of Dr. Mercedes Muriedas and of Dr. René Jordan.
5) The jury will announce its decision by July 11. This decision will be *final* and no individual will be permitted to challenge it.
6) The texts will be returned to their authors in the offices of Fox Film de Cuba, S.A. during the five days following the publication of the jury's decision. Thereafter, they will be destroyed.
7) Fox Film de Cuba, S.A. will give to the winners a letter stating that they have won one of the scholarships offered. In this letter will appear the number of the check sent by Fox Film de Cuba to the summer school in payment of the tuition corresponding to the contestant in question.
8) The failure of the interested party to collect the letter, or to register within the registration period of the summer school for the 1956 session will be taken as a forfeiture of the scholarship granted by Fox Film de Cuba, which will be absolved of any commitment to the contestant in question.
9) Each text should contain, clearly written, the name, address, and telephone number of the author.

FOX FILM DE CUBA, S.A.
Thomas E. Sibert
President

Havana, June 8, 1956.

Translated by Rielle Navitski

RIELLE NAVITSKI is Assistant Professor of Theater and Film Studies at the University of Georgia. She is the author of *Public Spectacles of Violence: Sensational Cinema and Journalism in Early Twentieth-Century Mexico and Brazil* (Duke University Press, 2017).

Chapter 10

Film Culture and Education in Republican Cuba: The Legacy of José Manuel Valdés-Rodríguez

Irene Rozsa

THE UNIVERSITY OF HAVANA offered the film course El Cine: Industria y Arte de Nuestro Tiempo (Cinema: Industry and Art of Our Times) from 1942 to 1956. José Manuel Valdés-Rodríguez (1896–1971), who created and taught the course for its full duration, proudly asserted that it was the first of its kind in Latin America.[1] Cuba's importance as a site of international exchanges for Latin American filmmakers from the 1960s onward is widely recognized. However, much less is known about the cosmopolitan aspects of the Cuban film culture of the preceding period, in particular, the pioneering role it has played in the history of film education. During the first half of the twentieth century, important discussions took place around the world concerning cinema's aesthetic and social dimensions. Valdés-Rodríguez's critical and pedagogical practice demonstrates that this dialogue was not restricted to the metropolitan sites of Europe, the Soviet Union, and the United States but also found resonance in Latin American countries.[2] His work as a film critic, archivist, and educator had a great impact on the evolution of Cuban film culture, and it shows the unexpected continuity between the avant-garde movement of the 1920s and the institutional developments of the 1940s and 1950s.

Historical accounts of Republican Cuba (1902–1958) have demonstrated the complex dynamic of progressive potential and political frustration that characterized this then young nation.[3] During this period, cultural life depended on individual initiative, private patronage, and institutional support, the latter being, for the most part, short lived. In this context, the longevity of Valdés-Rodríguez's film course, offered over fourteen consecutive years, and his ability to secure a stable university position as director of the Department of Cinematography in 1949, is remarkable. This analysis seeks to situate his pioneering efforts within the political and cultural conditions of his time, while illustrating the transnational logics of film education and noncommercial film exhibition in Latin America.

The crucial importance of Valdés-Rodríguez's course has been recognized in Cuban film histories, but more attention has been devoted to his film criticism than to the context in which his teaching took place.[4] Two book collections have been published in Cuba compiling a selection of his writings. The first, prepared in 1982 and published in 1989, covered a three-decade span with a small sample of his commentary on international films, chosen from many thousands of reviews.[5] These film reviews, like those of other Latin American intellectuals, worked as local reinterpretations of foreign cultural products.[6] In 2010, a new compilation focused on the texts in which Valdés-Rodríguez discussed Cuban cinema, thus salvaging from oblivion a crucial part of the critic's legacy.[7] This body of work, which until recently has been mostly ignored, offers important clues to interpreting the challenges and achievements of Cuban filmmakers and film enthusiasts of the first half of the twentieth century.

The story of how Cuba's most important institution of higher learning accommodated the study of cinema provides evidence of the increasing heterogeneity of Latin American film publics. Through his initiative and perseverance, Valdés-Rodríguez contributed to the formation of a sophisticated film audience, cognizant of the landmarks of film history, and aware of the artistic and social characteristics of film. He played an essential role in guiding the young cinephiles of the 1950s, many of whom became key figures of the celebrated Cuban cinema of the 1960s, and had further impact on the formation of the New Latin American Cinema.[8] For that generation, cinephilia and the desire to write about or make films were closely interconnected. Its encounter with cinema in the late 1940s and throughout the 1950s took place in an environment where the possibility of creating a national film industry seemed remote. At the same time, the constant circulation of people, texts, and artworks made Cuban artists and intellectuals see themselves as part of a world of innovation and modernization. The creative and intellectual effervescence of that period shaped many of their views and aspirations in important ways.[9]

I will discuss Valdés-Rodríguez's early contact with progressive pedagogical theories and with the avant-garde projects of the 1920s as a preamble to his ideological and intellectual commitment to a Marxist view of art and society. Throughout the 1930s, his connections to the international Left helped shape his views about cinema and created unusual opportunities for film instruction. In particular, his familiarity with Harry Alan Potamkin's 1932 course, his meeting with Sergei Eisenstein in 1934, and his collaboration with exiled Spanish Republicans in 1939 all played an important role in his outlook toward film education.[10] These transnational links crucially contributed to his knowledge and prestige, facilitating the institutional credentials that made him an essential figure of Cuban and Latin American film culture.

Valdés-Rodríguez and the Intellectual Community of the 1920s and 1930s

Valdés-Rodríguez's family background indicates that he was introduced to innovative ideas about pedagogy from an early age. His father, Manuel Valdés-Rodríguez (1849–1914), was a prominent teacher and education reformer and one of the first proponents of a scientific approach to education. From 1877 onward, he worked as an educator and director at various schools linked to the Sociedad Económica de Amigos del País. On more than one occasion, he traveled to the United States as a representative of that institution in order to learn about the most advanced educational theories of his time. In 1885 he visited the public school system in New York, later translating their teacher's manual into Spanish. His approach to teaching revealed an understanding of the latest developments in experimental psychology, as well as a progressive attitude toward education. For instance, he was the first Cuban teacher to advocate for a racially integrated classroom. He published the sum of his pedagogical insights in 1898 and continued to campaign for professional teacher training until his death.[11] His revolutionary contributions to Cuban pedagogical practice and theory were recognized on the centenary of his birth in 1949 through a series of conferences, publications, and events.[12]

Both by virtue of his family background and through his own accomplishments, Valdés-Rodríguez was in close contact with the learned circles of 1920s Havana. From 1927 onward, he published social chronicles, translations of North American writers, critical essays, as well as theater, film, and literary reviews for various publications.[13] He was close to the new generation of writers, artists, and essayists who converged around the creation of *Revista de Avance* (1927–1930). The editors of this noteworthy avant-garde magazine conceived of their collective project as an expression of their intellectual and political inconformity with the status quo.¹⁴ The focus and main interest of this publication concerned the renewal of literary and artistic practice in opposition to the voices of tradition.

Revista de Avance's cosmopolitan outlook did not preclude its concern with national matters, but rather generated a well-informed intellectual dialogue with the most important artistic and literary currents of its time.¹⁵ In addition to publishing many significant pieces penned by the youngest generation of Cuban writers and essayists, the magazine included a wide range of international artists and authors. Its pages were illustrated with works by Jean Cocteau, Salvador Dalí, Henri Matisse, Pablo Picasso, Diego Rivera, and many others.¹⁶ The magazine published—for the first time in Cuba—many European and North American writers such as Blaise Cendrars, Waldo Frank, André Gide, Jean Giraudoux, Maxim Gorky, Paul Morand, Eugene O'Neill, John Dos Passos, Ezra Pound, Arthur Rimbaud, Bertrand Russell, George Santayana, and Paul Valéry. Spanish and Latin American writers were also well represented, including pieces by Federico García Lorca, José Carlos Mariátegui, José Ortega y Gasset, Horacio Quiroga, Alfonso Reyes, Miguel de Unamuno, and César Vallejo.¹⁷

The magazine's editors and most of its collaborators were politically active and opposed the highly unpopular Gerardo Machado regime, which ruled the island from 1924 to 1933.¹⁸ The corruption and despotism that characterized this government triggered waves of opposition from all sectors of society. The most radical intellectuals engaged in clandestine activities and eventually suffered prison and exile, while others channeled their activism by working with various oppositional political parties. Valdés-Rodríguez's family's respectability served him well during these turbulent years. His large house, located in the wealthy Havana neighborhood of Vedado, became a clandestine meeting place for young agitators such as Raúl Roa, then an active member of student and communist organizations.¹⁹ During this time he also organized a rudimentary cineclub, holding film screenings at his residence with borrowed projection equipment and using his neighbor's white garage wall as a screen.²⁰

Valdés-Rodríguez's involvement with cinema was always dually conditioned. On the one hand, his critical appraisals responded to his aesthetic and intellectual preferences. On the other, he depended on it as a source of income and employment. During the early part of the 1920s, he worked in the management of Cine Fausto, one of the largest and most impressive theaters in 1920s Havana.²¹ At the end of that decade, he started publishing film and theater reviews in newspapers and magazines such as *El Mundo, El País, Revista de La Habana,* and *Social.* He secured a permanent column in *El Mundo* in 1935, where he ran the weekly column Tablas y Pantalla (Stage and Screen) until 1967.[22] Thus, he remained tied to the industrial and public relations imperatives of the press, while pursuing other endeavors.

Like other important intellectuals of his generation, Valdés-Rodríguez was openly involved in Communist activity between 1931 and 1935. He became a member of the Cuban Anti-Imperialist League in 1931 and of the Cuban Communist Party in 1934.[23] That year he became one of the editors of the Communist magazine *Masas,* for which he was incarcerated in 1935.[24] During this period he was also very much implicated in international exchanges of ideas about cinema. He was a foreign correspondent for the leftist US film journal *Experimental Cinema,* which played a significant role in the film culture of the United States, especially through its translation and dissemination of Soviet texts. In 1932 he published an article in the journal, and on that occasion the Contributors page introduced him as "a young Cuban" whose "essays have appeared in various issues of the foremost Cuban intellectual journal, *La Revista de La Habana*" and who "has also made several translations of stories and books by John Reed." He is also presented as "General Secretary of the Cine Club of Cuba."[25] The article "Hollywood: Sales Agent of American Imperialism" is an accusatory text responding as much to Hollywood movies as to the American control of Cuba's economy.[26] Recent scholarship has demonstrated that many Cuban film critics articulated their anti-imperialist sentiment through their analysis of American films, and Valdés-Rodríguez's writing offers a good example of this trend.[27]

It is in the context of his Communist involvement that Valdés-Rodríguez first encounters the possibilities of pedagogy regarding cinema. In April 1932, he delivered a lecture at the Lyceum Society of Havana entitled "The New Cinematographic Technique." This was one of the first known instances of public discussion about the aesthetic and social aspects of cinema on the island. It was well received for its interest and novelty and recognized by the organizers as a topic "of relevant modernity."[28] Although it is not possible to ascertain the exact content of that foundational conference, it is quite likely that it focused on Soviet cinema. This is suggested by Valdés-Rodríguez's conclusion to the talk where he shared his hope that Sergei Eisenstein, the Soviet director he most deeply admired, could travel through Cuba once he finished his *¡Que Viva México!* project.[29]

Eisenstein never visited Cuba, but Valdés-Rodríguez was able to meet him in person during his trip to the Soviet Union between April and September 1934. He traveled as a correspondent for the magazines *Ahora* and *Bohemia* covering the Soviet Writers' Congress of 1934.[30] Valdés-Rodríguez was part of the international committee organized by *Experimental Cinema* to campaign in defense of Eisenstein's unfinished Mexico film throughout 1933.[31] Through common friends he was able to get in touch with Eisenstein directly and visited him at his Moscow apartment in August 1934. He remembered having had long conversations with him, obtaining an autograph, and even talking to him about making a film in Cuba.[32] In some of his recollections he also described spending time with Eisenstein throughout the spring and summer of that year and learning firsthand about the film curriculum he was developing for the State Institute of Cinematography (GIK).[33]

The Academy of Dramatic Arts: The First Iteration of the Film Course

Valdés-Rodríguez's strong connection to the international Left, initiated during the early 1930s, continued into the following decade. Writing theater and film criticism earned him continuous employment as well as the recognition of his peers. His steady contributions to *El Mundo* won him several honors and accolades for his journalistic work. At this more mature stage of his life, as he was forty-two years old, Valdés-Rodríguez became involved in new educational initiatives. He was part of the network of Cuban intellectuals who supported the arrival of Spanish émigrés in 1939. They founded the Escuela Libre de La Habana (Free School of Havana), an institution that housed the Academy of Dramatic Arts, which provided the context for the first iteration of his film course.

The Spanish Civil War had an impact on transatlantic contact in important ways. The defeat of the Republican army forced a large number of Spaniards into exile, and many leftist artists and intellectuals sought refuge in Cuba. Although they arrived on the island in smaller numbers than they did in other Latin American countries such as Mexico and Argentina, their impact on Cuban cultural and artistic activity should not be underestimated. In addition to abundant family ties facilitating Spanish immigration to the island, other links, forged through political, professional, and regional associations, created welcoming networks of support. Several architects and visual artists took permanent residence, while others, including university professors, dancers, playwrights, and theater promoters only stayed for a short time. However, they all left their mark on national culture through their interaction with Cuban artists and intellectuals, their publications, and their creative and educational activities.[34]

The Spanish émigrés played a crucial role in Cuban artistic education during this period. Although exiled university professors faced great difficulties in teaching in Cuba without proper validation of their credentials, legal conditions allowed for private education. They were able to create the Escuela Libre de La Habana, with the help of leftist friends such as Raúl Roa, the support of prominent intellectuals such as Fernando Ortiz and José María Chacón y Calvo, and the generosity of the wealthy patron María Luisa Gómez Mena. This independent learning center was modeled on the progressive ideals about modern, secular education of the Spanish Institución Libre de Enseñanza.[35]

The school opened in October 1939 with an ambitious plan to offer an alternative setting for both secondary and postsecondary educational programs. Initially, it was divided into five sections that aspired to cover subjects in science, business, languages, and the arts.[36] Three of the five sections were under the administrative supervision of Cuban collaborators while the other two were headed by Spaniards.[37] The school benefited from experienced teachers, but their ambitions greatly surpassed their means. The large number of professors and collaborators, both foreign and national, was greater than the number of students they could recruit, and this experimental institution did not last long. However, one of its branches, the Academia de Artes Dramáticas de la Escuela Libre (Academy of Dramatic Arts of the Open School), known as ADADEL, had a long-lasting impact. Founded by José Rubia Barcia in June 1940, ADADEL was the first to introduce a systematic approach to the study of theater in Cuba and among the first of its kind in Latin America.

Rubia Barcia was a Spanish playwright, theater director, and literature professor who arrived in Havana in May 1939. During his four years on the island, he delivered conferences, published articles, and befriended like-minded Cubans such as Roa and Valdés-Rodríguez. From June 1940 until his departure for a teaching position at Princeton University in August 1943, Rubia Barcia trained many Cuban actors and directors.[38] Other instructors at the academy included the Austrian Ludwig Schajowicz and the Cuban Luis A. Baralt. A group of ADADEL's ex-students continued their theatrical work by forming the ADAD Group, which was active from 1945 to 1950. The stage where ADAD performed was named "the Valdés-Rodríguez," most likely in honor of José Manuel's father, the late educator Manuel Valdés-Rodríguez.[39]

The Academy of Dramatic Arts has been recognized for its importance in theater studies in Cuba, but this setting should also be credited for housing the country's first course on film appreciation.[40] Given his long association with theater criticism and creation, it is not surprising that Valdés-Rodríguez's first students were training to be theater actors and directors.[41] During the late 1920s and early 1930s, he had been part of a group of avant-garde enthusiasts, linked to *Revista de Avance*, who staged plays and later formed a short-lived theater group called "La Cueva."[42] As both film and theater reviewer for the newspaper *El Mundo*, he was knowledgeable in the historical and creative dimensions of the theater, and he was always in contact with new plays and new ideas about this medium.[43]

The relationship between actors' training and the study of film can be traced back to the early days of the State Institute of Cinematography in the USSR. This Soviet film school, founded in 1919 as a technical school (GIK), and turned into a higher education institution in 1934 (VGIK), was initially associated with actors training for the Moscow Art Theater.[44] The school's program covered filmmaking skills as well as the study of the history of art, literature, and culture at large, but the performance aspect was key, especially at its inception. For instance, Lev Kuleshov's experiments with actor Ivan Mozzhukhin took place there during the early 1920s,[45] and Sergei Eisenstein taught a workshop in 1928 examining how the techniques of Japan's kabuki theater could be applied to film acting.[46]

VGIK served as model and inspiration for European film schools of the 1930s and 1940s such as the National Film School in Rome (renamed the Centro Sperimentale di Cinematografia) and L'Institut des Hautes Études Cinématographiques in France (IDHEC). These institutions were funded by the Italian and French states and responded to specific nationalist policies.[47] In contrast, the institutional settings provided by ADADEL, and later by the University of Havana Summer School, were small-scale projects with limited resources and modest objectives. Although the Cuban example is not comparable to the full-fledged European film schools, keeping them in mind allows us to recognize that film culture was acquiring enough importance on the island for an embryonic film pedagogy to emerge.

This film pedagogy shares some traits with the isolated film courses that were offered in institutions of higher education in the United States during the interwar years. Those educational initiatives, along with the existence of noncommercial or niche film exhibition sites and the expansion of the film society movement, contributed to the growth of American film culture.[48] In some instances, film instruction in American universities was connected to the film industry, as was the case for courses offered at Harvard Business School and at the University of Southern California. In other cases, the focus was on the recognition of film's social and aesthetic aspects, independent of any professionalization objectives. One key example of this tendency was the course offered by Harry Alan Potamkin at the end of 1932 for the New School of Social Research in New York.[49]

Valdés-Rodríguez drew inspiration from both the Soviet and the American experiences.[50] Eisenstein's teaching methods concerned the training of filmmakers and were therefore not fully applicable to the Cuban situation, but his ideas and film practice lay at the heart of the theoretical and ideological background of Valdés-Rodríguez's teaching approach. Potamkin's course, on the other hand, was addressed to the adult student with a general interest in cultural and artistic matters and therefore offers the most pertinent point of reference for the Havana course. It is possible that Valdés-Rodríguez may have met Potamkin in person during a trip to the United States before the latter's untimely death in 1933. They were both associated with the journal *Experimental Cinema*, so they may have met at a gathering or event. If not, Potamkin's course description was in any case available in print form in the *National Board of Review* and in the *New School Bulletin* for 1932–1933.[51]

Film Pedagogy at the University of Havana Summer School

Valdés-Rodríguez was ideally situated to be part of the renovation of institutionalized education that took place during the early forties. Cuban politics stabilized after several years of unstable governments following the ousting of Machado in 1933. In 1939 a constitutional assembly was formed and general elections were called. The populist government of Fulgencio Batista was elected and inaugurated in 1940. During the early part of that year, the delegates to the constitutional assembly, representing various political parties—including the Communists—collaborated in the drafting of the new constitution. This was a rare historical moment in which intellectuals and politicians from a wide range of ideological positions debated together the democratic future of the nation.[52] As a result, the Constitution of 1940 established important social reforms as well as political and civil rights, creating the legal basis for optimal relations between citizen and state. In practice, these principles or laws were not always implemented or respected, thus waves of conflict and resistance continued to exist. Nevertheless, the progressive forces behind constitutional change had great impact on the development of the young nation. One of the ways in which this potential was realized was through the modernization of the educational system.

In this context, the status and structure of the University of Havana went through an intense period of transformation. The revolutionary impetus of the student movement had demanded university reforms for almost two decades. The Constitution of 1940 finally recognized the much desired university autonomy and made ample budget allocations. As part of this environment of renewal, the University of Havana founded its Summer School on March 26, 1941.[53] The school focused on cultural enrichment, offering non-credit courses in literature, humanities, Cuban and foreign cultures, geography, history, languages, and the arts. Valdés-Rodríguez's course, El Cine: Industria y Arte de Nuestro Tiempo, was included in the Arts section.[54] Its future was secured by this new institutional alternative and so was its long-term impact in Cuba's cultural history.

Throughout the forties and fifties the university opened up to new types of instruction, incorporating for the first time the presence of theater and film. The evidence suggests that these new developments were closely related to the legacy of the Escuela Libre. Links of friendship and camaraderie with University of Havana professors facilitated the gradual insertion of Spanish exiles and their collaborators into this reputable institution. For instance, Rubia Barcia was able to teach Spanish Grammar and Literature at the Summer School between 1941 and 1943.[55] Theater instructors Ludwig Schajowicz and Luis A. Baralt, originally associated with ADADEL, created the Teatro Universitario and the Seminario de Artes Dramáticas.[56] These teaching positions were financially beneficial as they guaranteed a more stable income than the minimal enrollment the Escuela Libre could secure.

Besides these developments in his teaching career, Valdés-Rodríguez also took an active part in the professionalization of journalism that took place during these years. From 1940 to 1942, he was the president of the Agrupación de Redactores Teatrales y Cinematográficos (Theater and Film

Writers' Association), or ARTYC. He was also a member of the Asociación de Reporters de La Habana (Havana Reporters' Association), and led its Foreign Relations Commission from 1941 to 1945. In addition, he presided over the organizing committee for the First Journalists' Congress hosted in Havana in December 1941.[57] At this congress, journalists made the case for professional journalistic training, and in 1942 they were granted official authorization. The Manuel Márquez Sterling School of Journalism was inaugurated in October 1943. Throughout the rest of the decade, Valdés-Rodríguez earned various certificates and diplomas from the school, culminating in the title of professional journalist in 1949, and eventually becoming an adjunct professor.[58]

Valdés-Rodríguez's professional reputation grew not only through his participation in new institutional spaces but also through his writing. He won various awards both for his critical essays and for his journalistic pieces.[59] At the same time that his intellectual prestige expanded, he cultivated his professional relationship with film industry representatives. Hollywood film distributors in Havana lent their films for the course screenings, and they also collaborated by offering scholarships covering the course fees. Every year, Fox Film de Cuba conferred ten scholarships through a writing contest.[60] The contest was open to anyone not directly involved with the theater, film, or journalistic fields, whether or not they were students. Applicants needed to submit a critical piece regarding a film that had recently premiered in Havana, as specified by Fox.[61] Through this mutually beneficial agreement, Fox enlarged its connection to the Cuban public, and many applicants who could not otherwise have afforded the course were able to enroll.

The pedagogical program of the university course started as an offshoot of the ADADEL course, but Valdés-Rodríguez's was able to refine it throughout fourteen uninterrupted years of teaching at the Summer School (1942–1956). The sporadic, stand-alone lectures he had delivered during the 1930s, although directed at interested audiences, did not require the same type of planning as a course of longer duration does. This summer course required the integration of several interrelated aspects and permitted a more sustained engagement with a diversity of topics. The book *El cine en la Universidad de La Habana* (*Film at the University of Havana*), published in 1966, allows us a glimpse of the scope and content of the course. However, by Valdés-Rodríguez's own admission, the program described should be regarded as reminiscence combined with guidelines for future teaching opportunities.[62]

The principal aims of the course were to familiarize students with important film classics and to provide them with a vocabulary and method useful not only for film analysis but for the critical appraisal of other artistic manifestations as well. The course was organized into twelve lectures and twelve screenings, but this structure may have been somewhat variable.[63] As he explained, the length of coverage for each topic could be adjusted according to the amount of time allotted to the overall course. In his synthesis of the course's history, written a posteriori, he affirms that the course was divided into the following eight sections: "The Birth of Cinema," "Social Technology and Cinema," "Cinema, Collective and Social Art," "Introduction to Film Criticism," "Cinema, Culminating Art," "The Novel and Cinema," "The Theater and Cinema," and "The Specifically Cinematographic."[64] Central to all the lessons was the belief that cinema is a superior art form capable of revealing aspects of human psychology and social reality that no other art form could properly represent. To support his arguments, Valdés-Rodríguez made extensive reference to literature and theater, ranging from the modernist literature of James Joyce and Marcel Proust to the plays of Eugene O'Neill. Although he insisted that cinema had not lived up to its full potential, he discussed Eisenstein's films as an exceptional realization of the medium's possibilities.[65]

Valdés-Rodríguez strived to create a balanced repertory where various modes of filmmaking such as newsreels, animation, documentaries, and feature film genres could be represented. He also incorporated a wide range of filmic traditions, and a typical film list included US, European, and Soviet productions. Several key American and British directors such as Orson Welles, Laurence Olivier, John Ford, Carol Reed, Vincente Minnelli, and Alfred Hitchcock were featured.[66] Latin American films by important Mexican and Argentine directors of the period such as Fernando de Fuentes, Emilio Fernández, and Lucas Demare were included.[67] Some Cuban short films were also screened. Consistent with the postwar relevance of Italian cinema, various Italian films were shown throughout the fifties, including those of Roberto Rossellini and Vittorio de Sica. European productions were most amply represented by French cinema, in particular through the films of Jean Renoir and Julien Duvivier, which were shown on several occasions. Only the films of Charles Chaplin and Eisenstein were shown with comparable frequency.[68] The screening selection depended in no small measure on the availability of the films through their local distributors. This created an irregular supply, which is why in many cases the films of significant directors of the period, such as Luis Buñuel and Akira Kurosawa, were only sporadically accessible.

The Department of Cinematography and the Extension of Film Activities

The university film course gained in popularity and prestige as the years went by. During its first six years, it functioned in a stable but modest manner. The screening sessions had first taken place with borrowed equipment in a classroom, but to improve on the substandard image and sound quality, they had to be moved to the facilities at a radio station.[69] In 1948, the university was going through a construction boom, and Valdés-Rodríguez managed to get sufficient administrative support to install proper film projection equipment in the amphitheater at the School of Education. The architectural and technical upgrades to the Enrique José Varona theater were completed in July 1948, and it became a permanent site for film projection within the university—hailed as the first of its kind in Latin America.[70]

A few months later, in March 1949, the branch in charge of the University Extension programs approved the creation of the Department of Cinematography, with a fixed salary for its director, a projectionist, and a secretary.[71] The department included the personal library of Valdés-Rodríguez, with hundreds of his books on film and other arts, as well as his collection of specialized film publications.[72] With these developments, the scope of film activities at the university was greatly enlarged. The department would henceforth be engaged in four principal types of activities: the film course at the Summer School, the promotion of film as an educational tool, the creation of a film archive, and regular screenings for the general public.

One of the department's stated goals was to function as a lending service for the use of film as a teaching aid for university professors in any discipline.[73] Valdés-Rodríguez was attuned to ideas about the pedagogical value of visual images and promoted their use as a necessary tool in modern teaching strategies.[74] University professors such as Roa employed the services of the department, using films to illustrate certain topics in social science classes.[75] At the Department of Art History, Professor Luis de Soto frequently utilized visual media, including photographs, slides, and the screening of documentaries.[76]

Film Culture and Education in Republican Cuba | 311

Fig. 10.1 The Enrique José Varona Theater, considered the first permanent university screening room in Latin America. (The images in this essay have been preserved thanks to the admirable labor of the researcher Pedro Noa Romero in his digitization of materials belonging to the archives of the Extension School of the Universidad de La Habana.)

The institutional credentials of working within the university setting allowed Valdés-Rodríguez to create a film archive. The refurbishment of the Teatro Varona included a film storage area with proper air-conditioning and dehumidification.[77] This became the location of the Filmoteca Universitaria, the first Cuban film archive, which by 1957 included a total of 150 titles, including documentaries, feature films, and newsreels, in thirty-five-millimeter and sixteen-millimeter formats.[78] The first acquisition was Eisenstein's 1938 film *Alexander Nevsky*.[79] Other prominent titles included copies of *Battleship Potemkin* (*Bronenosets Potyomkin*, dir. Sergei Eisenstein, 1925), *La grande illusion* (dir. Jean Renoir, 1937), and *Germany Year Zero* (*Deutschland im Jahre Null*, dir. Roberto Rossellini, 1948).[80] In addition, the Filmoteca was an important repository holding the only copies of key Cuban films from the 1920s and 1930s.[81]

Fig. 10.2a and Fig. 10.2b Details of the decorative panels in the Varona Theater showing quotations from Dante, Charles Baudelaire, and Sergei Eisenstein and a list of revered directors.

To obtain the funds for growing the film collection, in 1949 the Department of Cinematography started offering an alternative, but regular, film exhibition program called Cine de Arte (Art Cinema). By paying a small membership fee, subscribers could attend two film projections per month. They received printed program notes, and the screenings were preceded by a short introduction, sometimes delivered by Valdés-Rodríguez, and other times by specialists in topics relevant to the film. After the film, spectators participated in the ensuing debate.[82] The films were provided either by film distributors or by embassies, which collaborated with the university in the promotion of their country's cultural heritage.[83]

In the 1950s, Havana's active filmgoers had access to a vast network of commercial cinemas that regularly projected contemporary films from Hollywood, Mexico, and various European countries. This exposure to international films was mostly the result of the logics of market-driven entertainment. In contrast, the institutional setting of the university film programs generated an intellectual attitude toward film viewing. The film course furnished a basic knowledge of film history and sharpened the students' critical sense. The Cine de Arte screenings provided further opportunities for refining a systematic understanding of cinema's technical, social, and aesthetic elements. This exercise of their analytical capacity did not preclude a pleasurable engagement with the films. Rather, it defined a new type of collective spectatorship, an emerging Cuban art cinema audience.

When the Department of Cinematography was first created, one commentator ventured to propose that the university could become a filmmaking training facility.[84] This was never seriously considered, and cinephiles with filmmaking aspirations acquired their technical skills either through the local television and advertising industries or abroad. On the other hand, the University of Havana program effectively became the training ground for professional film criticism. As a key member of ARTYC, Valdés-Rodríguez was able to establish and convey the professional standards he valued.[85] One of his most prominent disciples, Guillermo Cabrera Infante, became the most influential Cuban film critic of the 1950s. He had won one of the Fox scholarships and took the film course in 1948, later embarking on a very significant journalistic and literary career.[86] He developed his own style of writing about contemporary cinema, and his views differed greatly from those of his old teacher. Their divergent opinions are a testament to the generational shift that would inevitably occur.

The course and the screening sessions enabled a platform for discussion and interaction where many friendships and collaborations were formed. For instance, Germán Puig, Ricardo Vigón, Néstor Almendros, and Cabrera Infante, who all met through the film course, formed a cineclub in 1948.[87] In this case, the ex-students had a falling out with Valdés-Rodríguez as the youngsters came into their own and developed their own tastes, preferences, and cultural projects.[88] In other cases, the direct mentorship and support of the professor was instrumental. One example of this was the film section of the Nuestro Tiempo (Our Times) cultural society, helmed by Julio García Espinosa and Alfredo Guevara who borrowed films from the Filmoteca for their cineclub.[89] This group would later form the nucleus of the Instituto Cubano de Arte e Industria Cinematográficos (ICAIC). Nelson Rodríguez, one of the course's students in 1955, founded another left-leaning group, called Cine Visión (Vision Cinema). He later became an important film editor at ICAIC, and credits Valdés-Rodríguez with inspiring him to form the cineclub and to pursue a professional film career.[90]

Conclusion

For two decades, Valdés-Rodríguez mediated the encounter of many Cuban cinephiles with the most provocative aspects of international cinema. At the Varona theater the professor ensured that they learned essential critical tools to discuss films with an informed, open-minded outlook. In the absence of film festivals or stable cinémathèque screenings, he fulfilled the role of arbiter of an alternative circuit of film programming. The conditions that made this possible depended very heavily on the initiative, determination, and perseverance of this man, who had the remarkable capacity to successfully navigate the worlds of intellectual pedigree, leftist politics, cultural journalism, industry imperatives, and institutional labyrinths.

The University of Havana was closed in 1957 because of the tense political climate during the last years of Fulgencio Batista's unconstitutional regime (1952–1958). When it reopened under the new revolutionary government, the university structure, as well as its faculty and staff appointments, underwent drastic changes. Valdés-Rodríguez taught the course as part of the Summer School once again in 1960, but the Department of Cinematography did not survive despite an initial intention to improve it.[91] In 1962, two new entities were created: the Department of Audiovisual Media, dealing mostly with teaching aid materials, and the Cinema section of the University Extension Commission, which continued the work of organizing film screenings on campus.[92] However, no provisions were made for continuation of the traditional film course. Valdés-Rodríguez, who was sixty-six years old by then, would only teach the course again in 1963, exclusively for students in the School of History.[93]

In contrast to North American universities during the 1960s, when new film programs were established, film-related academic endeavors at the University of Havana did not solidify into disciplinary formations.[94] Valdés-Rodríguez was able to propel the study of cinema from within the purview of independent learned societies and teaching centers to the more stable and prestigious setting of a Department of Cinematography in an institution of higher education. This gradual movement toward the formalization of the study of cinema ensured a permanent place from which to conduct his educational activities and an enduring environment that could house a growing film collection. However, this institutional basis for the study of film did not coalesce into the formation of a film studies discipline within the University of Havana curriculum.

This situation was symptomatic of the generational shift that had occurred. Whereas establishing a film department in the 1940s was an innovative and forward-thinking development, by the early 1960s other priorities were at stake. In Cuba, the academic setting for the study of film was at odds with the cultural project of the revolution. Popular culture became a matter of the highest concern for the state, and the redefinition of the scope and importance of film culture and film knowledge went far beyond the university walls. The overriding concern was a political task of enormous implications—it concerned the ideological reorientation of revolutionary citizens in the making, as well as the construction of a new national identity.

Valdés-Rodríguez collaborated with preexisting as well as post-revolutionary institutions. The official position of the newly formed state-funded ICAIC was to categorically deny the ongoing or future value of any preceding film-related efforts in Cuba. It was important to the film institute to start from a blank slate, and this applied to everything from filmmaking and film criticism to practices of film viewing in any form.[95] Yet, Valdés-Rodríguez's work could be adapted to new objectives, and some of the initiatives he pioneered were repurposed. For instance, the post-screening discussion model that he adopted for the Cine de Arte sessions, and which had been embraced by several independent cineclubs, inspired massive-scale film viewing gatherings known as popular cine-debates.[96] Furthermore, one of his most significant contributions to post-revolutionary film culture was his willingness to lend the holdings of the Filmoteca Universitaria to the incipient Cuban cinémathèque founded by ICAIC in 1960. Thus, many of the screenings organized by cinémathèque during these years were possible thanks to the pre-revolutionary institutional and financial structures that he had ingeniously established.[97]

Valdés-Rodríguez did not occupy any administrative positions at ICAIC, but he cooperated with the film institute in many capacities and officially represented Cuba at various international film festivals in the early 1960s. Initially he was a useful resource given his extensive contacts with film distributors, local and international filmmakers, and foreign embassies. When the process of nationalization severed many of these connections, his association with the Communist Party and his knowledge of Soviet cinema became useful assets for promoting the filmography of socialist countries. However, during this time of complex allegiances, he also represented an ossified version of film taste and a more orthodox view of culture than the one supported by younger cultural administrators.

Examining Valdés-Rodríguez's legacy allows us to acknowledge some of the cultural projects, large and small, that preceded the state-funded film institute, and to recognize their part in the ensuing consolidation of institutionalized revolutionary film culture. Even the reference to both "art" and "industry" in the names of ICAIC and in the film course (Cinema: Industry and Art of Our Times) reminds us of Valdés-Rodríguez's importance as historical link. Understanding his crucial role in creating the first Cuban sites of specialized film knowledge enlarges the frame of reference connecting film education and exhibition initiatives, the impulse to preserve and screen the films of the past, the formation of cineclubs, and the emergence of a new autochthonous critical discourse during Cuba's Republican era.

> IRENE ROZSA is a doctoral candidate in Film and Moving Image Studies at Concordia University. Her dissertation focuses on the transition from pre-revolutionary to post-revolutionary Cuban film culture.

NOTES

1. José Manuel Valdés-Rodríguez, *El cine en la Universidad de La Habana (1942–1965)* (La Habana: Empresa de Publicaciones Mined, 1966), xiv.

2. Recent publications explore how these ideas circulated in avant-garde and institutional settings. For the European context, see Malte Hagener, *Moving Forward,*

Looking Back. The European Avant-Garde and the Invention of Film Culture, 1919–1939 (Amsterdam: Amsterdam University Press, 2007); Malte Hagener, ed., *The Emergence of Film Culture: Knowledge Production, Institution Building, and the Fate of the Avant-Garde in Europe, 1919–1945* (New York: Berghahn Books, 2014). For the North American context, see Lee Grieveson and Haidee Wasson, eds., *Inventing Film Studies* (Durham, NC: Duke University Press, 2008).

3. Louis A. Pérez, *Cuba: Between Reform and Revolution* (New York: Oxford University Press, 2006); Hugh Thomas, *Cuba or the Pursuit of Freedom* (New York: Da Capo Press, 1998).

4. Michael Chanan, *Cuban Cinema* (Minneapolis: University of Minnesota Press, 2004), 99–100, 104–105.

5. José Manuel Valdés-Rodríguez, *El cine: industria y arte de nuestro tiempo*, ed. Romualdo Santos (La Habana: Editorial Letras Cubanas, 1989), 16.

6. For an illuminating analysis of the role of writers and intellectuals in negotiating the influence of Hollywood cinema in Latin America, see Jason Borge, *Latin American Writers and the Rise of Hollywood Cinema* (New York: Routledge, 2008).

7. Pedro R. Noa Romero, *Ojeada al cine cubano: José Manuel Valdés-Rodríguez* (La Habana: Ediciones ICAIC, 2010).

8. Students of Valdés-Rodríguez included Néstor Almendros, Guillermo Cabrera Infante, Fausto Canel, Julio García Espinosa, Alfredo Guevara, Orlando Jiménez Leal, Eduardo Manet, José Massip, Walfredo Piñera, Germán Puig, Mario Rodríguez Alemán, and Ricardo Vigón, among many others. Many of them wrote film criticism during the 1950s and early 1960s, while others became filmmakers in Cuba but pursued their later careers in exile. Their stories merit a separate in-depth study. The work of García Espinosa and Guevara is better known because of their long-term contributions to the Cuban Film Institute, or Instituto Cubano de Arte e Industria Cinematográficos (ICAIC). For instance, under Guevara's leadership, ICAIC became a crucial nexus in the transnational network of collaboration between filmmakers of the New Latin American Cinema by sponsoring publications, documentaries, coproductions, and film festivals. García Espinosa's 1967 essay "Por un cine imperfecto" ("For an Imperfect Cinema") is a key example of the revolutionary ideals that resonated throughout Third World filmmaking in the 1960s and 1970s. For the prevailing history of ICAIC, see Chanan, *Cuban Cinema*. For a translation of the text mentioned, see Julio García Espinosa, "For an Imperfect Cinema," in *New Latin American Cinema*, vol. 1, ed. Michael T. Martin (Detroit: Wayne State University Press, 1997), 71–82.

9. Scholars have recently explored aspects of 1950s Cuban cultural history. See Hyde on modernist architecture, and Rivero on television. Timothy Hyde, *Constitutional Modernism: Architecture and Civil Society in Cuba, 1933–1959* (Minneapolis: University of Minnesota Press, 2012); Yeidy Rivero, *Broadcasting Modernity: Cuban Commercial Television, 1950–1960* (Durham, NC: Duke University Press, 2015).

10. These interactions are explained in detail in this essay's sections: "Valdés-Rodríguez and the Intellectual Community of the 1920s and 1930s" and "The Academy of Dramatic Arts: First Iteration of the Film Course."

11. Manuel Valdés-Rodríguez, *Ensayos sobre educación: teórica, práctica y experimental* (Habana: Imprenta El Figaro, 1898).

12. Dulce María Escalona, "Manuel Valdés-Rodríguez," in *El maestro y la educación popular*, ed. Dulce María Escalona (La Habana: Ministerio de Educacion, Direccion de Cultura, 1950), 7–19.

13. Noa Romero, *Ojeada al cine cubano*, 263.

14. Francine Masiello, "Rethinking Neocolonial Esthetics: Literature, Politics, and Intellectual Community in Cuba's *Revista de Avance*," *Latin American Research Review* 28, no. 2 (1993): 15.

15. Ibid., 3.

16. Carlos Ripoll, "*La Revista de Avance* (1927–1930). Vocero de vanguardismo y pórtico de revolución," *Revista Iberoamericana* 30, no. 58 (1964): 267.

17. Ibid., 265; Rosario Rexach, "*La Revista de Avance* publicada en Habana, 1927–1930." *Caribbean Studies* 3, no. 3 (1963): 3–16.

18. The original editors were Alejo Carpentier, Martí Casanovas, Francisco Ichaso, Jorge Mañach, and Juan Marinello. José Zacarías Tallet and Félix Lizaso substituted Carpentier and Casanaovas, respectively.

19. Raúl Roa, "Firmeza y continuidad de una conducta," in Valdés-Rodríguez, *El cine: industria y arte*, 434.

20. María Eulalia Douglas. *La tienda negra: el cine en Cuba, 1897–1990* (La Habana: Cinemateca de Cuba, 1996), 51.

21. Louis A. Pérez, *On Becoming Cuban: Identity, Nationality, and Culture* (Chapel Hill: University of North Carolina Press, 1999), PDF e-book, chap. 5.

22. Noa Romero, *Ojeada al cine cubano*, 264.

23. Ibid.

24. After the six-month prison term, he returned to the professional milieu unscathed. He remained faithful to socialist ideals, and his writing became more ideologically overt after the 1959 Cuban Revolution. This position was celebrated in most tributes to his legacy throughout the 1960s, 1970s, and 1980s. See Romualdo Santos, "Historia de una pasión cinematográfica," in Valdés-Rodríguez, *El cine: industria y arte*, 5–25.

25. *Experimental Cinema* 4 (1932), 2.

26. José Manuel Valdés-Rodríguez, "Hollywood: Sales Agent of American Imperialism," *Experimental Cinema* 4 (1932), 18–20, 52–53.

27. Megan Feeney, "'Enseñándolos a ver': Hollywood in Havana and the Birth of a Critical Practice, 1897–1933," *Journal of Latin American Cultural Studies* 15, no. 3 (2006): 321–339.

28. Lyceum and Lawn Tennis Club Collection, Cuban Heritage Collection, University of Miami Libraries, Coral Gables, Florida.

29. Noa Romero, *Ojeada al cine cubano*, 48.

30. Ministerio de Defensa Nacional, "J. M. Valdés-Rodríguez," in *Premio Varona* (La Habana: Impresores P. Fernández, 1945), 40.

31. "Notes on Activities of Experimental Cinema during 1933," *Experimental Cinema* 5 (1934), 2.

32. José Manuel Valdés-Rodríguez, "El hombre, el creador, el técnico: Sergei Mijailovich Eisenstein," *Lunes de Revolución*, February 6, 1961, 24–26.

33. Noa Romero, *Ojeada al cine cubano*, 13.

34. Miguel Cabañas Bravo, "Lazos y ensanches del arte español a través del exilio de 1939: el caso de Cuba," in *Las redes hispanas del arte desde 1900*, eds. Miguel Cabañas Bravo and Wifredo Rincón García (Madrid: Consejo Superior de Investigaciones Científicas, 2014), 89–106.

35. Dania Vázquez Matos, "La Escuela Libre de La Habana: vivero de inquietudes y desvelos renovadores," *Ágora: Boletín Digital Dirección de Información Universidad de La Habana* 3 (2012): 10–15.

36. Ibid., 14.

37. The Cubans who were involved with the administration of the Escuela Libre were all professors at the University of Havana. Alfonso Bernal del Riesgo was responsible for the section dedicated to Secondary Studies, José Elías Entralgo Vallina for Free Courses, and Raúl Roa García for Cultural Relations and Publications. The other two sections, Advanced and University Studies and Arts and Languages, were headed by Spaniards Luis Tobío Fernández and José Rubia Barcia, respectively. Rubia Barcia took over the leadership of the school after its first director, Cuban lawyer José Miguel Irisarri, stepped down.

38. Jorge Domingo, *El exilio Republicano español en Cuba* (Madrid: Siglo XXI de España, 2009), 503–504.

39. Luis A. Baralt, "Cincuenta años de teatro en Cuba," in *El Libro de Cuba* (La Habana: Artes Gráficas, 1954), 614.

40. Valdés-Rodríguez, *El cine en la Universidad*, xiii.

41. Among his first students were actors Violeta Casal, Marisabel Sáenz, Alejandro Lugo, Ana Saínz, Juanita Caldevilla, and directors Modesto Centeno and Francisco Morín. See Valdés-Rodríguez, *El cine en la Universidad*, xiv.

42. Baralt, "Cincuenta años de teatro en Cuba," 614.

43. Valdés-Rodríguez, *El cine en la Universidad*, 456–485.

44. Duncan Petrie, "A New Art for a New Society? The Emergence and Development of Film Schools in Europe," in *Emergence of Film Culture*, ed. Hagener, 270.

45. Ibid., 271.

46. Sergei Eisenstein, "The GTK Teaching and Research Workshop," in *Selected Works*, vol. 1, ed. Richard Taylor (London: British Film Institute, 1988), 127–130.

47. For analyses of film education in Europe during this period, see Masha Salazkina, "Soviet-Italian Cinematic Exchanges: Transnational Film Education in the 1930s," in *Emergence of Film Culture*, ed. Hagener, 180–198; also Petrie, "Film Schools in Europe," in *Emergence of Film Culture*, ed. Hagener, 268–282.

48. For a collection addressing various aspects of American film culture in the first half of the twentieth century, see Grieveson and Wasson, eds., *Inventing Film Studies*.

49. Dana Polan, *Scenes of Instruction: The Beginnings of the U.S. Study of Film* (Berkeley: University of California Press, 2007), 6.

50. Mirta Aguirre, "Cine en la Universidad," in *Crónicas de Cine*, ed. Marcia Castillo and Olivia Miranda (La Habana: Editorial Letras Cubanas, 1988), 249.

51. Polan, *Scenes of Instruction*, 240.
52. Thomas, *Cuba or the Pursuit of Freedom*, 716–723; Pérez, *Cuba: Between Reform and Revolution*, 214.
53. Ramón de Armas, Ana Cairo Ballester, and Eduardo Torres-Cuevas, *Historia de la Universidad de La Habana, 1930–1978* (La Habana: Editorial de Ciencias Sociales, 1984), 502; Alfonso Bernal del Riesgo, "La enseñanza universitaria en Cuba," in *El Libro de Cuba* (La Habana: Artes Gráficas, 1954), 546.
54. I am grateful to Pedro Noa Romero for generously sharing materials related to Valdés-Rodríguez's film course that are held at the University of Havana's Extension Department. These documents have been digitized and preserved thanks to his arduous and laudable archival work. Throughout this essay, I will refer to these sources as Valdés-Rodríguez Digital Archive.
55. Domingo, *El exilio Republicano español*, 503–504.
56. Baralt, "Cincuenta años de teatro en Cuba," 614.
57. *Premio Varona*, 41.
58. Octavio de la Suareé, "Escuela Profesional de Periodismo Manuel Márquez Sterling," in *El Libro de Cuba* (La Habana: Artes Gráficas, 1954), 527.
59. *Premio Varona*, 40–41.
60. Valdés-Rodríguez, *El cine en la Universidad*, xv.
61. Valdés-Rodríguez Digital Archive.
62. Valdés-Rodríguez, *El cine en la Universidad*, 368–371.
63. Ibid., xiv.
64. Ibid., 369–371.
65. Ibid., 393–429, 456–485.
66. Ibid., 381–386.
67. Ibid. The Mexican films *Janitzio* (dir. Carlos Navarro, 1935), *Doña Bárbara* (dir. Fernando de Fuentes, 1943), *María Candelaria* (dir. Emilio Fernández, 1944), and *La perla* (*The Pearl*, dir. Emilio Fernández, 1947) were shown in the 1940s, while Luis Buñuel's *Los olvidados* (1950) was screened in the 1950s. Argentine films included *La guerra gaucha* (*The Gaucho War*, dir. Lucas Demare, 1942), *Todo un hombre* (*A Real Man*, dir. Pierre Chenal, 1943), *Su mejor alumno* (*His Best Pupil*, dir. Lucas Demare, 1944), *La casta Susana* (*Chaste Susan*, dir. Benito Perojo, 1944), and *La dama duende* (*The Ghost Lady*, dir. Luis Saslavsky, 1945). It is interesting to note that in some instances, the film information provided by Valdés-Rodríguez is imprecise. For example, he incorrectly credits the Argentine film *El matrero* (*The Outlaw*, dir. Orestes Caviglia, 1939) to Lucas Demare. In another confusing case, he lists "'Muralla de Pasiones.' Est. San Miguel. Director: Mario Soffici." He may have been referring to the Mexican film *Murallas de pasión* (*Walls of Passion*, dir. Víctor Urruchúa, 1944), or to the Argentine film made for Estudios San Miguel *Tres hombres del río* (*Three Men of the River*, dir. Mario Soffici, 1943).
68. Ibid., 381–386.
69. Ibid., xiv.
70. Ibid., xv–xvi.
71. Ibid., xiii–xv.

72. Valdés-Rodríguez Digital Archive.
73. Valdés-Rodríguez, *El cine en la Universidad*, xvii.
74. Aguirre, "Cine en la Universidad," 249.
75. Raúl Roa, "Firmeza y continuidad de una conducta," in Valdés-Rodríguez, *El cine: industria y arte*, 436.
76. José Manuel Valdés-Rodríguez, *La Reforma Universitaria y los medios audiovisuales*. (Habana: Servicio de Medios Audiovisuales, Universidad de La Habana, 1963), 17; Valdés-Rodríguez, *El cine en la Universidad*, 20–23.
77. Valdés-Rodríguez, *El cine en la Universidad*, xvii.
78. Pedro Noa Romero, "La primera savia nutricia: La filmoteca universitaria," *Revista Cine Cubano*, nos. 181–182 (2011), 110–115.
79. Valdés-Rodríguez, *El cine en la Universidad*, xvii.
80. Ibid., 372–380.
81. Noa Romero, "La primera savia nutricia," 110–115.
82. Valdés-Rodríguez, *El cine en la Universidad*, xvi.
83. Ibid., 71.
84. Aguirre, "Cine en la Universidad," 251.
85. For Valdés-Rodríguez, a good film review should address five essential components: the thematic quality of the film; the specifically filmic elements displayed; the presence of other artistic values; the significance of the work in terms of its technical and aesthetic contribution to its historical period; and the philosophical, social, and political outlook of the film's writers and director. See Valdés-Rodríguez, *El cine en la Universidad*, 369.
86. Antoni Munné, "Retrato del crítico como ente de ficción," in *El cronista de cine: un oficio del siglo XX y otros escritos cinematográficos*, by Guillermo Cabrera Infante (Barcelona: Galaxia Gutenberg, 2012), 15.
87. Other active members included Tomás Gutiérrez Alea, who later became the most important Cuban filmmaker of his generation, and cinematographer Ramón F. Suárez. They collaborated on *Memorias del subsdesarrollo* (*Memories of Underdevelopment*, 1968), one of the most significant Cuban films of the 1960s.
88. The history of this organization is fraught with controversy, as has been recently explained by Emmanuel Vincenot, "Germán Puig, Ricardo Vigón et Henri Langlois, pionniers de la Cinemateca de Cuba," *Caravelle*, no. 83 (2004): 11–42.
89. Noa Romero, *Ojeada al cine cubano*, 265–266.
90. Valdés-Rodríguez Digital Archive.
91. Eduardo Manet, "Cine y cultura en la Universidad de La Habana," *Cine Cubano* no. 2 (1960), 54–55.
92. Valdés-Rodríguez, *La Reforma Universitaria*, 3.
93. Noa Romero, *Ojeada al cine cubano*, 266–267.
94. Lee Grieveson and Haidee Wasson, "The Academy and Motion Pictures," in Grieveson and Wasson, *Inventing Film Studies*, xi–xxxii.
95. Alfredo Guevara, "Realidades y perspectivas de un nuevo cine," *Cine Cubano* no. 1 (1960), 1–3.

96. In my dissertation I analyze the relationship between cineclubs, the cine-debates, and ICAIC's cinémathèque during the post-revolutionary period. For an early mention of this, see Manet, "Cine y cultura en la Universidad de La Habana," 55.

97. Noa Romero, "La primera savia nutricia," 110–115.

Chapter 11

The Secret History of Aztlán: Speculative Histories, Transnational Exploitation Film, and Unexpected Cultural Flows

Colin Gunckel

IN THEIR 2002 FILM *The Great Mojado Invasion, Part 2 (The Second U.S.–Mexico War)*, Guillermo Gómez-Peña and Gustavo Vázquez construct a speculative fiction about the history of US–Mexico relations. Narrated as a history told from the future, this self-proclaimed "uncensored version of the director's cut of the Chicana/o sci-fi classic banned in sixty-nine festivals" uses clips from low-budget cinema on both sides of the border to trace a satirical narrative that begins with the Conquest and continues through the Mexican Revolution, the Chicana/o movement, the so-called Reconquista (the proposed reconquering of the Southwest by Mexico), and the subsequent formation of a rebel army opposed to all exclusionary nationalisms. By constructing the film entirely of found footage interspersed with Gómez-Peña's direct address to the spectator—in a performance channeling the ghoulish hosts of creature features on late night television—the film's hybrid nature and economic resourcefulness resonate with a tradition of so-called rasquache cinema (a "do it yourself" aesthetic practice by which artists make the most of scarce resources and limited budgets) produced by Chicana/o filmmakers since the 1960s.[1]

While its construction as a montage of existing material might situate it within a film historical legacy that begins with *I Am Joaquín* (dir. Luis Valdez, 1969), it nonetheless departs from the solemn nationalism of such films and their reliance on the Mesoamerican past as the foundation for claims of identity and place. By working between traditions of Chicana/o cinema, exploitation, and found footage films, Gómez-Peña and Vázquez disrupt the interrelated boundaries of nation, history, and race through a raucous mélange of Mexican wrestling clips, Hollywood B westerns, soft porn, and musical numbers repurposed as "amazing, uncensored archival footage." In a scene labeled "Aztlan 2000 and One," for instance, a futuristic Aztec robot promises a group of indigenous men that "when I become emperor of Mexico, you will again be free to live on the lands of your fathers." Not only is this fantasy of the recent past visualized through a dubbed clip of an unnamed science fiction film, but at several points in the piece, history is also conflated with its representation in cinema. In talking about the conquering Spanish, Gómez-Peña explains, "According to Chicana/o fundamentalist historians, these bad actors were hairy, smelly, neurotic and very horny." Narrating the history of the Americas by referencing the ways that US–Mexico relations have been mediated through transnational popular culture, the filmmakers are, among other things, proposing parodic parallels between the uses and appropriation of Mexico's indigenous cultures by the state, the culture industries, and social justice movements.[2]

The reference here to exploitation films and other "bad cinema" as archival footage, while clearly a parody of authoritative histories, also perhaps inadvertently registers the recent interest in such films as legitimate objects of scholarly inquiry. Once considered unworthy of serious consideration on intellectual or aesthetic grounds, the Mexican exploitation films of the mid-twentieth century have generated within the last decade a growing body of scholarship and new generation of home video rereleases. In keeping with emergent areas of cinema studies that depart from an attachment to canonical histories and aesthetic hierarchies, such work has argued for so-called Mexploitation cinema as undervalued allegories of nation and gender, or as a curious episode of transnational cinematic exchange.[3]

Building upon the considerable insights of such work, this essay seeks to situate low-budget exploitation films as a telling instance of the long-standing, transnational circulation of ideas about indigenous Mexico. As films that were transnational in both conception and distribution, their evocations of ancient Mexico in particular sustain an unlikely dialogue with existing representations on both sides of the border. In Mexico, selective imagery of Mesoamerica—from murals to monuments and cinema—composed a

Fig. 11.1 *The Great Mojado Invasion, Part 2 (The Second U.S.-Mexico War)*, (dir. Gustavo Vázquez and Guillermo Gómez-Peña, 2002). Image copyright of the artist, courtesy of Video Data Bank, www.vdb.org.

keystone of cultural nationalism in the post-revolutionary era. This array of imagery in turn influenced Aztec apparitions in the popular culture of the United States, which was also greatly shaped by the emergence of the discipline of archaeology and the trappings of tourism. The Chicana/o concept of Aztlán, which placed the Aztec homeland in the southwestern United States, drew from and reframed both of these extant repertoires as the basis of new formations of identity, community, and belonging.

While several authors have productively mapped the emergence of Chicana/o or Latina/o futurism through science fiction genres, this essay focuses upon the way so-called speculative fictions or horror fantasies are turned toward history.[4] Many of the ideas and images in all three spheres, regardless of their differences, situate indigenous Mexico as a figment of the past, while proposing a selective version of time travel, whether literal or conceptual. The artifacts and stories that circulate between both nations are also often united by historical speculation, whether the subject is the location of hidden treasure, the actual site of the Aztec homeland, or the historical foundations of Mexican or Chicana/o nationalisms. In embarking upon these quests, they extract mythical Aztecs from history to fulfill a narrative or conceptual function in the present. Whether this trope is framed as the incompatibility of the indigenous with the modern or as the basis of national or ethnic identity, the apparently fluid temporality in these instances is almost consistently unidirectional. This brand of temporality is also deceptively premised upon fixed notions of the past that produce reductive caricatures or erasures of indigenous Mexico, both historical and contemporary.

Mexican exploitation film, while certainly partaking of these tendencies, also unwittingly constitutes an alternative trajectory and another way of thinking through intertwined conceptions of race, nation, and transnationality. As Jeffrey Sconce has argued, the imperfect, incomplete, and at times incoherent nature of low-budget films inadvertently produces ruptures and juxtapositions that may align them with the provocations of radical or experimental cinema.[5] In the case of Mexican exploitation films, these impoverished aesthetics often produce a kind of simultaneity or disjuncture in which disparate spaces and temporalities improbably coexist or overlap. By perhaps unintentionally disrupting the unidirectional past-within-the-present that structures other representations, such films offer a burlesque of nationalisms and other mythologies undergirded by frozen versions of the Aztec past. The translation and reediting of these films as they traveled to the United States added another layer of textual transnationality and fragmentation, while sometimes resignifying or scrambling nationalist iconography in the process.

In examining transnational circulation of imagery and ideas about indigenous Mexico, I use Aztlán (the mythical Aztec homeland, believed by some to be in the Southwest) as a touchstone through which to map transnational representations of indigenous Mexico, from the colonial mind-set of Spanish explorers and popular literature, to the alternative cultural and geographical cartographies variously present in both low-budget cinema and the Chicana/o movement. This spectrum includes an admittedly extreme range of motivations, intentionality, and representational strategies. What binds all of these artifacts across multiple centuries is the concept of Aztlán as the basis of transnational imaginaries and the enduring, compelling power it has exerted over the cultural production of the continent. That Aztecs adopted an origin story that would then be adapted as a script for Spanish expeditions, a range of popular culture texts, and a social justice movement is nothing short of remarkable. Even more remarkable is that it continually serves as a reminder of the arbitrary and violent nature of geopolitical borders, and the centuries of exchange, migration, and movement between Mexico and the US Southwest. If Aztlán has been the product of a range of projected desires and motivations, however, its cultural manifestations over the last century have also typically relegated the indigenous to symbols.

Understanding the travels of Aztec mummies and sinister sacrifices across centuries allows us to productively rethink the history and legacy of midcentury exploitation film. As the *Great Mojado Invasion* suggests, these works constitute an overlooked influence upon artists and filmmakers working between Mexico and the United States. In fact, a number of artists have produced works about colonialism, US-Mexico relations, and the construction of history that employ juxtaposition, hybridity, assemblage, or montage to propose a similar effect of simultaneity or atemporality. By incorporating references to popular culture—from comic books to bad science fiction—and remixing them with pre-Conquest and colonial imagery, such works also explicitly situate these "lowbrow" products as texts through which lofty notions about race, nation, and history have been negotiated across borders. In other words, one might argue that midcentury Aztec horror films perhaps counterintuitively mark a pivotal moment in the cinematic representation of indigenous Mexico. This essay, by drawing parallels between Aztlán and B-movie Aztecs, thus constitutes a speculative rethinking of the unexpected importance and impact of Mexican exploitation films of the 1950s and 1960s.

Aztec Horror in Midcentury Mexico

In the late 1950s, the Mexican film industry began producing a cycle of horror, science fiction, and *lucha libre* (Mexican wrestling) films, along with a number of features that combined conventions of all three. Coincident with the decline of the Golden Age, these films were produced cheaply and quickly to generate maximum profit from an emerging youth market. Among these were *El vampiro* (*The Vampire*, dir. Fernando Méndez, 1957), *El barón del terror* (*Braniac*, dir. Chano Urueta, 1962), *La maldición de la llorona* (*The Curse of the Crying Woman*, dir. Rafael Baledón, 1963), *El espejo de la bruja* (*The Witch's Mirror*, dir. Chano Urueta, 1962), and *El hombre y el monstruo* (*The Man and the Monster*, dir. Rafael Baledón, 1959). A significant number of these productions explicitly traded upon the Aztec past as horror: *La cabeza viviente* (*The Living Head*, dir. Chano Urueta, 1963), the Aztec Mummy Trilogy (dir. Rafael Portillo, 1957–1958), *Las luchadoras contra la momia* (*Wrestling Women vs. the Aztec Mummy*, dir. René Cardona, 1964), and *Santo en la venganza de la momia* (*Santo and the Vengeance of the Mummy*, dir. René Cardona, 1971), among others. With remarkable consistency, the mummies in these films are typically awakened by the discovery or robbery of an ancient Aztec treasure. Consistent with colonial accounts of indigenous savagery, this awakening is then often accompanied by the threat of human sacrifice.

For example, in the first film of the aforementioned trilogy, *La momia azteca* (*The Aztec Mummy*, 1957), a hypnotherapist, Dr. Eduardo Almada (Ramón Gay) accidentally resurrects an Aztec mummy by conducting an experiment upon his wife Flor (Rosita Arenas) in which she regresses to a past life as the intended victim of Aztec sacrifice. Her revelations during this session reveal the location of a hidden vault in which Popoca, an Aztec warrior and her lover in this past life, has been guarding a valuable breastplate and bracelet for centuries. When Almada and his companions remove the breastplate to display it as proof of his past-life theories on hypnotherapy, they awaken an angered Popoca and activate an ancient curse. The resolution of the entire trilogy thus hinges on the restoration of the breastplate and the return of Popoca to his eternal slumber.

As I have argued elsewhere, the terror-inducing resurrection of Aztec mummies in exploitation film constituted a sort of "return of the oppressed" whereby an indigenous heritage relegated to the past threatens the present, and is typically contained or eliminated by the film's conclusion.[6] Such narrative trajectories often emphasize the incompatibility of the indigenous with the modern. Indeed, the science-oriented discourses and characters in the film resonate with the dichotomous split between the modern and traditional proposed by concurrent strains of modernization theory that had taken hold in international relations, Mexican nationalism, and the cultural sphere.[7] For instance, Almada's colleague Dr. Sepulveda (Jorge Mondragón) initially scoffs at the curse, assuring those present that science will have to conquer the superstition and myth passed down by the Aztecs. In fact, when read as national allegory, the films demonstrate a decided ambivalence about the place of the indigenous in modern Mexico. While elevated as a cultural "treasure," the resurrection of Aztecs in the present is nonetheless regarded as undesirable and, through the risk of human sacrifice and mummy attacks, potentially dangerous.

There are a number of cultural precedents that might account for the emergence of these films as a body of work with identifiable and consistent

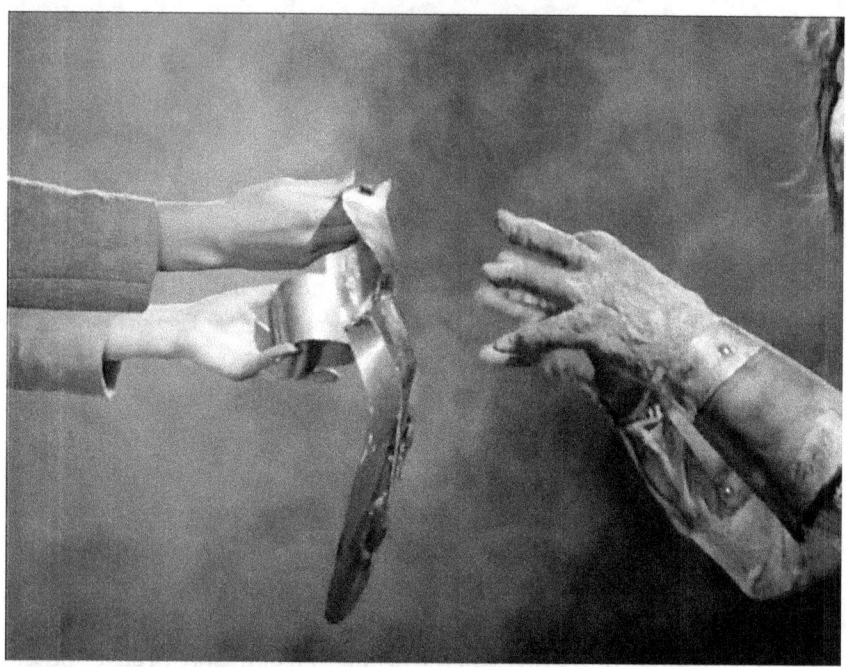

Fig. 11.2 Flor (Rosita Arenas) returns a breastplate and bracelet to the Aztec mummy: "Popoca, in memory of the great love that once existed between us, stop all this death and destruction. Take these objects that are yours to guard and go back to the grave of our ancestors, where we should never have interrupted your eternal sleep." *La momia azteca contra el robot humano* (*The Robot vs. the Aztec Mummy*, dir. Rafael Portillo, 1958).

conventions. Perhaps most obviously, they are heavily indebted on a conceptual and aesthetic level to forms of *indigenismo* tied to state-sponsored nationalism in Mexico since at least the early nineteenth century. The regime of Porfirio Díaz coincided with the emergence of archaeology as a discipline and undertook the excavation and restoration of spectacular sites such as Teotihuacán as evidence of the nation's cosmopolitan modernity.[8] This tendency intensified further during the post-revolutionary period, when scholars and public figures such as José Vasconcelos and Manuel Gamio situated indigenous heritage as a cornerstone of a uniquely Mexican national identity. From the 1920s onward, this impulse became apparent in grandiose visual displays of national history, from the epic murals of Diego Rivera to the 1964 foundation of the National Museum of Anthropology, both of which would later become key visual sources for the development of Chicana/o art and identity, as I discuss further in this essay.[9]

This official embrace of the indigenous by the Mexican state, however, remained largely rhetorical. In other words, while Mexico's indigenous history functioned as a unifying symbol, its indigenous population continued to be disenfranchised. Federico Navarrete describes this version of Mexican history as "'monolithic,' both because of its love of large stone monuments... and because of an equally monolithic identification between the pre-Hispanic indigenous peoples and modern mestizo Mexicans, from which contemporary indigenous groups are paradoxically excluded."[10] Within this dynamic, the indigenous remain symbols, incorporated in to a vision of the nation's distant history or, racially speaking, folded into the nation's population via the process of *mestizaje* (racial mixture) a la Vasconcelos. As with the Aztec mummies, the indigenous in this formulation are simply not supposed to intrude upon the present, or at least to do so only as relics.

Both the visualization of ancient Mexico via murals and discourses of indigenismo greatly influenced the cinematic representations of the indigenous in Mexican cinema. Beginning in the 1930s and through the Golden Age, a number of films dealt explicitly with the place of the indigenous in Mexican history and identity. These included, most notably, *Redes* (dir. Emilio Gómez Muriel and Fred Zinnemann, 1934), *Janitzio* (dir. Carlos Navarro, 1935), *La noche de los mayas* (*Night of the Mayas*, dir. Chano Urueta, 1939), and *María Candelaria* (dir. Emilio Fernández, 1944). As Dolores Tierney has compellingly argued, these films vary in their engagements with indigenismo, insofar as they are more or less contradictory, progressive, folkloric, or anthropological in their evocation of the indigenous.[11] While not aspiring to arbitrate, per Tierney, between authentic or inauthentic representations, I would suggest that despite the apparent differences between such films, they are largely indebted to a set of conventions tied to nationalism, conventions that relegate indigenous characters to the realm of archetype or symbol. Thus while acknowledging that Mexican cinema's historical representation of the indigenous may be limited yet not monolithic, I nonetheless concur with Charles Ramírez Berg that this cinema has typically answered the "Indian question" with stereotypical and demeaning portrayals.[12] Aztec mummies are one perhaps exaggerated example of the variation among this repertoire of imagery.

Cinematic indigenismo, however, was not the only celluloid precursor of midcentury Aztec mummies. During the 1930s, as filmmakers experimented with a variety of genres in search of a viable Mexican cinema, a number of films planted the seeds for culturally specific Mexican horror film: *La llorona* (*The Crying Woman*, dir. Ramón Peón, 1933), *La fantasma del convento* (*The Phantom of the Convent*, dir. Fernando de Fuentes, 1934), *El baúl macabro* (*The Macabre Trunk*, dir. Miguel Zacarías, 1936), and *El signo de la muerte* (*The Sign of Death*, dir. Chano Urueta, 1939), among others. The characters, conventions, and settings of such films doubtless influenced their subsequent cinematic counterparts. Not coincidentally, a number of the directors responsible for midcentury exploitation films, including René Cardona and Chano Urueta, had directed generic precursors in the 1930s.[13] If cinematic indigenismo hews closely to canonical constructions of Mexican cinema and nationalism, these 1930s preexploitation films by contrast constitute a parallel undercurrent; Aztec mummy films and their ilk occupy a position in Mexican cinema that is thus generically hybrid and, as we shall see, fundamentally transnational.

The fact that many Mexploitation films reach into the pre-Conquest or colonial past is hardly coincidental, as their visual vocabulary and conceptual basis originates centuries ago. Rather than being born with the advent of cinema, "Aztec horror," as the mirror image of the glorified Mesoamerican past, first emerged as a trope during the Spanish rule of Mexico. Accounts of human sacrifice in Bernal Díaz del Castillo's well-known account of the Conquest is accompanied, for instance, by a gruesome description of indigenous priests: "They wore their hair very long, down to the waist, with some even reaching down to the feet, covered with blood and so matted together that it could not be separated, and their ears were cut to pieces by way of sacrifice, and they stank like sulphur, and they had another bad smell like carrion."[14] Gaspar Pérez de Villagrá's 1610 account of Spanish incursions into New Mexico reiterated the belief that the area was indeed the ancient homeland of the Aztecs and includes the description of a supernatural event. According to Pérez de Villagrá, the Mexica, while migrating south to present-day Mexico, encountered a "frightful demon in the guise of an old and withered hag" that he described thus: "a mass of long, disheveled hair of ashen gray almost hid her fleshless face; long, crooked teeth peered forward from two misshapen, protruding lips which enclosed a leering, grinning mouth, extending from ear to ear."[15] Such representations have continued to influence conceptions of indigenous Mexico. As Cuauhtémoc Medina has compellingly argued, for instance, the conception of the Aztecs as horrific and bloodthirsty, although originating with the Conquest and colonialism, contributed to a sensibility embraced by mid-twentieth-century artists and intellectuals—from painter Gunther Gerzso to poet Octavio Paz and novelist Carlos Fuentes—that he describes as the "Indo-American Gothic."[16] Indeed, if Jesse Lerner has identified key representational paradigms by which the Mayan were placed in relation to modernity, "Aztec horror" is a clearly identifiable construct in the parallel representation of Aztecs.[17]

Despite this constellation of precedents and influence, the evocation of the indigenous in exploitation cinema marks a distinct departure within this history of representation, regardless of their mutual resonance. In particular, Aztec mummy films certainly do not read as solemn expressions of cultural nationalism, or as earnest expositions of Mexican history. If their campy address, bad acting, low production values and fragmented narratives did not sufficiently distance them from official indigenismo, the mummy characters themselves appear as rotting, putrid, and lumbering deformations of the exalted Aztecs that appear in Diego Rivera's murals. Furthermore, as scholars like Ernesto R. Acevedo-Muñoz have pointed out, the decline of Mexico's Golden Age in the 1950s coincided with a growing dissatisfaction with the lack of reform in the post-revolutionary era, backlash against the uneven effects of modernization, and a general distrust of the symbols and rhetoric of official nationalism.[18] In terms of culture, this tendency was apparent both in the work of a new generation of artists—José Luis Cuevas and Rufino Tamayo among them—that rejected the grandiose and didactic nature of Mexican muralism and through a new generation of independent film productions that deconstructed or rejected Golden Age conventions.[19] In this regard, Aztec mummies and their ilk might be construed as participants in a broader cultural zeitgeist occupied with skewering of cultural nationalism, as embodiments of decaying mythologies that should be put to rest.

While such an interpretation is somewhat compelling, it is also the case that even as potential parodies or critiques, these films have significant limitations. In the first place, Aztecs, as textual representatives of indigenous Mexico, here remain rather symbolic figures, whether acting in the service of nationalism or a burlesque thereof. In other words, contemporary indigenous Mexicans are mostly absent from these films in a way that somewhat counterintuitively aligns them with official versions of nationalism. Secondly, when indigenous Mexicans do appear in cinema before 1960, it is typically as anonymous background, noble or tragic symbols of the nation, exotic spectacle, or as an angry, irrational mob. In the latter case, Golden Age films like *María*

Candelaria suggest that despite the differences between such films and the low-budget features of the 1950s and 1960s, the idea of the indigenous as symbol, stereotype, or terror also remains an important continuity.[20] This perspective, however, is indebted largely to an analysis that adopts an exclusively national frame of reference, a prevalent tendency within the study of Mexican cinema. Considering the transnational nature of these films at multiple levels by contrast allows us to understand them and their potential impact in a different light. Whether as texts shaped by conventions within and beyond Mexico, as products that were distributed across borders (and altered in the process), or as an instance of the circulation of indigenous representation between the United States and Mexico, the multifarious nature and life cycle of these films allow us to appreciate the interrelatedness of representational regimes in both countries, while perhaps holding the potential to denaturalize and reconceive them.

Aztec Horror across the Border

To declare the low-budget sci-fi and horror films produced in Mexico to be one instance of ongoing transnational exchange should hardly constitute a revelation. Since at least the 1920s, Mexican cinema has been a transnational endeavor, defined by the changing relationships between the film industries in Mexico and the United States, along with the socioeconomic and political circumstances that shaped them. Despite significant changes across decades, there are also notable continuities that have structured these transnational cinematic exchanges between the United States and Mexico. Perhaps most obviously, Hollywood feature films have unquestionably dominated Mexican screens since the 1920s. One of the most curious exceptions to this typically unidirectional cultural flow are the low-budget horror and science fiction films produced in Mexico beginning in the 1950s. K. Gordon Murray, American International Pictures, and other enterprising purveyors of exploitation films dubbed many of them into English for distribution on US television. It is probably no exaggeration to say that this practice still constitutes perhaps the most extensive distribution of Mexican cinema in the United States directed at an English-speaking audience. One factor that greatly facilitated this crossing of borders was the decided lack of cultural specificity, or indeterminacy, within many of these films. A significant number of them take place in rather nondescript nineteenth-century locales and easily qualify as gothic horror. Aside from a few and often indirect cultural references, the overlay of

English dialogue produces a text that potentially could have been originally produced almost anywhere. While this textual malleability accounts for the ability of these films to traverse borders, I would argue that an additional set of factors facilitated the transnational travel of the Aztec horror narratives and images.

First, their success in the United States can at least partially be attributed to their recycling of Hollywood conventions and characters. In fact, many of these films might be regarded as a revival and partial Mexicanization of the aesthetics, characters, and narratives of classic Universal horror films. Seen in this light, the proliferation of Aztec mummies in the postwar period clearly refers to and resuscitates the horrific Egyptian mummy made popular by Boris Karloff in 1932. As a set of characters and conventions, Aztec mummies arriving in the United States were thus already cross-cultural intertexts traveling between the two countries. In addition to these influences, there is also at least one US film that marks an early example of shared representational conventions that circulated across borders. In the 1946 film *The Flying Serpent* (dir. Sam Newfield), a nefarious archaeologist discovers emperor Moctezuma's hidden treasure in the Aztec ruins of San Juan, New Mexico. To keep this discovery to himself, he uses the treasure's guardian, the Aztec god Quetzalcoatl, to murder those that would intrude upon his scheme. This film, which was remade as *Q* (dir. Larry Cohen) in 1982, also builds upon pre-existing conceptions of ancient Mexico and associated imagery circulating within the United States. Indeed, it situates New Mexico as the site of Aztlán: the ancestral homeland of the Aztecs and a supposed repository of treasure coveted by colonial Spain.

If *The Flying Serpent*'s curious postulation of Mexico within the United States seems to trouble geopolitical boundaries, it is also coded as problematic and terrifying in a way that resonates with Mexican texts. This familiar, dichotomous trope—treasure and terror—is succinctly visualized early in the film. As Forbes surveys the hidden vault beneath the Aztec pyramid, Moctezuma's treasure occupies one side of the room, while the caged Quetzalcoatl shrieks on the opposite side. Forbes is physically situated between these two conceptions of the Aztec past. As with the later mummy films, this production adopts the past-within-the-present familiar to Mexican nationalism, while coding it as a problem. Indeed, the film's resolution hinges on the death of Quetzalcoatl and a return to normalcy. Although we might consider *The Flying Serpent* somewhat of an anomaly, it clearly emulates a series

Fig. 11.3 Dr. Forbes arrives at the Aztec pyramids located in New Mexico in *The Flying Serpent* (dir. Sam Newfield, 1946).

of conventions that are echoed in midcentury Mexican exploitation. In fact, to make the transnational flows of Aztec horror even more convoluted, one could argue that this film contributed to the conventions of the later exploitation films.

Furthermore, the visual iconography of the later Mexican films—including monumental ruins, costumes, hidden treasure, sacrificial altars, and decaying Aztec royalty—clearly resonate with the kind of imagery of and ideas about indigenous Mexico that had already circulated between the two countries from at least the early twentieth century. The recycling of these narratives is quite likely indebted to literary and cinematic precursors, from issues of *Weird Tales* to young novels such as Thomas A. Janvier's 1890 *Aztec Treasure House for Boys*. To this extent, the low-budget exploitation films relied upon a degree of audience familiarity as they were broadcast on television across the border. Curiously enough, their place in the televisual landscape of the 1960s and 1970s was hardly singular. In fact, a surprising number of popular television shows in the United States—particularly western, adventure, and supernatural genres emulating the low-budget films targeting teens—dedicated one or more episodes to stories of Aztec treasure and sacrifice. Among these were *Kolchak: Night Stalker* (1975), *Kung Fu* (1974), *My Favorite Martian* (1965), *Time Tunnel* (1967), *Wagon Train* (1960), and *The Wild, Wild West* (1967). To this extent, films such as *La momia azteca contra el robot humano* (*The Robot vs. The Aztec Mummy*, dir. Rafael Portillo, 1958) and television westerns not only joined a legion of cheaply produced and youth-oriented media in the twentieth century, but also constituted another instance in a long trajectory of ancient Mexico's cross-border travels in popular culture.

Chicana/o Aztlán

Within recent history, the mythical Aztec homeland of Aztlán is perhaps most recognizable as a key facet of the Chicana/o movement of the late 1960s and 1970s and its brand of cultural nationalism. Introduced as a unifying declaration at the National Chicana/o Youth Liberation Conference in 1969 and widely influential within the Chicana/o movement, "El plan espiritual de Aztlán" solidified the Southwest as the location of the site from which the Mexica people migrated south to Tenochtitlán (present-day Mexico City). By claiming ancient origins north of the border and a national community that transcended borders, Chicana/os consciously rejected their status as outsiders or foreigners. This powerful sense of national belonging, while effecting a reversal that implicitly situated Euro-Americans as immigrants, also acknowledged and validated migration as a long-standing part of the Chicana/o/Mexicano experience.

By connecting this sense of belonging to Aztec history, Chicana/os in the movement also explicitly identified themselves as indigenous. Part of this maneuver most certainly was motivated by the ability to stake a claim to being descendants of the continent's original inhabitants. The embrace of Aztlán was also at least implicitly a rejection of Spanish ancestry and the brutal legacy of European colonialism. Crucially, this conception of identity also reversed racial hierarchies. By celebrating the Aztec past, asserting pride in indigenous ancestry, and declaring that "brown is beautiful," Chicana/os bestowed value upon the traits that have historically been the grounds for discrimination and exclusion, both in the United States and Mexico. The concept also serves as a powerful reminder of the historical migration and trade among indigenous peoples throughout the North American continent, movement that denaturalizes a contemporary geography defined by national borders.

Nonetheless, the idea of Aztlán, and its fixation upon the Aztecs in particular, converges uncomfortably with problematic conceptions of Mexican indigeneity on both sides of the border. The idea of positing Aztlán as a mythical Chicana/o homeland, for instance, is at least in part indebted to the Spanish colonial obsession with Aztlán as a city of untold treasure and the numerous expeditions, maps, and other documentation this obsession produced. A key 1538 Spanish expedition in search of the Seven Cities of Cíbola, according to John R. Chávez, "would lead to the centuries-old myth that Aztlán was in the Southwest."[21] The Spanish quest for "wondrous peoples and great wealth somewhere in the unknown north" is not only a central component of Aztlán's persistence but also has shaped the travels of ancient and indigenous Mexico in popular culture.[22]

Even more obviously, however, the concept is heavily indebted to forms of indigenismo tied to state-sponsored nationalism in Mexico since at least the early nineteenth century. Drawing upon this array of "monolithic" imagery stage managed by the Mexican state, early Chicana/o artists often reproduced imagery such as the so-called Aztec calendar, images of virile Aztec warriors, renderings of gods like Quetzalcoatl, and versions of Aztec and Mayan pyramids. If Aztec treasure and mummy narratives position Aztecs in the present as a threat, Chicana/o cultural production—from the film *I Am Joaquín* to the reworking of goddesses Coyalxauqui and Coatlicue by Chicana artists such as Yolanda Lopez, Santa Barraza, and Alma Lopez—propose a simultaneity or fluidity between past and present that informs contemporary conceptions of Chicana and Chicano identity.

As the product of a social justice movement, the Chicana/o concept of Aztlán can certainly not be accused of exerting the same impact as the indigenismo of the Mexican state. Nonetheless, by insisting upon a linkage between Chicana/o identity and the Aztec past, it likewise flattened out the history of indigenous Mexico while often denying or simply overlooking its contemporary existence. To this extent, the borrowing of Mexican nationalism's "past-within-the-present" obscures complex histories of migration, cultural exchange, and identity formation on both sides of the border in favor of a selective embrace of a glorious and distant Aztec past that borrows from the trappings of one exclusionary nationalism to craft another.[23] At the same time, the Aztec-centric nature of Aztlán also resonates with, and at times inadvertently borrows from, the circulation of ancient Mexican imagery within the United States. Although indicative of the inventive hybridity and eclecticism of early Chicana/o art, this tendency nonetheless visualized the relationship between indigenous Mexico, Chicana/o identity and the history of Greater Mexico in highly selective ways.[24] The Chicana/o claim to indigenous identity via Aztlán, while rooted in a speculative history, also (at least in its most literal manifestations) romanticizes the past while situating Chicana/os within the overarching space of the "bronze continent" that collapses important distinctions between Chicana/os, other mestizos, native peoples in the United States, and indigenous Mexicans.[25] So if the concept of Aztlán proposes an alternative temporality, these rhetorical and visual maneuvers rely on a reductive and binary form of "time travel." Its mobilization of the Aztec past as "symbol and archetype" also resonates unexpectedly with the fictions of Mexican Golden Age cinema and its bastard offspring: the low-budget horror and sci-fi films that traveled between the two countries in the 1950s and 1960s.[26]

Aztec Remix

It is certainly tempting and perhaps even justifiable to dismiss the representation of ancient Aztecs, whether they appear in Mexican exploitation, Chicana/o art, or US television, as somehow meaningless or regressive in their racial politics. The persistent construction of indigenous Mexico as noble yet irredeemably savage, relegated to the past, and almost invariably Aztec would certainly support such an argument. A more nuanced reading of these texts and their transnational conception and circulation, however, suggests that they perhaps unintentionally provide alternative ways of imagining exchanges and movements that predate or transcend the US-Mexico border. To this extent, their visions of Aztlán resonate with (as they diverge from) conceptions of Aztlán in the Chicana/o movement and the cultural production that both preceded and accompanied it. The significance of low-budget exploitation cinema, from *The Flying Serpent* to *The Living Head*, is not only the evocation of alternative temporalities or geographies, but the fundamentally transnational nature of their subject matter, production, and distribution. By wearing their transnationality on their sleeves, their low-budget productions reveal the seams and intersections that have structured cinematic and cultural exchanges between the United States and Mexico in the twentieth century and beyond.

Again, the way both these hybrid films and the later exploitation films explicitly call attention to their transnationality holds important consequences for the study of midcentury Mexican cinema, a body of work that is always already transnational. In other words, rather than constituting exceptions or deviations, these films might constitute key texts, or at least important touchstones through which we are able to productively rewrite the history of Mexican cinema culture. So while Doyle Greene has argued that exploitation films have been undervalued and overlooked as allegories of the nation, they might even more appropriately be understood as allegories and instances of transnationality.[27] More than being transnational in subject matter, construction and distribution, the hybrid nature of these films produces juxtapositions that further complicate the issue of national origins. If these films both participate in an overlooked cultural flow and constitute yet another instance of indigenous Mexico in popular culture, they also at times inadvertently suggest unexpected and alternative cultural geographies. Although marked as hopelessly and clumsily transnational, the creative and even jarring hybridity of these artifacts resonate with a kind of discursive and visual space explored by a number of cross-border artists who use similar strategies to reimagine the relationship and exchange between the United States and Mexico at multiple levels.

In the case of exploitation cinema, these texts even more obviously (and sometimes painfully) exhibit the traces of their circulation across borders. Regardless of their somewhat generic and culturally unmarked gothic settings, for instance, the cheap dubbing to which they were subjected serves as a constant reminder of their foreign origins. Other films take this logic to a perplexing and somewhat disorienting extreme. *La marca del muerto* (dir. Fernando Cortés, 1961) was released in the United States as *Creature of the Walking Dead*. While it included dubbing and narration in English, the distributor, Jerry Warren, also filmed scenes in English with actors that never appeared in the original. *Face of the Screaming Werewolf* (dir. Gilberto Martínez Solares, Rafael Portillo, and Jerry Warren, 1964) likewise combines footage of two Mexican exploitation films: *The Aztec Mummy* and the Tin Tan vehicle *La casa del terror* (*The House of Terror*, dir. Gilberto Martínez Solares, 1961). This footage is then interspersed with new English language scenes starring Lon Chaney Jr. in his last known screen appearances as a werewolf. This peculiar cinematic "mash-up" consists of multiple layers of intertextual reference, cross-border travel, and spatial confusions. The Aztec mummy is already an amalgamation of nationalist mythology, Mexicana, and Egyptiana via Hollywood horror. Through cleverly stitching together two films and additional footage, the creature here is placed alongside an Egyptian-style mummy stored in the same pyramid, a monster that then is resurrected in a laboratory only to transform into a werewolf. These additional creatures are characters in *La casa del terror*, much of which takes place in a wax museum. In other words, the Mexican film is already a translation and conglomeration of Hollywood horror staples. *Screaming Werewolf* returns these reworked stock characters to the United States through a film spoken in English, with an Aztec mummy along for the ride.

This bewildering palimpsest of transnational intertexts is mirrored by geographical impossibilities. As the two mummies were discovered on an archaeological excursion in the Yucatán and brought to Pasadena for scientific study, a majority of the film takes place in latter location. Nonetheless, this narrative border crossing is undermined by visual slippages; not only are the relations between individual spaces entirely unclear, but exterior shots from the multiple films shuttle between Southern California and Mexico City. In other words, the distinction between films, spaces, nations, and even characters are thrown into question. In this context, the Aztec mummy—who is, like many of the characters, abruptly and summarily killed off—functions less as an evocation of, or commentary on, Mexican nationalism. Instead, he is one transnational intertext rubbing up against and colliding with a range of others that have been (re)appropriated and (re)translated to expose multiple layers of cinematic exchange between the United States and Mexico.

This hybrid and even confusing style of montage, while not intentionally experimental in a conventional sense, nonetheless exists as a cinematic precursor to more recent imaginings of transnational relations and exchanges. Of course, the most obvious and oft-cited cinematic precedent for and influence upon early Chicana/o cultural production (and cinema in particular) is the radical impulse of New Latin American Cinema. Embracing the idea of an "imperfect cinema" whose production values and urgency would draw upon and reflect the socioeconomic circumstances of working-class Chicana/os, filmmakers adopted aesthetic and economic solutions born of a decided lack of resources.[28] Until recently, genealogies of influence citing New Latin American Cinema implicitly position it against the melodramatic, ostensibly bourgeois tendencies of classical Latin American cinema and Golden Age Mexico in particular. As Victoria Ruétalo and Dolores Tierney have argued, this historiographic formulation has almost entirely excluded the impact and circulation of equally "imperfect" low-budget exploitation films that typically have been marginalized in prestige-oriented or politically motivated histories of national cinemas in Latin America.[29]

Significantly, a number of artists and filmmakers working at the interstices of the Latina/o, Mexican, and mainstream art worlds have built equally upon other cinematic and aesthetic tendencies that, rather than relying upon documentary or social realism associated with New Latin American Cinema, engage in the articulation of speculative fictions of the past and present. Furthermore, instead of trading upon romanticized or fixed categories of difference (and indigeneity in particular), they participate in an aesthetic akin to what Virginia M. Fields and Victor Zamudio-Taylor have identified in the indigenous cultural production of the early colonial period: "Intermingled visual languages, along with the coexistence of styles, represent epistemologically, and in terms of social imaginary, the negotiation and translation of different histories and universes," a conception of this artistic production that departs from conventional ideas of "authenticity."[30] If we add the disruption and complication of temporality to this equation, the affinity between such works, low-budget exploitation film, and alternative cultural production becomes rather counterintuitively apparent as other ways of thinking through race, nation, and identity in the Americas. Again, this is not to suggest any equivalence or direct causality between these practices or objects, but instead that they each in their own manner suggest aesthetic and conceptual challenges to fixed borders and categories.

The B-movie montage of Gómez-Peña and Vázquez's film is consequently part of a body of work that not only draws aesthetic inspiration from popular culture but also situates these mass-produced narratives and images as a fundamental part of the transnational imaginary of both indigenous Mexico and US-Mexico relations. Furthermore, by channeling and participating in this unruly circulation, these works often engage in the kind of fragmentation and juxtaposition reminiscent of low budget exploitation film. By doing so, such works highlight the often chaotic and unexpected nature of transnational exchange while problematizing the past-present temporality upon which nationalisms and their evocations of the Aztec past hinge. Through montage, collage, and juxtaposition, disparate artifacts and images coexist on a simultaneous plane, allowing for a provocative, open-ended interplay of cultural signifiers. These works posit bad movies, comic books, and science fiction as factors mediating both dynamics and borrow from them an aesthetic that disrupts divisions between past/present, United States/Mexico, modern/premodern, history/fiction, and authentic/inauthentic. As in the case of *The Great Mojado Invasion*, these works also suggest that cultural complexes girding nationalisms—from murals to Golden Age cinema—are themselves speculative fantasies and, at worst, "bad cinema." Appropriately, many of the artists producing art and films along these lines work between the two countries, drawing upon and freely intermingling a rich set of cultural and historical references. Aesthetically and structurally, these works resonate with the way certain experimental films interrogate the construction of history, films that Jeffrey Skoller argues foster "an awareness of other temporalities in which linear chronologies are called into question in favor of other temporal structures such as simultaneity and virtuality."[31]

Enrique Chagoya, for instance, has produced works based upon the Mesoamerican codices, precisely the documents often referenced as evidence of Aztlán's existence. Rather than transparent transmissions of pre-Conquest history or myth, however, Chagoya's works become multilayered surfaces upon which images and artifacts cross borders and temporalities to occupy the same space. His collaboration with Gómez-Peña and Felicia Rice, *Codex Espanglienses*, is one such project.[32] In this work, as Jennifer González points out, the artists defy narrative linearity and playfully disrupt boundaries, producing a provocative, multimedia collage that "employ[s] iconic figures and persistent stereotypes to overturn the fantasies of nationalism, ethnocentrism, and historical amnesia that cloud international relations in the present."[33] Producing palimpsestic collages that freely mix images from comic books on both sides of the border, pre-Conquest art, contemporary politics, and a healthy dose of science fiction, Chagoya fashions his own "alternative historical possibilities."[34] Conceiving of his codex works in general as speculative evocations of the indigenous writings destroyed by the Spanish, the artist describes such works as "reverse anthropology" that regards the colonizers from the perspective of the colonized, while also reversing the terms of modern art's appropriative "primitivism."[35] Rather than presenting either a straightforward counternarrative or a postmodern play of pastiche, however, "the artist proposes to deconstruct and simultaneously construct mythologies that reside in our fractured memories," through these juxtapositions.[36]

In their film *La piedra ausente* (*The Absent Stone*, 2012), Sandra Rozental and Jesse Lerner and also freely mix temporalities and modes of address to recount the historic relocation of the largest carved stone in the Americas from the Mexican village of San Miguel Coatlinchán to the Museum of National Anthropology in 1964. The film narrates this event through interviews with the town's inhabitants, archival footage, images from a 1960s comic book adaptation of the stone's journey, and animated sequences. What the film traces are the multiple narratives and mediations involved in the process of transforming an indigenous sculpture into national patrimony. By giving voice to the townspeople (who worked at one point to sabotage its removal), the film also presents a critical view of the process, making painfully apparent the distance between the exaltation of the indigenous past as national symbol and the marginalization of the indigenous population. The film's animated sequences, drawing aesthetically from both pre-Conquest and colonial art, also establish a critical distance from and parody of the state's "monolithic" history. Characterized by a perverse collage of science fiction, photography, comedy, and episodes of national history a la Chagoya, these sequences culminate in a speculative fiction as the film closes, depicting the future return of the stone to its original location. Throughout, the film mobilizes multiple modes of address, collage, and humor to not only trace the various narratives about this episode, but to propose a different means of narrating the place of the indigenous within Mexican constructions of race, history, and nation.

The point of this essay, once again, is not to propose an all-encompassing or linear account of the ways Aztecs and indigenous Mexico have traveled through popular culture. On the one hand, it might function as a way of tracing the references present within a certain body of contemporary art and cinema that intervenes in this lineage. Aside from those mentioned here, sculptors Einar and Jamex de la Torre also draw upon the circulation of indigenous imagery across borders, as do the multiple artists included in the recent *Pre-Columbian Remix* exhibition.[37] On the other hand, this essay demonstrates the value of rethinking the significance and legacy of low-budget exploitation, both within and beyond the frame of Mexican cinema. In both cases, I hope to have traced a long-standing body of images and ideas that, through widely varying manifestations, impacted ideas about indigenous Mexico for centuries. On both counts, juxtaposition, imperfection, and improbability unmask nationalist narratives as speculative fantasies, while staging colonialism and its legacy as a poorly acted horror movies that speak multiple languages. Nonetheless, even the recycling and reappropriation of these symbols images by contemporary artists hints at the exhaustion and inadequacy of this iconography. In other words, as *La piedra ausente* suggests, the absence or exclusions of indigenous Mexican voices from all of these representations is what enables and perpetuates the persistence of these mythologies into the present.

> COLIN GUNCKEL is Associate Professor of Screen Arts and Cultures, American Culture, and Latina/o Studies at the University of Michigan and the author of *Mexico on Main Street: Transnational Film Culture in Los Angeles before World War II* (Rutgers University Press, 2015). He has published essays in a number of scholarly journals, including *American Quarterly*, *Aztlán: A Journal of Chicana/o Studies*, *Film History*, and *Velvet Light Trap*. He also serves as Associate Editor of the A Ver: Revisioning Art History monograph series on individual Latino/a artists.

NOTES

1. For a discussion of this tendency in Chicana/o cinema, see Rita Gonzalez, "Surplus Memories: From the Slide Show to the Digital Bulletin Board in Jim Mendiola's *Speeder Kills*," in *Still Moving: Between Cinema and Photography*, eds. Karen Beckman and Jean Ma (Durham, NC: Duke University Press, 2008), 158–171.

2. For a more extensive analysis of this film in relation to Gómez-Peña's body of work, see Catherine Leen, "The Final Frontier: Guillermo Gómez-Peña's *The Great Mojado Invasion*," in *Imagined Transnationalism: U.S. Latino/a Literature, Culture, and Identity*, eds. Kevin Concannon, Francisco A. Lomelí, and Marc Priewe (New York: Palgrave Macmillan, 2009), 221–236.

3. Key book-length contributions to this emerging area include Doyle Greene, *Mexploitation Cinema: A Critical History of Mexican Vampire, Wrestler, Ape-Man and Similar Films, 1957–1977* (Jefferson, NC: McFarland, 2005); Victoria Ruétalo and Dolores Tierney, eds., *Latsploitation, Exploitation Cinemas, and Latin America* (New York: Routledge, 2009).

4. See, for instance, Catherine S. Ramírez, "Deus ex Machina: Tradition, Technology and the Chicanafuturist art of Marion C. Martinez," *Aztlán: A Journal of Chicana/o Studies* 29, no. 2 (2004): 55–92; Lysa Rivera, "Future Histories and Cyborg Labor: Reading Borderlands Science after NAFTA," *Science Fiction Studies* 39, no. 3 (2012): 415–436.

5. See Jeffrey Sconce, "'Trashing' the Academy: Taste, Excess, and an Emerging Politics of Cinematic Style," *Screen* 36, no. 4 (1995): 371–393.

6. See Colin Gunckel, "*El signo de la muerte* and the Birth of a Genre," in *Sleaze Artists: Cinema at the Margins of Taste, Style, and Politics*, ed. Jeffrey Sconce (Durham, NC: Duke University Press, 2007), 122–143.

7. See Claire Fox, *Making Art Panamerican: Cultural Policy and the Cold War*, (Minneapolis: University of Minnesota Press, 2013), 125–126.

8. See Christina Bueno, "Teotihuacán: Showcase for the Centennial," in *Holiday in Mexico: Critical Reflections on Tourism and Tourist Encounters*, eds. Dina Berger and Andrew Grant Wood (Durham, NC: Duke University Press, 2010), 54–76.

9. Néstor García Canclini, *Hybrid Cultures: Strategies for Entering and Leaving Modernity* (Minneapolis: University of Minnesota Press, 1995), 123.

10. Federico Navarrete, "Ruins and the State: Archaeology of a Mexican Symbiosis," in *Indigenous Peoples and Archaeology in Latin America*, eds. Cristóbal Gnecco and Patricio Ayala (Walnut Creek, CA: Left Coast Press, 2011), 40.

11. See Dolores Tierney, *Emilio Fernández: Pictures in the Margins* (Manchester: Manchester University Press, 2007), 73–103.

12. Charles Ramírez Berg, *Cinema of Solitude: A Critical Study of Mexican Film, 1967–1983* (Austin: University of Texas Press, 1992), 137–156.

13. For a discussion of this earlier generation of filmmakers, see Ana M. López, "Before Exploitation: Three Men of the Cinema in Mexico," in *Latsploitation, Exploitation Cinemas, and Latin America*, eds. Victoria Ruétalo and Dolores Tierney (New York: Routledge, 2009), 13–33.

14. Bernal Díaz del Castillo, *The Discovery and Conquest of Mexico* (New York: Farrar, Straus and Cudahay, 1956), 104.

15. Gaspar Pérez de Villagrá, *History of New Mexico* (Los Angeles: Quivira Society, 1933), 46.

16. See Cuauhtémoc Medina, "Gerzso and the Indo-American Gothic: From Eccentric Surrealism to Parallel Modernism," in *Risking the Abstract: Mexican Modernism and the Art of Gunther Gerzso*, ed. Diana C. Du Pont (Santa Barbara, CA: Santa Barbara Museum of Art, 2003), 195–213.

17. Jesse Lerner, *The Maya of Modernism: Art, Architecture, and Film* (Albuquerque: University of New Mexico Press, 2011.

18. See Ernesto R. Acevedo-Muñoz, *Buñuel and Mexico: The Crisis of National Cinema* (Berkeley: University of California Press, 2003), 57–79.

19. For a compelling account of this shift in the politics of Mexican muralism, see Mary K. Coffeey, *How a Revolutionary Art Became Official Culture: Murals, Museums, and the Mexican State* (Durham, NC: Duke University Press, 2012), 25–77.

20. For a later example of an irrational indigenous mob and the use of indigenous language as a terror-inducing device, see Felipe Cazal's film *Canoa* (1976).

21. John R. Chávez, "Aztlán, Cíbola, and Frontier New Spain," in *Aztlán: Essays on the Chicana/o Homeland*, eds. Rudolfo A. Anaya and Francisco Lomelí (Albuquerque: University of New Mexico Press, 1989), 57.

22. Carroll L. Riley, "Spaniards in Aztlan," in *The Road to Aztlan: Art from a Mythic Homeland* [exhibition catalog], eds. Virginia M. Fields and Victor Zamudio-Taylor (Los Angeles: Los Angeles County Museum of Art, 2001), 236.

23. For other critiques along these lines, see Josefina Saldaña-Portillo, "Who's the Indian in Aztlán? Re-Writing Mestizaje, Indianism, and Chicanismo from Lacandón," in *The Latin American Subaltern Studies Reader*, ed. Ileana Rodríguez (Durham, NC: Duke University Press), 413; Alicia Gaspar de Alba, "There's No Place Like

Aztlán: Embodied Aesthetics in Chicana Art," *New Centennial Review* 4, no. 2 (2004): 103–140; Cherríe Moraga, "Queer Aztlán: The Re-Formation of Chicana/o Tribe," in *The Last Generation: Prose and Poetry* (Boston: South End Press, 1993).

24. Guisela Latorre has most thoroughly discussed the presence of indigenous imagery and themes in Chicana/o art in *Walls of Empowerment: Chicana/o Indigenist Murals of California* (Austin: University of Texas Press, 2008).

25. "El Plan Espiritual de Aztlán," in *Aztlán: Essays on the Chicana/o Homeland*, eds. Rudolfo A. Anaya and Francisco A. Lomelí (Albuquerque: University of New Mexico Press, 1991), 1. For related critiques of the Chicana/o use of Aztlán, see Patricia Penn-Hilden, "How the Border Lies: Some Historical Reflections," in *Decolonial Voices: Chicana and Chicana/o Cultural Studies in the 21st Century*, eds. Arturo J. Aldama and Naomi H. Quiñonez (Bloomington: Indiana University Press, 2002), 154–155. For a more recent defense of Aztlán and, more generally speaking, the Chicana/o invocation of indigenous identity, see Rafael Pérez-Torres, *Mestizaje: Critical Uses of Race in Chicana/o Culture* (Minneapolis: University of Minnesota Press, 2006), 3–50.

26. Anaya and Lomelí, "Introduction," iii.

27. See Greene, *Mexploitation Cinema*, 12–19.

28. Relative to the influence of this cinema on Chicana/o filmmakers, see Francisco X. Camplis, "Towards the Development of a Raza Cinema (1975)," in *Chicana/os and Film: Representation and Resistance*, ed. Chon A. Noriega (Minneapolis: University of Minnesota Press, 1992), 284–302.

29. Victorial Ruétalo and Dolores Tierney, "Introduction: Reinventing the Frame: Exploitation and Latin America," in *Latsploitation, Exploitation Cinemas, and Latin America*, eds. Victoria Ruétalo and Dolores Tierney (New York: Routledge, 2009), 1–12. See also Andrew Syder and Dolores Tierney, "Importation/Mexploitation, or, How a Crime-Fighting, Vampire-Slaying Mexican Wrestler Almost Found Himself in an Italian Sword-and-Sandals Epic," in *Horror International*, eds. Steven J. Schneider and Tony Williams (Detroit: Wayne State University Press, 2005), 33–55.

30. Virginia M. Fields and Victor Zamudio-Taylor, "Aztlan: Destination and Point of Departure," in Fields and Zamudio-Taylor, *Road to Aztlan: Art from a Mythic Homeland*, 53.

31. Jeffrey Skoller, *Shadows, Specters, Shards: Making History in Avant-Garde Film* (Minneapolis: University of Minnesota Press, 2005), xvi.

32. See Guillermo Gómez-Peña, Enrique Chagoya, and Felicia Rice, *Codex Espanglienses: From Columbus to the Border Patrol* (San Francisco: City Lights Books, 2000).

33. Jennifer González, review of *Codex Espangliensis: From Columbus to the Border Patrol*, by Guillermo Gómez-Peña, Enrique Chagoya, and Felicia Rice, *Aztlán: A Journal of Chicana/o Studies* 24, no. 1 (1999), 212–213.

34. Daniela Pérez, "Simultaneous Dimensions," in *Enrique Chagoya: Borderlandia* [exhibition catalog], ed. Patricia Hickson (Des Moines: Des Moines Art Center, 2007), 37.

35. See oral history interview with Enrique Chagoya, Paul Kalstrom, Archives of American Art, July 25–August 6, 2001, accessed July 24, 2014, http://www.aaa.si.edu/collections/interviews/oral-history-interview-enrique-chagoya-12495.

36. Pérez, "Simultaneous Dimensions," 40.

37. See *Einar and Jamex de la Torre: Intersecting Time and Place* (Tacoma, WA: Museum of Glass: International Center for Contemporary Art and Seattle: University of Washington Press, 2005); *Pre-Columbian Remix: The Art of Enrique Chagoya, Demián Flores, Rubén Ortiz-Torres and Nadín Ospina* (Purchase, NY: Neuberger Museum of Art, 2013).

INDEX

The Absent Stone (*La piedra ausente*) (film), 343–344
Academia de Artes Dramáticas de la Escuela Libre (ADADEL) (Academy of Dramatic Arts of the Open School of Havana), 303–306, 307
accents, Spanish-language films and, 213–216
Acevedo-Muñoz, Ernesto R., 242, 333
Actualidades Argentinas (newsreel), 77
Agrupación de Redactores Teatrales y Cinematográficos (ARTYC) (Theater and Film Writers' Association), 307–308, 314
Aguirre, Ignacio, 27
Ahora (periodical), 303
Aín, Casimiro, 89
Airaldi, Roberto, 233
Albertini, Luciano, 42
Alemán (Miguel) administration, 244, 261, 274
Alexander Nevsky (film), 173n21, 311
Almendros, Néstor, 315
Alonso, Carlos J., 54
Alonso, Luis, 128
Al son del mambo (*To the Sound of Mambo*) (film), 271, 278–281, 279f, 286–287
Alton, John J.: at Argentina Sono Film, 220, 221, 224–234; background, 218; Hollywood, return to, 218; *los locos de la azotea* and, 218; at Lumiton, 220; Lumiton creation and, 218; "Motion Picture Production in South America," 8, 213–216, 219, 221, 224; "Motion Picture Production in South America Up to Date," 234; "News Letter from South America," 224; *Painting with Light*, 235; photography, 234–235; at SIFAL, 221, 223
Alton, John J., cinematography: Academy Award, 218; comedy, 225–226; crime drama, 225, 229; described, 221–222; emotionality in, 225–226; experimental phase, 220–221, 229; film noir, 218–219, 229; glamour lighting, 229, 230, 231; inky blacks, 219, 229, 232; interiors, 222, 227; lattice lighting, 229; melodramas, 225, 227–228, 230–234; restrictions on, 220, 226, 229; shadows, 219, 222–224, 226–230
Alton, John J., films by title: *Amalia*, 225, 227f; *Cadetes de San Martín* (*Cadets of San Martín*), 226–227; *Caminito de gloria* (*Little Path to Glory*), 220, 233; *Compañeros* (*Mates*), 221; *Crimen a las 3* (*Crime at Three O'Clock*), 221, 223; *Escala en la ciudad* (*Layover in the City*), 221, 222–223; *¡Goal!* 225; *El hijo de papá* (*Father's Son*) (director), 220–221, 223; *Loco lindo* (*Crazy Dandy*), 225, 226; *Madreselva* (*Honeysuckle*), 230–232, 233; *El matrero* (*The Outlaw*), 232–233; *Palermo*, 229; *El pobre Pérez* (*Poor Pérez*), 226; *Puerta cerrada* (*Closed Door*), 232, 233; *Tararira* (*La bohemia de hoy/The Bohemia of Today*), 221; *Los tres berretines* (*The Three Whims*), 220, 221–222; *12 mujeres* (*12 Women*), 232; *El último encuentro* (*The Last Encounter*), 229–230
Álvarez, Santiago: *Hasta la victoria siempre* (*Until Victory*) (film), 288
Álvarez Bravo, Manuel, 188; *Disparos en el Istmo* (*Shots Fired on the Isthmus*) (film), 181

Álvarez del Vayo, Julio: *Rusia a los doce años*, 155
Alvear, Gil: "Where Is Costa Roja?," 129–130
Amador, María Luisa, 243
Amadori, Luis César, 230–232; *Caminito de gloria* (*Little Path to Glory*) (film), 220, 233–234; *Madreselva* (*Honeysuckle*) (film), 231*f*, 233; *El pobre Pérez* (*Poor Pérez*) (film), 226
Amalia (film), 225–226, 227*f*
Amalia (novel) (Mármol), 225
Ambrosio, 50, 56
Ameche, Don, 249
American Cinematographer (periodical), 224, 226; "John Alton Returns to Hollywood from Abroad," 234–235
"The American Danger" (Angeli), 53–56
An American in Paris (film), 218
Amero, Emilio: *777* (film), 181
Anderson, Benedict, 167
de Andrade, Oswald, 164
Andrew, Dudley, 5, 163
Angeli, Diego: "The American Danger," 53–56
"Añoranzas de Hollywood" (Longing for Hollywood) (Aragón Leiva), 89
Antes y ahora (*The General Line/Old and New* [*Staroye i novoye*]) (film), 156, 161, 163, 166
À propos de Nice (film), 190, 204
Aragón Leiva, Agustín, 115; "Memoirs of an Extra," 101–110, 132; "Añoranzas de Hollywood" (Longing for Hollywood), 89
Arcaño y sus Maravillas orchestra, 272
Arenas, Rosita, 329, 330*f*
Argentina: accent of, 214; the gaucho in, 78; immigrants, Italian, 78; intellectual culture, Hollywood and, 87–89; music as unifying emblem of, 271; national identity, 74–76, 78, 81–86, 88–91, 271; photography, avant-garde, 181, 199–206; tango in, 88; US cultural hegemony and imperialism in, 76, 87, 89; Valentino and, 74–75, 81–86, 88–91
Argentina, film audiences: film fandom of, 126; film magazines for, 140; foreign films, appreciation of, 151–153, 177–178, 190–191; press influence on, 215; social stratification in, 87–88; for Soviet films, 151–153; for Spanish-language films, 215
Argentina, film culture in: anti-imperialistic function of, 76; art cinema, 221, 222–223; avant-garde influences on, 181; censorship of, 151–152; cosmopolitanism of, 151–153, 177–178, 190–191; gender balance, threats to, 84, 89–91; Hollywood and, 84–91; inclusivity of, 76–79, 87–88; nationalism and, 75–81, 87, 271
Argentina, film industry: Alton on, 213–216, 219, 221, 224, 234, 235; Argentina Sono Film, 220, 221, 224–234; development of, 217–218, 219–220; Hollywood collaborations, 76–77; industrial developments, 234; Lumiton, 218, 220; newspaper coverage, 81–83, 84*f*; recreating the western frontier, 76–77; SIFAL, 221, 223; Spanish-language films, 214–216
Argentina, stage entertainment: *circo criollo*, 78; *cocoliche*, 75, 78–79, 87; *sainete*, 78, 93n16, 222
Argentina Sono Film, 8, 218, 220, 221, 224–234
Arias, Pepe, 226
Arlt, Roberto: "El discurso del astrólogo" ("The Astrologer's Discourse"), 88; *Los siete locos* (novel), 88
Armendáriz, Pedro, 243, 255, 257, 259
Arnaz, Desi, 280
Arnheim, Rudolph, 192
Arnold, John, 226
The Arrival of a Train (*L'Arrivée d'un train en gare de La Ciotat*) (film), 20
Arrival of the Historic Bell on September 16 (film), 24, 27
L'Arroseur arrosé (*The Gardener and the Boy*) (film), 20
L'Art Cinématographique (periodical), 192
L'art dans la Russie nouvelle: le cinéma (March- and Weinstein), 156
Artaud, Antonin, 194
art cinema, 160–163, 188–189, 221, 222–223, 314–315, 342–344
Así nació el obelisco (*Thus the Obelisk Was Born*) (film), 202, 203*f*, 204, 204*f*, 205
Asociación de Reporters de La Habana (Havana Reporters' Association), 308
Astor, Mary, 257
"The Astrologer's Discourse" ("El discurso del astrólogo") (Arlt), 88
Atget, Eugène, 183
Atlántida (periodical), 87
Aub, Max, 256
audiences: Americanization of, 161; cosmopolitanism of, 151–153, 156, 173n21, 177–178, 190–191, 243, 245–252, 260; female, concerns about, 47; film as a danger to, 47; film fandom, 126; gift economy exchanges (ñapa practices), 48–49; heterogeneity of,

299; ideal spectator, construction of an, 48–50, 60; immigrant, 74; literary classics, exposure to, 250–252; modernization of, 259; movie stars, affection for, 126–127; options available to, 243–244, 253, 259, 260; preferences of, 245–246; press influence on, 215; regulating the, 46; social stratification in, 40, 52–53, 87–88; social stratification of, 58–59; sophisticated, formation of, 299; for Spanish-language films, 215; Spanish-speaking market for Hollywood films, 129–130, 133, 139, 213; transgressions of the public/private divide, 35–36, 46. *See also specific countries*

Auer, John, 217

Auerbach, Ellen, 181

Auerbach, Walter, 194

avant-garde cinema: aesthetic alternative, 193–194; El CineClub de Buenos Aires and, 189–191; city symphony genre, 204–205; Coppola's work, 194–206; *Film und Foto* (FiFo) exposition, 183, 186; of Moholy-Nagy, 186–187; photography, influence on, 180–182, 185, 187–192, 205–206

avant-garde photography: Argentina, 199–206; Coppola's work, 187–193; Direct Photography movement, 184; film, influence on, 180–182, 185, 187–192, 205–206; Moholy-Nagy's work, 187; New Objectivity (*Neues Sachlichkeit*) movement, 184, 194; New Vision (*Neues Sehen*) movement, 181, 184–187, 193–194

avant-garde writing: 164–165, 300–303

"Aventuras de la Familia Pérez en Nueva York" (Martínez), 121–122

Aventurera (film), 270, 274, 275*f*, 278

Ávila Camacho, Manuel, 250–251, 256

Aztec horror films: directors of, 332; history and legacy of, 328; the indigenous, evocation of, 328–334; past-present temporality, 342–344; precursors, 332; transnationality of, 325–329, 334–337, 342–344

The Aztec Mummy (*La momia azteca*) (film), 329, 337, 340

Aztec Treasure House for Boys (Janvier), 336

Aztlán, 325–329, 326*f*, 337–339

Babies' Quarrel (*Querelle enfantine*) (film), 20

Baby ryazanskie (*Peasant Women of Ryazan*), 171n4, 178

Baby's Breakfast (*Repas de bébé/Baby's Meal*) (film), 20

Bad Boy (film), 243

Baignade en mer (*Bathing in the Sea*) (film), 20

Balázs, Béla, 192

Baledón, Rafael, 257; *El hombre y el monstruo* (*The Man and the Monster*) (film), 328; *La maldición de la llorona* (*The Curse of the Crying Woman*) (film), 328

de Baños, Ricardo: *Sangre y arena* (*Blood and Sand*) (1917) (film), 122

Baralt, Luis A., 304, 307

Barcelona y sus misterios (*Barcelona and Its Mysteries*) (film), 122

Barnes, George, 224

Baroncelli, Jacques de: *Les mystères de Paris* (*The Mysteries of Paris*) (film), 244, 250, 253

El barón del terror (*Braniac*) (film), 328

Barraza, Santa, 338

Barro humano (*Human Filth*) (film), 128

Barth, Luis Moglia: *Amalia* (film), 225–226, 227*f*; *¡Goal!* (film), 225, 226; *Tango!* (film), 221; *12 mujeres* (*12 Women*) (film), 232

Barty, Billy, 284

Bassin des Tuileries (*The Tuileries Palace of Paris*) (film), 20

Bataille de femmes (*Fight amongst Women*) (film), 20

Bathing in the Sea (*Baignade en mer*) (film), 20

Batista, Fulgencio, 306, 315

Battleship Potemkin (*Bronenosets Potyomkin*) (film), 107, 151, 153, 155, 158*f*, 159–162, 165–166, 171n2, 172n10, 172n14, 173n21, 178, 183, 190, 311

Bauhaus school, 181–182, 186, 192–193, 208n28

El baúl macabro (*The Macabre Trunk*) (film), 332

Baur, Harry, 250

Bed and Sofa (*Tretya meshchanskaya*) (film), 155

Belgrano, Manuel, 76

Bence, Amelia, 233

Berkeley, Busby: *The Gang's All Here* (film), 134, 269

Berlin, die Symphonie der Großstadt (*Berlin, Symphony of a Great City*) (film), 177, 183, 190, 204

Bermúdez Zatarain, Rafael, 39

Bernard, Claude Fernand Bon, 6, 18–20, 24, 26–27

Bernard, Raymold: *Les misérables* (film), 250

Berriozábal, Felipe, 19, 25, 26–27

Bertellini, Giorgio, 7, 73–97

Bertini, Francesca, 35, 38n4, 39, 51, 52*f*, 83

Biermann, Aenne, 183
The Big Combo (film), 219, 234
Bird of Paradise (film), 286
The Birth of a Nation (film), 77
Blackton, J. Stuart, 127
Blanco, Jorge Ayala, 243
Blaze O'Glory (film), 137
Blood and Sand (film) (1922), 121
Blood and Sand (Sangre y arena) (film) (1917), 122
Blood and Sand (Sangre y arena) (novel) (Ibáñez), 122
Boero, Felipe: *El matrero (The Outlaw)*, 232
Bogart, Humphrey, 257
Bogotá, Colombia, 43–46
Bohemia (periodical), 272, 303
La bohemia de hoy/The Bohemia of Today (Tararira) (film), 221
Bohr, José: *Luponini (el terror de Chicago) (Luponini [The Terror of Chicago])* (film), 229–230; *Sombras de Gloria* (film), 137
Boletín de la Sociedad de Embellecimiento de Bogotá (Bulletin of the Bogotá Beautification Society), 45
Bolewslawski, Richard: *Les misèrables* (film), 250
Bombal, María Luisa, 232
Border Incident (film), 219
Borelli, Lyda, 39, 51, 83
Borge, Jason, 9, 269–292
Borges, Jorge Luis, 87, 93n16, 165–166, 189, 191, 201; *Evaristo Carriego*, 209n46
Borges, Norah, 188
Borgnetto, Luigi Romano: *Maciste* (film), 53
Borrasca en las almas (Stormy Souls) (film), 256
Boudu Saved from Drowning (Boudu sauvé des eaux) (film), 222
Boval, Bruno, 234
Bowers, Charles, 177
Boytler, Arcady: *La mujer del puerto (The Woman of the Port)* (1934 film), 255, 256
Bracho, Julio, 242, 260; *Distinto amanecer (A New Dawn)* (film), 255–258, 259–260
Braniac (El barón del terror) (film), 328
Brazil: avant-garde influences in, 181; cineclubs, 156, 157, 161, 169, 173n21; cinema in, de Faria on, 147–149; national film industry, development of, 217; Soviet cinema in, 154, 156, 160, 169
Brecht, Bertolt: *The Life of Galileo*, 88

British cinema, 309
Brizuela, Natalia, 181–182, 205
Bronenosets Potyomkin (Battleship Potemkin) (film), 107, 151, 153, 155, 158f, 159–162, 165–166, 171n2, 172n10, 172n14, 173n21, 178, 183, 190, 311
A Bronx Morning (film), 204
Les Brûleurs d'herbe (Grass Burners) (film), 20
Brulier, Nigel de, 109, 110
Bruno, Guiliana: "Siteseeing: Architecture and the Moving Image," 221
Bryher (Annie Winifred Ellerman): *Film Problems of Soviet Russia*, 156
Buenos Aires 1936. Una visión fotográfica (Buenos Aires 1936: A Photographic Vision), (Coppola), 200, 202
Bulletin of the Bogotá Beautification Society (*Boletín de la Sociedad de Embellecimiento de Bogotá*), 45
Buñuel, Luis, 3, 194, 242, 256, 310; *Los olvidados* (film), 244; *Un chien andalou* (film), 177
Bush, W. Stephen, 120
Bushman, Francis X., 76
Bustillo Oro, Juan: *Canaima* (film), 252; *En tiempos de la Inquisición (In the Times of the Inquisition)* (film), 251
Butler, Horacio, 189
Buzzell, Edward: *Neptune's Daughter* (film), 243

cabaretera film, 278
La cabeza viviente (The Living Head) (film), 328, 339
Cabinet of Dr. Caligari (Das Kabinett des Dr. Caligari) (film), 177, 183, 190
Cabiria (film), 50, 53, 56, 58
Cabrera Infante, Guillermo, 314, 315
Cachao (Orestes López), 272
Cadets of San Martín (Cadetes de San Martín) (film), 226–229
Cadorna, Luigi, 57f
Café de chinos (Chinese Café) (film), 243
Cagney, James, 257
Cairo, Humberto: *Nobleza gaucha (Gaucho Nobility)* (film), 7, 75, 77–81, 122
Calle Corrientes (Corrientes Street) (photograph), 182
Caminito de gloria (Little Path to Glory) (film), 220, 233–234
Camisas negras (A noi!) (film), 82, 84f
Canaima (film), 252

Canaima (novel) (Gallego), 252
Cantinflas. See Mario Moreno (pseud. Cantinflas)
Caras y Caretas (periodical), 161
Cara-Walker, Ana, 78
Cárdenas, Lázaro, 253–254
Cardona, René, 332; *Las luchadoras contra la momia* (*Wrestling Women vs. the Aztec Mummy*) (film), 329; *Santo en la venganza de la momia* (*Santo and the Vengeance of the Mummy*) (film), 329
The Card Players (*Partie de cartes*) (film), 20
Carmina, Rosa, 261
Carousel (film), 295
carpa, 248
Carpentier, Alejo, 155, 160, 283; "El cine en la nueva Rusia" (Cinema in the New Russia), 166
Carranza, Luis Romero, 218
Carril, Hugo del, 230
Cartelera cinemotográfica, 1950-1959 (Amador & Blanco), 243
Caruggi, Eduardo, 124*f*
Caruggi, Pedro, 124*f*
Caruso, Enrico, 81
Casablanca (film), 257
Cascarita (Orlando Guerra), 273
Caserini, Mario: *Gli ultimi giorni di Pompeii* (*The Last Days of Pompeii*) (film), 56
Castagnino, Juan Carlos, 189
Castro, Almir, 173n21
Castro, Fidel, 288–289
Castro Ricalde, Maricruz, 3
Cataruza, Héctor, 223
Catholic Church, 40, 47–48, 282
La cautiva del caudillo moro (*The Sheik*) (film), 85
Cavalcade (film), 215
Cavalry Charge (perhaps *Lanciers de la reine, défilé*) (film), 20
Caviglia, Orestes, 229; *El matrero* (*The Outlaw*) (film), 232–233
Cendrars, Blaise, 301
censorship: Mexican film industry fight against, 280–281; Liga de Decencia, 280–281; Colombian periodicals fight against, 47; of Soviet films, 151–152, 154, 160, 171n2, 171n14
Centro Sperimentale di Cinematografia (Italy), 305
cha-cha-chá, 277, 288

Cha-Cha-Cha-Boom! (film), 271, 285–287, 288
Chacón y Calvo, José María, 304
Chagoya, Enrique, 344; *Codex Espanglienses* (book), 343
chanchada, 273
Chaney, Lon Jr., 340
Chaplin, Charlie, 109, 162, 190, 309; *The Circus* (film), 183; *Shoulder Arms* (film), 190
Chaplin-Club, 156, 157, 161, 169, 173n21
Chapperon, Emilio, 126
The Charge of the Gauchos/The Beautiful Spy (*Una nueva y gloriosa nación*) (film), 76
Charge of the Rurales in the Village of Guadalupe (film), 25
Chávez, John R., 338
Chelovek s kinoapparatom (*The Man with a Movie Camera*) (film), 159, 183, 204
"Cherry Pink and Apple Blossom White" (Pérez Prado), 285
Chicana/o cultural production: art and identity, 330; cultural nationalism in Mexico and, 337–339; filmmakers, 324; New Latin American Cinema, 341–342
Chicana/o movement, Aztlán and the, 337–339
Un chien andalou (film), 177
Child's Play (perhaps *Scène d'enfants*) (film), 20
Chinatown at Midnight (film), 243
Chinese Café (*Café de chinos*) (film), 243
Chiola, Sebastián, 232
La chute de la Maison Usher (*The Fall of the House of Usher*) (film), 190
Cinearte (periodical), 159–160, 161, 167
Cine Club de México, 101
"The 'Cineclub' of Buenos Aires" (Torre), 8, 176–178
Cine Club of Cuba, 302
CineClub of Buenos Aires (CineClub of the Amigos del Arte), 8, 151, 156, 161, 171n20; 176–178, 189–191
cineclubs: 171n20; Brazil, 156–157, 161, 169, 173n21; Cuba, 302, 315, 316; Mexico, 101; Soviet cinema and, 156, 173n21, 177–178, 191
Cine Cosmos, 171n20
"El cine en la nueva Rusia" (Cinema in the New Russia) (Carpentier), 166
El cine en la Universidad de La Habana (*Film at the University of Havana*) (Valdés-Rodríguez), 308
Cine Fausto, 301
Cinegraf (periodical), 223
El Cine Gráfico (periodical), 46, 47, 48–49, 50

Cinelandia (periodical): beauty products, advertisements for, 129; beginnings, 112–113, 127, 140, 141n5; circulation, 127; decline and end, 140–141; discourse of progress, 117, 127, 138–139; fan magazine structure, 114; Hollywood studios, alignment with, 134; influence of, 137; intermediary role, 7, 136–137, 139; legacy, 141; "Añoranzas de Hollywood" (Longing for Hollywood) (Aragón Leiva), 88–89; scholarship on, 116; sponsorship, 127; "Where Is Costa Roja?" (Alvear), 129–130

Cinelandia (periodical), columns and sections: columnists, 115; contributors from outside Hollywood, 114; "La Moda en Hollywood" (Fashion in Hollywood), 129; "Notas Hispanoamericanas," 138; "Notas Panamericanas," 138; "Por Otras Tierras" (In Other Lands), 138

Cinelandia (periodical), contributions to: construction of film culture, 116–117; expansion of US film culture, 112–114; fan culture, 114–115, 127; Spanish-language film production, 137–138; transition to sound, 134–137

Cinelandia (periodical), coverage of: film labor, 131–132; Good Neighbor policy films, 134–135; Latin America, 128; Latin American actors, 128–129, 134; Latin American film industry, 134, 138; movie stars, 127–134, 139

Cinelandia (periodical), readership: collaboration with, 138–139; orientation to their, 113–114, 116–117, 127, 128–129, 134; participation in construction of film culture, 116–117; target audience, 113

"Cinema in the Argentine" (Tew), 151
"Cinema in the New Russia" ("El cine en la nueva Rusia") (Carpentier), 166
cinéma pur, 160–163, 165
Cinema Quarterly (periodical), 192
Cinema Repórter (periodical), 140
Le Cinéma Soviétique (Moussinac), 147–148
Cinematograph (Lumière), 18–31
Cine-Mundial (periodical): beginnings, 112; circulation, 120, 127; decline and end, 140–141; discourse of progress, 124, 127; film and modernity in, 116; focus of, 117; hemispheric orientation, 118, 119f, 130, 139; imported cinema, position on, 39–40; influence of, 138; intermediary role, 7, 136–137, 139–140; legacy, 141; Películas, argument with, 39–40; scholarship on, 116

Cine-Mundial (periodical), columns and sections: "El Arte de la Proyección" (Richardson), 120; "Aventuras de la Familia Pérez en Nueva York" (Martínez), 121–122; "Baturillo Neoyorquino" (New York Mishmash), 121; columnists, 115; contributors from outside Hollywood, 114, 124–125; crónicas, focus of, 114, 122; crónicas gráficas, 122, 139; "Favoritos del Cine" (Movie Favorites), 126; "De Plateros a la Quinta Avenida" (From Plateros Street to Fifth Avenue), 138; "Preguntas y Respuestas" (Questions and Answers), 126; "El Teatro Moderno" (Kinsilia), 120; "Ventana de Buenos Aires" (Window on Buenos Aires), 138

Cine-Mundial (periodical), contribution to: construction of film culture, 116–117; expansion of US film culture, 112–114; fan culture, 126–127; film journalism, 122; modernization, 116, 124; transition to sound, 134–137

Cine-Mundial (periodical), coverage of: European features vs. US serials in Colombia, 51; Good Neighbor policy films, 134–135; Latin American actors, 134; Latin American film industry, 122, 134, 138; movie stars, 128, 134

Cine-Mundial (periodical), readership: collaborations, 138–139; orientation to their, 113–114, 116–117, 134; participation in construction of film culture, 116–117; photo competition, 139; target audience, 113, 120
Cine Visión (Vision Cinema), 315
circo criollo, 78
The Circus (film), 183
city symphony films, 204–205
Clair, René, 194
Clave del Sol (periodical), 200
Closed Door (Puerta cerrada) (film), 232, 233
Close Up (periodical), 151, 156, 192
Cobra (film), 85
Cockfight (film), 26
cocoliche, 75, 78–79, 87
Cocteau, Jean, 301
Codex Espanglienses (book), 343
Cohen, Larry: Q (film), 335

Cold War era, 140, 261, 283, 287
Colombia: Bogotá's transformation in, 43–46; conservative modernization, 44, 47, 55; fascism, foundation for, 40
Colombia, film audiences in: 40–42, 44–50, 59–60
Colombia, film in; historical films, 41; imported films, exhibition and distribution practices, 40–41; serial cinema, 48, 50–53, 55–56, 58–59, 60; strongman films, 41, 42f, 50, 53
Colombia, film magazines in: censorship, fight against, 47; exhibitors-distributors use of, 47–53; ideal spectator, production of, 48–50, 60; ideology promoting European films over US serials, 48, 50–53, 55–56, 58–59, 60; nationalism and film in, 53–59; protofascist rhetoric in, 57–58; purpose of, 47–48; racist discourse in, 58; social structures, reproducing, 49–50; US films in Columbia, position on, 40–41
comedia ranchera, 245, 249, 252, 262, 273–274, 291n18
comedic films, 244, 245–251, 286
comedy lighting, 225–226
Communism: in Cuba, 302; *Dicen que soy comunista* (*They Say I'm a Communist*) (film), 256; Eisenstein and, 148; Valdés-Rodríguez and, 302–303
Compañeros (*Mates*) (film), 221
El conde de Montecristo (*The Count of Monte Cristo*) (film), 250–251, 252
El conde de Montecristo (*The Count of Monte Cristo*) (novel) (Dumas), 250
Constructivist movements, 184
Coppola, Armando, 188
Coppola, Horacio: in Argentina, 199–206; avant-garde cinema, 194–206; avant-garde photography, 184, 187–193; at Bauhaus, 181–182; CineClub of Buenos Aires and, 178, 189–190; European initiation, 192–198; influence of, 181–182; mentioned, 8; Moholy-Nagy's influence on, 182; tradition and modernity, synthesis of, 200–202, 204
Coppola, Horacio, works: *Así nació el obelisco* (*Thus the Obelisk Was Born*) (film), 202, 203f, 204, 204f, 205; *Avenida Juan B. Justo* (photograph), 200; *Bartolomé Mitre, esquina Maipú* (*Corner of Bartolomé Mitré and Maipú*) (photograph), 202; *Buenos Aires 1936. Una visión fotográfica* (*Buenos Aires 1936: A Photographic Vision*), 200, 202; *Calle Corrientes* (*Corrientes Street*) (photograph), 182; *Do de pecho* (*Falsetto Note*) (film), 209n49; *Dream* (*Traum*) (film), 194–195, 195f, 198; *Iglesia de Nuestra Señora de Monserrat* (*The Church of Our Lady of Montserrat*) (photograph), 202; *Imagema*, 180; *Mateo y su victoria* (*Mateo and His Victory*) (photograph), 182; "Seven Themes: Buenos Aires" (photo-essay), 191; *Study No. 2* (photograph), 193; *Un domingo en Hampstead Heath* (*A Sunday on Hampstead Heath*) (film), 196, 198, 198f; *Un muelle del Sena* (*A Dock on the Seine*) (film), 195–196, 197f; *Vestir al bebé* (*Dressing Baby*) (film), 209n49; *Victoria esquina Bolívar* (*Corner of Victoria and Bolívar*) (photograph), 182
Le Corbusier, 189, 191
Córdova, Arturo de, 243, 250, 252
Corner of Victoria and Bolívar (*Victoria esquina Bolívar*) (photograph), 182
Correio da Manhã (newspaper), 160
El Correo Español, 22
Corrientes Street (*Calle Corrientes*) (photograph), 182
Cortège de la couronne or *Cortège du sceptre royal* (*Imperial Procession in Budapest*) (film), 20
Cortés, Fernando: *La marca del muerto* (film), 340
Cosimi, Nelo, 86
cosmopolitan, meaning of, 3, 4
cosmopolitanism: of audiences, 151–153, 156, 173n21, 177–178, 190–191, 243, 245–252, 260; and modernity in Mexico, 243–244, 247–248; transnationalism of film culture, 5, 151–160, 177–178, 190–191, 217
The Count of Monte Cristo (*El conde de Montecristo*) (film), 250–251, 252
The Count of Monte Cristo (novel) (Dumas), 250
Crazy Dandy (*Loco lindo*) (film), 225, 226
The Creation of the Hymn (*La creación del himno*) (film), 77
Creature of the Walking Dead (*La marca del muerto*) (film), 340
Crime at Three O'Clock (*Crimen a las 3*) (film), 221

crime dramas, 225, 229, 244, 257, 258–259
crime serials, 53, 64n24
criollista films, 222–223
The Crowd (film), 168
The Crying Woman (*La llorona*) (film), 332
Cuando acaba la noche (*When the Night Ends*) (film), 244, 257–258, 260
Cuarterolo, Andrea, 8, 180–210
Los cuatro jinetes del Apocalipsis (Ibañez), 76
Cuba: Communism in, 302; Constitution of 1940, 306–307; Hollywood's version of, 280; intellectual community (1920s-1930s), 300–303; music in, 271–272, 275–276; national culture, 303–304; propagandistic documentary films, 288–289; Republican era (1902-1958), 298; Spanish émigrés in, 303–304, 307
Cuba, education in: arts education, 303–307; journalism, professionalization of, 307–308, 314; modernization of, 306–307; Spanish émigrés contribution to, 304, 307; theater studies, 305. See also University of Havana
Cuba, film culture: art cinema, 314–315; cineclubs, 315, 316; cine-debates, 316; international films, availability of, 314; post-revolutionary, 316–317. See also University of Havana Summer School
Cuban Anti-Imperialist League, 302
Cuban Communist Party, 302
Cuevas, José Luis, 333
Cunard, Grace, 126
The Curse of the Crying Woman (*La maldición de la llorona*) (film), 328
Curtiz, Michael: *Casablanca* (film), 257
Curwood, Robert, 217

Dalí, Salvador, 301
Dall'Asta, Monica, 50, 51
Dalton, Dorothy, 130
D'Annunzio, Gabriele, 57–58, 82
D'Annunzio, Gabriellino: *Quo Vadis?* (1924 film), 83
Dance of the Spanish Procession at the Tívoli del Eliseo (film), 27
Dante Alighieri, 249
danzón, 272
Deas, Malcolm, 44
Debernardi, Felipe, 178
Decoine, Henri: *Non coupable* (*Not Guilty*) (film), 243

del Amo, Sebastián: *El fantástico mundo de Juan Orol* (*The Fantastic World of Juan Orol*) (film), 261
Delbene, Floren, 225, 230
Del can-can al mambo (*From the Can-Can to the Mambo*) (film), 271, 280–281, 281f, 287
Delgado, Miguel M.: *Romeo and Juliet* (film), 249; *The Three Musketeers* (film), 249
Dell'Oro Maini, Atilio, 199
Demare, Lucas, 309
De Mille, Cecil B.: *The Sign of the Cross* (film), 215
Demolition of a Wall (*Démolition d'un mur*) (film), 20
Dempsey, Jack, 105
Denizot, Vincenzo: *Maciste* (film), 53
Desnos, Robert, 160
Deutschland im Jahre Null (*Germany, Year Zero*), 311
Deutscher Werkbund (DWB), 182
The Devil's Money (*Los dineros del diablo*) (film), 256
El Diablo santificado (*A Sainted Devil*) (film), 85
Diagonal Symphony (*Diagonal-Symphonie*) (film), 183
Diamant-Berger, Henri, 192
El Diario Nacional (newspaper), 34
Díaz (Porfirio) and administration, 20, 22–24, 26–27, 330
Díaz del Castillo, Bernal, 332
Díaz López, Mercedes, 251
Dicen que soy comunista (*They Say I'm a Communist*) (film), 256
Di Domenico, Francesco, 43–46
Di Domenico, Vincenzo, 43–46
Di Domenico entertainment empire, 6–7, 34, 39–46, 56, 59–60
Diegues, Carlos, 168
Dietrich, Marlene, 257
The Dinah Shore Show (TV show), 285
Los dineros del diablo (*The Devil's Money*) (film), 256
Di Núbila, Domingo, 226, 233
DiPaulo, Dante, 286
Direct Photography movement, 184
Diricio, Cornelio, 132
"El discurso del astrólogo" ("The Astrologer's Discourse") (Arlt), 88
Disney, Walt, 134, 135f

Disney studios: *Saludos Amigos* (film), 134, 269; *The Three Caballeros* (film), 269
Disparos en el Istmo (*Shots Fired on the Isthmus*) (film), 181
Distinto amanecer (*A New Dawn*) (film), 255–260
divas of Italian cinema, 35, 39, 41, 51, 52f, 83
A Dock on the Seine (*Un muelle del Sena*) (film), 195–196, 197f
Do de pecho (*Falsetto Note*) (film), 209n49
Un domingo en Hampstead Heath (*A Sunday on Hampstead Heath*) (film), 196, 198f
Doña Bárbara (film), 252
Don Casto (Marcel Lévesque), 35, 38n4
Dos Passos, John, 301
The Dove (*La Paloma*) (film), 129–130
Downey, Wallace, 217
Dream (*Traum*) (film), 194–195, 195f, 198
Dressing Baby (*Vestir al bebé*) (film), 209n49
Dreyer, Carl Theodor: *The Passion of Joan of Arc* (*La Passion de Jeanne d'Arc*) (film), 177, 183, 190
Dudow, Slatan, 193
Dulac, Germaine, 194
Dumas, Alexandre: *The Count of Monte Cristo*, 250; *The Three Musketeers*, 249
Dunne, Stephen, 285–286
Durán, Javier, 246
Ďurovičová, Nastaša, 3–4, 221
Duse, Eleonora, 81
Dussel, Enrique, 4
Duvivier, Julien, 309
Dwan, Allan: *The Three Musketeers* (film), 249

Eandi, Héctor, 178
"Early Cinema and Modernity in Latin America" (López), 115
Edison Vitascope, 19, 25
The Ed Sullivan Show (TV show), 285
education through film, 53, 126, 149, 164–165, 279–280. *See also* film pedagogy
Egan, Richard, 285
Eggeling, Viking: *Diagonal Symphony* (*Diagonal-Symphonie*) (film), 183
Eisenstein, Sergei: Cine Club de México, 101; Communist affiliation, 148; dialectics, 155; film pedagogy, 305, 306; friends of, 89; influence of, 153, 164, 167–168, 188, 306; mentioned, 3, 147; Ocampo and 168, 175n59; periodicals coverage of, 159–162, 159f, 167–168; staging of oppositions, 165–166; Valdés-Rodríguez and, 155, 300, 302–303, 306, 309
Eisenstein, Sergei, works: *Alexander Nevsky* (film), 173n21, 311; *Battleship Potemkin* (*Bronenosets Potyomkin*) (film), 107, 151, 153, 155, 158f, 159–162, 165–166, 171n2, 172n10, 172n14, 173n21, 178, 183, 190, 311; censorship of, 151, 160, 171n2, 171n14; cineclub showings of, 156; *The General Line* (*Old and New* [*Staroye i novoye*]) (film), 155-156, 161, 163, 166; "Messiah or Threat" interview (*Cinearte*), 167–168; "Montage as Conflict," 165; *October* (*Oktyabr*) (film), 151, 155, 161, 165, 178; periodicals promoting, 158f; ¡*Que Viva México!* (film), 101, 181, 302
"Eisenstein em Hollywood" (Marinho), 159f
Elippi, Elías, 228f
Elizondo, José Francisco "Pepe," 138
Ellerman, Annie Winifred (Bryher), 156
Ellington, Duke: "The Mooch," 221
Elsaesser, Thomas, 218
Emir, the Police Horse (*Emir, cavallo de circo*) (film), 34, 36–37, 37n1
"La enamorada de Rudolfo Valentino" ("The Lover of Rudolph Valentino") (Méndez Calzada), 7, 66–71, 90
The End of St. Petersburg (film), 178
Enrique José Varona Theater, 310–311, 311–313f
En tiempos de la Inquisición (*In the Times of the Inquisition*) (film), 251
Entr'acte (film), 190, 194
Epstein, Jean, 192; *The Fall of the House of Usher* (*La chute de la Maison Usher*) (film), 190; "On Some Aspects of *Photogénie*," 161
Escala en la ciudad (*Layover in the City*) (film), 221, 222–223
Escuela Libre de la Habana (Open School of Havana), 303–306
España, Claudio, 224
El Espectador (newspaper), 267
El espejo de la bruja (*The Witch's Mirror*) (film), 328
European cinema, 41, 50, 309, 311
Evans, Gil, 288
Evaristo Carriego (Borges), 209n46
exhibition culture in Latin America. *See specific countries*
Experimental Cinema (periodical), 302, 303, 306

extras in Hollywood, 101–111, 132, 133f
Ezra, Elizabeth, 1

Face of the Screaming Werewolf (film), 340–341
Fairbanks, Douglas, 51, 76, 85, 101, 107–109
Fairbanks, Douglas, Jr., 101, 249, 252, 253
The Fallen Idol (film), 243, 260
The Fall of the House of Usher (*La chute de la Maison Usher*) (film), 190
Falma Film, 234
Falsetto Note (*Do de pecho*) (film), 209n49
fan culture, 2–3, 114–115, 126–127. *See also specific countries*
La fantasma del convento (*The Phantom of the Convent*) (film), 332
The Fantastic World of Juan Orol (*El fantástico mundo de Juan Orol*) (film), 261
Fantômas (film), 56
de Faria, Octávio, 156, 163, 173n21; "Russian Cinema and Brazilian Cinema," 7–8, 147–149
Father's Son (*El hijo de papá*) (film), 220–221, 223
Fauré, Felix, 22
Feininger, Andreas, 183
Félix, Maria, 252
Fernández, Emilio, 242, 245, 273, 309; *Flor silvestre* (*Wildflower*) (film), 251, 259–260; *María Candelaria* (film), 255, 331, 333–334; *Víctimas del pecado* (*Victims of Sin*) (film), 270, 274, 275–276, 278
Fernández, Maria, 4–5
Fernández Reyes, Álvaro, 258–259
Ferrari Pérez, Fernando, 19
Ferreyra, José Agustín, 209n46, 230; *Mi último tango* (*My Last Tango*) (film), 86; *El tango de la muerte* (*The Tango of Death*) (film), 86–87
Ferro, Helen, 88–89
Feuillade, Louis: *Fantômas* (film), 56; *Judex* (film), 51
feuilleton, 50, 53
Féval, Paul: *The Hunchback*, 251
Fields, Virginia M., 342
Figari, Pedro, 201
Fight amongst Women (*Bataille de femmes*) (film), 20
Figueroa, Gabriel, 241–242
Film Art (periodical), 192
Film at the University of Havana (*El cine en la Universidad de La Habana*) (Valdés-Rodríguez), 308

film audiences. *See* audiences
film clubs. *See* cineclubs
film culture: avant-garde influences, 181; construction of, 116–117; cosmopolitanism of, 5, 151–160, 177–178, 190–191, 217; film criticism, training for, 314; global distribution of films, 43-46; heterogeneity of, 153, 245; inclusivity vs. social stratification in, 40–42, 44–46, 47, 48, 59–60, 76–79, 87–88; Spanish-language film magazines role in, 116. *See also specific countries*
film fandom. *See* audiences; movie stars
film labor: income inequality, 103–104, 105; Mexican, in Hollywood, 101–111; racialized, 131–133, 133f
film magazines: English-language. *See Cinelandia* (periodical); *Cine-Mundial* (periodical). *See also specific magazines*
film magazines, Spanish-language: censorship, fight against, 47; columnists role, 115–116; decline and end, 140–141; exhibitors-distributors use of, 47–53; film culture, role in, 116; film industry in Latin America, coverage of, 122, 133, 138; ideal spectator, production of, 48–50, 60; ideology promoting European films over US serials, 48, 50–53, 55–56, 58–59, 60; imported films, position on, 39–40, 41, 46, 50–51; modernity and, 117, 124; nationalism and film in, 53–59; protofascist rhetoric in, 57–58; purpose of, 47–48; racist discourse in, 58; social structures, reproducing, 49–50, 56; US takeover of world markets and retention of control, role in, 112–114, 118–127. *See also specific magazines*
film noir, 218–219, 229, 256, 257, 258–259, 260
Filmoteca Universitaria film archive (University of Havana), 311, 314, 316–317
film pedagogy: audience, 41; Europe, 305; Italy, 305; transnationalism in, 300, 303–304; United States, 306; USSR, 305; of Valdés-Rodríguez, José Manuel, 299–300, 302–310, 316–317. *See also* University of Havana Summer School
Film Problems of Soviet Russia (Bryher), 156
Film Revista Valle (newsreel), 77
Film und Foto (FiFo) exposition, 182–184, 186, 190
Firmat, Pérez, 277
First Journalist Congress, Havana, 308
Fitzmaurice, George: *The Son of the Sheik* (film), 85, 86f
Flaherty, Robert: *Moana* (film), 190

Flor silvestre (*Wildflower*) (film), 251, 259–260
The Flying Serpent (film), 335–336, 336f, 339
Folha de São Paulo (newspaper), 168–169
Fondane, Benjamin, 177, 221; *Tararira* (*La bohemia de hoy/The Bohemia of Today*) (film), 221
Ford, Francis, 126
Ford, John, 309
The Four Horsemen of the Apocalypse (film), 7, 74, 76, 79, 85, 87, 88, 121, 223
Fox, 137
Fox Film de Cuba, S. A., 295–297, 308
"Fox Film de Cuba, S.A.'s Continuing Competition for Scholarships to Summer School at the Universidad de la Habana" (Sibert), 9, 295–297
Franco, Herminia, 225
Francy, Nedda, 228f, 229
Frank, Waldo, 301
Franken, Mannus: *Rain* (*Regen*) (film), 190
French cinema, 305, 309
Frend, Charles: *San Demetrio London* (film), 243
Friedman, Seymour: *Chinatown at Midnight* (film), 243
Froelich, Carl: *Second Youth* (*Reifende Jugend*) (film), 193
From the Can-Can to the Mambo (*Del can-can al mambo*) (film), 271, 280–281, 281f, 287
From the Radio Tower of Berlín (film), 182
Fuentes, Carlos, 333
Fuentes, Fernando de, 309; *Doña Bárbara* (film), 252; *La fantasma del convento* (*The Phantom of the Convent*) (film), 332
Full Speed Ahead (*A toda máquina*) (film), 250

Gabin, Jean, 252
"Gabriel Veyre and Fernand Bon Bernard, Representatives of the Lumière Brothers in Mexico" (Reyes), 18–33
La Gaceta Literaria (periodical), 151–152, 176–178, 190
Gaido, Domenico: *Samson against the Philistines* (*Sansone contro i filistei*) (film), 42
Galaor films, 50
Galeen, Henrik: *The Student of Prague* (*Der Student von Prag*) (1926 film), 190
Galindo, Alejandro, 242, 260; *Dicen que soy comunista* (*They Say I'm a Communist*) (film), 256; *Los dineros del diablo* (*The Devil's Money*) (film), 256
Galindo, Marco Aurelio, 138

Gallego, Rómulo: *Canaima* (novel), 252
Gallo, Mario: *La creación del himno* (*The Creation of the Hymn*) (film), 77; *Güemes y sus gauchos* (*Güemes and His Gauchos*) (film), 77; *Juan Moreira* (film), 77; *La revolución de Mayo* (*The May Revolution*) (film), 77
Galvão, Patrícia, 164
Gamio, Manual, 330
Ganga bruta (film), 181
The Gang's All Here (film), 134, 269
gangster films, 257–258, 262
Gángsters contra charros (film), 261
Garbo, Greta, 76, 165
García, David F., 272
García, Sara, 251
García Canclini, Néstor, 5
García Espinosa, Julio, 315
García Lorca, Federico, 189, 301
García Márquez, Gabriel, 282, 283; "The Mambo," 9, 267–268
García Ortega, Francisco, 115, 118, 122, 125, 135f
García Riera, Emilio, 249, 251, 254, 257, 261
Gardel, Carlos, 87, 135
The Gardener and the Boy (*L'Arroseur arrosé*) (film), 20
Garmes, Lee, 232
Gasnier, Louis: *Las luces de Buenos Aires* (*The Lights of Buenos Aires*) (film), 223
The Gaucho (film), 76, 101, 105–110
Gaucho Nobility (*Nobleza gaucha*) (film), 7, 75, 77–81, 122
Gaumont, 56
Gavaldón, Roberto, 255
Gay, Ramón, 329
The General Line (*Old and New* [*Staroye i novoye*]) (film), 155
Germany, Year Zero (*Deutschland im Jahre Null*) (film), 311
Gerzso, Gunther, 333
Getino, Octavio, 2
Ghosts before Breakfast (*Vormittagspuk*) (film), 194
Gide, André, 301
Gil Blas (newspaper), 20, 22, 24
Gillespie, Dizzy, 275
Giraudoux, Jean, 301
glamour lighting, 229, 230, 231
Gliks, Alfred, 218
globalization: cosmopolitan transnationalism of film culture, 5, 151–160, 177–178, 190–191, 217; defined, 4; of film trade, 112–114; serial cinema and, 51–52

Glücksmann, Max, 77, 239n31
¡Goal! (film), 225, 226
Goddard, Paulette, 134
Goity, Elena, 229
Gola, José, 229
Gómez Bao, Miguel, 233
Gómez Landero, Humberto: *Músico, poeta y loco* (*Musician, Poet, and Madman*) (film), 249–250
Gómez Mena, María Luisa, 304
Gómez Muriel, Emilio, 242; *Cuando acaba la noche* (*When the Night Ends*) (film), 244, 257–258, 260; *Redes* (film), 331
Gómez-Peña, Guillermo, 342; *Codex Espanglienses* (book), 343; *The Great Mojado Invasion, Part 2* (*The Second U.S.–Mexico War*) (film), 324–325, 326f, 328
Goñi, Santos, 89
Gonzaga, Adhemar: *Barro humano* (*Human Filth*) (film), 128
González González, José, 286
Good Neighbor era, 116–117, 133, 140, 270, 283
Good Neighbor films, 134–135, 139, 269, 278, 285, 287
Gorelik, Adrián, 200–201
Gorky, Maxim, 301
Gout, Alberto, 273; *Aventurera* (film), 270, 274, 275f, 278
La grande illusion (film), 311
Grass Burners (*Les Brûleurs d'herbe*) (film), 20
The Great Mojado Invasion, Part 2 (*The Second U.S.–Mexico War*) (film), 324–325, 326f, 328, 343
Greca, Alcides: *El último malón* (*The Last Indian Uprising*) (film), 77
Greene, Doyle, 340
Greene, Graham: *The Fallen Idol* (film), 260
Grifell, Maruja, 281f
Griffith, D. W., 105; *The Birth of a Nation* (film), 77
Gropius, Walter, 186
guaguancó, 276, 285–286
Guazzoni, Enrico: *Messalina* (film), 83
Güemes and His Gauchos (*Güemes y sus gauchos*) (film), 77
Guerra, Orlando (Cascarita), 273
Guerrero, Luis Juan, 192
Guerrico, César José, 218
Guevara, Alfredo, 315
Guevara, Ernesto "Che," 288
Guevara, Juan Gualberto, 282

Guffey, Burnett, 219
Guilherme, Olympio, 161
Gunche, Ernesto, 122; *Nobleza gaucha* (*Gaucho Nobility*) (film), 75, 77–81
Gunckel, Colin, 9–10, 324–348
Guzmán, Domingo, 46
Gymnastics Class at the Colegio de la Paz, Formerly Vizcaínas (film), 27

Hamann, Richard, 192
Hamlet (film), 249
Hansen, Miriam, 5, 46, 49, 169, 170; "The Mass Production of the Senses," 169; "Vernacular Modernism: Tracking Cinema on a Global Scale," 169
Harem of Death (film), 147
Hasta la victoria siempre (*Until Victory*) (film), 288
Hathaway, Henry: *Peter Ibbetson* (film), 232
Haussmann, George-Eugène, 44
Havana Reporters' Association (Asociación de Reporters de La Habana), 308
Heartfield, John, 183
Heller, Fritz, 192
Henabery, Joseph: *Cobra* (film), 85; *A Sainted Devil* (*El Diablo santificado*) (film), 85
El Heraldo (newspaper), 267–268, 282
Heraldo del Cinematografista (periodical), 223
Hernández, José, 77–78; "Martín Fierro," 77
Herrand, Marcel, 250
Hidalgo, Bartolomé, 78
Higbee, Will, 4
El hijo de papá (*Father's Son*) (film), 220–221, 223
Hindi cinema, 169–170
historical films, 41, 76, 53–56
Hitchcock, Alfred, 260, 309
Höch, Hannah, 183
Hoffman, Renaud: *Blaze O'Glory* (film), 137
Holiday in Havana (film), 280
Hollywood film distributors, 308
Hollywood film industry: competitors, post-WW II, 122, 140; Cuba-as-primitive-playground ideology, 280; film labor, Mexican, 101–111; foreign newspaper coverage of, 82; Good Neighbor films, 134–135, 139, 269, 278, 285, 287; Latin Americans/Latino actors, stereotyping of, 117, 125, 129–130, 134, 285; Soviet cinema compared, 161–162, 165–166; Spanish-language films, production of, 136–138, 213–216;

Spanish-speaking market, 129–130, 133, 139, 213; World War II, 117, 118. *See also* United States, film industry
Hollywood in Latin America: Argentine film culture and, 84–91; film scholarships, Cuba, 308; Mexican film industry, attempts to obstruct, 245; US cultural hegemony and imperialism and, 73, 87, 89, 169–170; World War I, 112; World War II, 117–118
Hollywood Lighting from the Silent Era to Film Noir (Keating), 224
El hombre y el monstruo (The Man and the Monster) (film), 328
Honeysuckle (Madreselva) (film), 230–232, 231f, 233
Horak, Jan-Christopher, 205
horror films, 325–337, 342–344
A Horse Breaker (film), 26
Horses Bathing (film), 26
Howe, James Wong, 224
Hugo, Victor: *Les misèrables*, 250
Human Filth (Barro humano) (film), 128
The Hunchback (El jorobado) (film), 251
The Hunchback (novel) (Féval), 251
Hurricane, or Tempest in Veracruz (film), 28, 33n37
Huston, John: *The Maltese Falcon* (film), 256–257, 260
Húttula, Gerardo: *Compañeros (Mates)* (film), 221

I Am Joaquín (film), 324, 338
Ibañez, Vicente Blasco: *Los cuatro jinetes del Apocalipsis*, 76; *Sangre y arena (Blood and Sand)*, 122
Ibarra, Jesús, 259
Ibarra, Néstor, 178, 191
Illuminati, Ivo: *Emir, the Police Horse (Emir, cavallo de circo)* (film), 37n1
Imagema (Coppola), 180
immigration: to Argentina, 74–75, 78, 93n16, 94n17; to Colombia, 40, 43, 59; to Cuba, 303; to Mexico, 243; to United States, 46, 74, 81, 103, 114–115, 117, 122, 131–133, 337
Imparcial Film (periodical), 223
Imperial Procession in Budapest (likely *Cortège de la couronne* or *Cortège du sceptre royal*) (film), 20
Impressions of the Old Port of Marseille (Impressionen vom alten Marseiller Hafen) (film), 186–187, 196

Indo-American Gothic, 328–334
Infante, Pedro, 241, 242, 243, 245, 249, 250, 251, 254–255
Inflation (film), 183
Ingram, Rex: *The Four Horsemen of the Apocalypse* (film), 7, 74, 76, 79, 85, 87, 88, 121, 223
Instituto Cubano de Arte e Industria Cinematográficos (ICAIC), 288, 315, 316–317
International Photographer (periodical), 8, 218, 223; "Motion Picture Production in South America" (Alton), 213–216, 219, 221, 224; "Motion Picture Production in South America Up to Date" (Alton), 234; "News Letter from South America" (Alton), 224
In the Times of the Inquisition (En tiempos de la Inquisición) (film), 251
Invernizio, Carolina, 50
Irusta, Augustín, 232, 233
Irwin, Robert McKee, 3
Italy, 53–59, 81–82, 305, 309
Italy, cinema of: 39–41, 42f, 50–56, 58, 69, 76, 82–84, 309
Ivan the Terrible (Krylya kholopa/Wings of a Serf) (1926 film), 147, 165
Ivens, Joris: *The Bridge (De brug)*, 183; *Rain (Regen)*, 190

Jackson, Pat: *Shadow on the Wall* (film), 243
Jacoby, George: *Quo Vadis?* (1924 film), 83
Jacquier, Philippe, 31
Janitzio (film), 331
Janvier, Thomas A.: *Aztec Treasure House for Boys*, 336
Jasset, Victorin: *Zigomar, roi de voleurs (Zigomar, King of Thieves)* (film), 62n24
jazz, 221, 270–271, 275, 282
Jones, F. Richard: *The Gaucho* (film), 76, 101, 105–110
Jones, Spike, 283–284
Jordán, Anita, 225
El jorobado (The Hunchback) (film), 251
José, Edward: *My Cousin* (film), 81
journalism, professionalization of, 307–308, 314
Joyce, James, 309
Juan Moreira (film), 77
Judex (film), 51
Jurado, Kathy, 256

Das Kabinett des Dr. Caligari (Cabinet of Dr. Caligari) (film), 177, 183, 190

Kanellos, Nicolás, 113
Kant, Immanuel, 4
Karl Marx University, 193
Karloff, Boris, 335
Keating, Patrick, 226; *Hollywood Lighting from the Silent Era to Film Noir*, 224
Keaton, Buster, 190
Kelley, Albert H.: *The Charge of the Gauchos/The Beautiful Spy* (*Una nueva y gloriosa nación*) (film), 76
Kelly, Gene, 249
Kemeny, Adalberto: *São Paulo, A Sinfonia da metrópole* (*São Paulo, Symphony of the Metropolis*) (film), 181
Kent, Robert E., 286
Kenton, Stan, 272–273, 283; "Viva Prado!," 273
El Kine (periodical), 46
El Kine Universal (periodical), 47, 50
King, Henry: *Carousel* (film), 295
The King of the Neighborhood (*El rey del barrio*) (film), 248
Kinsilia, Edward, 120
A Kiss Before the Mirror (film), 215
Klimovsky, León, 178, 188, 189, 191
Knight, Alan, 253
Kolchak: Night Stalker (TV show), 337
Krull, Germain, 183
Krylya kholopa (*Wings of a Serf/Ivan the Terrible*) (film), 165
Kuleshov, Lev, 305
Kun, Josh, 271
Kung Fu (TV show), 337
Kurosawa, Akira, 310
El laberinto de la soledad (*The Labyrinth of Solitude*) (Paz), 244, 246

labor-themed films, 244, 254, 255–256
Laffon, Yolande, 250
Lamarque, Libertad, 136, 230, 231, 232, 233
Lanciers de la reine, défilé (*Cavalry Charge*) (film), 20
Lang, Fritz: *Destiny*, 190; *Metropolis*, 193, 223
Lang, Walter: *Week-End in Havana* (film), 280, 285
Langdon, Harry, 177
Lanzetta, Rafael, 254
Larkin, Brian, 169–170
Lassoing (film), 26, 30
Lassoing of a Wild Horse (film), 26, 30
Lassoing of a Wild Ox (film), 26, 30

The Last Days of Pompeii (*Gli ultimi giorni di Pompeii*) (1913 film), 56
The Last Encounter (*El último encuentro*) (film), 229–230
The Last Indian Uprising (*El último malón*) (film), 77
Latin America: avant-garde influences in, 181; cinema in, scholarship on, 1; exhibition culture in, 121; film and modernity in, 115–116, 154; film in the advancement of US political and economic interests, 117; film magazines coverage of, 128, 134, 138; US cultural hegemony and imperialism in, 54–56, 73, 87, 89, 169–170, 270. See also specific countries
Latin America, film production in: Alton on, 213–216, 219, 221, 224; film magazines coverage of, 122, 133, 134, 138; funding, 1; influence of Euro-American film labor, 217, 219–220
Latin American Cinematographic Industrial Society (SICLA) (Sociedad Industrial Cinematográfica Latinoamericana), 43
Latin American/Latino actors: film magazines coverage of, 128–129, 134; stereotyping of, 117, 125, 129–130, 134, 285
lattice lighting, 229
Layover in the City (*Escala en la ciudad*) (film), 221, 222–223
L'Echo de Mexique (newspaper), 19
Ledesma, Amanda, 230
Leger, Fernand: *Ballet mécanique*, 183
Leiva, Felipe de (pseud.): "Memoirs of an Extra," 7, 101–110, 132
Lenin, Vladimir, 147, 156
Leopardos poetry circle, 40
Lerner, Jesse, 333; *La piedra ausente* (*The Absent Stone*) (film), 343–344
Lerski, Helmar, 183
L'étoile de mer (film), 177, 190
Lévesque, Marcel (Don Casto), 35, 38n4
Lewis, Joseph H.: *The Big Combo* (film), 219, 234
Lewis, Sylvia, 286
Leyda, Jay: *A Bronx Morning* (film), 204
libertadores, 76
The Life of Galileo (Brecht), 88
Liga de Decencia, 280–281
lighting, Alton's use of: comedy, 225–226; crime drama, 225; film noir, 218–219, 229; glamour lighting, 229, 230, 231; lattice

lighting, 229; melodramas, 225, 227–228, 230–234; shadows, 219, 222–224, 226–230
The Lights of Buenos Aires (*Las luces de Buenos Aires*) (film), 223
Lim, Song Hwee, 4
Limite (film), 168–169, 181
Linder, Max, 48
L'Institut des Hautes Études Cinématographiques (IDHEC) (France), 305
El Lissitzky, 183, 185
literary adaptations to film, 245–249, 251–252
literary classics, parody of, 245–249
Little Path to Glory (*Caminito de gloria*) (film), 220, 233–234
The Living Head (*La cabeza viviente*) (film), 328, 339
Llanderas, Nicolás de las, 222
La llorona (*The Crying Woman*) (film), 332
Lloyd, Harold, 83
Loco lindo (*Crazy Dandy*) (film), 225, 226
los locos de la azotea (the fools on the roof), 218
Longhi, Enzo: *La Perricholi* (film), 128
"Longing for Hollywood" ("Añoranzas de Hollywood") (Aragón Leiva), 89
López, Alma, 338
López, Ana M., 154, 278; "Early Cinema and Modernity in Latin America," 115
López, Orestes (Cachao), 272
López, Yolanda, 338
Lo que le pasó a Sansón (*What Happened to Samson*) (film), 277
The Lost City of the African Jungle (film), 55–56
Louis Lumière (Sadoul), 31
"The Lover of Rudolph Valentino" ("La enamorada de Rodolfo Valentino") (Méndez Calzada), 7, 66–71, 90
The Loves of Carmen (film), 133
Lubitsch, Ernst, 127
Las luces de Buenos Aires (*The Lights of Buenos Aires*) (film), 223
Las luchadoras contra la momia (*Wrestling Women vs. the Aztec Mummy*) (film), 329
lucha libre films, 261, 328
Lumière (film), 31
Lumière Cinématographe, 18–31
Lumiton, 218
Lumiton, Equipo: *Los tres berretines* (*The Three Whims*) (film), 220, 221–222
Luponini (*The Terror of Chicago*) (*Luponini (el terror de Chicago*)) (film), 229–230

Lusnich, Ana Laura, 226
Lustig, Rodolfo: *São Paulo, A Sinfonia da metrópole* (*São Paulo, Symphony of the Metropolis*) (film), 181
Lyceum Society of Havana, 302

The Macabre Trunk (*El baúl macabro*) (film), 332
Machado (Gerardo) administration, 301, 306
Maciste (character), 50–51, 53, 58
Maciste the Tourist (*Maciste turista*) (film), 63n40
Madreselva (*Honeysuckle*) (film), 230–232, 231f, 233
Magaña, Ángel, 228f
Malcomson, Scott, 4
La maldición de la llorona (*The Curse of the Crying Woman*) (film), 328
Malerei, Photographie, Film (*Painting, Photography, Film*) (Moholy-Nagy), 185
Malfatti, Arnaldo, 222
The Maltese Falcon (film), 256–257, 260
mambo: 271–272, 279–280; García Márquez on, 267–268, 282; Mexican film industry and, 273–274; in national identity, 271–272; North American phase, 282–288; origins of, 272, 283; Pérez Prado's version of, 272; threat of, 282; transnationality of, 277–278, 280, 282–289; US public's ambivalence toward, 282–284; youth culture, appeal to, 282
"The Mambo" (García Márquez), 9, 267–268
"Mambo a la Kenton" (Pérez Prado), 272–273
mambo films: *Al son del mambo* (*To the Sound of Mambo*), 271, 278–280, 279f, 286, 287; *Aventurera*, 270, 274, 278; *Cha-Cha-Cha-Boom!* 285–287; comedies, 286; *Del can-can al mambo* (*From the Can-Can to the Mambo*), 271, 280–282; incorporation of US popular culture in, 280; message of Cuban-Mexican fraternity, 280; Mexicanidad in, 278; moral subtext, 280–282; musical pedagogy in, 279–280; *El revoltoso* (*The Rebellious One*), 277; *Simbad el mareado* (*Simbad the Seasick*), 277; *Underwater!* 285, 287; *Víctimas del pecado* (*Victims of Sin*), 270, 274, 278
"Mambo no. 5" (Pérez Prado), 268, 282
Mamoulian, Rouben: *The Mark of Zorro* (film), 244, 245
The Man and the Monster (*El hombre y el monstruo*) (film), 328

A Manhã (newspaper), 163, 173n21
Manhatta (film), 204–205
Mann, Anthony: *Border Incident* (film), 219; *T-Men* (film), 219
Man Ray, 183, 195; *L'étoile de mer* (film), 177, 183, 190
Manuel Márquez Sterling School of Journalism, 307–308
The Man with a Movie Camera (*Chelovek s kinoapparatom*) (film), 159, 183, 204
Marano, Mario, 128
La marca del muerto (*Creature of the Walking Dead*) (film), 340
La marca del zorrillo (*The Mark of the Skunk*) (film), 244, 245–249, 247f, 248f, 250, 253
March, Frederic, 250
Marchand, René, 148, 156
María Candelaria (film), 255, 331, 333–334
El mariachi desconocido (*Unknown Mariachi*) (film), 278
Mariátegui, José Carlos, 301
Marinho, L.S., 159–160; "Eisenstein em Hollywood," 159f
Maris, Mona, 139
The Mark of the Skunk (*La marca del zorrillo*) (film), 244, 245–249, 247f, 248f, 250, 253
The Mark of Zorro (film), 244, 245
Mármol, José: *Amalia*, 225
Marodon, Pierre: *Mascamor* (film), 51
Marqués, María Elena, 256
Marro, Albert: *Barcelona y sus misterios* (*Barcelona and Its Mysteries*) (film), 122
Martin, E. A.: *The Lost City of the African Jungle* (film), 55–56
Martínez, Modesto: "Aventuras de la Familia Pérez en Nueva York," 121–122
Martínez de la Pera, Eduardo, 122; *Nobleza gaucha* (*Gaucho Nobility*) (film), 75, 77–81
Martínez Solares, Gilberto: *La casa del terror* (*The House of Terror*), 340–341; *Face of the Screaming Werewolf* (film), 340–341; *Lo que le pasó a Sansón* (*What Happened to Samson*) (film), 277; *La marca del zorrillo* (*The Mark of the Skunk*) (film), 244, 245–249, 247f, 248f, 250, 253; *El mariachi desconocido* (*Unknown Mariachi*) (film), 278; *El revoltoso* (*The Rebellious One*) (film), 277; *El rey del barrio* (*The King of the Neighborhood*) (film), 248; *Simbad el mareado* (*Simbad the Seasick*) (film), 249, 253, 277; *Los tres mosqueteros y medio* (*Three and a Half Musketeers*) (film), 249; *El vizconde de Montecristo* (*The Viscount of Monte Cristo*) (film), 251

"Martín Fierro" (poem) (Hernández), 77
Masas (periodical), 302
Mascamor (film), 51
"The Mass Production of the Senses" (Hansen), 169
"Masters of Russian Cinematography" (Mom), 156
Mat (*Mother*) (film), 155
Maté, Rudolph, 224
Mateo and His Victory (*Mateo y su victoria*) (photograph), 182
Mates (*Compañeros*) (film), 221
Matisse, Henri, 301
El matrero (*The Outlaw*) (film), 232–233
El matrero (*The Outlaw*) (opera) (Boero), 232
Mauro, Humberto, 167; *Ganga bruta* (film), 181
Max Factor, 129, 234
Mayakovsky, Vladimir, 163
The May Revolution (*La revolución de Mayo*) (film), 77
McCarthy, Todd, 219, 222, 225–226
Medina, Cuauhtémoc, 332
Melford, George: *The Sheik* (*La cautiva del caudillo moro*) (film), 85
Mello, Cláudio, 173n21
melodramas, 76–78, 209n46, 225, 227–228, 230–234, 248, 253, 255–257
"Memoirs of an Extra" (Leiva), 7, 101–110, 132
Méndez, Fernando: *El vampiro* (*The Vampire*) (film), 328
Méndez Calzada, Enrique: "La enamorada de Rudolfo Valentino" ("The Lover of Rudolph Valentino"), 7, 66–71, 90
Mendoza, Víctor Manuel, 254
Menichelli, Pina, 39, 51, 83
Merayo, Antonio, 227, 233
Messalina (film), 83
"Messiah or Threat" (Eisenstein interview) (*Cinearte*), 167–168
Mexican Dance (film), 26
Mexico, cultural production: art, evocation of the indigenous in, 333; avant-garde influences in, 181
Mexico, film audiences: cosmopolitanism of, 242–252, 260; literary classics, exposure to, 250–252; for Mexican vs. Hollywood films, 243; options available to, 243–244, 253, 259,

260; social stratification in, 52–53; topics preferred by, 245–246

Mexico, film genres: *cabaretera*, 270, 273, 278; *comedias rancheras*, 245, 249, 252, 262, 273–274, 291n18; comedic films, 244, 245–251; crime dramas, 244, 257, 258–259; film noir, 256, 257, 258–259, 260; gangster films, 257–258, 262; horror films, 325–337; 342–344; literary adaptations, 245–249, 251–252; *lucha libre*, 261, 328; mambo, 274–278, 286; melodrama, 248, 253, 255–257; romance, 251, 256–257; *rumbera*, 261, 262, 273–275, 278; science fiction films, 324–327, 328, 334; suspense, 258; thrillers, 244, 255, 257, 261; transnationality of, 324–327; wrestling films, 261, 238

Mexico, film in: art cinema, 342–344; avant-garde influences, 181; characters embodiment of transcultural intersections, 252–253; class bias illustrated, 274; Golden Age (1940s-1950s), 243–263; language used in, 247–248; modern-traditional dichotomy, 329; past-present temporality, 342–344; political language in, 256; post-revolutionary era, 326; transnationality of, 249–250, 251, 273–278, 276f, 325–327, 334–337, 342–344

Mexico, film industry: censorship, fight against, 280–281; competitiveness of the, 122, 140; institutional role served by, 279; international influences on, 153, 217, 244, 249–252, 256–257; mambo's success and the, 273–278; Mexican films, percent of total releases, 242; national film industry, development of, 153, 217; Spanish-language film magazines coverage of, 138; star system, construction of, 252; US relations, 125, 242–243, 245, 334, 340–341

Mexico: film magazines in, 140, 263n7

Mexico, film themes: capitalist development, 241–242, 244, 247; contemporary political reality, 259; cultural nationalism, 245, 247; economic conflict and reforms, 254–256; industrialization, perils of, 256; labor-themed, 244, 254, 255–256; urbanization, 255, 259, 274–275; visual representation of Spanish culture, 251–252

Mexico, national identity and film in: as compromised by US urban culture, 274–276; construction of, 241–242; cosmopolitanism in conflict, 259–260, 262; indigenismo tied to, 325–334, 338, 342–344; in labor-themed films, 254; music underlying, 271; performative humor, 245–247; unifying identity through film, 254–255

Mexico, stage entertainments: carpa, 248

Mexico-US relations: film boycott, 125; *The Great Mojado Invasion, Part 2 (The Second U.S.–Mexico War)* (film), 324–325, 326f, 328, 343; Hollywood obstructionism, 245; mambo films and, 270–271; Mexploitation films, 334, 336–337, 340–341; US domination of film market, 242–243, 334

Mexploitation films: directors of, 332; history and legacy of, 328; the indigenous, evocation of, 328–334; past-present temporality, 342–344; precursors, 332; transnationality of, 325–329, 334–337, 342–344

MGM, 218

Mignolo, Walter, 4

Military Exercises by the Cadets at the Mexican Academy (film), 33n37

Milner, Victor, 226

Minnelli, Vincente, 309; *An American in Paris* (film), 218

Mino García, Fernando, 255

Miranda, Carmen, 134, 139, 233, 269, 278, 280, 285

Miró, Clemente, 26

Les misèrables (film), 250

Les misèrables (novel) (Hugo), 250

Mi último tango (My Last Tango) (film), 86

Mix, Tom, 103, 104

Moana (film), 190

Moctezuma, Carlos López, 261

modernism: 6–8, 10, 168, 181, 198, 205; vernacular (Hansen), 5, 169. *See also* avant-garde cinema; avant-garde photography; avant-garde writing

modernity: of audiences, 259; cinema's function in, 115–116, 121, 154, 170; conservation modernization in Colombia, 44, 47, 55; and cosmopolitanism in Mexico, 243–244, 247–248; film magazines contribution to, 116, 124; modernity-indigenous dichotomy, 329; parallel, 169; thematization in film, 241–244, 247–250, 254–257, 259, 262, 277–278; and tradition, Coppola's synthesis of, 200–202, 204; transnational imaginaries of, 117

Moglia Barth, Luis: *El último encuentro (The Last Encounter)* (film), 229–230

Moholy-Nagy, Lázló, 181–182, 183, 188, 191, 193, 195; *7am New year's Day* (photograph), 182; *From the Radio Tower of Berlín* (photograph), 182; *Impressions of the Old Port of Marseille (Impressionen vom alten Marseiller Hafen)* (film), 186–187, 196; *Malerei, Photographie, Film* (Painting, Photography, Film), 185
Mojica, José, 136
Mom, Arturo: *Loco lindo (Crazy Dandy)* (film), 225, 226; "Masters of Russian Cinematography," 156; *Palermo* (film), 228f, 229
La momia azteca (The Aztec Mummy) (film), 329, 337, 340
La momia azteca contra el robot humano (The Robot vs. the Aztec Mummy) (film), 330f
Mondragón, Jorge, 329
El Monitor Republicano (newspaper), 20
Monsiváis, Carlos, 247, 280–281
"Montage as Conflict" (Eisenstein), 165
Montagnes russes sur l'eau (Rollercoasters) (film), 20
Montaldo, Graciela, 49
"The Mooch" (Ellington), 221
Moore, Robin, 275
Mora, Carl J., 244
Moraes, Vinícius de, 163
Morales, Noro, 272
Morand, Paul, 301
Moré, Benny, 273
Moreno, Antonio, 76, 128, 130; *Santa* (film), 255
Moreno, Juan J., 128, 137
Moreno, Mario (pseud. Cantinflas), 138, 241, 242, 243, 245, 249, 251, 252
Morgan, Janice, 218
Morphine (film), 149
Mother (Mat) (film), 155
"Motion Picture Production in South America" (Alton), 8, 213–216, 219, 221, 224
"Motion Picture Production in South America Up to Date" (Alton), 234
Moussinac, Léon, 156, 192; *Le Cinéma Soviétique*, 147–149, 155
movie stars: fan culture, development of, 126–127; film magazines coverage of, 127–134, 139; income, 103–104; Latin American audiences, affection for, 126–127; star system, construction of, 252. *See also specific actors*

Moving Picture World (periodical), 39, 113, 117, 118–119, 122
Mozzhukhin, Ivan, 305
Un muelle del Sena (A Dock on the Seine) (film), 195–196, 197f
Mugica, Miguel, 218
Muiño, Enrique, 227
Una mujer de Oriente (A Woman of the East) (film), 244, 261–262
La mujer del puerto (The Woman of the Port) (film), 255, 256
Munby, Jonathan, 218
El Mundo (newspaper), 302, 303, 305; "Tablas y Pantalla" ("Stage and Screen") column (Valdés-Rodríguez), 302
Murray, K. Gordon, 334
muscle-man genre, 41, 42f, 50–51, 53, 63n40. *See also* Maciste
music: "blackening" of, 275; Cuban, 267–268, 271–272, 275–276; in national identity, 271. *See also specific genres of*
Musician, Poet, and Madman (Músico, poeta y loco) (film), 249–250
Mussolini, Benito, 82
Musuraca, Nicholas, 219
Múzquiz, Carlos, 257, 258f
My Cousin (film), 81
My Favorite Martian (TV show), 337
My Last Tango (Mi último tango) (film), 86
The Mysteries of Paris (Les mystères de París) (film), 244, 250, 253
The Mysteries of Paris (Les mystères de París) (novel) (Sue), 244, 250

La Nación (newspaper), 189
Naldi, Nita, 76
National Chicana/o Youth Liberation Conference, 337–339
National Film School (Italy), 305
Navarrete, Federico, 331
Navarro, Antonio, 25
Navarro, Carlos: *Janitzio* (film), 331
Navitski, Rielle, 53, 112–146
Negrete, Jorge, 243, 249, 251–252
Negri, Pola, 85
Neptune's Daughter (film), 243
Neues Sachlichkeit (New Objectivity) movement, 184, 194
Neues Sehen (New Vision) movement, 181, 184–187, 193–194

Neumann, Kurt: *Bad Boy* (film), 243
A New Dawn (*Distinto amanecer*) (film), 255–260
Newfield, Sam: *The Flying Serpent* (film), 335–336, 336f, 339
New Latin American Cinema, 6, 299, 341–342
New Objectivity (*Neues Sachlichkeit*) movement, 184, 194
New Vision (*Neues Sehen*) movement, 181, 184–187, 193–194
"News Letter from South America" (Alton), 224
newspapers: film industry coverage, 81–83, 84f; influence of, 215. *See also specific newspapers*
New Vision (*Neues Sehen*) movement, 181, 184–187, 193–194
Niblo, Fred: *Blood and Sand* (1922 film), 121
Nigeria, 169–170
Night of the Mayas (*La noche de los mayas*) (film), 331
Nobleza gaucha (*Gaucho Nobility*) (film), 7, 75, 77–81, 122
La noche de los mayas (*Night of the Mayas*) (film), 331
A noi! (*Camisas negras*) (film), 82, 84f
Non coupable (*Not Guilty*) (film), 243
North Wind in Veracruz (film), 33n37
Nosotros los pobres (*We the Poor*) (film), 243
Not Guilty (*Non coupable*) (film), 243
Novarro, Ramón, 128, 129, 130
Nuestro Tiempo (Our Times) cultural society, 315

Obligado, Rafael: "Santos Vega" (poem), 77
Obregón, Álvaro, 125
O'Brien, Charles, 218
Ocampo, Victoria, 156, 168, 189, 199
October (*Oktyabr*) (film), 151, 155, 161, 165, 178
O Fan (periodical), 173n21
O'Farrill, Chico, 288
Old and New (*Staroye i novoye*) (*Antes y ahora/ The General Line*) (film), 155–156, 161, 163, 166
Olivari, Nicolás, 189
Olivier, Laurence, 249, 309
Los olvidados (film) (Buñuel), 244
O'Neill, Eugene, 301, 309
"On Some Aspects of *Photogénie*" (Epstein), 161
La Opinión (newspaper), 132

O'Quigley, Robert, 217
Orgeron, Marsha, 126
Orientalist fantasy films, 253
The Origins of Cinema in Mexico, 1896–1900 (*Los orígenes del cine en México 1896–1900*) (Reyes), 18
Orol, Juan, 242; *Gángsters contra charros* (film), 261; *Una mujer de Oriente* (*A Woman of the East*) (film), 244, 261–262
Ortega y Gasset, José, 301
Ortiz, Fernando, 304
Osborne, Marie, 34, 35, 36
Ospina León, Juan Sebastián, 6–7, 39–65
Oubiña, David, 191, 194, 198
Our Times (Nuestro Tiempo) cultural society, 315
The Outlaw (*El matrero*) (film), 232–233
The Outlaw (*El matrero*) (opera) (Boero), 232
Ozep, Fedor, 155; *Living Corpse* (*Zhivoy trup*), 156, 160

pachuco subculture, 246–247
Pagano, Bartolomeo, 50
Painting, Photography, Film (*Malerei, Photographie, Film*) (Moholy-Nagy), 185
Painting with Light (Alton), 235
El País (newspaper), 302
The Palace Governor and Honor Guard on Horses (film), 27
Palermo (film), 228f, 229
Palma, Andrea, 256–257
La Paloma (*The Dove*) (film), 129–130
Pan-Americanism, 53–56, 130, 134, 138–139, 142n7
Parade of Peasants in the Fiestas Patrias (film), 24
Parade of Rurales at a Gallop on September 16 (film), 24, 26
Paradisi, Umberto: *Camisas negras* (*A noi!*) (film), 82, 84f
Paramount, 137, 140, 218, 234
Parker, Charlie, 275
Partie de cartes (*The Card Players*) (film), 20
Pasión jarocha (*Veracruz Passion*) (film), 244
The Passion of Joan of Arc (*La Passion de Jeanne d'Arc*) (film), 177, 183, 190
Pastrone, Giovanni: *Cabiria* (1914 film), 50, 53, 56, 58
Pathé Exchange productions, 56
Pathé Journal newsreels, 36

La Patria degli Italiani (newspaper), 75, 81–82; "Arte e Artisti" (Art and Artists) column, 82; "Tra Cinematografie e "Films"" (Between Movie Theaters and "Films") section, 82
Paxman, Andrew, 245
Paz, Octavio, 333; *El laberinto de la soledad* (The Labyrinth of Solitude), 244, 246
Peasant Women of Ryazan (*Baby ryazanskie/ The Village of Sin*) (film), 171n4, 178
pedagogy: film as, 53, 126, 149, 164–165; musical, 279–280. *See also* film pedagogy
Peixoto, Mário: *Limite* (film), 168–169, 181; "Um filme da América do Sul," 168–169
Películas (periodical): "The American Danger," 53–56; *Cine-Mundial*, argument with, 39–40; Colombian-Italian nationalist discourse, 53–59; "For the Glory and Greatness of Italy" section, 56–58; immigration position, 59; imported films, position on, 39–40, 41, 46, 50–51; on Maciste films, 53; mentioned, 6; publisher of, 47; race, essentialist discourses of, 58–59; regulating film spectatorship, 46; Salavarrieta monument petition, 45; "The Show on June 15th" (Tic Tac), 34–38
La Película: Semanario Cinematográfico Sud-Americano, 84–85
Peón, Ramón: *La llorona* (*The Crying Woman*) (film), 332
Peña, Fernando Martín, 190
Peredo Castro, Francisco, 256
Perelli, Carlos, 233
Pérez de Villagrá, Gaspar, 332
Pérez Prado, Dámaso, 9; *Cha-Cha-Cha-Boom!* 285–287; "Cherry Pink and Apple Blossom White," 285; García Márquez on, 267–268; "Mambo a la Kenton," 272–273; "Mambo no. 5," 268, 282; mambo of, 272–273; popularity, 267; propagandistic documentary films, 288–289; "Qué rico el mambo," 273; signature grunt, 277; *Spike Jones Show* appearance, 283–284, 284f; success in Mexico, 273, 288; "Suite de las Américas," 288; "Voodoo Suite," 285–287, 288
Pérez Prado, Dámaso, film appearances: *Al son del mambo* (*To the Sound of Mambo*), 271, 278–280, 279f; *Aventurera*, 270; *Del can-can al mambo* (*From the Can-Can to the Mambo*), 271; *Underwater!* 285; *Víctimas del pecado* (*Victims of Sin*), 270

Pérez Prado orchestra, 276, 282–284
La Perricholi (film), 128
Peru, 154
Peterhans, Walter, 181, 183, 185, 192–193, 199
Peter Ibbetson (film), 232
Petit de Murat, Ulises, 189
The Phantom of the Convent (*La fantasma del convento*) (film), 332
Phocea Film, 42f
photography: avant-garde influences in, 181–182, 187–192, 205–206; Bauhaus school, 186; Direct Photography movement, 184; *Film und Foto* (FiFo) exposition, 182–184; New Objectivity (*Neues Sachlichkeit*) movement, 184; New Vision (*Neues Sehen*) movement, 184–187; pictorialism, rejection of, 182, 184–187
"Photography and the New God" (Strand), 205
Picasso, Pablo, 301
Pick, Lupu: *St. Sylvester's Night* (*New Year's Eve*) (film), 177
Pickford, Mary, 85, 108
La piedra ausente (*The Absent Stone*) (film), 343–344
Pinal, Silvia, 248–249
Piqueras, Juan: "Veinte películas soviéticas en Suramérica" (Twenty Soviet Films in South America), 152
Place Bellecour (*A Plaza in Lyon*) (film), 20
La Pluma (periodical), 162
El pobre Pérez (*Poor Pérez*) (film), 226
Podestá, José María, 162
Polo, Eddie, 51
Pondal Ríos, Sixto, 189
Pool at the Moment in which Large Numbers of Swimmers Enter (film), 33n37
Poor Pérez (*El pobre Pérez*) (film), 226
Poppe, Nicolas, 8, 217–240
Pork Butcher in Chicago (film), 20
Portillo, Rafael: *Face of the Screaming Werewolf* (film), 340–341; *La momia azteca* (*The Aztec Mummy*) (film), 329, 337, 340; *La momia azteca contra el robot humano* (*The Robot vs. the Aztec Mummy*) (film), 330f
Potamkin, Harry Alan, 300, 306
Potemkin (film), 107, 151, 153, 155, 158f, 159–162, 165–166, 171n2, 172n10, 172n14, 173n21, 178, 183, 190, 311
Potomok Chingis-Khana (*Storm over Asia*) (film), 155, 156

Pound, Ezra, 301
Power, Tyrone, 252
Prado, Lilia, 257, 258f
La Prensa (newspaper), 223, 282
Preobrazhenskaya, Olga: *The Village of Sin (Baby ryazanskie/Peasant Women of Ryazan)* (film), 171n4, 178
The President and his Retinue on September 16 (film), 24
The President of the Republic and his Ministers at Chapultepec Castle on September 16 (film), 26–27
The President of the Republic Crossing the Plaza de la Constitución on September 16 (film), 24, 27
The President of the Republic Returning to Chapultepec in a Carriage (film), 26
The President of the Republic Riding a Horse in the Forest at Chapultepec Castle (film), 24
Príamo, Luis, 192
Prison of Dreams (Prisión de sueños) (film), 256
propaganda films, 148, 161, 288–289
À propos de Nice (film), 190
Proust, Marcel, 309
Púa, Carlos de la, 88–89
Pudovkin, Vsevolod, 156, 157, 162, 188, 192; *The End of St. Petersburg* (film), 178; *Mother (Mat)* (film), 155; *Storm over Asia (Potomok Chingis-Khana)* (film), 155–156
Puerta cerrada (Closed Door) (film), 232, 233
Puig, Germán, 315
Pujol, Sergio: *Valentino en Buenos Aires: Los años veinte y el espectáculo*, 89–90
Pulido, José, 261
Py, Eugenio, 77

Q (film), 335
Querelle enfantine (Babies' Quarrel) (film), 20
"Qué rico el mambo" (Pérez Prado), 273
¡*Que Viva México!* (film), 101, 181, 302
Quijano, Aníbal, 270, 289
Quiñones, Eduardo, 126
Quiroga, Horacio, 87, 126, 301
Quo Vadis? (1913 film), 50
Quo Vadis? (1924 film), 83

Radiolandia (periodical), 140
Rain (Regen) (film), 190
Ramírez Berg, Charles, 241, 331
ranchera films, 245, 249, 252, 262, 273–274, 291n18

rasquache cinema, 324
RCA Victor, 273
Re, Lucia, 58
Reachi, Manuel, 130
The Rebel (film), 215
The Rebellious One (El revoltoso) (film), 277
Redes (film), 181, 331
Reed, Carol, 309; *The Fallen Idol* (film), 243, 260
Reed, John, 302
Regen (Rain) (film), 190
Reifende Jugend (Second Youth) (film), 193
Renger-Patzsch, Albert, 183
Renoir, Jean, 222, 309; *Boudu Saved from Drowning (Boudu sauvé des eaux)* (film), 222; *La grande illusion* (film), 311
Repas de bébé (Baby's Meal/Baby's Breakfast) (film), 20
Republican Cuba, 298
Restivo, Mariano: *Galaor* films, 50
Revista de Arte y Variedades (periodical), 47
Revista de Avance (periodical), 155, 300–301, 305
Revista de La Habana (periodical), 302
El revoltoso (The Rebellious One) (film), 277
La revolución de Mayo (The May Revolution) (film), 77
El rey del barrio (The King of the Neighborhood) (film), 248
Reyes, Alfonso, 301
Reyes, Aurelio de los, 6, 121; "Gabriel Veyre and Fernand Bon Bernard, Representatives of the Lumière Brothers in Mexico," 18–33; *The Origins of Cinema in Mexico, 1896–1900 (Los orígenes del cine en México 1896–1900)*, 18, 31
Rice, Felicia: *Codex Espanglienses* (book), 343
Richardson, F. H., 120
Richter, Hans, 183; *Ghosts before Breakfast (Vormittagspuk)* (film), 194; *Inflation* (film), 183
Rico, Mona, 128
Rimbaud, Arthur, 301
Río, Dolores del, 128–130, 131f, 133, 286
Ritchie, Billie, 127
Rivera, Diego, 301, 330, 333
Rivero, Fernando: *Les misèrables* (film), 250
Roa, Raúl, 301, 304, 310
The Robot vs. the Aztec Mummy (La momia azteca contra el robot humano) (film), 330f
Rockefeller, Nelson, 134, 271, 287, 288

Rodchenko, Alexander, 185
Rodríguez, Arsenio, 272
Rodríguez, Ismael, 242, 245; *Borrasca en las almas* (*Stormy Souls*) (film), 256; *Nosotros los pobres* (*We the Poor*) (film), 243; *A toda máquina* (*Full Speed Ahead*) (film), 250; *Los tres huastecos* (*The Three Huastecans*) (film), 254–255
Rodríguez, Joselito: *Café de chinos* (*Chinese Café*) (film), 243
Rodríguez, Nelson, 315
Rojas, Ricardo, 78
Rojas Castro, Armando: *Santiago* (film), 181
Roland, Gilbert, 128, 130, 285
Roland, Ruth, 39
Rollercoasters (*Montagnes russes sur l'eau*) (film), 20
Romaña, Roberto, 278–279, 279f
romantic drama films, 251, 256–257
Romeo and Juliet (film), 249
Romero, José Luis, 156, 178, 189
Romero Brest, Jorge, 178, 189, 199
Romero Rubio de Díaz, Carmen, 24, 26
Room, Abram: *Bed and Sofa* (*Tretya meshchanskaya*) (film), 155
Roosevelt, Franklin D., 134, 269, 271, 287
Rosas, Juan Manuel de, 225
Rosauro Castro (film), 255
Rosenberg, Ellen, 194
Rossellini, Roberto, 309; *Germany, Year Zero* (*Deutschland im Jahre Null*) (film), 311
Rotha, Paul, 192
Rowden, Terry, 1
Rozental, Sandra: *La piedra ausente* (*The Absent Stone*) (film), 343–344
Rozsa, Irene, 9, 298–317
Rubia Barcia, José, 304
Ruétalo, Victoria, 341
Ruíz Vásquez, Juan Carlos, 40, 58
rumba, 275–276
rumbera films, 261, 262, 273–275, 278
Rusia a los doce años (Álvarez del Vayo), 155
Russell, Bertrand, 301
Russell, Jayne, 285
Russian cinema, 7–8, 147–149. *See also* Soviet film
"Russian Cinema and Brazilian Cinema" (Faria), 7–8, 147–149
Ruttmann, Walter: *Berlin, Symphony of a Great City* (*Berlin, die Symphonie der Großstadt*) (film), 177, 183, 190, 204

Sadoul, Georges: *Louis Lumière*, 31
The Saga of Gosta Berling (film), 177
sainete, 78, 93n16
A Sainted Devil (*El Diablo santificado*) (film), 85
Salavarrieta, Policarpa, 45
Salazkina, Masha, 155
Saldívar, José David, 289
Salón Olympia, 34–38, 44–46
Saludos Amigos (film), 134, 269
Salvador, Jaime: *El jorobado* (*The Hunchback*) (film), 251
The Salvation Hunters (film), 177
samba, 271, 273
Simbad the Seasick (*Simbad el mareado*) (film), 249, 253, 277
Samson against the Philistines (*Sansone contro i filistei*) (film), 42
Sánchez García, José María, 115
Sánchez Prado, Ignacio M., 8–9, 241–266
San Demetrio London (film), 243
Sandrini, Luis, 221, 225
Sangre y arena (*Blood and Sand*) (1917 film), 122
Sangre y arena (*Blood and Sand*) (novel) (Ibáñez), 122
Sansone contro i filistei (*Samson against the Philistines*) (film), 42
Santa (1931 film), 255
Santayana, George, 301
Santiago (film), 181
Santo and the Vengeance of the Mummy (*Santo en la venganza de la momia*) (film), 329
"Santos Vega" (Obligado), 77
São Paulo, Symphony of the Metropolis (*São Paulo, A Sinfonia da metrópole*) (film), 181
Sarlo, Beatriz, 88, 202, 220
Saslavsky, Luis: *Crimen a las 3* (*Crime at Three O'Clock*) (film), 221; *Puerta cerrada* (*Closed Door*) (film), 232, 233
A Scena Muda (periodical), 168
Scene at the Pane Baths (film), 33n37
Scène d'enfants (*Child's Play*) (film), 20
Schajowicz, Ludwig, 304, 307
Schifrin, Lalo, 288
Schroeder Rodríguez, Paul, 181
Schwartz, Jorge, 187–188
science fiction films, 324–327, 328, 334
Sconce, Jeffrey, 327
Sears, Fred F.: *Cha-Cha-Cha-Boom!* (film), 271, 285–287, 288

Second Youth (*Reifende Jugend*) (film), 193
Seitz, John F., 219
Selection of Yokes for a Drove of Oxen (film), 26
Selznick, David O., 243
Semon, Larry, 177
Sennett, Mack, 177
Señorita Andrea (film), 27
serial cinema: in Mexico, 51–53; muscle-man genre, 63n40; periodicals promoting European films over US serials, 48, 50–53, 55–56, 58–60; realism in, 63n35; transnationality of, 51–53
Serna, Laura Isabel, 3, 52, 116, 126, 132–133
7am New year's Day (photograph), 182
777 (film), 181
"Seven Themes: Buenos Aires" (Coppola), 191
Sevilla, Ninón, 273, 274, 275f, 276, 279
Shadow on the Wall (film), 243
shadows, Alton's use of, 219, 222–224, 226–230
Shakespeare, William: *Hamlet*, 249; *Romeo and Juliet*, 249
Shamroy, Leon, 224
The Sheik (*La cautiva del caudillo moro*) (film), 85
Sheller, Charles: *Manhatta* (film), 204–205
Shestaia chast' mira (*The Sixth Part of the World*) (film), 151, 178, 190
Shots Fired on the Isthmus (*Disparos en el Istmo*) (film), 181
Shoulder Arms (film), 190
"The Show on June 15th" (Villafañe), 7, 34–38
Sibert, Thomas E., 295; "Fox Film de Cuba, S.A.'s Continuing Competition for Scholarships to Summer School at the Universidad de la Habana," 9, 295–297
Sica, Vittorio de, 309
Sierra, Santiago: *Maciste turista* (*Maciste the Tourist*) (film), 63n40
Los siete locos (novel), 88
The Sign of Death (*El signo de la muerte*) (film), 332
The Sign of the Cross (film), 215
Silva, David, 257
Simbad el mareado (*Simbad the Seasick*) (film), 249, 253, 277
Sinbad the Sailor (film), 249
Sinclair, Upton, 103
Singer, Ben, 40–41
"Siteseeing: Architecture and the Moving Image" (Bruno), 221

The Sixth Part of the World (*Shestaia chast' mira*) (film), 151, 178, 190
Skoller, Jeffrey, 343
Social (periodical), 155, 302
social stratification of film audiences, 40, 52–53, 58–59, 87–88
Sociedad Económica de Amigos del País, 300
Sociedad Fotográfica Argentina de Aficionados, 200
Sociedad Impresora de Discos Electrofónicos (SIDE), 230
Sociedad Industrial Cinematográfica Latinoamericana (SICLA) (Latin American Cinematographic Industrial Society), 43
Sociedad Industrial Fotográfica Argentina Limitada (SIFAL), 221, 222–223
Soffici, Mario: *Cadetes de San Martín* (*Cadets of San Martín*) (film), 226–229
Solanas, Fernando, 2
Soldi, Raul, 230
Soler, Domingo, 250
Sombras de Gloria (film), 137
son (musical genre), 267, 274
The Son of the Sheik (film), 85, 86f
Sortie d'usine (*Workers Leaving the Lumière Factory*), 20
Soto, Luis de, 35, 310
Southern, Eve, 110
Soviet film: actors training, 305; debates engendered by, 155–157, 162–163; film as pedagogy, 149; film distribution, 153; French intellectuals and, 155; Hollywood films compared, 161–162, 165–166; the masses in, 163–166; national consciousness imprinted in, 166–169; possibilities of, 154; promise and possibility in, 170; propagandist, 148, 161; as pure cinema, 160–163, 165; silent films, 162–163; sound, commitment to, 162; supporters of, 155; as world cinema, 157–160. *See also* USSR
Soviet film in Latin America: artists' and intellectuals' responses to, 153; censorship of, 151, 154, 160, 171n2, 171n14; cineclubs and, 156, 173n21, 177–178, 191; cosmopolitan film culture, creating a, 157–160; half-life of, 170; leftist reception, 163–166; national cinema, impact on, 166–169; print culture, impact on, 163–166, 171n8
Spanish Civil War, 303–306
Spanish-language Hollywood films, 136–138, 213–216, 235

Spike Jones Show (TV show), 283–284, 284f
Spilimbergo, Lino, 189
Spottiswoode, Raymond, 192
Staroye i novoye (*The General Line/Old and New*) (film), 155
State Institute of Cinematography (GIK), 305
Stern, Grete, 181, 193, 194, 198–199
Sternberg, Josef von: *The Salvation Hunters* (film), 177
Stevens, Charles, 101–107, 109–110
Stiller, Mauritz: *The Saga of Gosta Berling* (film), 177
Storm over Asia (*Potomok Chingis-Khana*) (film), 155–156
Stormy Souls (*Borrasca en las almas*) (film), 256
Strand, Paul, 183; *Manhatta* (film), 204–205; "Photography and the New God," 205; *Redes* (film), 181
Stravinsky, Igor, 156
strongman films, 41, 42f, 50–51, 53, 63n40
St. Sylvester's Night (*New Year's Eve*) (film), 177
The Student of Prague (*Der Student von Prag*) (1926 film), 190
Students of Chapultepec on Parade (film), 25
Students of Chapultepec with Bayonets (film), 25, 33n37
Der Student von Prag (*The Student of Prague*) (film), 190
Stull, William, 229
Sturges, John: *Underwater!* (film), 271, 285, 287
Suárez, Gonzálo, 25
Sublette, Ned, 272
subtitles, 213
suburb, motif of the, 209n46
Sue, Eugène: *Les mystères de Paris* (*The Mysteries of Paris*), 244, 250
"Suite de las Américas" (Pérez Prado), 288
A Sunday on Hampstead Heath (*Un domingo en Hampstead Heath*) (film), 196, 198, 198f
Sur (periodical), 156, 188, 191, 199, 232
surrealism, 160, 193–195, 237
Susini, Enrique Telémaco, 218
suspense films, 258
Süssekind Rocha, Plínio, 173n21
Swanson, Gloria, 76
Sydney, George: *The Three Musketeers* (film), 249

Tálice, Roberto, 88–89
Talmadge, Norma, 85
Tamayo, Rufino, 333
tango: national identity and the, 88–89, 271; Valentino and the, 74–75, 81, 88–89
Tango! (film), 221
El tango de la muerte (*The Tango of Death*) (film), 86–87
tango films, 86–89, 221, 278
Tararira (*La bohemia de hoy/The Bohemia of Today*) (film), 221
Tarich, Yuri, 155; *Ivan the Terrible* (most likely *Wings of a Serf* [*Krylya kholopa*]) (1926 film), 165
The Tattler (periodical), 168
Teige, Karel, 183
Tell, Veronica, 199
Tempest in Veracruz (film), 33n37
el terror de Chicago (*Luponini*) (*Luponini* [*The Terror of Chicago*]) (film), 229–230
Tew, H. P., 152, 156, 157; "Cinema in the Argentine," 151
Theater and Film Writers' Association (Agrupación de Redactores Teatrales y Cinematográficos), 307–308, 314
They Say I'm a Communist (*Dicen que soy comunista*) (film), 256
Third Cinema, 2, 154
Thompson, Kristin, 160
Three and a Half Musketeers (*Los tres mosqueteros y medio*) (film), 249
The Three Caballeros (1942 film), 269
The Three Huastecans (*Los tres huastecos*) (film), 254–255
The Three Musketeers (1921 film), 101
The Three Musketeers (1942 film), 249
The Three Musketeers (novel) (Dumas), 249
The Three Whims (*Los tres berretines*) (film), 220, 221–222
thrillers, 244, 255, 257, 261
Thus the Obelisk Was Born (*Así nació el obelisco*) (film), 202, 203f, 204, 204f, 205
Tic-Tac. *See* Villafañe, Carlos (pseud. Tic-Tac)
El Tiempo (newspaper), 24
Tiempo, César, 189
Tierney, Dolores, 242, 331, 341
Time Tunnel (TV show), 337
Tin Tan. *See* Valdés, Germán (pseud. Tin Tan)

T-Men (film), 219
A toda máquina (*Full Speed Ahead*) (film), 250
Torre, Einar de la, 344
Torre, Elena de la, 136
Torre, Guillermo de, 151, 154, 156, 176, 188, 190–191; "The 'Cineclub' of Buenos Aires," 8, 176–178
Torre, Jamex de la, 344
Torres, Irma, 254
Torres, Raquel, 128, 129
To the Sound of Mambo (*Al son del mambo*) (film), 271, 278–281, 279f, 286–287
Tovar, Lupita, 128
transnational cinema: Aztec horror/Mexploitation films, 325–329, 334–337, 342–344; cultural significance of, 39–40; defining, 1–4; scholarship on, 2–4; serial cinema, 51–53
transnationalism: of film culture, 5, 151–160, 177–178, 190–191, 217; in film pedagogy, 300, 303–304; mambo and, 277–278, 280, 282–289
Traum (*Dream*) (film), 194–195, 195f, 198
Los tres berretines (*The Three Whims*) (film), 220, 221–222
Los tres huastecos (*The Three Huastecans*) (film), 254–255
Los tres mosqueteros y medio (*Three and a Half Musketeers*) (film), 249
The Tuileries Palace of Paris (*Bassin des Tuileries*) (film), 20
Tunney, Gene, 105
Turner, Lana, 249
12 mujeres (*12 Women*) (film), 232

Uhoff, Enrique, 255
Gli ultimi giorni di Pompeii (*The Last Days of Pompeii*) (film), 56
El último encuentro (*The Last Encounter*) (film), 229–230
El último malón (*The Last Indian Uprising*) (film), 77
Umbo, 183
"Um filme da América do Sul" (Peixoto), 168–169
Unamumo, Miguel de, 34, 37, 301
Una nueva y gloriosa nación (*The Charge of the Gauchos/The Beautiful Spy*) (film), 76
Underwater! (film), 271, 285, 287
United Artists, 234

United States: cultural hegemony and imperialism in Latin America, 54–56, 73, 76, 87, 89, 169–170, 270; film pedagogy in, 306; Good Neighbor era, 116–117, 133, 140, 270, 283; popular culture, Aztec apparitions in, 326; television, Mexploitation/Aztec horror films on, 334, 336–337
United States, film industry: in the advancement of US political and economic interests, 117, 134–135, 139, 269, 278, 285, 287; Angeli on "The American Danger," 53–56; higher education, ties to, 306; Latin American audiences, reliance on, 134; racialized labor, use of, 131–133, 133f; takeover of world markets and retention of control, 73, 112–114, 118–127. *See also* Hollywood film industry
United States-Mexico relations: Aztec horror/Mexploitation films, 334, 336–337, 340–341; film boycott, 125; *The Great Mojado Invasion, Part 2* (*The Second U.S.–Mexico War*) (film), 324–325, 326f, 328, 343; Hollywood obstructionism, 245; mambo films and, 270–271; US domination of film market, 242–243, 334
El Universal (newspaper), 27, 159
University of Havana: Batista regime, changes during, 315; Cine de Arte (Art Cinema) film exhibition program, 314–315; Department of Art History, 310; Department of Audiovisual Media, 315; Department of Cinematography, 310–311, 314, 315–316; Enrique José Varona Theater, 310–311, 311–313f; Filmoteca Universitaria film archive, 311, 314; School of History, 316; University Extension Commission Cinema section, 315–316
University of Havana Summer School: "Cinema: Industry and Art of Our Times" course (Valdés-Rodríguez), 295–296, 298, 307–310; film pedagogy, 306–310; focus of, 307; Fox Film de Cuba, S. A. scholarship competition, 295–297, 308; "Seminario de Artes Dramáticas" course (Baralt), 307; "Spanish Grammar and Literature" course (Barcia), 307; "Teatro Universitario" course (Scajowicz), 307
Unknown Mariachi (*El mariachi desconocido*) (film), 278
Until Victory (*Hasta la victoria siempre*) (film), 288

Urfé, Odilio, 272
Urruchúa, Victor: *Prisión de sueños* (*Prison of Dreams*) (film), 256
URSS Films, 153
Urueta, Chano, 273, 284; *Al son del mambo* (*To the Sound of Mambo*) (film), 271, 278–281, 279f, 286–287; *El barón del terror* (*Braniac*) (film), 328; *La cabeza viviente* (*The Living Head*) (film), 328, 339; *El conde de Montecristo* (*The Count of Monte Cristo*) (film), 250–251, 252; *Del can-can al mambo* (*From the Can-Can to the Mambo*) (film), 271, 280–281, 281f, 287; *El espejo de la bruja* (*The Witch's Mirror*) (film), 328; *La noche de los mayas* (*Night of the Mayas*) (film), 331; *El signo de la muerte* (*The Sign of Death*) (film), 332
USSR: film pedagogy, 305; propaganda films, 148, 161. *See also* Soviet cinema

Valdés, Germán (pseud. Tin Tan), 243, 244–253, 248f, 277–278, 284, 340
Valdés-Rodríguez, José Manuel: 1920s-1930s intellectual community and, 300–303, 305; awards/honors/accolades, 303, 308; background, 300; cineclub organized by, 301; collected writings, 299; Communism, involvement in, 302–303; Eisenstein and, 155, 300, 302–303, 306, 309; film audience, formation of, 299; film industry, relationship with, 303; Filmoteca Universitaria film archive, 311, 314, 316–317; "Hollywood: Sales Agent of American Imperialism," 302; journalism, professionalization of, 307–308, 314; legacy, 298–299, 307–308, 311, 314, 316–317, 318n8; mentioned, 9; publications, 300, 302, 303; reputation, professional, 308; School of History, University of Havana, 316; on Soviet film, 155; teaching, approach to, 300
Valdés-Rodríguez, José Manuel, film pedagogy: The Academy of Dramatic Arts (Open School of Havana), 303–306; beginnings, 302; *El cine en la Universidad de La Habana* (*Film at the University of Havana*), 308; "El Cine: Industria y Arte de Nuestro Tiempo" course, 295–296, 298, 307–310; formation of a sophisticated film audience, 299; legacy, 299, 316–317; "The New Cinematographic Technique," 302; State Institute of Cinematography (GIK), 303; "Tablas y Pantalla" (Stage and Screen) column, 302; theoretical and ideological background, 306; transnational links, 300, 303–304; University of Havana Summer School, 306–310
Valdés-Rodríguez, Manuel, 300, 305
Valdez, Luis: *I Am Joaquín* (film), 324, 338
Valentino, Rudolph: actor, 75, 76, 104; as Argentina's national representative, resistance to, 74–75, 81–86, 88–91; death and funeral, 85, 130; "La enamorada de Rudolfo Valentino" (Méndez Calzada), 7, 66–71, 90; gender balance, threat to, 84, 89–91; Italian Americans and, 74; Italian Argentines and, 81–84; overview, 71n1; press coverage, 81–86, 86f; tango and, 74–75, 81, 88–89
Valentino en Buenos Aires: Los años veinte y el espectáculo (Pujol), 89–90
Valéry, Paul, 301
Valle, Federico, 77
Valle Inclán, Ramón del, 121
Vallejo, César, 162, 163–164, 166, 301
The Vampire (*El vampiro*) (film), 328
La Vanguardia (newspaper), 223
Vani, Ester, 223
Vargas de la Maza, Armando, 115
Variety Theater, 47
Vasconcelos, José, 330–331
Vásquez, Alexandra, 283
Vázquez, Gustavo, 342; *The Great Mojado Invasion, Part 2* (*The Second U.S.–Mexico War*) (film), 324–325, 326f, 328, 343
Vedia y Mitre, Mariano de, 199
"Veinte películas soviéticas en Suramérica" (Twenty Soviet Films in South America) (Piqueras), 152
Véjar, Carlos: *Pasión jarocha* (*Veracruz Passion*) (film), 244
Vélez, Lupe, 110, 128–129
Veracruz Passion (*Pasión jarocha*) (film), 244
Verga, Giovanni, 82
"Vernacular Modernism: Tracking Cinema on a Global Scale" (Hansen), 169
Vertov, Dziga, 155, 157, 188; *The Man with a Movie Camera* (*Chelovek s kinoapparatom*) (film), 159, 183, 204; *The Sixth Part of the World* (*Shestaia chast' mira*) (film), 151, 178, 190
Vestir al bebé (*Dressing Baby*) (film), 209n49

Veyre, Gabriel, 6, 18–31; *Arrival of the Historic Bell on September 16* (film), 24, 27; *Charge of the Rurales in the Village of Guadalupe* (film), 25; *Child's Play* (perhaps *Scène d'enfants*) (film), 20; *Cockfight* (film), 26; executions captured by, 25; fiestas patrias filmed by, 24; films shot in Mexico, list of, 28–35; *Dance of the Spanish Procession at the Tívoli del Eliseo* (film), 27; *Gymnastics Class at the Colegio de la Paz, Formerly Vizcaínas* (film), 27; *A Horse Breaker* (film), 26; *Horses Bathing* (film), 26; *Hurricane, or Tempest in Veracruz* (film), 28, 33n37; *Lassoing* (film), 26; *Lassoing of a Wild Ox* (film), 26; *Mexican Dance* (film), 26; *Military Exercises by the Cadets at the Mexican Academy* (film), 33n37; *The Palace Governor and Honor Guard on Horses* (film), 27; *Parade of Peasants in the Fiestas Patrias* (film), 24; *Parade of Rurales at a Gallop on September 16* (film), 24, 26; *Pool at the Moment in which Large Numbers of Swimmers Enter* (film), 33n37; *The President and his Retinue on September 16* (film), 24; *The President of the Republic and his Ministers at Chapultepec Castle on September 16* (film), 26–27; *The President of the Republic Crossing the Plaza de la Constitución on September 16* (film), 24, 27; *The President of the Republic Returning to Chapultepec in a Carriage* (film), 26; *The President of the Republic Riding a Horse in the Forest at Chapultepec Castle* (film), 24; *Scene at the Pane Baths* (film), 33n37; *Selection of Yokes for a Drove of Oxen* (film), 26; *Señorita Andrea* (film), 27; *Students of Chapultepec on Parade* (film), 25; *Students of Chapultepec with Bayonets* (film), 25, 33n37
Vice and Beauty (film), 149
Victims of Sin (*Víctimas del pecado*) (film), 270, 274, 275–276, 278
Victoria esquina Bolívar (*Corner of Victoria and Bolívar*) (photograph), 182
Vidor, King, 127; *Bird of Paradise* (film), 286; *The Crowd* (film), 168
Vigo, Jean: *À propos de Nice* (film), 190, 204
Vigón, Ricardo, 315
Villafañe, Carlos (pseud. Tic-Tac): on Salón Olympia, 46; "The Show on June 15th," 7, 34–38

The Village of Sin (*Baby ryazanskie/Peasant Women of Ryazan*) (film), 171n4, 178
Villa-Lobos, Heitor, 288
Villegas, Lucío, 127, 130, 136
Vincendeau, Ginette, 218
The Viscount of Monte Cristo (*El vizconde de Montecristo*) (film), 251
Vitascope, 19, 25
"Viva Prado!" (Kenton), 273
Vizcaíno, Manuel Cuéllar, 281–282
El vizconde de Montecristo (*The Viscount of Monte Cristo*) (film), 251
"Voodoo Suite" (Pérez Prado), 285–287, 288
Vormittagspuk (*Ghosts before Breakfast*) (film), 194

Wagon Train (TV show), 337
Wallace, Richard: *Sinbad the Sailor* (film), 249
Wallerstein, Emmanuel, 270, 289
Walsh, Raoul: *The Loves of Carmen* (film), 133
Warner Brothers, 56, 222
Warren, Jerry, 340; *Face of the Screaming Werewolf* (film), 340–341
Week-End in Havana (film), 280, 285
Weinstein, Pierre, 148, 156
Welles, Orson, 3, 309
Wells, Sarah Ann, 7–8, 151–175
Werker, Alfred L.: *Border Incident* (film), 219
West, Roland: *La Paloma* (*The Dove*) (film), 129–130
Weston, Brett, 183
Weston, Edward, 183
We the Poor (*Nosotros los pobres*) (film), 243
What Happened to Samson (*Lo que le pasó a Sansón*) (film), 277
When the Night Ends (*Cuando acaba la noche*) (film), 244, 257–258, 260
"Where Is Costa Roja?" (Alvear), 129–130
White, Pearl, 39
White, Tom, 234
Whitman, Walt, 205
Wiene, Robert: *Cabinet of Dr. Caligari* (*Das Kabinett des Dr. Caligari*) (film), 177, 183, 190
The Wild, Wild West (TV show), 337
Wildflower (*Flor silvestre*) (film), 251, 259–260
Williams, Esther, 243
Wings of a Serf (*Krylya kholopa*) (film), 165
Winning Grandma (film), 34–36
A Woman of the East (*Una mujer de Oriente*) (film), 244, 261–262

The Woman of the Port (*La mujer del puerto*) (1934 film), 255, 256
Wong, Anna May, 261
Workers Leaving the Lumière Factory (*Sortie d'usine*)
wrestling films, 261, 328
Wrestling Women vs. the Aztec Mummy (*Las luchadoras contra la momia*) (film), 329

Yarbrough, Jean: *Holiday in Havana* (film), 280

Zacarías, Miguel: *El baúl macabro* (*The Macabre Trunk*) (film), 332
Zamudio-Taylor, Victor, 342
Zárraga, Miguel de, 136
Zavalía, Alberto de: *Escala en la ciudad* (*Layover in the City*) (film), 221, 222–223
Zigomar, roi des voleurs (*Zigomar, King of Thieves*) (film), 62n24
Zini, Malisa, 230
Zinnemann, Fred: *Redes* (film), 331
Zwart, Piet, 183

www.ingramcontent.com/pod-product-compliance
Lightning Source LLC
Chambersburg PA
CBHW071358300426
44114CB00016B/2097